AGING IN CULTURE AND SOCIETY

Comparative Viewpoints and Strategies

To my Great Uncle
OTTO E. MOORE

Through the portions of his over 40 years in retirement that I have seen, I have come to appreciate the complexities of aging, its losses and its rewards. When I asked if he would like me to use his name, he replied, "All I can say is that, that name has been in use for over 86 years and is about used up. So please use it any way you want." I thus dedicate this book to Otto E. Moore with the hope that the readers will come to appreciate the resourcefulness, vitality, and humanity of older adults everywhere.

AGING IN CULTURE AND SOCIETY

CHRISTINE L. FRY
and Contributors

Comparative

Viewpoints

and

Foreword by
PAUL BOHANNAN

Strategies

PRAEGER SPECIAL STUDIES • PRAEGER SCIENTIFIC
A J.F. BERGIN PUBLISHERS BOOK

Library of Congress Cataloging in Publication Data
Aging in culture and society.

A J.F. Bergin Publishers Book.

Bibliography: p.
Includes index.
1. Aged—Addresses, essays, lectures. 2. Old age—
Addresses, essays, lectures. I. Fry, Christine L.
II. American Anthropological Association.

GN485.A343   301.43'5   79-13198
ISBN 0-03-052726-0
ISBN 0-89789-001-9 pbk.

Published in 1980 by Praeger Publishers
A division of Holt, Rinehart and Winston / CBS, Inc.
383 Madison Avenue, New York, New York 10017 U.S.A.

0 056 987654321
Printed in the United States of America

Old and Together on the Island of Paros, Greece
Photo by Jeff Beaubier.

Contents

Foreword

Old people and anthropologists need each other—indeed, they deserve each other. Old people need someone who can understand their individuality and variety—and anthropologists thrive on variation.

Authorities agree (several in this volume mention it) that old people are more different from one another than are people at any younger ages. The cultural input to the growing human organism starts at birth or even before, and has an immense impact on the personality of the adult. By the time people are very old, long experience of culture overwhelms the mere somatic base in determining what they have become.

Anthropology, of all the social sciences, is by far the one most concerned with variation in human experience. Anthropologists, as the essays in this book make amply clear, can use many methods of research and analysis. But the core of their method is, and will remain, participant observation. No other method could be so effective for studying the differences that living—living a long time—makes in human beings. There is no substitute for, as Jennie Keith puts it, "moving in on them."

When anthropologists move in on old people they find more than mere personal and cultural variation, however. They have devised a set of field work principles by which they can elicit not mere answers but also the right questions. As the ads used to say, "Ask the man who owns one," today anthropologists can ask the person who owns one what to ask. The major danger if this essential stage is omitted is that the researchers' interests will dictate the questions, not the experience in living of the respondents. Discovering the right questions is the most vital single task any social scientist can perform. Only then is it profitable to turn to surveys or other forms of quantification or hard data.

By using the traditional anthropological methods of "moving in on them," anthropologists ultimately discover that "some do and some don't" whatever the right question is. It is at that point that other methods (usually, in studying old people, survey research methods) come into play. How many do and how many don't?—provides the data needed for policy discussions.

Because these studies were done in this way, the questions they ask and answer vary widely—far more than would be the case if the authors had merely begun with survey methods. Myths are shattered; unlikely byways are explored. The focus is softer and more diffuse, and we learn a lot more about old people. We begin to reshape our myths and to sharpen our stereotypes so that services to the old can be provided from a far more comprehensive basis of awareness of the many dimensions of aging.

Thus, the major reason that aging is an anthropologist's subject is that anthropology covers the entire range of subdisciplines that are relevant to successful gerontology—as, again, this book illustrates. Biological anthropologists are concerned about the growth and variation of the human body; social anthropologists about the variations in human social systems and their detailed principles of organization. Cultural anthropologists concern themselves with the cultural medium in which people live and experience life. And psychological anthropologists focus on the individual experiences of living one's life, given one's physical endowment and one's place in history and society. All of these specialties can be—and here, they are—brought to focus on a single phenomenon: aging.

There are other "anthropologists' subjects" (aggression and alcoholism come to mind) that require such holistic approaches. But aging is the holistic topic par excellence. The other social and biological sciences are, of course, just as vital. Indeed, some of these subjects will continue to be dominated by these other disciplines. The point here is that anthropologists are only just now beginning seriously to discover that these subjects are some of the places where they belong. It is, in all cases, the holism of anthropology that makes it so essential in putting together an adequate set of solutions and understandings.

Like studies in child development, studies in gerontology have limited themselves to one arc of the life-span. Ultimately, of course, these specialties must grow together. Aging, after all, begins at conception. Growth, after all, stops only at death. To distinguish growth from aging is an artifact of our language—as well, probably, as a recognition that one feels differently when one is growing up than one does when one is "growing down," and that the different life stages pose different policy problems. Yet, for all the linguistic niceties reflecting the feelings and policy needs instead of the mere facts, it is a single set of processes.

With this book, it seems to me, the beginnings of a mature anthropology of aging are reaffirmed; set as they were by the preliminary work of Simmons, the pioneering achievement of Clark and Anderson, the beginning of real comparison in Cowgill and Holmes, and the case studies that have been appearing in recent years. A new professional society has been formed—the Association of Anthropology and Aging—and the new specialty has reached take off. May it have a long life.

Paul Bohannan
University of California
Santa Barbara

Preface

Anthropologists frequently rely upon aged informants, but anthropological studies of aging, with few exceptions, are a comparatively recent phenomenon. Older adults have provided many of the fascinating accounts of the cultures they remembered when they were young. It is now the culture, the experience, and the activities of these older people that we are beginning to investigate. This is a book about aging. It is also a book about anthropology. In the past few years the subjects of age and anthropology have merged. As the merger becomes more complete, we can see a "tradition" solidifying and taking form. This tradition is firmly planted in anthropology, but it also transcends anthropology. It takes us to another area, the interdisciplinary domain of gerontology. In this marriage between anthropology and gerontology we find a dynamic tension as disciplines collide, peer into each other's perspectives, question, challenge, and come back rejuvenated and enriched. The research in this volume is a product of that dynamic tension and the emergent tradition of an anthropology of aging.

Unfortunately, there is a paucity of distinctive anthropological literature on aging. In part, this is because our tradition is still in its infancy. On the other hand, publications on aging from an anthropological perspective and using crosscultural data are not totally absent. Certainly, such works as Simmons' 1945 classic, *The Aged in Primitive Society;* Cowgill and Holmes' *Aging and Modernization;* the essays in Kleemeir's *Aging and Leisure;* Clark and Anderson's *Culture and Aging,* along with scattered articles, chapters in ethnographies, or a few ethnographies such as Benet's *Abkhasians: Long-Living People of the Caucasus* or Ross's *Old People: New Lives* are landmarks in this growing literature. This new study is directed toward meeting two recognized needs in the discipline. First, the bibliography is more than a list of references cited. Containing over 500 bibliographic entries, this is a true resource in searching out the elusive literature on aging and anthropology. Second, this book is oriented toward students and teachers. With the scattered literature, teachers must search, collect, and then integrate disparate points of view. Students, on the other hand, must either spend a fortune on copying or live in the reserve book rooms of their libraries. This volume rectifies this situation by integrating new research with both the established anthropological tradition and the emergent tradition of anthropology and aging.

Anthropology traditionally embraces four major subfields which study origins, persistence, and modifications of humans and the cultures they create. These are physical anthropology, ethnology, archeology, and linguistics. Not all of these subdisciplines are represented in this book. Although archeologists study old things, we at present have little input to our tradition from the archeological record. Linguistics is only marginally represented in Chapters 3 and 4, which use a linguistic approach to culture in their ethnoscientific analysis of age in two cultures. Physical anthropology is represented by Chapter 2 on the biological factors in aging. The majority of research in this volume is ethnological. It raises rather basic issues about aging, about culture, and about our view of older adults. How is age cognitively coded or classified in the culture? What are the values which define the "good life" in old age? How are value conflicts and discrepancies between ideals and the compromises that must occur in real life resolved? What is it like to be old in different cultures and different settings? What resources are available to enable older adults to remain in charge of their lives and to maintain their self-esteem? How may our anthropological methodology contribute to our understanding of aging? And, finally, how may we use this knowledge in resolving some of the difficulties associated with advanced age?

A pervasive theme, and what the Editor considers a primary strength of this book, is that all of the contributors have a very positive view of old age. All are literally furious with the negative stereotype and imagery projected onto older adults. Each anthropologist has asked why. Each anthropologist has seen beyond the stereotype and beyond the age border. They have found things that were unanticipated. They were successful in this endeavor because they are also social scientists, trained to see into and to understand other cultures. In this book we will analyze the culture of the aging in many different contexts.

A volume like this is not the exclusive work of the Editor and the contributors, although it is their names which are associated with the book and its individual sections. It is only fair and proper that the people who made this book possible be acknowledged. I especially extend my appreciation to Arlene Ranalli, of the Office of the Dean of Arts and Sciences, Loyola University of Chicago, who typed several chapters of the manuscript and who prepared the bibliography. For the latter she deserves a medal of honor. I am also grateful to Jeanette Steurich, Secretary, Department of Anthropology, Loyola University of Chicago, who assisted and facilitated the extensive correspondence which must take place if such an endeavor is to succeed. To Dean Ronald Walker, Dean of the College of Arts and Sciences, Loyola University of Chicago, I extend my appreciation of his support of this project in terms of duplication, typing, mailing, and encouragement. I gratefully acknowledge the work of Janet Fletcher, Graduate Research Assistant, Department of Anthropology, Loyola University of Chicago, who proofread, assisted in the assembling of the bibliography, and who read and commented upon the manuscript from a student perspective. Without her commentary, this book would not be as clear and readable for students first encountering anthropology and aging. Finally, I wish to thank all the unnamed informants who shared their lives with their anthropologist and made possible the research upon which this book is based.

Christine L. Fry
Chicago, Illinois

1 Toward an Anthropology of Aging

CHRISTINE L. FRY
Loyola University of Chicago

Anthropology has a long history of being interested in age, but not in aging or the aged. Age has been investigated as a principle of social organization which, along with sex, differentiates roles and status in all human culture. Although many older men and women have served as anthropological informants, ethnographers usually were not interested in the immediate experiences of these informants as anthropological data. These were incidental to the primary issues of reconstructing a rapidly disappearing culture through the memories of these older informants and their knowledge of that culture. Until recently we have not been concerned with the experiences of becoming and being old.

Anthropology also has an established tradition of investigating human development; however, like the other social and psychological sciences, the focus has been on childhood rather than adulthood. In anthropology this takes the form of enculturation studies. As Margaret Clark comments, ". . . if one is to judge from typical anthropological accounts, the span of years between the achievement of adult status and one's funerary rites is either an ethnographic vacuum or is a vast monotonous plateau of invariable behavior" (Clark 1973:86). Anthropology is interested in culture, primarily the culture of adults and the social institutions adults have to negotiate. We have not directly asked questions of how people progress through various cultures as they age or what happens to them as they approach the concluding phases of that progression. We have not been interested in aging as a cognitive domain in our own or other cultures. Only recently have we asked the question of how do people in a culture view the elderly.

ORIGINS OF THE ANTHROPOLOGY OF AGING

Anthropological interests in aging roughly parallel the national concerns of the 1930's and the post-World War II years. As older people were defined as a vulnerable group with special problems, social programs and research intensified. In 1945 the earliest synthetic work on aging in a crosscultural perspective was published. This is the monograph by Leo Simmons, *The Role of the Aged in Primitive Society*. Although prior work had been done in this area, it did not form the basis of Simmons' research (Holmes 1976). Simmons, working at Yale with what was then the recently compiled Human Relations Area Files (HRAF), was able to bring together information from 71 different ethnographically known non-Western cultures. Over 100 sociocultural variables were correlated with 112 variables related to the status and treatment of the elderly. His goal was to discover crosscultural regularities and to ascertain the determinants of favorable or unfavorable conditions for older members of primitive societies. Although the reactions to, and reviews of this work were mixed (Hallowell 1946), this work remains a cornerstone of anthropological investigations of the aged. It also is a classic in the gerontological literature and a landmark in the very early development of mathematical anthropology.

For nearly twenty years, we see a hiatus as remarkably few scholars followed the lead of Leo Simmons. The postwar decades were ones of ferment in anthropology as universities expanded and America's position in the world became that of the leader among nations. Anthropology expanded and flourished. Anthropologists put their minds to the exciting breakthroughs that were being made on all fronts: evolutionary theory, systems theory, cognitive anthropology, the new archeology, transformational linguistics, and the new physical anthropology. Also ethnologists were in the process of discovering peasants and eventually the urban environment. Methodologies and theories were further enriched and became more sophisticated. In the midst of all this, aging and the aged got lost or were a minor part of other issues. Simmons' pioneering work, his monograph and several articles, along with a few scattered reports by anthropologists became a part of the gerontological, rather than anthropological literature.

In the second half of the 1960's, we find the initial crystallization of a commitment to investigate aging and the aged from an anthropological perspective. 1967 witnesses the publication of Margaret Clark's and Barbara Anderson's *Culture and Aging*. During that same year, Margaret Clark also published in *The Gerontologist* an article, "The Anthropology of Aging, A New Area for Studies of Culture and Personality," which was later reprinted in Bernice Neugarten's *Middle Age and Aging* (1968). The pace of research, the scope of commitment, and the involvement of anthropologists has intensified or quickened in the intervening years. Organized symposia and sessions devoted to aging and the aged are now a very regular occurrence at the national meetings of both the gerontological and anthropological associations. Publications, reporting this research, are on the upswing in professional journals in anthropology and in gerontology. Several anthropologists were among the social scientists in attendance at two institutes on Research Priorities on Aging which were held at the University of Chicago in 1976 and 1977. With the realization that "they were not alone in the world" or working outside their discipline, they created the Association for Anthropology and Gerontology (AAGE). Besides sponsoring symposia at national and regional meetings, AAGE maintains a Directory of Anthropologists and Anthropological Research on Aging, and publishes a newsletter and a bibliographic resource file.

Anthropological research on aging is diverse, reflecting the catholic interests of anthropologists and the cultures they study. In spite of the diversity, our investigations are united in a quest to understand culture and cultures. Within the social sciences, anthropology has been the cultural specialist, studying cultural processes and making crosscultural comparisons. Thus, when we approach a neglected or relatively unexplored area, we take with us the theories, approaches and methodologies which have been our strengths as we have explored other cultural domains. In the next two sections we will examine what we know about aging and the aged, first from the comparative perspective and then as a part of cultural processes.

AGING AND CROSSCULTURAL COMPARISONS

A first question of comparative studies is, what are we comparing? For those studies examining aging in a crosscultural perspective, the early work of Simmons led the way. Roles, statuses, treatment, and prestige are the areas of concern. The comparative method is a valuable tool in anthropological research. Before we begin, however, we must ask, What do we want to accomplish through the use of the comparative method? Two basic issues may be effectively explored through crosscultural comparisons. First, by ethnographically examining a wide variety of cultural contexts, we isolate regularities and patterns in the prestige and treatment of older individuals. This involves the search for factors and variables which are present in large numbers of cultures and which may be restricted to particular cultural types. Second, we can investigate the effects of major cultural changes upon how the elderly are integrated and treated in their respective cultures. Initially one must establish the directionality of change (i.e., industrialization or modernization) and then select or arrange known ethnographic cases to represent a sequence or progression toward cultures that have been most affected by the process one is trying to understand.

Among those to consider the effect of major social structural changes upon the elderly, the most comprehensive work is that of Cowgill and Holmes, *Aging and Modernization* (1972a and Cowgill 1974). Modernization is the major transformation of recent history. Numerous scholars have sought to understand the impact of industry. Through the collective research of 18 scholars conducted in a wide variety of cultures, Cowgill and Holmes carefully ordered these cultures according to the degree of modernization. Since similar questions were asked of each scholar discussing the position of the aged in their respective culture, a pattern associated with modernization emerges. In general, they conclude that modernization and the associated features are inversely related to the status and treatment of the elderly. Although depressed prestige of older people is associated with industrializing societies, mature industrial systems appear to support higher prestige for the elderly, especially as cohorts having better education, health, and finances reach old age (Palmore and Manton 1974).

With somewhat less emphasis on change and process, two other studies have isolated factors shaping the relative prestige of older adults. Press and McKool (1972) in a study of the aged in Mesoamerican peasant communities isolate prestige-generating components of roles and statuses in these communities. Roles and statuses generate prestige. Older people are not granted or denied prestige simply because they are old. Four basic prestige-generating components are isolated by Press and McKool as follows:

(1) *Advisory*, as manifest in seeking out and obtaining advice from older people as well as the degree to which it is heeded.

(2) *Contributory*, as apparent in older people participating in and contributing to social activities.

(3) *Control*, as seen in the influence an older individual exerts over others through a monopoly over resources and supernatural sanctions.

(4) *Residual*, as evidenced in the retention of prestige through association with former statuses and competencies.

Maxwell and Silverman (1970) using an information theory, have investigated the status of the elderly in 26 widely distributed societies through the HRAF files. They conclude that the esteem of the elderly is related to the useful knowledge they control. However, when we consider the effects of change and industrialization, information may be outmoded and the prestige components of statuses eroded.

Prestige and esteem are not the only questions anthropologists have considered crossculturally. Jack Goody (1976) presents examples of what is ethnographically known (primarily from African data) of aging within the social groups in preindustrial societies. The domestic group is of primary importance since families control production and consumption (i.e. they act much like a domestic corporation). As an individual ages, his position in the group changes. It is through the old that the young obtain their rightful claims to family resources and consequently older adults find themselves in considerably different social situations in nonindustrial societies than their counterparts in industrial societies. In industrial societies we find greater social differentiation and many areas of social life organized by principles other than kinship.

More elusive qualities have also been examined crossculturally. Crosscultural images and attitudes have been investigated by Arnhoff, Leon, and Lorge (1964) and by Bengston, Dowd, Smith, and Inkeles (1975). Negative images of aging tend to be associated with modernization. Conceptualizations of time and aging have also been considered crossculturally (Smith et. al. 1961). In cultures that are not regulated by the clock, natural rhythms and periodicities are expressed in views of time and the life cycle. Senility and attitudes toward aging have been extensively examined among the Ibo (Shelton 1965, Arth 1968a, 1968b). Senility is rare because of increased involvement in the most prestigious affairs of the community on the part of the elderly and interdependency is a value emphasized in childhood, thus dependency is mutual and subsequently is not despised (See also Palmore 1975).

AGING AND CULTURE

Age is an essential ingredient of all cultures since age is an ascribed characteristic of all individuals. Consequently age is incorporated, elaborated upon and interpreted by that complex world of symbols. Age is a cultural domain. It, however, is not a neat, tightly organized, well bounded or unambiguous domain. Anthropologists have found age grades in all cultures denoting the progression of individuals through the major divisions of the life cycle. These age categories index the life cycle, but that index is imprecise with considerable latitude for idiosyncratic interpretation in both tribal and urban cultures. (Fry 1976). In spite of this lack of clearcut age distinctions, there is order. Anthropologists have found that order in studies of age differentiation; aging, culture, and personality; subcultural variation in aging, aging, and cultural values; and in ethnographic investigations of older people.

Age Differentiation. Age is a rather basic component of socio-cultural life; yet at the present we do not have an integrated theory of age differentiation. At least, anthropologists have not proposed a theory as comprehensive as that of Riley and her associates (1972) on age stratification. Early researches in age differentiation noted continuities and discontinuities over the life cycle (Benedict 1938). Discontinuities punctuate the life cycle, dividing it into culturally significant portions or age grades. Public acknowledgment of these discontinuities occurs through rites of passage (Van Gennep 1960, Webster 1908). An individual is symbolically transformed in the ritual and ceremony surrounding the disjunctures of status transitions. He or she becomes a "new" person with new responsibilities and prerogatives. Age heterogeneity is, thereby, recognized as individuals progress through their life courses.

All cultures must resolve the question of how to structure age differences (Gulliver 1968, Linton 1942). Undoubtedly, the resolution of this problem is as variable as the institutions in which age differences are salient criteria for interaction and allocation of responsibilities. Vast amounts of anthropological research have been invested in the panhuman institution of kinship which is age heterogeneous. A gold mine of information is available on the domestic structuring of age differences and similarities; intergenerational relations; intergenerational transferal of wealth and power; and the cyclical nature of domestic units and the like. Marital gerontocracies are one of the more exotic aspects of aging to receive the attentions of social anthropologists. In several polygynous Australian cultures (Warner 1958, Hart and Pilling 1961, Goodale 1971) and African societies (Goody 1969), a man's career and power does not mature until he is old. Only at that time is he able to embark on his marital career by marrying several young ladies. The bachelorhood of younger men, in turn, is prolonged until they are at the peak of their careers when they are old. At the other extreme, in other societies a man may be stripped of his wealth in providing the obligatory gifts that accompany the marriages of his sons. Upon the marriage of the last son, his wealth depleted, he takes up residence with an adult child and figuratively "sleeps on his own grave" (Stenning 1971).

Age differentiation in other institutions is only incompletely understood. In age-heterogeneous institutions such as politics and religion, advanced age does not appear to be an impediment in attaining office. In fact, it may be an asset as some elderly become clan leaders, political specialists, adjudicators and even senators. Some of the aged may be the religious and ritual experts since they are generationally proximate to the ancestors and the supernatural.

Age is salient to the productive organization and the division of labor in every society. This may be entwined in kinship and the domestic organization or in the corporate structure of industrialized societies. Other institutions are noted for their homogeneity. These are formal and informal associations where an individual exercises choice in deciding to participate or not. Friendship cliques and most voluntary associations are noted for their commonalities in interests and other features, including age.

Age itself is a very important principle of group formation. Anthropologists investigating cultures primarily in East Africa and on the Great Plains of the United States have found homogeneous groups formed exclusively by age (Evans-Prichard 1968, Dyson Hudson 1963, Prins 1953, Lowie 1916). These are called "age sets," which are defined as corporate groups composed of people belonging to the same age category or age grade. Age sets take many forms ranging from age societies to age villages (Wilson 1951a, 1951b). Even in this variety, anthropologists have worked out conceptual schemes to understand the structure of age groups (Stewart 1977). Age sets have many apparent functions in allocating and mobilizing work on public projects, constituting the army, or in forming the public arena itself. Although we have no one reason for the appearance of age sets, they do serve as important integrative institutions. They counterbalance the potential centrifugal tendencies in powerful, autonomous lineages by uniting all males of the same age into one association. Eisenstadt in *From Generation to Generation* argues that age-homogenous groups (age sets and even grades in school) function to transfer loyalties from a particularistic orientation (i.e., in families) to a more universalistic orientation (i.e., in tribal politics or in occupational structures). Societies in which age is such an apparent and important principle of social organization are exciting laboratories for the development of theories of age differentiation and understanding the dynamics of relations between peers and other age groups. For instance, transitions from one age or age set to another are not always "smooth" in these societies (Foner and Kertzer 1978). With the ambivalencies associated with transitions into and out of the most rewarding roles, we find generations negotiating and drawing alliances with one another to transact generational succession (Spencer 1965, Bowers 1965). Age set societies make explicit that which is more covert and diffuse about age in other kinds of societies.

Culture, Personality, and Age: Anthropology, with its focus on culture and cultural processes, is also interested in how these shape human development and ultimately the individual and his or her personality. Culture and personality studies are concerned with the psychological aspects of culture and the effect of a sociocultural environment upon personality configurations (Clark 1967). Margaret Clark and Barbara Anderson effectively employed this perspective in their study of the mentally ill and mentally well elderly in San Francisco (1967). Differences in adjustment are examined in the interplay between psychological variables in the sociocultural matrix of American society. Aging is seen as continuing development within this milieu. Development involves change and adaptation. As a part of a psychological and cultural process, Clark and Anderson identify five adaptive tasks for the aged (also see Clark 1973):

> (1) Recognition of aging and definition of instrumental limitations.
> (2) Redefinition of physical and social life space.
> (3) Substitution of alternate sources of need-Satisfaction.
> (4) Reassessment of criteria for evaluation of the self.
> (5) Reintegration of values and life goals.

Recognition, redefinition, substitution, reassessment, and reintegration are all parts of the process of accomodating to aging. Older informants who were mentally ill had difficulties in meeting one or several of these adaptive tasks. Interestingly, those informants who cling most rigidly to the core American values, were the ones with the most difficulty.

Aging and Subcultural Variation: Anthropologists are contributing to our understanding of the complex web of relationships between poverty, minority group status, ethnicity, and the varying patterns of aging within groups characterized by all three factors. This is especially critical since age in urban societies is often identified with and compounded by poverty. Many impoverished old are members of ethnic or minority groups who have different cultural and historical experiences than the Anglo population. Also, they may have experienced a lifetime of discrimination, prejudice and stereotyping.

Ethnic minorities in accomodating to poverty and discrimination have used strengths in their respective cultures. These strengths are expressed in social networks and cultural values. Kiefer (1971) has noted that "structural intimacy" characterizes the culture of many working class and ethnic subcultures. The quality of social relations and the cohesiveness of the social group are valued. Solidarity and continuity of the group rather than any immediate benefit that membership may bring to the individual is emphasized. An individual's fate is inseparable from the group since both success and failure are collectively shared. A "collectivism," as distinguished from the individualism which pervades Anglo America, is a value orientation among many minorities. One is not judged alone in a competitive arena. One does not have to measure up to universal and abstract criteria. Instead, one is a part of a network of mutually binding relationships where one is judged according to role specific and personal criteria. Of course, this has implications for the aging process, cultural styles of aging, and for the self-esteem of minority elderly. Studies of specific minority elderly in America include the American Indian (Levy 1967), Mexican-Americans (Clark and Mendelson 1969, Moore 1971a), black Americans (Jackson 1971a, 1971b), and Asian-Americans (Kalish and Yuen 1971, Keifer 1971).

Cultural Values and Esteem: A very difficult area to study, but one that anthropologists have investigated, is the value structure of a culture. American society is noted for its emphasis on rugged individualism and the associated values of freedom and independence. If one is not self-reliant, one's humanity is reduced and one's morality is questioned. Independence/dependence are the positive/negative contrasts of a value which produces deeply ingrained conflicts for older Americans and older adults in other cultures. Independence is rooted in expectations of roles and statuses which pertain to the reciprocity or give-and-take involved in those social positions. To be independent is to be able to give and maintain a balance in a relationship as one also takes. In contrast, dependence is nonreciprocal taking. Margaret Clark points out (1972) that nonreciprocity is tolerated in certain roles with definite limitations, such as illness, rites of passage, or infancy and childhood. Chronic dependency, voluntary or involuntary, borders on freeloading. In many nonindustrial societies, the roles and statuses of older people enable them to give something of immediate use to others (i.e., the prestige-generating components). Thus they can take without remorse. As we have seen in industrial societies, the prestige-generating components of the statuses of older adults are reduced. Often what they have to give is of little value. When others are needed, little remains to give in exchange for their help. Reciprocity is out of balance, thereby jeopardizing integrity and self-esteem. Dependency is not exclusively an American problem, but is faced and resolved in various ways by all cultures.

Ethnography of Old Age: Anthropologists do not rely exclusively upon surveys to ascertain the state of affairs in a culture, subculture, or community under investigation. More often than not, the anthropologist uses his or her own personality, lives with the people, shares food with informants, develops intense relationships, and listens, watches, and records ethnographic information. To employ this technique in exploring the cultural world of older people requires that these people be a part of an interactive setting, perhaps even living together in the same location. Recently, anthropologists have ethnographically explored retirement residences, retirement communities, age-graded trailer parks, public housing for the elderly, and inner-city aged.

Retirement facilities, especially retirement communities, appeared as a specialized residential development in the post-World War II housing boom. Social scientists noted their variety and proposed theories on the dire effects of age segregation (Mumford 1956). Inspite of these early pleas for the integration of older people with other age groups, subsequent sociological research has indicated age concentration has benefits in terms of the social integration for working-class elderly (Rosow 1961, 1967). Ethnographic studies of these settings have been conducted by gerontologists and sociologists as well as anthropologists (Carp 1966, Jacobs 1974, 1975). Anthropological studies of age-homogenous residences, employing participant observation, emphasize the formation of a communal life. Such studies include: Idle Haven, a trailer park for working class retired (Johnson 1971); two adult mobil home estates in Arizona (Fry 1979); Arden, a retirement community of over 500 apartments in California (Byrne 1974); Merrill Court, an apartment building of elderly in San Francisco (Hochschild 1973); Les Floralies, a French retirement residence for CNRO workers (Ross 1974a, 1974b, 1977); a Sephardic home for the elderly (Hendel-Sebestyen 1979) and multiethnic housing units (Kandel and Heider 1979, Wellin and Boyer 1979). Ethnographic investigations of residential settings have also embraced single-room occupancy hotels in American inner cities (Sokolovsky and Cohen 1976).

Contrary to the early projections for geriatric ghettos, ethnographers report the existence of viable communities (Keith 1979). The attractiveness of age-homogeneous residential arrangements is in part attested by the long waiting list for openings in public housing for the old, but is more irrefutable in the success of age-restricted condominiums and retirement communities that have mushroomed in the Sun Belt of the United States during the past two decades. In minimizing risk, overcoming negative images, and attracting the more affluent older market, developers have packaged and sold more than residential units. They have designed, allocated space, built facilities, and made provisions for the maintenance of a social organization. Consequently, the social organization of many age-graded units is the result of planning (Fry

1977). The formal aspects of life are most directly affected by decisions made in the planning process, while the more informal arenas are only marginally influenced.

Age-homogeneous communities may be described as a combination of friendship and factions. As elsewhere, friendship cliques are formed on the basis of residential proximity and mutual interests. Factions serve as social borders in further shaping friendship networks. For instance, socialization to retirement in Les Floralies begins when cues to one's political identification (Communist/non-Communist) becomes apparent (Ross 1974a). Then one is actively recruited into the respective factions, networks, and activities. This and other studies have revealed that factions focus their disputes on administrative policy and its implementation within the community as it affects everyday life. Factionalism is not a socially disruptive force (except for the administrators and resident council presidents). Instead, it is socially creative with residents articulating into a social order which is concerned about its present and future.

Elderly are also concentrated in the inner city. The older people living in single-room occupancy hotels are known to be physically and psychologically sicker than their age peers. Yet they survive. Until recently, very little was known about the social networks of these older people who meet their needs in the decaying centers of American cities. Network analysis indicates that isolation and lack of significant networks among this elderly population is another myth (Sokolovsky and Cohen 1976). Networks are significant, but they are of low density and are highly compartmentalized. Intimacy and the willingness to invest themselves in other people is a characteristic which is lacking in the social relations of single-room occupancy hotel residents. This may be in response to lifelong difficulties or to different ways of meeting needs for intimacy and the meanings of intimacy (Erickson and Eckert 1977).

EMERGENT TRENDS AND CONCERNS

Age, aging, and the aged are within the province of anthropological investigations. Anthropology of aging and the aged, however, is a relatively youthful part of our discipline. It is maturing at a time when our nation is becoming conscious of inequalities and problems as we as a nation age. Other disciplines, too, are awakening to the challenge and need to understand age and older people. Gerontology, the study of the old, is by definition multidisciplinary. The contributions and research of many disciplines are welcome and are incorporated into a growing body of knowledge. As we have seen, anthropologists are participating in this endeavor. With active involvement and commitment, new problems and concerns emerge. Our encounter with the research and interpretations of other disciplines lead us to reflect upon our anthropological foundations; to evaluate critically and incorporate new ideas into our perspective; and to see the old in a new light. The chapters in this volume combined the perennial interests of anthropology with issues crystalizing in our studies of aging.

Anthropology is almost unique among all the disciplines studying all of humanity. Our perspective is comprehensive, limiting itself only to *Homo sapiens sapiens:* humans at all times and in all places. The importance of anthropology for the study of aging is that it is panhuman, evolutionary, and uncompromisingly comparative. With such an ecumenical viewpoint, anthropologists provide distinctive insights into the panhuman experience of aging. These insights are not generated simply because anthropologists are blessed with this perspective. Our perspective leads anthropologists to ask certain questions and to ask them in a particular way. With this in mind, I will discuss the chapters in this volume in terms of the recurrent themes in the research from all over the world. These I identify as (1) culture and the comparative viewpoint; (2) anthropological methodologies; (3) age and culture: the ideal and the real; and (4) cultural images of older people. The first two stem from the nature of anthropology, while the latter are emerging from the investigation of aging.

CULTURE AND THE COMPARATIVE VIEWPOINT

Culture is *the* most basic concept of anthropology and is the outstanding contribution of anthropology to the sciences in the twentieth century. Defining culture as a word is an empty intellectual activity. As a factor affecting the lives of people, culture is the symbolic dimension through which we comprehend order and predictability in our world. Every chapter in this book is concerned with culture, including the chapter by Jeff Beaubier on the biological factors in aging. The research in this volume sees culture as something humans use in negotiating each other and their environment. People manage their affairs by manipulating their cultural rules. Strategies are generated; situations are transacted. Cultural norms, learned through enculturation, guide peoples lives, but they are not mindlessly and blindly followed. Humans, including older humans, are seen as active participants rather than passive puppets.

Active older people are to be found everywhere utilizing and creating cultural resources. In Chapter 7, Virginia Kerns reports that older Black Carib women are quite competent in managing their own affairs to the benefit of their adult children as well as themselves. Elderly Corsican migrants, described by Linda Cool in Chapter 9, are actively engaged in social networks and maintain an ethnic identity. Even in India, where one is supposed to withdraw in old age, Sylvia Vatuk (Chapter 8) finds older informants involved in shopping, litigation, supervising building contractors, and taking care of spiritual matters. From places and cultures as far apart as peasant villages in Colombia (Chapter 4) and American Indians in Oklahoma (Chapter 6), we find older people integrated into and actively contributing to the social life of their communities. Some older adults have even created communities of their own (Chapter 10) and are actively involved in making each of those communities better according to the image of a favorite faction.

In viewing cultures, anthropologists maintain a goal of "holism" (Lowell Holmes discusses this and other characteristics of anthropology in more detail in his assessment in Chapter 15). This generally means we emphasize the context and focus on a wide range of interacting components in that context. Behavior and the meaning of that behavior are not studied in isolation. The classic ethnography is holistic in that it is a "descriptive integration" of all relevant factors. Chapters 3-10 of this book contain ethnographic descriptions and analyses of cultural contexts and factors pertinent to aging. Chapters 11-14 focus on contextual factors in creating and alleviating problems.

An ultimate goal of anthropology is the testing of anthropological theory through comparative cultural analysis. If we are to understand the human experience, we must see it in all its variety and find principles for unity and diversity. Cultures or subcultures are the anthropological laboratory or testing ground for theories about human behavior. By examining a number of ethnographic cases it is possible to isolate factors salient to a particular issue. Virtually every chapter references and compares what is known about aging in the United States and Europe with the particular cultural or subcultural group being studied. Theories about aging developed in these societies are subjected to the anthropological test. Sylvia Vatuk (Chapter 8) and Linda Cool (Chapter 9) evaluate disengagement theory in India and among Corsican migrants to

Paris. Jennie Keith (Chapter 10) evaluates her theory of communi-ty creation through the comparative data from eight age-homoge-neous communities. In Chapter 5, Charlotte Ikels investigates the ideal of filial piety and support for the old in three different con-texts in Chinese society. Christine Fry (Chapter 3) compares the dimensions of the American life cycle with those of the Maasai. American Indians (Chapter 6) and Polish-Americans (Chapter 14) are contrasted with Anglo-Americans. Comparisons are the back-bone of anthropological theory, yet cross-cultural material on aging is scattered and downright scarce. This book is comparative in that only two chapters are based on data from middle-class Americans. If we are to understand the panhuman experience of aging, we must base it on the data from a wide variety of cultures and use those cultures to evaluate our theories.

ANTHROPOLOGICAL METHODOLOGIES

With a tradition of investigating cultural diversity in all corners of the world, anthropological fieldwork is noted for involvement with data, the primacy of the data in our interpretations, and the diversity in the techniques through which we gather that data. A primary goal of anthropological research is to comprehend the world as our informants see it and to grasp the important features in that context. If the culture is totally alien, obviously one does not immediately proceed by testing hypotheses and building com-plicated models. Instead, one tries to become informed by observ-ing and inquiring of people living in that culture. The role of in-formant in anthropological research is considerably different from respondant or subject in sociological or psychological research. In-formants act as enculturating agents by explaining why things are as they are. They are more active in shaping the research than either respondants who answer questionnaires or subjects who participate in experiments. The data our informants provide are primary to our descriptions and to any hypothesis or model we wish to evaluate. They tell us what questions are most productive and how to ask those questions in a manner that is culturally meaningful. An ethnographer is concerned about the adequacy of any representation of an ethnographic setting and the appropriate-ness of any instrument developed to evaluate a theoretical model.

Anthropologists are most concerned about the quality of their data. A major rift in the social sciences centers on the question of quality versus quantity. It is an unfortunate dichotomy since the complementarity of both types of research is obscured. Qualitative research is just as we have described for anthropology. An ethnographer asks the question of what qualities are in a particular context. Informants tell us. Ethnographers build models of that context through continued probing and observing. This is much like children as they build theories of language and the culture of adults in trying to interact with adults. The process is intensive and involves long-term interaction with informants. Quantitative research, on the other hand, asks the question, how much? It, too, tries to build models of a culture, but these models are very different in that they are much more abstract. A researcher isolates a few aspects from the potentially many features in a context and tries to see how they are related by the number of times they are associated. Consequently, large amounts of data are needed and these data must be in a standardized form. Surveys are conducted with questionnaires or interview guides, with the massing of large quantities of data to be digested in the local computer and interpreted by the investigator. Survey research is extensive since large numbers of respondents participate in the research, but contacts are of short duration and of less intensity.

Both research strategies have their advantages and drawbacks. Qualitative research enables one to ask, What is there?—a rather basic question. It enables us to see things differently and to find new variables that may have been overlooked previously. If we restrict ourselves to qualitative research, we cannot find out to what extent our new knowledge is true. Also, we may be biased because our key informants may be biased. Quantitative research requires an adequate and preferably a probability sample and enables an investigator to ascertain to what extent the hypothesized relationship between variables is or is not apparent. An inherent danger in survey research is another kind of bias. This bias is toward the normative or ideal. Respondents often tend to reply in terms of what they think they should do rather than what they actually do. Also, questionnaires sometimes are biased toward the culture of the discipline and the investigator. Although this may have congruencies with the culture of the respondents, many of the finer nuances and potentially significant factors may be lost. Quantitative-qualitative, or intensive-extensive, may be viewed as complementary rather than in opposition. As complementary approaches they become sequential phases in research with the qualitative telling us what to look for and how to phrase culturally relevant hypotheses and the quantitative revealing the extent and the degree of association between appropriate variables.

The ethnographic techniques used are almost as varied as the cultural settings in which they are used. Participant observation, the most renowned of anthropological tools, is a label for heterogeneous research procedures. Within this tradition of exploring cultural variation, a "cookbook" of research procedures is useless. The procedures actually used arise through the interaction between the cultural context and the problem the ethnographer is investigating. In some settings and for certain problems, a variant of participant observation may be ideal, but in other contexts with different problems a survey or formal interviewing may be the best data-collection technique. In many of the chapters of this book, we see effective and complementary use of participant observation and survey techniques to answer some of our basic questions about aging.

The variety of techniques used to obtain the data upon which the chapters in this book are based clearly indicate that anthropologists have a variety of recipies in their methodological cookbook. The techniques used by Fry (Chapter 3) and Kagan (Chapter 4) to look at age as a cultural domain and the meanings of age are cognitive anthropological procedures. They elicit an "emic" or "inside view" through an analysis of native classifications (Romney and D'Andrade 1964, Tyler 1969). Both use standardized procedures appropriate for the context, Kagan asking a formal set of questions of her informants in Colombia and Fry administering a card sort as a part of a larger survey. In Chapters 5-10, our concern is with older adults in specific contexts. Virginia Kerns' insights among the Black Caribs, as she indicates, could only be obtained by participant observation and interviewing (Chapter 7). Jennie Keith (Chapter 10) is one of the few scholars investigating life in a retirement community to have "moved in on them." Formal interviews combined with a longer-term involvement provides the information about aging in Chinese society, India, Oklahoma Indians, and Parisian Corsicans is based.

Chapters 11-13 involve a consideration of problems and potential resolutions. Consequently, the focus is narrow and survey strategies are used to examine patterns and associations. These patterns, however, are always explained and related to what the ethnographer has learned qualitatively about the context. Eunice Boyer (Chapter 11) relates improved health perception to the roles and activities she found in a community which developed in public housing for the elderly. Jonas and Wellin discover and document the mutual aid networks in the same community, but because they did not restrict themselves to the formal interview they are able to see the finer differences in the male and female patterns of reciprocity. Similarly, Carol Schulz (Chapter 13) documents sex differences in the acceptance or rejection and anxiety about death. Her year's study of community life permitted her to see the reasons for the pattern in her data. Knowledge of the Polish-American family led Maria Siemaszko to document such differences and to contrast these differences with those in Anglo families in a way relevant for social service planning. Through combinations of appropriate methodologies to study aging and the aged in a variety of cultures, anthropologists are seeing the elderly in a new light. We now turn to these issues.

AGE AND CULTURE: THE IDEAL AND THE REAL

Culture is the symbolic medium through which we comprehend our world and negotiate it. As such, it is ideational, a cognitive code we use to guide our behavior. We use that code to evaluate our behavior and the behavior of others. Through this guide, or "design for living," we know the good life, and can readily express the qualities of the world as it should be. This is what anthropologists call "ideal culture." Ideal cultures are just that, when contrasted to actual behavior. Compromises are made as people's abilities and skills are used in going about making a living and interacting in a "real" world. When compromises are extreme or where two evaluative standards point in different directions, people experience value conflicts. Advanced age is often associated with ambivalence because of increased difficulties in affirming the ideals in everyday life.

Values are expressed as dualities with the positive and negative contrasting. The positive is the good and we try to realize and incorporate the positive. Dependency-independency is a major value orientation which has been investigated by anthropologists (see above). It is a value which is rooted in the panhuman basis for exchange, reciprocity. Charlotte Ikels (Chapter 5) examines this problem in China within the ideal of filial piety. Although she identifies the ideal of filial piety, she also finds that the ideal is not always actualized, especially in urban Hong Kong. Karen Jonas and Edward Wellin (Chapter 12) focus on the problem of dependency and how it is resolved in public housing for the elderly. Here they found older adults continuing the give-and-take of social life through mutual support networks. Although life is the positive to be affirmed, death is a reality occuring at any time, but with increased probability as age advances. Carol Schulz (Chapter 13) examines this duality in a small town in rural America. The role structure and life long patterns contribute to the successful or unsuccessful resolution of death anxiety. What is the good life?

Obviously, we cannot provide a universal answer, but for older Colombian peasants (Chapter 4) we find such qualities as care and affection, responsibilities, and respect are rather basic values.

The ideal and the real are also a basic duality in anthropology. Primarily because of our longer-term involvement with informants we realize that what they tell us is not always what they do. Ideal culture is easily expressed as the "shoulds," the "oughts," or the rules and norms. As people interact, these are compromised. Thus by our "moving in" and participating in the culture of our informants we see both the real and the ideal. By seeing both, we see intracultural variation. We become increasingly hesitant to describe *the* Chinese, *the* Corsicans, *the* Black Caribs, or even *the* aged, as if everyone so designated believes and behaves in the same way. This is especially important when we consider older people. We refer to them as "*the* aged" or "*the* elderly," but they, in every culture of the world, are the most heterogeneous, the most diverse age group.

It is primarily our methodology which enables us to grasp this variation. If we elicited only ideal culture, we would find uniformity. Among the Black Caribs, Virginia Kerns (Chapter 7) finds consensus in people's view of old age as a negative period of decline. She also found very active, competent women manipulating social networks for the mutual benefit of themselves and their children. Charlotte Ikels (Chapter 5) looks directly at the variation in treatment of older Chinese in village and urban contexts. Linda Cool (Chapter 9) finds variation among her informants in ethnic participation and identity. We should not be surprised that people vary, including older people, and that their behavior does not always measure up to the ideal. But by the very fact we are human, we use the short-cuts our culture provides by categorizing and classifying others in terms of ideals and shared characteristics. The aged, however, have only one characteristic in common—their age.

CULTURAL IMAGES OF OLDER PEOPLE

Categories simplify variation, but they also contain an evaluative dimension. The most pervasive theme in the chapters of this book is a deep concern over the negative images and stereotypes about the old. Stereotypes are barriers which maintain a social distance between people. Age boundaries exist and it is extremely difficult to see through or across these borders. The young cannot see, nor do they want to see, the old. The old cannot see the young or middle aged. Negativism reinforces and increases the gulf. As with other stereotypes, the few older adults we encounter are the exceptions, not the rule. The anthropologists in this volume sense something is wrong. They have seen through the stereotype. Older people are people. As our anthropological forefathers in their day championed unpopular causes such as the fight against scientific racism, we, today are advocating an end to ageism, both covert and overt.

Although images of older people are expressed differently in specific cultures, ageism is a common theme. It is a theme which becomes more intense in industrial societies. Our curiosity should lead us to ask the question, Why? We have not begun to explore this issue systematically, but we can offer possible reasons. First, on a psychological level we find individuals wrestling with the interplay of values, particularly those of life and death. If advanced age is associated with closer proximity to death, then old age is negative. This is reinforced by associated negative consequences of aging such as chronic health problems and poverty. Such an explanation, however, will encounter problems in the ethnographic laboratory of world cultures. Many older adults enjoy elevated prestige primarily because they are closest to the ancestors. Thus the association of age with death could well be a culturally specific interpretation, a rationalization, the product of a particular value configuration.

When we look at negative images as a product of sociocultural processes, we ask other questions. We can look at roles and statuses, as has been done, when we consider the aged and the effects of modernization. We can also ask, What does a negative stereotype accomplish? Who (what age group) stands to benefit the most? On the basis of our current information, the answer is unclear. In this volume, Virginia Kerns tells us (Chapter 7) that elderly Black Carib women use the stereotype to make demands on their children. Siemaszko (Chapter 14) sees the stereotype as mobilizing public support for the elderly in need of social services. On the other hand, in India (Chapter 8) the ideology of withdrawal in old age reinforces an intergenerational transfer of family resources (about which both the young and old are ambivalent). The negativism, the image of the sick, impoverished old, comes between and separates the generations. As we develop an answer, we most likely will be turning our attention to the problems of generational succession. People perceive and respond to the world in terms of their cultural images. Their passions, their fears, their motivations are shaped by these perceptions. People are rewarded when they ascend into life's rewarding roles, and then move on to allow their children the same privilege. Images of age and the ways in which they are used by respective age groups will provide insights into generational integration and conflict.

AGE, AGING, AND THE AGED

In concluding, two further issues must be raised. Our anthropological investigations of aging are maturing to a point where we can pull scattered studies together. To do this, we need a theory, one that will become a significant part of the anthropological tradition. As Jennie Keith argues (Chapter 10), this should be a theory of age differentiation. We cannot separate older people from younger people and treat them as an isolated phenomenon. We must consider age in its totality. What is age doing in the social organization? How is age culturally structured and organized? What are the qualities of intergeneratonal relations? What are the qualities of peer relations? As we find the answers to these questions, we will find more issues and problems. This will become especially true as we use our anthropological perspective which is panhuman, evolutionary, and comparative.

Another issue that cannot be overemphasized is that older people are people. They are people who happen to have been here a long time. The anthropologists contributing to this volume have discovered that. Our anthropology of aging will be predicated on that simple fact. We should not be surprised when older adults find enjoyment in dancing, singing, horseback riding, hunting, and many other activities associated with younger people. Nor should we be puzzled when an older person says, "I am happy." A few years ago, following an interview an older woman escorted me to the lobby of her apartment house. In the elevator we were joined by another woman, whom my informant later identified as being 75 years old. As the elevator descended, it became apparent that the woman was slightly senile. In the lobby, my informant grabbed my arm and guided me to the door. Once out of ear shot, she exclaimed, "That is what age does to you! Thank God, I am only 83!" Most of the older adults represented in the research in this volume are like her. They, too, are saying, "Thank God." They are intact, and even if they suffer some impairment, they are managing their own affairs. It is only with the extremes of old age that the problems become extreme, and even then there is variation.

2 Biological Factors in Aging

JEFF BEAUBIER
Sweet Briar College

Aging is a phenomena which human beings have been concerned about, resisted, and ultimately have had to accept. *Ever since our distant Neanderthal relatives recognized death and acknowledged it by interring the dead and including thoughtful gifts of tools and even flowers, our species has been blessed with a dichotomy: life-death, positive-negative. Age is an indicator of our progression between these dualities. As culture became more complex and the exact and predictive sciences emerged, humans have tried to comprehend, to understand, and somehow to intervene to slow the aging process. The goal is to prolong the positive–life. Our primordial question is what causes aging and what can we do about it.*

Biologically our answer cannot be divorced from the developmental sequences set in motion at conception. Genetic information sequentially differentiates cells and builds an embryo, a fetus, an infant, a child, an adolescent, and finally an adult. However, as Jeff Beaubier points out everything known wears out, including the adult. For humans, the physical state of the organism is at its highest level between the chronological ages of eighteen and thirty. Growth is complete; skills and reaction times are at their best, and biologically the organism stabilizes. Between thirty and forty-two the signs of age begin to make their appearance. Reaction times increase; the lens of the eye begins to harden, making focusing more of a problem; and the efficiency of oxygen transfer in the lungs begins to decline. Blood pressure begins to rise as the tissue in the arteries becomes more ineleastic. Strength and endurance, however, remain fairly constant into the forties with some sacrifice in speed. By the fourth and fifth decade of life, the signs of age become more pronounced. Strength and endurance decline; the number of muscle cells decline; tissues become less elastic; blood pressures rise; oxygen transfer becomes increasingly inefficient; and females go through menopause.

From the sixth decade on the effects of prior health, nutrition, exercise, and quality of life are most pronounced. In spite of tremendous variability, physiologically the tissues are less capable of carrying out functions. Metabolic rates decline as does cardiac function. Lungs further decline in size and ability to oxygenate the blood. Kidneys receive less blood and as membranes become less permeable, they remove fewer wastes from the blood. It takes a longer time for nerves to transmit their messages and stronger stimuli are needed to trigger sensory information. Consequently the senses through which we articulate with the world, begin to convey less or incomplete information. Thus, the pattern is of a biological organization which establishes and maintains itself and its integrity. This is followed by a gradual and then increased inability to maintain its integrity.

To understand aging in an animal as complex as a human being requires an analysis of both the biological processes and the socio-cultural context. Jeff Beaubier elaborates on the theme developed in the previous chapter. Humans are animals and, like all animals, are continuous with and products of nature. Our species is also distinctive in that our behavior is conditioned by something we call culture. We learn, we share with others, and we perceive and respond to our world through symbols. Although this ability is based upon our biological capabilities, it is extra somatic or beyond the body. Culture, however, is not independent of the biological organism as the biological organism is not independent of culture. Instead, they are intertwined in the complicated phenomena of human behavior. Since the way we behave affects our biological well-being and our biological well-being affects our behavior and identity, we must, then consider both sides of the coin.

As a physical anthropologist who has conducted research on human longevity, Jeff Beaubier focuses upon biological factors. In the past few decades our understanding of biological processes has been revolutionized by discoveries in molecular genetics and biology. Systematic changes occur in the aging organism. Are we genetically programmed to age and die? Jeff Beaubier responds with a resounding no. If anything, we are genetically programmed to live and reproduce. Through natural selection populations consist of individuals who are best able to live in a given environment. Aging is an increasing interference in the transmission of genetic information and consequent randomness in the biological organization.

As an anthropologist, puzzled by this phenomena, Jeff Beaubier directly looks at the interface between biology and culture. It is one's genetic endowment combined with the available cultural resources and patterns that accounts for longevity. He dramatically transmits this message through comparative biographies of two men he recognized as being old. The message is clear. With attention to nutrition, exercise, and avoidance of toxic substances and undue stress (all cultural factors or influenced by culture), while young, the genetic endowment (biological factors) can maximally be expressed.

Although we can preserve the integrity of our biological being, we still have the question whether we will ever cure aging. First of all, aging is not a disease. The often used phrase, "No one ever died of old age", is true. Aging is a natural process. We have made strides in increasing the life expectancy for the majority of human beings in the industrialized nations of the world. During the past century, years have been added to the lives of the average person, while the maximum life span remains unchanged at 120-150 years. Through the application of medical technology, the acute diseases of childhood and young adulthood have effectively been combated, permitting more people to live longer. Demographically, the effects of this are quite apparent in that population has increased. Currently 10 percent of the population of the United States are over sixty-five, with some projections of between 15 to 17 percent older adults by as early as the year 2000. Industrialized nations are justifiably concerned about the effects of an aging population upon their economies and social service programs.

If we could slow the processes of aging or find an anti-aging drug, we would completely transform our world as we know it. What are the consequences of extending the human life span for any society? What would our society look like without age or with life spans that extend for three and four centuries? It is very difficult to fathom an answer since age and generational succession are basic ingredients of all societies. With markedly increased life spans, we do know that population will increase and that generational competition for resources will also intensify.

We desire longevity, since this is the continued affirmation of a positive, life, as contrasted with a negative, death. We also desire a lot of positives we can loosely call quality of life. By blindly pursuing a single goal of near-immortality, without consideration of the consequences for the social organization and the culture that makes life worth living, we may short change ourselves and future generations.

The basic problem in unraveling potential for human *longevity* and thereby increasing adaptability of populations lies in what causes aging. Are species specific longevity rates in humans and other highly evolved plant and animal species the result of processes of wear and tear or due to a small specific set of genes or a combination of both of these? That is the central problem pursued by biological gerontologists today. Its solution depends on new research into causes for longevity, laboratory findings, and epidemiologic evaluations of relevant studies, including why people in different communities and cultures live as long as they do.

Two directions are evident in attempts to unravel the mysteries of aging. First is a search for specific genes some gerontologists believe initiate aging. Other gerontologists believe aging is caused by processes that increase *randomness in biologic molecules.* This latter direction views the search for aging loci ("specific genes inducing aging") as looking for the nonexistent. The second view is supported by the fact of great variation in life expectancy rates of organic species having widely diverse habitats. This suggests environmental influences is the prime aging factor.

A comprehensive theory on what causes aging will certainly include notions of both genetics and environment. The genetic component, however, will probably not consist of genes that actively initiate aging changes. Rather aging will turn out to be due to the effects of environmental stresses (of many kinds) that work themselves out on the *weakest parts of the body*. For instance certain diseases, such as heart disease, arteriosclerosis, diabetes, and so on, occur over and over. The heart, blood vessels, and organ that produces insulin are more susceptible than other body parts to the insults, challenges, and wear and tear characteristic of our culture. In this sense we can say genes are involved. But this is a passive involvement, not one that actively, purposively ages the organism.

Although scientists seeking information on what causes aging experiment with rats, mice, and other small mammals, and even birds and fishes, man is of special interest. Unlike other species contemporary man and his transitional apelike ancestors survived in ecologic niches dependent upon nonbiological materials and processes. Homo sapiens evolved intricate patterns of tool making, language, customs, and values. This shared, learned behavior—*culture*—is our primary survival mechanism. Culture is a complex adaptive mechanism arising from a biologic base of bipedalism, evolution of hands, large brains, and language. How long a species characteristically lives depends on the survival mechanisms it acquired in evolution. But in humans this refers to our social behavior as well as our biological endowment. Thus to understand aging in our species we must deal simultaneously with biological as well as cultural factors.

Therefore, at least two goals of theoretical gerontology include elucidations of a theory of biologic aging (concerned with life span) and distribution, causes, and consequences of longevity, specifying forms of social life that promote it (concerned with life expectancy and performance).

LIFE SPAN VS. LIFE EXPECTANCY

Before examining the causes for longevity it is necessary to see what is possible versus what actually happens so far as how long people live is concerned. Of necessity we must deal with concepts of *life span* and *life expectancy*. Life span refers to the chronologic age of life for the oldest living members of species. It is a critical, limiting time boundary within which all will die. How long an individual organism actually lives, or *performs* depends on its life experiences. No matter how good were its environmental conditions, however, a species' specific life span is the inexorable limitation on life. As Hayflick (1975) has pointed out, since variations in life span between species is much greater than variations in life expectancy (average performance) within species, life span must be limited by universal biologic properties inherent in species. That is, life span is an inherent property of species and depends on their genes. This last point will be examined after a discussion of life expectancy and performance. Table 2.1 is an abbreviated list of life spans and expectancies well known by biologists.

TABLE 2.1 Selected Species' Maximum Life Spans and Average Life Expectancies

Species	Maximum Life Span	Average Life Expectancy
Galapagos tortoise	150 years	–
Man	120+ years	70
Elephant	77 years	40
Horse	62 years	30
Donkey	50 years	40
Gorilla	36 years	26
Dog	34 years	12
Pig	27 years	16
Nightingale	7 years	–
Mouse	3 years	2
Shrew	2 years	1
Fruitfly	37 days	–
Afagous insects	25 hours	–

Performance is the number of years *actually* lived by individuals and cohorts during their lifetimes. This is similar to life expectancy. The only difference is life expectancy is a future projection applied to populations. It lists how many years various age categories have left. Performance refers to the completed chronology or the *lifetime*.

Life expectancy and performance in human populations vary greatly within and between countries. Life expectancy rates are found in statistical tables called *life tables*. It is quite fascinating to thumb through a life table for the first time and discover, based on statistical averages of people of the same age, sex, race, occupation and state, how long you probably will live. It has spurred quite a few young people to see if they can beat the odds and lengthen their lives. To do that realistically means you have to know something about what causes longevity and shift from less healthy behaviors and exposures to strategies for health. The key is using one's intelligence and practicing preventive medicine.

Life expectancy rates listed in life tables depend on the condition of social institutions and level of social and economic development (See Table 2.2).

Life expectancy is a summary statistic produced by national statistical services of nations with statistical agencies. Conceptually, life expectancy is the total number of *person-years* lived by all persons born in the population being measured divided by the number of persons at risk of dying. This forms a ratio of the study population:

$$\frac{\text{person years lived}}{\text{persons born}}$$

If a person lives 100 years, he contributes 100 person-years to the numerator and 1 to the denominator, increasing the ratio. When a year-old infant dies, it contributes only 1 year to the numerator but adds 1 to the denominator, noticeably reducing the ratio.

As a key vital statistic this ratio summarizes in one figure the overall health conditions of the population under study whether it be a nation, state, or, for that matter, a particular occupation. In advanced countries long-term degenerative diseases (heart diseases, cancer, stroke, and so on) having complex etiologies, and accidents, poisonings, and violence predominate as major forces of mortality reducing this ratio. In developing countries acute infectious diseases (malaria, cholera, tuberculosis, and so on) are leading causes of death. In measuring life expectancy, emphasis is on adding group statistics of fairly large populations and calculating the leading causes of death (negative factors). This contrasts with the study of longevity, which requires elucidation of positive factors in life styles of longevous subpopulations and individuals that result in above-average life expectancy. This latter study considers medical factors such as public health services, doctor/patient ratio, cost of medical care, prenatal care, medical services at birth, and maternal and child care available. It also includes broad sociocultural influences such as real per-capita income and education as well as specific variables affecting individuals such as nutrition, exercise, good family life, life and work satisfaction, drug abuse (including tobacco), pollution exposure, attitudes toward the aged, and social stress. All of these factors influence how long people live. These patterns of variables, typical of various cultures and social classes, interact and put selective pressures on gene pools. They are pervasive, difficult to avoid, and operate throughout the lifetime to shorten or lengthen life. In societies where they have useful social roles and are respected and active, the aged live longer. Where attitudes and knowledge of good health practices are ingrained in the people, longevity is more common. A resulting consequence, besides longer life, is a better

TABLE 2.2 Life Expectancy by Level of Social and Economic Development

	Years
Island of Paros	77
Japanese women	76
Sweden	74
Japan	73
Cyprus	73
Netherlands	73
Greece	72
Norway and Iceland	72
Denmark	71
France, Germany, Switzerland	71
Russia	70
Finland	69
Portugal	67
Turkey	58
Indonesia	44
Kenya	43
India	41
Ethiopia	35
Gabon	32

LIFE EXPECTANCY IN THE U.S.

	Years
Total population	71
Nonwhite males	59
Nonwhite females	67
White males	69
White females	74
Hawaii	74
Ohio	71
South Carolina	68
Judges	78
Coal miners	65

Sources: DHEW Publication No: (HRA) 75-1150; Beaubier (1976)

quality of life. This is summarized in a phrase that has become well known among gerontologists: "Get more years out of life and more life out of years."

EVOLUTION, LONGEVITY, AND MAN

Linschitz (1953), Lwoff (1962), and Quastler (1946) have specifically discussed the significance of design features in biological organization. The organization of organic matter is initially unlikely because it requires a precise arrangement of random matter and an energy input. Once this organization attains capacity for reproduction, however, as long as adequate nucleotides and substrate (raw materials) are available, it will continue to evolve. Its evolution thereafter depends on information stored in its structure and energy from chemical bonds extracted from the environment. Enhancing the efficiency of biological structure and function depends on enlarging the store of information available to the organism and species. This information is present in the structure of informational macromolecules, cells, tissues, organs, and so on. Neurons which make up nervous tissue are a supreme organic development since they are by far the most efficient for acquisition, storage, transmission, and use of available information. Thus determinants of behavior based on the nervous system, Campbell's (1978) fourth great adaptive mammalian complex, are a significant design feature related to life span.

Prior to the evolution of sexuality, simple single-cell organisms exchanged genes through conjugation. Variations in completing clones depended on retention of rare beneficial mutations. Cells divided by mitosis in a sense were immortal since mother cells gave rise to a continuous line of identical daughter cells. Meiosis, the process of forming viable sex cells with one-half the number of chromosomes by reduction division, made possible sexual reproduction and greatly increased variation within populations, speeding evolutionary divergence. Through random assortment and crossover, species had increased variants as possible solutions for coping with environmental changes and exploiting new niches. A consequence of this biologic development was death of mitotic cell lines in the body but immortality for the germ plasma or reproductive lines. The cost of increased viability of species and immortality of germinal lines was cell death of mitotically derived cells.

Contemporary multicellular, sexually reproducing creatures are exquisite products of long evolutionary processes. Their constituent parts and populations are subject to rigid continuous selective pressures. The beginning of life for these creatures starts with fusion of a single viable sperm and egg cell forming a zygote. The resultant fertilized egg divides by mitosis to form all cells of various tissue types in the body. This entire process of cell differentiation is genetically controlled. There are over 100 human cell types with widely varying life spans. For example, young generalized stem cells in the blood forming system give rise to erythrocytes (red) and leukocytes(white) cells and all intermediate differentiating types. White cells live about 7 days, reds about 210. On the other hand, muscle and brain cells live as long as the host up to probably over 120 years. Thus some cells live thousands of times longer and have entirely different structures and functions, as indicated in Table 2.3. Yet all approximately 50 trillion cells in humans derive from a single fertilized egg (one cell).

TABLE 2.3 Maximum Life Spans for Selected Cell Types

Cell Types	Tissue Types	Life Span
Mitotic (i.e., stem cells)	Blood cells	7-120 days
Conditionally mitotic cells	Liver, pancreas	Mitosis begins if tissue is challenged
Post mitotic cells	Brain, muscle	120 years

Homo sapiens evolved from higher primates developing language and tool use as primary adaptations into a highly cooperative ground dwelling species possessing technology, kinship, social structure, and culture. As a consequence, in the last two million years our brains have enlarged 50 percent (cephalization), enabling us to analyze more data generated from our social existence. Maintaining stability and survival of our species now depends greatly on the social structure of the population. Analyses of homo sapiens' survival thus includes many systems and considers problems such as nutrition and infection (physical factors) solved through human interaction in society (cultural factors). For example, mechanized agriculture and modern medicine are advanced-nation traits but both are usually associated with stratified, competitive societies primarily powered by fossil fuels (Odum, 1971). These societies generate carcinogens, toxins, and pollution as negative side effects reducing life expectancy. Even though many infectious epidemics are under control and life expectancy has increased, explosive increases in chronic degenerative diseases take their place. Thus our view of aging and longevity must incorporate and integrate ecological, biological, and cultural factors effecting human populations.

SELECTED THEORIES OF AGING

Chemical Aging. A significant area of research on causal factors in senescence is chemical aging. Kohn's (1971) powerful argument for examination of changes in molecules is the proper focus of investigations into biological aging. Histologists are familiar with age changes in the extracellular space and ground substance between and within organs and tissues. The extracellular compartment of mammals composed of connective tissue comprises 23 percent of the whole organism giving structural rigidity to the body. Table 2.4 lists major connective tissue types and distributions at selective sites in humans as is estimated widely in the medical literature.

TABLE 2.4 Percent Connective Tissue at Various Sites in Humans

	Collagen	Elastin	Mucopolysaccharides
Mineral-free cortical bone	88		1
Achilles tendon	86		
Skin	72		
Cornea	68		5
Cartilage	64-46		37-21
Aorta	24-12	30	6
Whole cortical bone	23		1
Nuchal ligaments	17	75	
Lung	10	3-7	
Liver	4	30-16	

Much knowledge about collagen was formulated by industrial chemists since it is the source of leather, gelatin, and organically derived glue. Biologists, on the other hand, for years neglected its study, generally viewing the extracellular proteins as impediments to their research of organs. This bias has been corrected by a new research emphasis on the role of collagen and other connective tissue components in aging processes. About 40 percent of body protein is collagen. Collagen is extruded as long chains of amino acids forming heavy macromolecules that bind together into long twisted bundles (Verzar 1963). The assembly of these subunits proceeds to the formation of fibrils. The ultrastructure of these gross fibers was demonstrated by Gross (1961) with electron micrographs showing an ordered pattern of striated constituents. Particular combinations of collagen assembly give rise to and meet the demand for specific tissue types they comprise. For example, in tendons fibrils must be inelastic to transmit forces across joints without loss of precision as in rapid finger movement. In the lens the configuration of fibrils gives rise to tissue that transmits light with amazing lack of distortion.

Elastin and mucopolysaccharides also have mechanical properties suited to the structural and functional requirements of the tissues they are embedded in. Elastin stretches and is located in blood vessels and other distensible tissues that undergo constant bending such as the aorta. This major heart valve transmits contracting impulses of the left ventricle into usable power in the circulation. Old elastin becomes frayed, brittle, fragmented, and yellowish. The chemical changes with age are not precisely known but the effect is like the limpness of a worn out elastic bandage. Mucopolysaccharides like the hydrated chondroitin sulfates provide tissues with firmness and some flexibility while highly viscous hyaluronic acid is ubiquitous in heart valves and mobile tissues where lubrication is required. Age related changes in mucopolysaccharides have been studied by Sobel (1967), who reported declines in output in several tissues not including the human aorta.

When collagen is first synthesized, it is bound by simple hydrogen bonds and steric forces with very little crosslinking between strands of amino acids and no bonds among fibrils. Over the lifetime of the animal, however, many new crosslinks are formed producing rigidity, stiffness, and inflexibility in tendons and joints, "leathery"skin, decline of lens distension creating "near-sightedness," and other adverse local changes. Verzar completed several groups of experiments demonstrating rates of these changes. He calculated the biologic ages of humans (as opposed to their chronological ages) using progressive crosslinking as the index. This demonstrates that meaningful decrements in function and vitality vary greatly between equally aged members of the same species due to environmental effects.

He and Kohn have argued persuasively that increased crosslinkage of collagen as well as changes in elastin are major constraining factors of the human life span since essential diffusion of cellular gases, metabolites, hormones, nutrients, and accumulating residues through membranes are progressively impeded by these extensive crossconnections.

Free Radicals. The role of free radical formation in destruction of DNA, cell membranes, and protein synthetic machinery of cells is now well attested (Gordon 1971). Free radicals are elements and molecules in cells that have unpaired electrons and are extremely reactive. These chemicals combine readily with many parts of the cell causing damage, ruptures, and even mutations in the nucleus.

Free radicals often initiate chain reactions producing other free radicals. The source of free radicals is both from inside and outside the body. These sources include X-rays, irradiation, heat, drug administration, ozone (generated by automobile exhaust), and normal reactions in cells. In fact, all living cells produce a constant low level of free radicals as a byproduct of metabolism and energy production. Some simple common free radicals include potassium, sodium, and a molecule of oxygen called superoxide. Superoxide is currently the subject of important research in the biology of aging (Cocolas 1978). Fortunately, low levels of superoxide and other free radicals can be taken care of by still other chemicals. For example, there is an enzyme, superoxide dismustase, that combines quickly with superoxide to form a harmless neutral byproduct. This enzyme, also produced within cells, is a *free radical scavenger*. Some free radical scavengers can be obtained through nutrition such as vitamin C in citrus fruits, vitamin E in whole wheat bread and wheat germ oil, selenium in wheat germ oil and in plants grown in soil rich in this trace element. (In places where the element is absent or scarce in the soil, such as eastern North Carolina, it is interesting to observe, though not yet causally correlated, that the population ages more rapidly.) Another effective scavenger, reduced glutathione, is naturally metabolised by people with adequate health and normal nutrition. This is the kind of information nutritional biochemists like Steven G. Chaney of the University of North Carolina prove to see how nutritional intake might retard processes of aging. Basically free radicals are always generated but can be quickly neutralized if adequate scavengers are available. The problem is that the biochemistry of cells is very complex. There are many reactions occurring simultaneously.

In some contexts, scavengers are used up by third chemicals before they can react with free radicals. This leaves free radicals again available for cellular destruction. This is exactly what happens in Paraquot poisoning (commercial herbicide). Superoxide dismutase is completely overwhelmed. Left unchecked, superoxide then reacts directly on the lung to cause intra-alveolar fibrosis and pulmonary edema, a pathologic profile remarkably similar to the victims of Legionnaire's Disease. The aging effects of superoxide are numerous. It stimulates collagen synthesis in several lung diseases. Excess collagen then acts like scar tissue blocking normal organ functioning. It affects cell growth and differentiation, nucleoproteins, proteins, lipoproteins, and is directly involved in interactions with informational macromolecules causing genetic damage (Van Hemmer 1975). It is implicated in increased collagen deposition in lungs exposed to toxic levels of oxygen, ozone, and other agents. Another internal source of free radicals in cells is the mixed function oxidases. These molecules initiate normal, necessary reactions in biosynthetic pathways, for example, during production of steroid hormones. Normally the end product is pharmacologically inert substances and H_2O, but some superoxide and H_2O_2 may also be produced. Then lipid peroxides are formed when these free radicals combine with polyunsaturated fats that make up cell membranes. These highly reactive radicals damage cell organelles and membranes and include crosslinkage in collagen. Membranes may become less elastic or usually just rupture. This includes organelle membranes. The most harmful damage occurs when lysosomes are split causing massive spills of digestive enzymes destroying adjacent cells. Repair enzymes interact on damaged sites producing sluffed scar tissue (lipofusion or aging pigment) which accumulates especially in nondividing cells. Basically, one important feature of free radical pathways is that radicals react with certain protein groups, inactivating various enzymes and decreasing the activity of the protein synthetic machinery of the cells. They also react with DNA to cause mutations and with membranes causing loss of elasticity and cell rupture.

Error Cascades. Orgel and Holliday are proponents of a theory based on cellular aging due to an accumulation of error in the protein-synthesizing machinery of cells. The main events analogous to transcription and translation may be an important source of mistakes. Production of proteins in cells occurs thousands of times per minute and like any mechanical process is subject to small errors. The enzymes and hormones initiating protein synthesis are gene product themselves; therefore slight errors in some will lead to a cascade of increasing errors due to amplification properties of the genome. Holliday's brilliant research on neurospora (1975) is strong evidence for a role of error cascades in cellular aging. A radio-labeled mutant gene was induced; the onset of death of the culture correlated significantly with turnover of the marked enzyme. Minor alterations in proteins involved in simple metabolic pathways may have minor effects, but only minor alterations of enzymes concerned with transcription or translation are likely to result in increasing accumulations of errors in subsequent gene products leading to decreases in metabolic efficiency.

Mutations. Mutations are changes in DNA. They may occur in somatic (body) or germinal (sex) cell nuclei. The causes may be intrinsic such as crossover, or environmentally induced with heat or mutagenic chemicals such as radium. Chemicals, with their subato-

mic structure, pass through cell nuclei constantly creating alterations in DNA. All changes in somatic cells lead to functional decrements and/or death of postmitotic cells (neurons, etc.). Changes in
surviving germinal cells that form zygotes are the bases of evolutionary changes.

Autoimmunity. Specificity is the essential process of the immune system that permits us to combat infectious diseases. Stem
cells continually arise in bone marrow and diversify into T and B
lymphocytes (white blood cells) within the circulation. B cells give
rise to plasma cells that extrude serum antibody. T cells form adher-
ing antibody on their surface membranes. Immunoglobulins have
specificity for antigens. As long as immune ability is maintained, the
immune system can distinguish hundreds of thousands of invasive
foreign substances and neutralize them by an overwhelming immune response of T and B cell proliferation to end the infectious
threat. Memory and recognition are essential properties of the immune system. Upon reinfection the immune system recalls primary
contact with antigen and mounts a massive secondary response.
(Immunization is a priming of memory with a small attenuated
dose of antigen. Subsequent infection with wild-type pathogens
then results in a massive secondary response.) Recognition of highly specific antigenic determinants or cell surface markers is a prere-
quisite of secondary responses. The ability to distinguish indigenous (self) surface markers on tissues and cells is the fundamental
recognition requirement. The dichotomy—self vs. nonself—initially
stimulates immune response (organ transplants are rejected since
"nonself" is detected). When the immune system ages, functional
decrements in recognition ability occur. If recognition declines
drastically, T and B cells and macrophages attack "self" tissues
finding them indistinguishable from invasive antigens.

Senescence of Mitotic Cells. Hayflick (1975) has received much
attention in the past decade for his experiments on mitotic cell
lines. He demonstrated that mitotic cells *in vitro* have a limited proliferative potential and attempted to show that diminished capacity of renewal is the basic cause of aging. With Morehead (1961) he
cultured human fetal lung fibroblasts in a nutrient medium under
physiologic conditions favorable for their division. After four days
of incubation, individual cells began to divide and within a week
they covered the inside of bottles with a layer one cell deep. The
cells were then stripped off, separated with digestive enzyme tryp-
sin, and planted half each in two newly prepared bottles. Within a
week the bottles again filled with fresh monolayers meaning the

original culture seemingly had doubled. This procedure was repeated as fibroblasts continued division, doubling each time to fill new bottles. The mean number of doublings was 50 ± 10. In Stage III the culture slowed its renewal rate, showed accumulating residues and mutations, and died out. Hayflick concluded the number of population doublings of tissues of animals related to the life span of species.

Progeriac Diseases. Progeriac diseases are intensively studied by gerontologists because unraveling their origin may shed light on normal aging phenomena. Werner's syndrome and the Hutchinson-Gilford progeria syndrome are diseases that appear somewhat to caricature aging. The etiology of the progeriac diseases is uncertain. Epstein (1966) claims they are due to an autosomal recessive allele but conclusive evidence is lacking. DeBusk (1972) undertook an exhaustive review of all known cases of progeria and concluded many features associated with aging are absent as well there being insufficient data to verify its cause. Onset can appear prenatally and is usually detectable by age 3 or 4 due to a retardation of growth rate. Postmortem examinations indicate the first lesion appears as a deficiency of eosinophilic cells of the anterior pituitary. Since the pituitary is responsible for multiple functions in endocrine system regulation, this lesion obviously is a significant pathway in the developmental pathogenesis of progeria. The effects of progeria are so serious an afflicted individual experiences rapid degenerative changes and dies between the ages of 7 and 27. Only 60 confirmed cases of progeria have been diagnosed since 1886, when Jonathan Hutchinson reported the first. Incidence is approximately 1/8,000,000 births. Progeria is likely caused by a malfunction in a crucial early pathway in the development of the embryo.

Genes for Longevity or Senescence. The organization and function of organisms depends on every bit of available information. This information is coded in organic matter. It is the summary product of relentless changing environmental pressure on competing and symbiotic gene pools over time. In this open system, efficiency of every molecule, structure, and behavior, is, in a sense, "evaluated" through natural selection. For example, the weight/activity ratio of alternative possible enzymes and hormones, down to the last atom, is decisive in their selection. Watson (1975) has elegantly described this process as it applies to the Mammalian genome. All the present day mammalian orders, other than rodents and primates, have genes coding for the synthesis of vitamin C. The small generalized mammalian precursor also had this capacity. Eventually these genes were transformed to other more essential functions when rats and humans began habitually acquiring adequate vitamin C through nutritional intake in foraging behaviors. All the space set aside for the genes is crucial. If genetic functions can be achieved through behavioral analogues, this leaves available genes to be selected and switched to other functions. In other words, the genetic resources are under relentless pressure to produce viable individuals insuring survival of the population and better adapted animals. In this view, the complete set of genes is like an envelope containing the essential residue of information the species has retained during its long history of interactions in nature.

Thus we can see all the genes in a sense are genes for longevity. They enable the organism to exist against all probabilities of entropy resulting in dissipation of heat, energy, structure, and intelligence. Of course, some limited set of genes more specifically modify the life span, such as the genes for DNA repair mechanisms. This evolutionary perspective would lead us to believe a specific genetic locus for programmed senescence and death is a nonessential function. That is, the genes are under great pressure to produce an organism that, in the face of fierce requirements within its niche, remains viable. It seems unlikely in this fantastic struggle to achieve sufficient fecundity and fertility to offset high death rates that mutant genes for the self-destruction of their organisms' populations would be selected and retained. In fact, the opposite is the case. Species' life spans correlate much higher with their specific number of genes than with the proliferative capacity of their mitotic cells.

If there were a gene(s) that initiates aging processes, this gene would be subject to mutations just like any other. Why don't we see rare examples of individual plants and animals experiencing the pseudomutation, living two, three, four, or more times longer than the usual life span characteristic of their species? It seems more reasonable to assume our genes (the mechanism and storage facility of information) would exclusively select and retain information useful to the survival of the host.

Processes of Aging. Causal aging factors are numerous, probably acting on all organizational levels of intact animals. Biologists identify categories from subatomic particles, atoms, molecules, macromolecules (especially DNA), organelles, cells, tissues, organs, and systems, to the whole organism as sites of aging. Changes at the basic levels of organization induce aging effects on higher levels of structure. Thus irreversible transformations of subatomic particles, whether considered "aging" or death, reduce life expectancy and limit life span. All atoms have half-lives based on diminution of energy in atomic nuclei. Since the location of atoms in molecules does not seem to affect when transformations of atoms will result in loss of molecules, changes in subatomic particles are a primary stochastic aging effect.

Everything known to man wears out. Even platinum bars stored in vacuum as standards of weights and measures will change as time goes by. It is reasonable that inorganic and organic molecules also are doomed by bombardment of endless intrinsic and extrinsic simultaneous random events. The ontogeny of species probably ends at maturation; post-maturational changes are results of mesons, heat, irradiation, radicals, toxins, pathogens, stresses, and other noxious stimuli experienced throughout the lifetime.

LONGEVITY: BIOGRAPHICAL COMPARISONS

As I mentioned at the beginning of this chapter, longevity is determined by both genetic and environmental factors. This means for humans about 50 percent of how long one lives depends on one's genes. The other 50 percent depends on environmental factors and mental and physical health. If you have all the best genes for longevity and work out the best possible life-style, you could live to 120 or more years. If you have all the good genes but have gotten into a trap of mental and physical self-abuse, your life will be drastically shortened. On the other hand, you may have bad genes, but still attain longevity by adjusting with a life-style that minimizes your deficit. Through my research on longevity I have become very sensitive to these principles. I can easily spot people who have longevity or who are good candidates for it. Let me give you an example.

One day while I was doing field work in the countryside on the island of Paros, I stopped at a small farmhouse within a dispersed hamlet of vivid rustic beauty. I needed directions back to the main village. An ancient man came out and helped me. He was open, strong, logical, deliberate, and good humored. Since it was obvious he had longevity I made a point to ask him some questions and arranged to observe him for several days. It turned out he has an active, consistent routine that is healthy, satisfying and meaningful. He is practically self-sufficient. He works steadily every day on his small farm raising much of the food his family requires. He doesn't smoke or take any medications. His nutrition is excellent, mostly of fresh fruits and vegetables, light meats, fish, fresh baked bread, cheeses, yogurt, eggs, legumes, nuts, dried fruits, olive oil, onions and garlic (combat cholestrol), herbs, condiments and spices. He and his wife work side by side with harmony and affection. A brief catnap, or a glass of cool water on the shady veranda is a good rest break after completion of specific tasks. When work is done they often look out over fields, orchards, and vineyards of the small valley opening on the sea. Then they enjoy conversation with family and friends from the neighborhood. The hamlet is free of chemical and noise pollution and is safe at all times. The people adhere to the traditional cultural values of their pastoral community. Most seem to have a deep philosophical commitment and satisfaction. Time is marked by natural phases and completion of work, rather than by watching the clock.

In only the few days I was involved in this participant observation, the beauty, naturalness, and healthy existence rubbed off. I felt a strength, confidence and tranquility that was overwhelming and regretted when I had to depart. Back in the main village I found out the old man is 105 years old. He directs the three small farms promised to his sons (who are in their 60's and 70's). He has been married for 60 years to his present wife, who is 90. He works every day and is known and respected for his achievement of longevity. He hasn't been sick in 30 or 40 years and never sees a doctor. He doesn't wear glasses and hears well, and in fact appears to have a number of good years still left. This is an example of a person who has genes for longevity. But something else was crucial. He took the biological and cultural resources available to himself *when he was young* and brought it all together into a fine-tuned, flawless design for living. His model is purposeful, and personally meaningful within the context of his own culture. It is also healthy and free from random loss of energy and resources.

This brings to mind a contrasting experience. When I first began teaching I had to accept a position 500 miles away from my family. I drove home every two or three weekends and broke the journey halfway with a brief stop at a gasoline station that also had a restaurant. The place was run by a man who had married a German woman following World War II. It was extremely orderly and clean. Besides getting fuel for the car, I would have some fruit, bread and water. One weekend, instead of the German woman, a new person waited on me. He seemed old. He was bald with deep wrinkles on his face and neck with a ruddy complexion. He stooped obviously, and continually smoked and drank coffee. When he brought the food I decided to ask him a few questions. His name was Taylor Saltzman. He said he was working in the restaurant temporarily and vaguely hoped to get another job through someone in the building trades. We talked about the merits of different occupations, during which I mentioned working on ships. I related how I left college as an undergraduate and worked around the Orient on foreign flag tramp steamers, and that the sea was good. For the first time he brightened up considerably. He related how the merchant marine, in fact, had been his life's work.

He first shipped out when he was a teenager. He would stay on board for five or six months and then go ashore. But life on shore was boring and the people didn't understand or appreciate seamen. On board ship one could find a few good companions. There was always plenty of alcohol and drugs available, although ships could be confining. Almost after every voyage he had great debauches after getting paid off in port. His real troubles had begun in the Phillippines. He had jumped ship there to live with a woman he especially cared for. He went so far as to take care of her two children and get a job in a local slaughter house. For the first time he ate regular meals and enjoyed family life. The trouble was he lived incognito with no papers and continually in fear of deportation by the police. After about two years they caught him. He was put on an oil tanker to Arabia. The ship transferred crude oil from the Arabian Gulf to Japan. He would not be able to return to the United States or the Phillippines for 18 months, virtually a prisoner during the continual uneventful passages across the Indian Ocean. The roughest part was waiting to fill up in Arabia. There were so many tankers you had to wait two or three weeks anchored off shore.

The temperature got to 130° in the daytime, and the customs of Muslim Arabia were puritanical: no women, no alcohol. Consequently, the sailors stayed in their cabins, drank, and smoked hashish. Thus engaged, Taylor and his companion, Pedro, a small quiet cook from the Phillippines, wiled away their evenings. One night Pedro idly picked up a stack of photographs off Taylor's cluttered dresser. They were portraits of women Taylor knew from many parts of the world. Suddenly Pedro became extremely upset. He held the picture of Taylor's common-law wife. This woman was the very woman Pedro loved best. Was it the same name? Yes. Taylor was incredulous. He begged Pedro's forgiveness, saying he had no knowledge of Pedro's prior relationship. They discussed and argued and fought for several hours, all the while drinking on the fantail, bow, galley, cabins and all over the ship. Pedro's mild nature welled into a rage of macho jealously that could not be stemmed. He knew how to settle things with a knife. That is how it had to be settled, with a knife. Taylor's pleas and exasperation finally wore out. He vowed if Pedro insisted and came after him the fight would end in death. Spitting epithets they bared their concealed weapons. They slashed and stabbed until Pedro lay unconscious in a pool of blood. He was taken off the ship hanging to life by a thread. Taylor was arrested by the Arabian police the next morning and put in a cell with a dirt floor and no plumbing. He was told if Pedro died as expected he would be beheaded for the crime. Taylor waited several weeks in suspended uncertainty. His hair turned completely white. The United States consul told him the government would probably let the Arabians exercise jurisdiction. Taylor got down on his knees and for days on end cried to God to please let Pedro live. Pedro finally did not die and just before the ship was to sail an agreement was worked out. Taylor never understood it, but as a condition of being able to return to the States, he had to sign a paper barring him from ever again working in the merchant marine.

While Taylor related this story I noticed more about his appearance. He wore a complete set of false teeth. His hands shook and his muscular movements were slow and weak. He moved bowed down, with a shuffling gait. Around his iris was a film of grey pigment—usually a telltale sign of age. I guessed he looked about as old as the farmer from Paros.

"Yes, but despite the troubles," I said, "I miss the beauty and solitude of the sea." "Well," he replied with regret and longing, "you have a Z card, you're young, too. You can always go back. But me, I'm old. I'm 42." I was completely flabbergasted. I had guessed he must be at least 65 years old. This was a perfect negative example of longevity. He had smoked heavily since he was a teenager and used drugs and strong stimulants. He had been mostly idle and without exercise, especially walking and running. His nutrition was poor and irregular. He had no lasting friends or relatives. He had no interests or healthy activities. He was insecure. There had been many conflicts in his life. He worried about the future, and regretted the past. Overall his life seemed almost diametrically opposite to the farmer's. It lacked thoughtfulness, activity and conservation of scarce mental and physical resources.

CULTURE, SOCIETY, AND LONGEVITY

The foregoing biographical sketches represent two pathways that led to high longevity on one hand and rapid aging on the other. Persons interested in studying longevity have described many other lifestyles that can lead to longevity. One does not have to be a farmer, for example, to achieve longevity. But being a small farmer does almost certainly ensure the person will be physically active. In some cultures it probably assures the person will be sensitive to good nutrition as well. The most important variables in achieving longevity are high physical and mental activity and lack of smoking. Throughout 99 percent of man's existence, he was extremely active.

Physical anthropologists have demonstrated man evolved as a hunter. Early man acquired large amounts of protein through a technique called persistence hunting. He outwitted, outran, and then killed much larger animals than himself with a few simple tools and the help of his friends. That's why man lost his body hair. In the chase, it was advantageous to have a lack of it. Early man probably walked and ran hundreds, perhaps, even thousands of miles every year.

There are some special places on earth where longevity seems to be concentrated. In those places one immediately notices the people are especially physically active, engaged, and committed. They seem more alive and optimistic.

The island of Paros, Greece, has longevity. This longevity is demonstrated statistically through a life table (Beaubier 1976). It is also confirmed by a description of the culture. Paros is a society that requires physical work and rewards and prizes mental activity. There is good nutrition, lack of pollution, excellent medical care, folk medicine and preventative health, good family life, lack of crime and social strife. The people are proud of their families, homes and community. Several other places, with lifestyles similar to Paros, are noted for their longevity, including Swedish and Japanese villages, and Soviet Georgia, the home of the Abkhasians (Benet 1974).

3 Cultural Dimensions of Age: A Multidimensional Scaling Analysis

CHRISTINE L. FRY
Loyola University of Chicago

*W*hat *is age? This is a rather naive, but legitimate question. Age has something to do with time and the cumulative effects of processes occurring through time. People are complex biological and cultural creatures. If we had no culture and were of a simpler biological organization (like a tree), then time would be paramount and directly mirror age (our trunks would get bigger). Age becomes more complicated since humans live in a world of symbols. All cultures incorporate age into the possible ways individuals are differentiated. Names are given to the divisions of the life cycle reflecting a progression from infancy to old age. As early as 1929 Radcliffe-Brown recognized this by coining the term "age grade" to refer to these age categories. Although they are ideational, categories are not idle, passive entities existing in the realm of ideas since humans use them in charting the world, delineating what is good and bad, and deciding upon their courses of action or behavior.*

What makes us old, culturally? How is age differentiated and structured into a cultural system? What are the expectations and standards of acceptable behavior for different age groups? What does it mean to be old, and what values enable one to maintain a sense of self worth? These are large questions with only incomplete answers. Answers are incomplete because each culture has somewhat unique resolutions to the problems and because other issues have been more intriguing for anthropologists to investigate.

The next two chapters explore these questions in 2 different societies—Midwestern United States and a peasant village in Colombia. Both are concerned with the cultural meanings of age. Culture is covert and elusive. It is not something we can directly see, hear, taste, smell, or feel. Yet culture is very real, being manifest in the actions of our informants and in what they tell us about their world. Discovery of the order in another culture requires that the anthropologist guard against ethnocentrism or cultural centeredness. This applies not only to making value judgments about the other culture, but even to the concepts we use in describing and analyzing that culture. The techniques used to explore age in the United States and Colombia reflect a major concern in anthropology since the 1960's. Ethnocentrism is subtly present in that the investigator imposes his/her categories onto the cultural setting being studied. "Ethnoscience" or "cognitive anthropology" has spawned numerous analyses of native classifications and the semantic organization of these cognitive structures. More importantly, cognitive anthropology has developed explicit eliciting techniques to minimize the biases of the observer in the gathering and recording of data. Cognitive anthropology is by no means a monolithic battery of techniques, nor is it a whole subdiscipline of cultural anthropology. Instead, it offers a wide variety of elicitation procedures which may be utilized as the ethnographic context and the problem under investigation warrants.

Both Fry and Kagan are concerned about culture, the meaning and organization of age, and their informant's viewpoint. Christine Fry employs a strategy which is adapted for large scale urban societies noted for their variability. Early in her research Fry explored the question of aging and its markers through adulthood with a limited number of informants. On the basis of the persistent themes these informants suggested, she developed an instrument (an interview) to be used to collect information in a more efficient and standardized manner.

An interview guide, unless completely open ended and non-directive, by necessity imposes the investigator's categories in eliciting the informant's response. To minimize this, a card sort was developed on the basis of the early phases of research. Each card contained descriptions of people by different combinations of statuses. Informants used these cards to differentiate kinds of people according to age and to arrive at what they thought were the divisions in the adult portions of the American life cycle. With the responses of a large number of informants another problem surfaces. Management of a large quantity of data and analyzing it becomes insurmountable without the assistance of a computer. Computers "crunch" numbers and give us more numbers with which to interpret the relationships in the data. A technique, multidimensional scaling, uses numbers, but the computer draws pictures of the relationships of similarity/differences between points of data or objects. Since informants sorted cards (objects) on the basis of age similarity, this technique is used to analyze the underlying cultural dimensions of age in the Midwestern portion of America. It is chronology which is most apparent, but through multidimensional scaling we see there is more. Chronological age becomes bent and twisted by other dimensions identified by Fry as engagement-responsibility, reproductive cycle, and encumberment.

A similar responsibility dimension appears in a multidimensional scaling analysis of age terms from a simpler culture—the pas-

toral Maasai of East Africa. As more comparative work is done on the cultural organization of age, we will be able to better understand how age is interlaced with basic issues that must be resolved by all cultures. Differences in cultural organization of age should be expected, but similarities should not be surprising.

Meaning and values are aspects which are cultural. Age, as codified and interpreted culturally, has meanings and values directly affecting the behavior of individuals in all cultural systems. Before we can ask the questions of how older adults are treated, what resources are present for the resolution of the difficulties of old age, how older adults are articulated with younger adults and children, or any similar question, we must first ask the cultural question: How is age culturally organized and how is this reflected in the social organization? Older adults are members of a society, just as are children, young and middle aged adults, and babies. To construct a theory of aging, based exclusively upon the elderly is most unwise. It is almost as foolish as focusing exclusively upon biological processes. To understand old age, we first must ask what age is doing in the culture as a principle of social organization and in structuring the cultural world.

In spite of the obviousness of age and aging, investigators remain perplexed in understanding the phenomena. On the one hand, age is relatively easily measured in terms of years, but on the other, what do these mean? A persistent theme in gerontological research is a lament over the arbitrariness of chronological age (Baltes and Goulet 1970, Looft 1973, Robin 1971, Wohlwill 1970). The number of years elapsed since birth is an exact and simple indicator for large-scale bureaucratic organizations in making decisions about their membership or clientele. These include such decisions as when a person may enter or exit (i.e., retire) from the organization or when a person is entitled to certain benefits and rights (i.e., Social Security or the privileges of voting, driving, and drinking). Cain (1974) has demonstrated the increasing importance of chronological age and the resulting legal definitions in determining the status of the elderly. Chronology, however, masks an incredible amount of variation, much of which is not explainable by age alone. This is clear from medical and psychiatric research (R. Butler 1968). Recognition of this heterogeneity has stimulated social scientists to explore other dimensions of age.

In unraveling the complicated web that is masked by the facade of chronological age, social scientists have emphasized two research strategies in their investigations of aging in industrialized societies (Elder 1975). The first is represented by the work of Matilda White Riley and her associates (1972) on cohort analysis and age stratification. The second is the normative approach of Bernice Neugarten (1968). Both perspectives have been directed to an understanding of age as an important aspect of social organization. Riley and her associates seek to examine the impact of historical circumstance on age cohorts located in an age stratification structure, while Neugarten and her associates are concerned with the normative aspects of age statuses, the regulation of behavior and the implications for a developmental psychology.

On the surface, the central issues of age stratification appear to be at odds with the questions of age norms. This is not the case, however, since at a deeper level, they are complimentary. Neugarten and Datan, in clarifying this complementarity, have distinguished three dimensions of time: life time, social time, and historical time (1973:56-58). Life time is a series of orderly changes that occur in the life cycle, of which chronological age, despite its problems, is the index. Social time is the age-graded system of statuses and norms which underlie the major periods of life distinguished in a particular ethnographic setting. Historical time refers to the social, political, and economic events which occur through time and have impact upon the lives of people within that system. The cohort-historical approach is most directly concerned with the interplay between life time and social time. Since the different aspects of time are components of any social context, the two approaches merge to present a complementary and comprehensive view of the sociological aspects of the life cycle.

Although these sociological perspectives have different emphases, both have considered aging and the life course as a developmental sequence of statuses (Clausen 1972, Neugarten, Moore and Lowie 1965, Neugarten and Moore 1968, Neugarten and Hagestad 1976). Through these analyses we have obtained insight into the sociological dimensions of aging, especially in industrialized societies. How, on the other hand, do we get to the more elusive cultural dimensions of age other than through an analysis of the expectations or rules associated with the sequential status occupation? In other words, what is the cultural meaning or interpretation of life time and social time at a particular historical time? In this paper, I argue that a technique known as multidimensional scaling combined with standardized eliciting techniques is a productive avenue to examine the cognitive organization of aging in virtually any ethnographic context.

The purpose of this paper is to consider multidimensional scaling as a technique in the analysis and interpretation of cultural data. This technique is applied to cognitive data on aging elicited from 242 informants in a midwestern city in the United States. The resulting multidimensional scaling solutions are examined, interpreted, and conclusions drawn. The importance and the implications for this type of research and analysis in aging and for an anthropology of aging are assessed.

MULTIDIMENSIONAL SCALING

> The main functions of multidimensional scaling are . . . getting hold of whatever pattern or structure may otherwise be hidden in a matrix of empirical data . . . of representing that structure in a form that is much more accessible to the human eye—namely as a geometric model or picture. The objects under study . . . are represented by points in the spatial model in such a way that the significant features of the data about these objects are revealed in the geometrical relations among the points (Shepard 1972 (a):1).

Multidimensional scaling begins with a matrix of similarity or dissimilarity measure between the objects to be scaled. On the basis of these measures, coordinates are produced for the spatial representation. Multidimensional scaling enables the researcher to go beyond the flat unidimensional scales frequently encountered in statistical analysis. Instead, the data about the objects being scaled may be examined in any dimension. The number of dimensions is at the discretion of the investigator. This, however, is limited by two factors (Burton and Romney 1975). The first is the interpretability of the resulting configuration. Since it is difficult to visualize objects in four-dimensional or five-dimensional space, unless "tinker toy" models are built, the configurations are usually restricted to three dimensions. The second factor is the goodness of fit measurement. This, frequently called the stress measurement, indicates the degree of discrepancy between the data and the configuration. The closer the stress is to 0, the better the fit. These two factors not only determine the number of dimensions used, but also serve as criteria of acceptability for the spatial representations. The multidimensional scaling procedure used in this study is KYST, a combination of DMSCAL 5M and TORSCA 9 developed by Kruskal, Young, and Seery at Bell Labs.

RESEARCH DESIGN

The objects scaled in this study are cards which describe a person by means of age statuses. Age statuses were selected rather than age terms since Jeffers, Eisdorfer, and Busse (1962) have noted considerable ambiguity and lack of agreement in the ordering of age terms. Jeffers and her colleagues have suggested the creation of an instrument involving a card sort employing major life events or age statuses.

What life events should be incorporated into this instrument? With the possible number of individual "careers" in an industrial society, an infinite number of life events are conceivable. However, as suggested by investigations into the sociological aspects of the life cycle in American society (Cain 1964, Clausen 1972, Blau 1973, Neugarten, Moore, and Lowie 1965), the institutional spheres are (1) the private domestic sphere and (2) the more public, universalistic occupational or economic institutions. Preliminary interviewing indicated that the age-sensitive statuses in the domestic sphere are marital status, status of children, and residential status. The corresponding events in the public sphere are educational status and career status. The age events selected within the respective spheres and the way in which they were combined in describing people, hereafter referred to as social persona, are to be found in Appendix A at the end of this chapter. The resulting instrument consisted of 34 social persona cards. This instrument was used to explore the cultural dimensions of age in American society.

Each informant was instructed to read the social persona cards and to sort them into piles or groups according to their decisions regarding the appropriate age or similarity in age bracket. The number of resulting age groups, the number of cards included in each, and the cards placed in the subdivision was at the discretion of the informant. The instructions prior to the card sort contained the statement: "There are no correct number of piles or ways to sort and organize these cards. What we are interested in is how *you* would sort and organize the people described on these cards with respect to age." Once the informant had rechecked the sorted cards, he or she was asked to assign a chronological age or range of ages to the respective age groupings and if possible to give a name to the age bracket which would describe the people so classified.

The instrument was pretested and then administered to 242 men and women over the age of 18 years in a midwestern city, the Standard Metropolitan area of Lafayette-West Lafayette, Indiana, in the fall and winter of 1971-1972. Informants were selected on a probability basis through a multiphase sampling procedure. All the city blocks in the SMA were first numbered. The initial sampling phase involved the selection of city blocks using a random number table. In the second phase, households were identified and selected. The household units were identified through the street and address index of the city directory, appropriately numbered using a standard reference point (i.e., the northwest corner of the block), and then 1 in 10 were selected on a probability basis. The third sampling phase selected the individual in the household unit who would be contacted. Since a majority of households have two adults over 18, the sex of the respondent was selected on a probability basis. Only when single-individual households (i.e., single male or female or widowed) were contacted, this procedure was not followed. Known biases exist in the resulting sample with respect to the age and sex distribution of the total population as was determined by comparison with the 1970 Census. There are no other known biases in the data collected.

MEASURE OF AGE PROXIMITY

For the purposes of multidimensional scaling it is first necessary to construct measures of similarity or proximity. The measure can be direct in that it is based immediately on the pair of objects rather than being derived through calculations of other data. This includes a direct subjective judgment of the apparent similarity between two objects or the frequency with which two things co-occur or are sorted into the same category by a population (Shepard 1972(B)). The measure of proximity used here is a measure of direct proximity based on a method of subjective clustering and the resulting coincidence (Green and Carmone 1970). The informants were asked to sort the cards into groups so that those in any given group are thought to be more similar to each other than they are to any cards not in the group. From this an incidence matrix is constructed in which an "1" is inserted if any two cards appear in the same group and a "0" otherwise. The incidence matrix is thus limited to zero-one-type data. Table 3.1 is a truncated view of a 34 X 34 lower half matrix with the main diagonal absent reporting the age proximity between the social persona cards. This was calculated on a case-by-case basis and then aggregated across the total sample.

MULTIDIMENSIONAL SCALING SOLUTIONS AND INTERPRETATIONS

The incidence or age proximity matrix was read into the KYST program. The output is the cartesian coordinates between the social persona cards in N-dimensional space. Although the actual number of dimensions underlying the relationships between the

TABLE 3.1 Proximity measures among the social persona cards
(abbreviated table)

	A	B	C	D	E	F	G	H	I	J	...	Z	1	...	8
A	–														
B	.78	–													
C	.82	.82	–												
D	.84	.79	.84	–											
E	.80	.79	.76	.78	–										
F	.72	.74	.71	.70	.77	–									
G	.56	.55	.56	.55	.58	.62	–								
H	.45	.46	.43	.47	.44	.56	.56	–							
I	.34	.36	.31	.34	.36	.37	.48	.52	–						
J	.33	.36	.36	.33	.34	.36	.48	.50	.81	–					
.	.	.		.		.									
.	.	.		.		.									
.	.	.		.		.									
Z	.03	.02	.03	.03	.03	.02	.01	.02	.05	.05	...	–			
1	.02	.02	.01	.01	.02	.02	.01	.03	.04	.03	...	.74	–		
.	.	.		.		.		.		.					
.	.	.		.		.		.		.					
.	.	.		.		.		.		.					
8	.00	.00	.00	.00	.00	.00	.01	.02	.00	.01	...	.19	.19	...	–

items is unknown, the program was instructed to start with three dimensions and reduce by one dimension in each cycle until finally a unidimensional solution was reached. Figures 1, 2, and 3 present these multidimensional scaling solutions, respectively, in one, two, and three dimensions. As is characteristic of multidimensional scaling, the goodness of fit increases as the number of dimensions increases. Stress, which has a potential range of 0.0 to 1.0, drops from .111 in one dimension to .052 in two dimensions and to .036 in three dimensions. Based on the relatively large drop in stress between the one-dimensional and the two-dimensional solutions and the relatively small decrease in stress between the two-dimensional and the three-dimensional solutions, the two-dimensional solution is the "best" representation. The unidimensional solution is included here because it remains intact in both the two- and three-dimensional representations. The three-dimensional solution is included because of its interpretability and the importance of

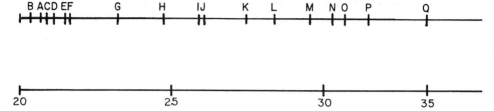

FIGURE 3.1.   One-dimensional representation of the interpoint distances among 34 social persona cards
with the equivalent chronological age indicated
in a parallel scale.

that interpretation for our understanding of the cultural organization of aging.

AGE IN ONE DIMENSION

Figure 3.1 is the representation of the one-dimensional solution.
As is to be expected, this unidimensional scale is an index which
mirrors chronological age. This is evident from the configuration
since the letter and number symbols were assigned to the cards on
the basis of the chronological ages the informants had given to the
social persona. Thus card A is the youngest (21.4) and card 8 is
the oldest (68.6). Below the one-dimensional solution is a scale of
chronological age in five-year nonequidistant brackets reflective of
the ages of the social persona appearing on the scale above. The
chronological age assigned to each social persona appears in Appendix A, end of chapter. In this representation only two cards are
out of order. Card B and card 2 are in "error" by less than .2 of a
year. The ordering of the social persona in one dimension indicates
that when we consider age alone, it is life time or chronological
age.
    Figure 3.1 contains the expected result in one dimension since
the informants were instructed to create age grades by sorting the
social persona into piles of age similarity and then to arrange these
piles by increasing age. Thus when the data is aggregated, there is a
high degree of correspondence between the scale informants used,
chronological age, and the scale the computer constructed. Multidimensional scaling has been used to scale unidimensional structures in both natural phenomena (Shepard 1962) and social
phenomena (Guttman 1961). It is not this one dimension, however, with which we are the most concerned. This dimension is all
too obvious and is the dimension we wish to go beyond.

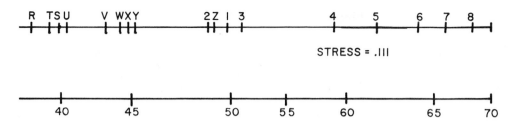

AGE IN TWO DIMENSIONS

The two-dimensional solution in Figure 3.2 indicates that the indexing by chronological age remains intact and if anything improves in ordering. Instead of remaining in a straight line, the chronological scale "bends" to form what is best described as a horseshoe. Now we must turn to the most important task in multidimensional scaling—the interpretation of the representation of the data. In an internal analysis of the configuration, two strategies have been used: (1) a search for clustering of the objects within geometric space, and (2) the search for axes or dimensions which have a substantive significance (Napior 1972, Shepard 1972a). In Figure 3.2 there are no apparent clusters and time, obviously, isn't the only dimension. Therefore, the second strategy is employed. The two dimensions are identified as responsibility-engagement on the vertical axis and the reproductive cycle on the horizontal axis. In discerning these dimensions it is necessary to consider both the content of the social persona cards and the similarities and differences in the social persona as they are plotted on the respective axis.

The vertical axis is identified as responsibility-engagement since an examination of the social persona cards reveals that the social persona on the far negative side of the axis are either students or are retired, while on the positive side we encounter social persona who are fully engaged in the domestic cycle and who are in responsible career positions. Closer to the central portion of the axis we find social persona who are entering domestic and occupational roles or who have begun withdrawal from these roles through retirement or widowhood. It is interesting to note in the figure that the social persona are positioned in nearly two straight lines on the negative side of the axis. On the positive side of this axis, the second dimension comes into play and the configuration is marked by a bend.

This second dimension is identified as the reproductive cycle. As we move from the negative to the positive side of this axis, we find that the developmental status of children, i.e., their involve-

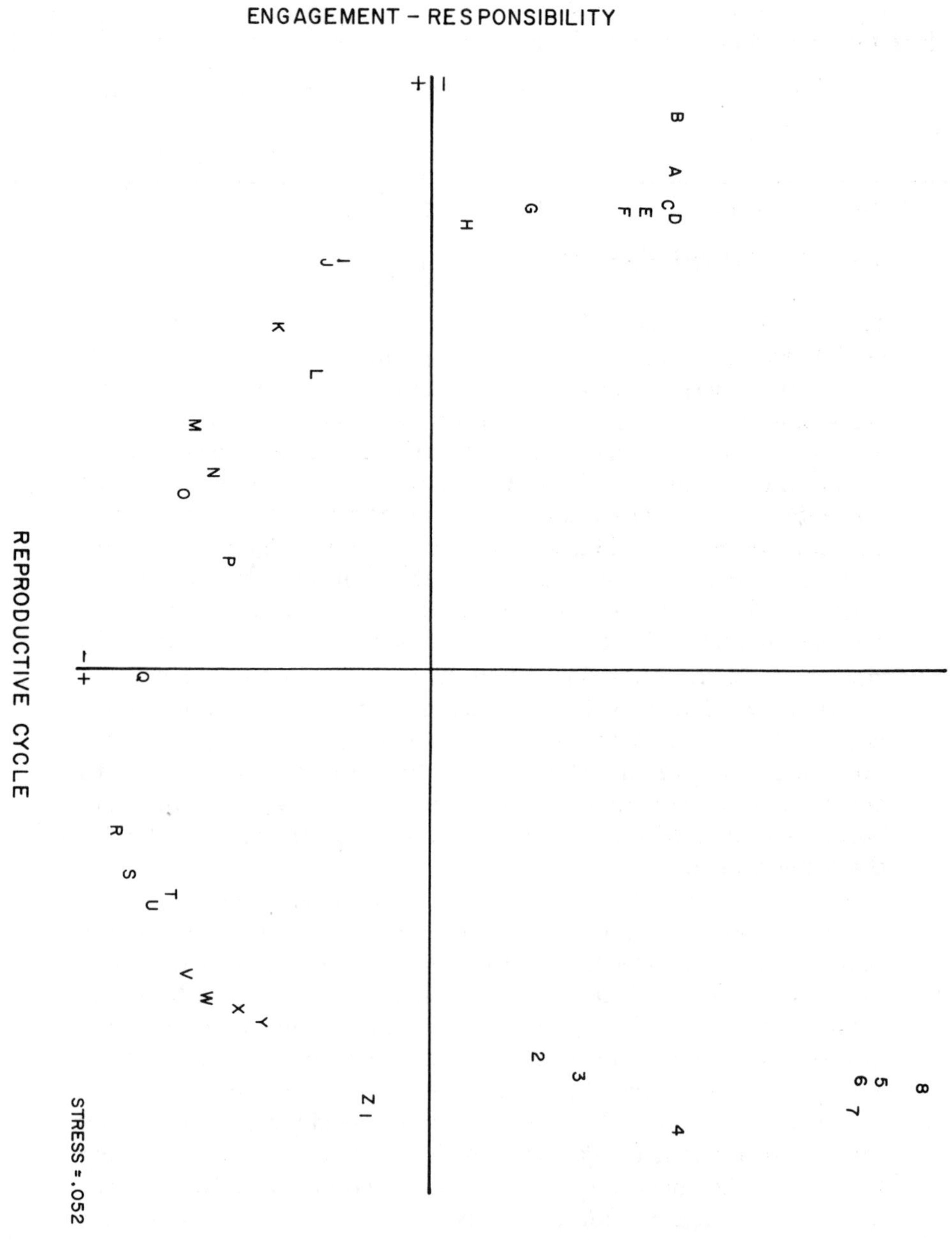

FIGURE 3.2. Two-dimensional representation of interpoint distances among 34 social persona cards. Chronological age remains intact, but is bent into the form of a horseshoe.

ment first in educational institutions and then in the domestic sphere, is sequenced: pre-school, school, high school, college, married, married with children. The reproductive cycle is intertwined with the responsibility-engagement dimension in that children are a responsibility reinforcing engagement in career or occupational roles. This is reflected in the gradualness of the "bend" and by the fact that the reproductive cycle comes into play only on the positive side of the responsibility-engagement axis.

Age in two dimensions is a chronological progression of statuses. As the life time becomes longer, the statuses are marked by increasing responsibilities and engagement in the social system. This progression is then "intersected" by further responsibilities with the possible arrival of children and then their maturation. Finally, the horseshoe is complete as the sequence of statuses are marked by an increasing withdrawal primarily from occupational engagement. Chronologically, prior to age 25 roles are frequent and marital status changes from single to married (A-H). Then 25-35 work roles and promotional sequences are apparent along with pre-school and school age children (I-P). The years 35-50 are marked by high-school children, highly productive jobs, and finally the empty nest (Q-1). Beyond 50, the reference to children disappears and widowhood and retirement are the most frequent statuses found in the social persona cards (2-8). Thus, in the two-dimensional representation of age, life time is clearly intertwined with social time.

AGE IN THREE DIMENSIONS

Finally, we turn to the three-dimensional solution. The stress decreases by only .016, indicating that the best and most parsimonious representation is the two-dimensional figure. The most important dimensions of aging are responsibility-engagement and the reproductive cycle. The three-dimensional solution is presented here since it transcends both the chronological and status dimensions. In this three-dimensional solution (See Figure 3.3) we find that the two dimensional configuration remains intact in that the indexing of the social persona by chronological age, bent in the form of a horseshoe, is still apparent. This, however, is further twisted by the third dimension in a "roller-coaster" pattern—it is first high, then low, then high, and then low again.

For the lack of a better term, this dimension is identified as "encumberment[2]." It is reflective of the burdens or obligations encountered during different portions of the life cycle. Although it may appear to be a totally new dimension, it is actually predictable from the two status dimensions. Those social persona (A-H) on the negative side of both the responsibility-engagement axes are also on the negative side of the encumberment dimension. They are not burdened by career responsibilities and obligations to children. The same is true of those social persons (Q-1) on the positive side of both status axes. Here children are becoming independent and one is at peak productivity in the career cycle. Thus one is becoming unencumbered in domestic roles and is established in occupational roles. On the other hand, those social persons (J-P) on the positive side of the responsibility-engagement axis, but who are beginning the reproductive cycle are far on the positive end of the encumberment dimension. They are encumbered since they are beginning careers and are simultaneously burdened by obligations to a developing family. Similarly, those on the negative side of the responsibility-engagement axis, but positive on the reproductive cycle, are seen as encumbered. This is mostly because of withdrawal from work roles and the problems which increase with older age—namely decrement in health and a fixed income. Figure 3.3 visually represents the chronological dimension intertwined with the status dimensions and encumberment in the form of a "roller coaster on a horseshoe curve."

This image is not a total surprise. We often hear the phrase "over the hill" used in a context of joking. The geometric representation in Figure 3.3 suggests that this indeed may be a deeper cognitive organization of age in American culture. This is reinforced by the terms many informants used in describing the social persona in the age grades they had generated. Of the over 200 terms collected (Fry 1973), most referred to the status dimensions or to a descriptive age dimension. However, many terms reflect patterns of responsibility, independence, or a life course. The terms mirroring the image presented in Figure 3.3 are: for the young—"Beginners," "Lot of Freedom with Few Responsibilities," "Getting Started," "Grasping Adults," and "Strugglers;" for middle age—"Hard-Up Middle Age," "Successful," "Just Beginning to Live," "Peak of Plateau," "Top of Ladder," "Beginning of Adult Freedom Years," "Freedom Group," and "Slightly Over the Hump;" and for the old—"Responsible Only for Themselves," "Over-the-Hill Years," and "Declining Adult." Thus the configuration of age in three dimensions is of youth "coming off the chute" only to find themselves in a "valley" of responsibility and obligations for career and family. They then climb out of the valley and up a hill into middle age where careers are established and family is maturing. Finally, there is a slight descent into old age which be-

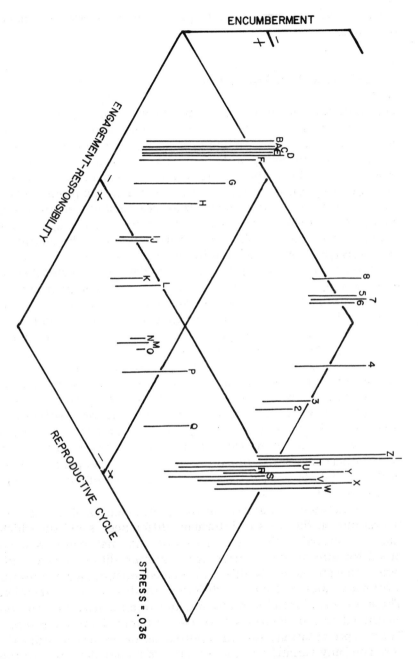

FIGURE 3.3. Three-dimensional representation of interpoint distances among 34 social persona cards. Note that chronological age is further twisted into a "roller coaster" on a horseshoe curve.

comes marked as chronic health problems necessitate dependence on others.

A QUESTION OF VARIATION

The multidimensional scaling solutions have enabled us to visualize chronological age bent and twisted in three dimensions and enabled the interpretation of the relationships that otherwise would have been embedded in a 34 X 34 matrix. Such representations, however, give the impression of a uniform structure and a structure which is subject to reification. In circumventing this tendency, two questions concerning variation are raised. The first is asking to what extent do these structures represent actual aging in our society? The second is directed to variation within the configuration on the part of individual informants.

The life course in industrialized societies is noteworthy for the heterogeneity in life careers. The variation is, in part, attributable to the multiplicity of timetables and to a complex interplay between individual choice and institutional constraints (Neugarten and Hagestad 1976). The question of how well does the geometric figure "fit" the actual life courses in American society cannot be adequately answered in this paper primarily because of the type of available data. The data upon which the multidimensional scaling solutions are based are normative. Informants sorted the cards by making judgments using what they thought were the cultural rules. As such, these geometric figures are a representation of this aspect of culture, often called ideal culture. Although this certainly influences peoples' actions, the question of what people actually do can only be answered with a different kind of data and a different research strategy.

The question of variation in the multidimensional scaling configurations on the basis of informant differences is an issue which can be answered in this paper. Age proximity matricies were computed for informants of different age groups, different sexes, different educational levels, different socioeconomic statuses, and for informants who had created different numbers of age categories. These were read into the KYST program and the resulting multidimensional scaling solutions have been examined and interpreted. These representations are not reported on or presented in this paper. The only variation in these figures is in the placement of the social persona which is exceptionally minor. The overall configuration—the horseshoe bend and the roller-coaster pattern—remains constant in these subpopulations.

COMPARATIVE VIEWPOINT

If one searches long enough and hard enough, it is possible to locate reports on the life cycle for most of the world's cultures. These are primarily descriptions of expectable status sequences in the predominant cultural institutions that individuals in that culture will experience as they age. Although they are valuable in their own right, for our purposes we lack comparability. Age statuses may be contrasted, but the type of analysis seldom takes us to the cultural dimensions. One exception to this is a study by Kirk and Burton (1977) of the Maasai. The Maasai are a pastoral, tribal people of East Africa. Age is an important component of Maasai social structure since each male and female belongs to an age set or a corporately organized age-homogenous group with distinctive names and appropriate behavior. These crosscut patrilineal clans which are the cattle-owning and all-powerful domestic and productive units.

Kirk and Burton's research is not directly concerned with aging, but their results provide some comparable data on cultural dimensions of age. The immediate objectives of their work is the evaluation of a series of explicit hypothesis concerning semantic domains and cognitive organization. The data they collected were not age-related, but presented similarities and differences in personality traits. Personality traits, however, do not exist outside of individuals except in terms of an abstract evaluative framework (i.e., desirability). In establishing the context for personality, Kirk and Burton utilized the age sets as social identities. This included the entire life cycle with the exception of the age sets for old men and old women. Also multidimensional scaling is used to analyze the personality data and the age sets. Thus, in spite of different purposes and different data, we do find a basis for comparison.

A point of similarity emerges in the dimensionality of the two-dimensional representation of the Maasai age sets (social identities). These are identified as "responsibility" and "marriageability" (see Figure 3.4) which parallel the "engagement-responsibility" and the "reproductive-cycle" dimensions in the two-dimensional solution of the American data. Engagement-responsibility are grouped since engagement more adequately describes the status transition process, while responsibility is a quality which is a product of being engaged in certain types of statuses. As has been noted, one of the more common adjectives used by American informants in describing the age grades they had created was responsibility.

"Marriageability" and the reproductive cycle are not the obvious parallel we find with the first dimension. In examining Figure

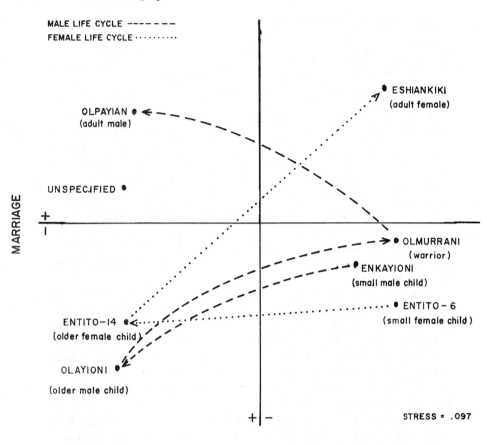

MARRIAGE

RESPONSIBILITY

FIGURE 3.4.   Two-dimensional-representation of Maasai age terms indicating male-female differentiation (after Kirk and Burton 1977:756, by permission).

3.2, we find that the intersection of the reproductive cycle (horizontal axis) with the engagement-responsibility axis (vertical axis), is reflective of the marital status of the social persona. For most of those above the horizontal line (i.e., either end of the horseshoe), marital status is single, widowed or not referenced, while those below the line are almost universally married. Marriage is not a dimension in the American cognitive organization of age. Instead, it is a component of the engagement-responsibility dimension, and seemingly is a precondition for the reproductive cycle. Otherwise, we would have a different configuration. Although the two are not causally connected, marriage and reproduction are linked, at least in ideal culture. The minor difference here is a product of differing types of data and the problems investigated in the two studies.

A significant point of contrast is the sequencing of the social identities along the dimensions, which is partially affected by the differences in the number of points (social persona) scaled and by the fact that not all portions of the life cycle are represented. The American analysis has 34 social persona with childhood and adolescence not represented, while the Maasai case is based on 9 social identities and old age is absent. Regardless of these biases, we still may see differences in the patterns resulting from the cultural contexts. In the two-dimensional representation, the American life cycle forms the image of a horseshoe curve with male and female social persona reinforcing the image. In contrast, the Maasai male and female life cycles are notably differentiated. Females, progressing from childhood to adolescence remain unmarried, but move from no responsibility to being responsible. Once a girl is married and becomes an adult, she moves to the no-responsibility-but-married quadrant of the representation (a V-shaped image). On the other hand, the male life cycle is a "zig-zag." Young boys leave the no-responsibility quadrant when they become herd boys. When a young boy enters the warrior age set, he returns to the no-responsibility quadrant and is still not marriageable. Only when he passes on to the householder set, and marries, will he enter the quadrant (married and responsible) opposite the adult female (Kirk and Burton 1977).

The patterns in the multidimensional scaling representations for the Maasai life cycle are attributable to the positions for the respective sexes in a patrilineal, pastoral society. Both adolescent boys and girls play important roles in the household economy of their fathers. Boys do the difficult work of herding and girls assist in domestic tasks. Upon marriage, a girl leaves her natal home to assume residence with her husband and his patrilineal kin. These people are virtual strangers who view her with suspicion and in whom she has little interest except through her husband and her offspring. Hence, she is married, but not responsible. Before a young boy marries, he goes through warriorhood. This is an anomalous status for young men who are expected to raid other Maasai segments, steal cattle, and receive the attentions of young unmarried women for their exploits in war. They are a threat to the households of the married men and their women. Consequently precautions are taken to separate them from domestic life. Warriorhood is a holding period of no responsibility prior to the responsibilities and powers of householding which are allocated to married adult men.

Responsibility and reproduction are rather basic issues any human society must resolve. Without them there would be little cooperative effort, production, or continuity of the species. Age structures are clearly entwined in these problems as individuals progress through their life cycles and society. Thus it is not surprising to find some similarity in the dimensionality of age statuses. Also it is quite expectable that the patterns will be different. In adapting to a wide variety of ecological pressures, each culture arrives at a solution to the questions of responsibility and reproduction. Age status structures are reflective of this accomodation and, hence, are understandably different.

CONCLUSIONS AND IMPLICATIONS

Multidimensional scaling has proved to be a useful technique in isolating the dimensions of aging in American culture. In all the multidimensional scaling solutions, the one-dimensional solution remains intact. This is the dimension which is predominant in American society, life time or chronological age. In the two- and three-dimensional representations this elementary temporal dimension is bent and twisted by nontemporal dimensions of responsibility-engagement, reproduction, and encumberment. Although these are reflective of status change occurring in a temporal dimension, we have transcended descriptions of status transition. Through multidimensional scaling, we have been able to discern the relationships between data from a card sort as images in Euclidian space. In interpreting these figures we have been able to isolate the more elusive cognitive dimensions and the cultural organization of an ubiquitous domain—aging.

This, however, is only a beginning. As anthropologists increasingly bring their expertise to issues of age, a societal priority area, we must apply the appropriate anthropological concepts and procedures, just as we would in any other cultural domain in a specific sociocultural context. In other words, we should begin by ethnographically exploring this domain. Even in an industrialized society, into which the ethnographers have been enculturated, we cannot assume *apriori* that our ethnography is done. This is especially critical in a domain such as age which is ambiguous and not highly standardized in urban-industrial societies if one is to rely on terminology alone (Fry 1976).

Multidimensional scaling has proved to be productive in charting the nontemporal cognitive organization of age in American society and has given us insights into one other society, the Maasai. It was multidimensional scaling which enabled us to see the similarities and differences. This technique has other advantages. The eliciting procedures and analytic techniques are highly replicable.

The instrument used here may either be refined or adapted to another cultural context. In order to replicate the analysis, all that is needed is a large enough computer and one of the many multi-dimensional scaling programs. Although this research was designed for an urban society, the methodology does have implications for crosscultural comparative research. Since techniques exist to facilitate the interpretation of relationships between two geometric representations (Shepard 1972(b)), the potential is there for the development of comparative work on aging as a cultural domain. Before this can happen, however, it is first necessary to collect appropriate data in a systematic fashion. This paper has been a step in that direction for a sample of American culture. Through analytical tools such as multidimensional scaling we may understand the underlying cultural organization, the commonalities and variations, of an issue which is universal for all humankind—aging.

APPENDIX A

In this Appendix we find the instrument used to investigate the dimensions of age. This instrument consists of 34 cards describing individuals by sex and life events or age statuses. Each card is identified by a letter or a number which corresponds to the letters and numbers in Figures 3.1-3.3. Here the social persona are arranged according to increments in chronological order as can be seen by the figures in parentheses. In the interview situation, the cards had been shuffled prior to sorting in order to randomize the sequence of social persona as informants sorted and imposed their order. Questions were answered concerning the mechanics of sorting the cards, but *no* directions were given in the sorting of particular cards into particular piles. This was the informant's decision alone. Following the sorting of the cards, Questions 1 and 2 were asked for each grouping and the content of that grouping was recorded.

Instructions:

"People classify other people according to a number of different things. For example, we classify people by sex. That is— male or female. We can classify people by the amount of money they have. Here we would have rich, poor, comfortable, and the like. We also classify people according to age.

I have here several cards. Each card contains a description of a person who has accomplished several things or has had several things happen to him in the course of his life. I would like you to take these cards and, on the basis of the brief description of the person on each card, sort them into piles based on your guess regarding their approximate age or similarity in age bracket. There are no correct number of piles or ways to sort and organize these cards. What we are interested in is how *you* would sort and organize the people described on these cards with respect to age. You might find it easier to arrange them in rough age brackets ranging from younger to older.

Once the respondent had completed the card sort he or she was asked:

1. What would you call or what name would you give to the age bracket or the age group of the people you have placed in this pile? Are there any other words you might use to describe this general age group?
2. Roughly, what is the age or range of age in terms of years of the people described in this pile?

Card Deck: The mean age assigned by the total sample is indicated in parentheses.

A. A female, high-school graduate, single, working, living with parents (21.4)

B. A male, high-school graduate, single, in the army (21.6)

C. A male, high-school graduate, single, living with parents (21.6)

D. A male, high-school graduate, single, is working, living with parents (21.8)

E. A female, high-school graduate, single, working, living with roommate (21.9)

F. A male, in college, single, living with a roommate (22.2)

G. A male, in college, married, no children (23.6)

H. A male, in college, single, a veteran (24.9)

I. A female, high-school graduate, married, two preschool children (26.0)

J. A male, high-school graduate, working, married two preschool children (26.1)

K. A male, college graduate, working, married, no children (27.5)

L. A female, college graduate, working, married, no children (27.7)

M. A male, recently promoted at work, married, living with wife and children (29.7)

N. A female, married, has two school children, and is working (30.2)

O. A male, a veteran, married, living with wife and children (30.9)

P. A female, college graduate, single, recently promoted to a job of great responsibility and productivity (31.8)

Q. A male, a college graduate, recently promoted to a job of great responsibility, married and living with wife and children (35.0)

R. A female, working, married, two high-school children (38.3)

S. A female, college graduate, married, two high-school children (38.3)

T. A male, working, married, two children who are recent high-school graduates (39.8)

U. A female, in college, married, two children who are recent high-school graduates (40.5)

V. A female, working, married, two children both of whom are in college (42.2)

W. A male, recently promoted to a job of great responsibility, married, two children both of whom are in college (42.8)

X. A female, working, married, two children both of whom have recently married. (45.2)

Y. A male, recently promoted to a job of great responsibility, married, two children both of whom have recently married (45.2)

    Z. A female, high-school graduate, working, married, two chil-
        dren both of whom are married and have children of their
        own (49.3)
    1. A male, recently promoted to a job of great responsibility,
        married, has two children both of whom are married and
        have children of their own (49.4)
    2. A female, widowed, working, and living alone (50.0)
    3. A male, widowed, working, living alone (51.5)
    4. A male, widowed, working, living with adult children (58.5)
    5. A male, single, retired, living alone (64.4)
    6. A female, widowed, retired and living alone (64.7)
    7. A male, widowed, retired, living with adult children (65.4)
    8. A female, widowed, retired, living in a nursing home (68.6)

NOTES

1. The research upon which this paper is based was sponsored by the Kathryn McHale Fellowship granted by the American Association of University Women.

2. The encumberment dimension may be more clearly seen in Figure 3.3 by visualizing that figure as a cube. Figure 3.3 is an isometric drawing in which only the outlines of the cube are presented in order not to interfere with the view of the data.

4 Activity and Aging in a Colombian Peasant Village

DIANNE KAGAN
Santa Rosa Junior College

As in an industrialized society, Dianne Kagan finds that age boundaries are vague in the peasant village of Bojacá. To get at the covert meaning of age, Kagan uses cognitive anthropological techniques to discover the age categories and their meanings in terms of intergenerational relations, age norms and values, especially for the old.

She began her work with a series of naive questions, but ones that were standardized for each informant. As an uninformed anthropologist in the local culture, she asked, "What kind of people are there? What kind of age groups are there? What kind of things are there to do in the world?" As the answers to these initial questions took a consistent form, new questions emerged which were directly answered by her informants and confirmed in their actions. By pursuing these intriguing leads, Dianne Kagan has collected a wealth of information. Not only does she tell us about age differentiation in this peasant village, but she gives us insights into the meaning of old age, the basis of intergenerational conflict and the values which reinforce the "good life." With intensive contact with a smaller number of informants, it is not necessary to resort to a computer. The patterns are clear and the cultural world is charted as the informants, themselves, tell us. It is through those long sixteen months, the interviews, the living with and observing of her informants that Dianne Kagan can discuss the dimensions of and the meaning of old age and associated values in Bojacá, Colombia.

In Bojacá older adults are referred to by a distinctive age term vejez and occasionally anciano (a). Being a viejo does not accord prestige, nor is it associated with isolation and abandonment. Instead there is a sense of esteem and some deference directed to a viejo. Kagan points to the integration of older adults into family and community life. Elderly Bojaquenos are not idle. They actively contribute to community life in very distinctive areas which are reinforced by age norms. Both young and old recognize these norms and the appropriateness of the associated behavior. When the age norms between age groups are violated, intergenerational

> *conflict emerges. Older informants, or their more junior family members, readily point to infractions in the cases they analyzed with the anthropologist and to their strategies for avoiding or resolving the conflict. To age successfully in Bojacá, one must be able to live in a fashion where the underlying values are affirmed. Such underlying values include living in an environment where there is affection and caring, where one has duties and responsibilities, and where one has respect.*

The village of Bojacá, a peasant community resting high in the Andes of Colombia, provides an instructive contrast for the numerous studies of old age conducted in complex industrialized cultures.[1] Questions concerning the innate or universal nature of the aging experience have appeared with frequency in recent gerontological literature and this study has been formulated because the data available to answer these questions come largely from research in industrialized settings. The specific topics to be explored in this chapter will include age group attitudes, family and community activities of the aged, intergenerational relationships, and value orientations. The cognitive elicitation procedures utilized have also provided data for the formulation of a model of the aging process which is summarized at the end of the chapter.

CULTURAL AND GEOGRAPHIC SETTING

The people of Bojacá call themselves *campesinos*, rural countrymen or peasants. Their village, with over 900 inhabitants, was a Chibcha Indian settlement when the Spanish first arrived on the savanna of Bogotá in 1537. Today Bojaqueños lead lives that recall far more of their Spanish colonial heritage than the lives of the Chibcha. Men and women farm small land holdings or work as wage laborers on larger *haciendas*. They grow corn, barley, potatoes and other garden crops and three families in town have been successful enough to purchase small farm equipment. For most other Bojaqueños, agricultural work is manual activity and their labor is accomplished in the cold damp air produced as the result of Bojacá's location 9000 feet in the central Andes.

The hills and fields that surround Bojacá are almost continuously green; natural pasture and cultivated fields cover the hills and extend down to the valley floor to the edge of town. The village itself is neither quaint nor wretched. Most Bojaqueños are poor by American standards and village poverty shows in the appearance of the streets and buildings. But the predominance of early colonial structures, chipped and stained with mud, lends a tired sense of dignity to the town. Electricity and water function in some buildings when the town generator is working, and more and more Bojaqueños are looking toward the city of Bogota' as a model for twentieth-century living.

Bojacá will not become a modern village too quickly. Although some of the very young like to affect city dress, there is still an abundance of traditional *ruanas* (ponchos) and *sombreros* (hats) in the streets of Bojacá. And most significantly, Bojacá's roots in the past reach far too deep to be transformed rapidly by simple material changes.

BEING OLD IN BOJACA

In Bojacá, old age is not considered to be an idle period in one's life. The intrinsic qualities of aging such as the onset of degenerative diseases or declining physical strength are not mediated by awesome respect or highly ritualized patterns of deference, but old age does provide some specific gratifications. The individual has more time to spend with children and grandchildren, and old age can be a tranquil period filled with reflections on past achievements and events. The aged in Bojacá do not constitute a gerontocracy with exceptional rights and privileges, but they are esteemed and respected participants in the day-to-day activities of family and community life. Deference for the aged is demonstrated in a quiet but sincere manner with respectful allowance being made for the childlike behavior of the senile.

The most readily observable feature of old age in Bojacá is that the aged retain a high level of integration in both family and community activities. They are neither discarded nor segregated as an age group and if physically capable, older Bojaqueños remain active in wage earning or household maintenance throughout their lives.

ETHNOGRAPHIC METHODS

The covert attitudes toward old age in Bojacá are more difficult to describe and assess. As old age is not a topic of frequent conversation and as age behavior boundaries tend to be vague, it was decided that cognitive elicitation procedures could best outline some of the more elusive concepts and values regarding old age and age-specific activities in the village. While these procedures have been utilized frequently in the study of activities and objects constituting categorically visible domains (cf. Conklin 1955, Frake 1962), they are also of value in understanding the components of dynamic processes such as aging.

The aged in Bojacá are a part of a community, and it was necessary to understand the dimensions of the community in which they lived before proceeding with a cognitive study focused on their individual lives. Through participant observation in village life over a period of 16 months and various ethnographic activities, a picture of life in Bojacá was recorded. The overt data concerning the aged in Bojacá were readily available through census information, interviews, and observations.

The cognitive methodologies selected were directed toward the elicitation of folk taxonomies describing the "kinds of people," "kinds of age groups," and "kinds of things to do" in the world. As Tylor (1969:26) has stated, "A folk taxonomy tells us what the categories are and how they are related to one another" from the perspective of the native informant, not the ethnographer. Using the relatively informal elicitation procedures described by Frake (1964) I would sit with informants and allow them to provide vocabulary appropriate to age grades in Bojacá. Their responses would be the basis for formulating new questions that would map out the life-span and age-related behavior. The end result was data very similar to what Neugarten and Hagestad (1976:44) describe as "awareness of age norms" but the distinction being that Bojaqueños had a maximum opportunity to structure the progress of each interview.

Each interview series began with the same question: "When a person is born, what do you call him besides his name?" All of my informants responded with either *"nené"* or *"bebé,"* the two common words for an infant in Bojacá. Having elicited an inital response from the informant, the remainder of the interview took its structure from the preceding statement. For example, when Sra. Pascuala responded that a newborn "person" was called a *"bebé,"* she was then asked "What other kinds of people are there besides babies?" This same procedure was followed until the informant could no longer assign words to identify individuals on the life span and all contrasts between the terms were clear.

THE STAGES OF LIFE

The terms most frequently used to refer to age grades in Bojacá are: *nenés* (babies), *niños* (children), *jovenes* (young people), *adultos* (adults), and *viejos* (old people). The word *bebé* was occasionally substituted for *nené* with no apparent change in meaning and the

word *madurez* (maturity) was sometimes used to refer to that period between *juventud* (youth) and *vejez* (old age).

The term *anciano (a)* (literally ancient one) is used occasionally in Bojacá to refer to the aged but it seems to indicate little variation from *viejo*. A few informants felt that *anciano* carries more
emotional content in both a positive and negative sense. Sra. Fidela offered:

> When my son comes home from driving the bus and he says to me
> *Como le fue su dia, anciana?* (How was your day, old woman?) I
> know that he was worried about me because I am sick and old. He
> has respect for me and he is a good son and takes care of me when
> I am too sick to work. When I go to the *tienda* (small store where
> beer is also served) to buy something and the men who drink there
> say, "Ah, the *anciana* has come to buy food for the house," I know
> they are thinking I am old and useless.

Ethnographers in other Spanish-speaking communities have indicated that the term *anciano (a)* can carry greater respect and refer to a very old or special person (Coles 1973:36).

After the appropriate terms for the stages within the life cycle
were elicited, informants were asked to outline the chronological
boundaries appropriate to each age grade. Informants were quick
to point out that this either could not or should not be done as behavior does not always conform to age-designated boundaries. The
most vigorous opponent to my questions concerning chronological
age behavior boundaries was Don Pedro, an 83-year-old informant.
He pointed out that many young women of 15 are married, have
children and meet all the responsibilities of an adult. He quickly
added that a man such as himself could have lived many years and
still be young in interests and active in spirit. There are almost no
legal or political traditions limiting or shaping age-related behavior
in Colombia which could contribute to age-group boundaries in the
future.

AGE-GROUP ATTITUDES

Qualitative analysis of the cognitive material from Bojacá shows
that attitudes shaping behavior of the old in Bojacá are characterized by at least two distinctive features. First, it is a period when
the young should demonstrate greater deference and respect for the
old, and second, it is a period of increasing dependency for the aged
as many experience a diminishment of physical strength and health.

Responses reflecting the notion of respect or reverence for the
aged were by far the most common reactions to questions such as

"How does old age differ from other times in one's life?" or "What is it like to be old?" When asked this latter question, Isabel, an 18-year-old informant replied, "It is the time when people recognize how hard you have worked during your life." Lucila, age 42, replied, "We respect old people for having lived many years." Lucila and her father, age 81, agree that "Old people have experienced many things. They have seen problems and they have learned from these problems. Young people would not repeat the same mistakes over and over if they would listen to old people."

Stated more broadly, the principle reasons these and other informants provide for respecting the aged are:

1. They have lived many years, the implication being clear that it is not always easy to live many years in Bojacá;

2. *Dios* (God) has seen fit to allow them to live longer lives for whatever reasons He may have;

3. Most older people have cared for others when they were young (e.g. children, parents, siblings) and now they should be cared for in return; and

4. There are things that old people have learned or experienced that are considered to be of practical or functional use.

Bojaqueños do not conceive of the aged as profoundly wise men and women capable of delivering sage judgements on all matters in the contemporary world. The knowledge particular to the aged is viewed in a very pragmatic light. They have experiential wisdom; they have known more sides of human character, dealt with more tragedies, and seen the world take both positive and negative turns. They can reflect on other times and other events to shed light on the present.

FAMILY AND COMMUNITY ACTIVITIES OF THE AGED

Because nuclear family or two-generational living is preferred in Bojacá, many older Bojaqueños remain the heads of their own households throughout old age. This is especially true of older men who will arrange to live with other relatives or friends only when they have been widowed and can no longer physically care for themselves.

The independent households headed by aged individuals are usually very small, averaging between three and four individuals per household group. Most often the additional members of the household are unmarried children or siblings of the older couple. In a few households, grandchildren have been "loaned" to their grandparents for the express purpose of keeping them company and keeping them independent. This is a mutually satisfying arrangement between older and younger nuclear family groups. Most often the "loaned" grandchild comes from an overcrowded household where his or her absence will constitute subsistence relief. In turn, the child's grandparents will be able to continue a pattern of independent subsistence with the additional labor contributed by the child.

When illness or the death of a spouse makes independent living impossible, aged Bojaqueños will seek residence with other kin or friends. More than half of the dependent aged in Bojacá live with their children and the remaining dependent aged live with siblings, nephews and nieces, or friends. Sra. Clemencia, a childless widow, was invited to live with Sra. Floralba and her family when she grew too old to maintain her own household. Although they share no kinship ties, Sra. Clemencia helps care for Floralba's four children, husband, and brother-in-law. Sra. Floralba explains why she took Clemencia into her home:

> Sra. Clemencia is very old and cannot work too hard but she can help me with my work. And Clemencia is very religious. She has more time to pray and attend mass. She prays for my children and asks the Virgin to look after us. This is very important to me . . . .

Whether or not they share a residence, the old and the young interact daily in Bojacá. Both family and community activities involve the aged, but cognitively, Bojaqueños have notions about what sorts of activities are more appropriate for the aged. Activity areas where old people are thought to be most capable of providing insight or assistance include:

Religion
Food preparation
Manual skills
Simple curing techniques practiced in the home
The growth and properties of regional plants
Questions of justice
Personal counseling over problems already present in an individual's life

Areas where the advice of the aged is rarely sought and sometimes actually avoided include:

Economic activities involving the exchange of cash and dealings with nonvillagers

The use of mechanical devices
Village planning such as road construction or renovation
Formal education and school activities
Future plans of a romantic or sexual nature

As not all villagers share exactly the same cognitive expectations regarding age-appropriate activity, conflict can result in both family and community groups. Intergenerational conflict is also fostered by patterns of urbanization entering the community. While intergenerational conflict is not a serious problem in Bojacá, it is interesting to examine as a pattern of conflicting cognitive expectations.

INTERGENERATIONAL CONFLICT

Many older Bojaqueños express concern that the aging process is preventing them from performing normal adult work activities and is causing them to become more dependent on others. The aged villager views an idle life as a tragic one. But data collected from younger informants shows that they do not always view diminishment of activity and increasing dependency in old age as particularly tragic or even problematic. In fact, it is felt that one appropriate means of demonstrating respect for the aged is to provide assistance or relief from duties. This attitude, while perceived to be respectful, contributes to the diminishing sense of self-worth and esteem among many aged individuals who search actively for those areas of daily life where they can make a contribution.

Occasionally, the particular skills of the aged are not priority activities in village life. Sra. Isabel recalling an incident with her goddaughter stated, "Pascualita used to come to my house to learn to weave. I was teaching her to make a blanket so she could make things for her family, but she doesn't come anymore. She doesn't care about me or the things I can teach her." Isabel knows that her goddaughter is enrolled in the local high school and that she also works for her uncle after school to earn cash for the family. Isabel even speaks highly of Pascualita's industriousness to her neighbors. But Isabel, because she has not found an appropriate way to share activity with Pascualita, persists in interpreting Pascualita's absence as rejection. The industriousness that Isabel boasts of to neighbors will obviate the need for Pascualita to learn to weave her own blankets.

Other examples of intergenerational tension are reflected in relatively mild forms of conflict. Valentina, age 93, will be avoided or possibly even scorned when she attempts to guide her grandson in the appropriate steps of courtship. Yet the same grandson will seek Valentina's advice on the proper care of young sheep and other livestock. Tomas, age 68, assists his sons in the important processes of storing seed for the following year's barley crop. But Tomas' concerns over the new delivery agreement with a brewery in Bogotá receive little serious attention. Carmenza, age 72, teaches her grandchildren how to pray the rosary, how to cook, and how to be a good husband or wife, but she must adjust to new beliefs that allow newborn babies to be bathed during the first precarious month of life.

Younger informants explain that in their desire to show appropriate deference for older individuals, they will frequently exclude or circumvent the aged when they know friction from differing opinions is likely to occur. A recent example of this attitude concerns Don Pedro, age 83, who had been a member of the town council for 40 years.

Disagreements between Pedro and other members of the council had increased over the past years. Pedro tended to emphasize old problems and old achievements that were not thought to be relevant by the younger council members. When Pedro's declining physical and mental abilities made it difficult for him to attend all the council functions, secret arrangements were made between Pedro's sons and other members to omit Pedro's name from the forthcoming ballot. Today, Pedro is unaware that he was not re-elected to the council. He still performs many of the informal roles of a *consejal* (council member): he leads informal discussions over current problems in the local *tiendas* in an oratorical fashion, and he appears and takes part in all festivities and special events. Occasionally he is confused by the changes that take place in the village without his knowledge, but he has yet to confront the other council members over his exclusion from the decision-making process. He tends to attribute the most recent changes to a quickening pace of life caused by increasing modernization and urbanization in the village of Bojacá.

VALUES AND THE AGED

The study of values is a difficult task. Every society and every individual within a social group possesses a notion of the good life as well as a particular recognition of bad times. The community of Bojacá and the aged as a specific category of Bojaqueños are no different.

Kluckhohn (1951:395) et al. have argued that:

> *Value* implies a code or a standard which has some persistence through time, or, more broadly put, which organizes a system of action. Value...places things, acts, ways of behaving, goals of action on approval-disapproval continuum.

Older Bojaqueños have standards or possess a code which reflect their membership within the larger value orientations of all Bojaqueños. There are however, variations in the emphasis and focus upon certain group values that help to define being old in Bojacá as well as point out the specific interests and concerns of the aged. Defining the "good life" or the ideal patterns of old age in Bojacá is difficult. The circumstances of each individual life can be influenced by the size of one's family, the economic resources of the individual, marital status, physical health, and one's relationships with others. But cognitively structured interviews with older Bojaqueños regarding their own lives seem to single out three basic but significant value orientations. When aged individuals felt they had little or no access to these values areas, they described their lives as unhappy:

1. *To live near or with individuals for whom one has cariño and from whom cariño is felt to be returned. Cariño*, in this context, would include concepts of affection, fondness, and the exchange of kindnesses. Sra. Fidela recalls years in her life that were without *cariño*:

> My husband and I were married for 17 years. After he died I lived in our house for awhile, then I lived with my son Jose Alejandro, ...before my other sons married they lived with us sometimes. When we moved to *el centro* (about 10 years ago), all my sons lived with me but now only my youngest, Didacio, stays here with me. Didacio is a good son and cares for me. Jose Alejandro understood me too...he comes to visit me sometimes. His wife does not like me or understand my character...she never comes to see me. I have not seen my son Luis for 10 years...I lived with him and his family but we fought all the time. His wife is a very good person and she understands me. She was more like a daughter than a *nuera* (daughter-in-law). She was very special to me and was very *cariñosa* (loving). When I lived with them my son fought with her a lot. It was for this that I fought with my son and left. Didacio and I are happy living with the Tovares. Lilia Tovare and I are *primas hermanas* (daughters of sisters); we are like a family. If Didacio marries I hope we can all live nearby.

2. *To have oficio, a term used in Bojacá to mean duties, obligations, responsibility, or work. Oficio* to the Bojaqueño is more than

a simple set of chores although *oficio* may be nothing more than mending a tool or preparing vegetables for the soup. Most importantly, *oficio* means that one is contributing to life, that one is necessary, and that one is participating in the ongoing activities of life. Sra. Paulina, age 61, complains frequently that:

> *No tengo oficio* (I have no *oficio*). Until my mother died, she was everything to me. My husband died 14 years ago and my only daughter three years later. I have other family but they do not live nearby. Now when I have taken care of the animals and cleaned my house, I go to visit Sra. Teresa. She is a widow too and she is often sick. I help her in the house and I accompany her so she does not have to be alone. Sometimes when it is too cold or it is raining, I cannot go. It is terrible to sit alone with nothing to do.

Another old man of more than 75 years pointed out:

> When you are old you are only half healthy. Others must take care of you...the old are very dependent on others. Sometimes you can do little things...care for the children or go to the *tienda* or make a small thing for the house...but many old people just go out and walk in the streets. When I have no *oficio* I walk to the plaza and I come home again. The people think I am going to do some business.

3. *To be shown respeto or respect.* It is thought that the aged were always the most respected age group in Bojacá. Many Bojaqueños believe that it reflects poorly on both the old and the young when the aged are not shown respect in contemporary times. Although many villagers would disagree, Sr. Pablo, age 72, feels there is not as much respect shown the aged as there once was:

> Today is very different. The *viejos* pass by on the street like cars on the road. Before the young people would stop and greet them or step aside to allow them to pass. It is not like that now. Old people are respected because they have many years. But old people also have experience and many are very *juicioso* (wise) in regard to some things.

Sra. Luisa, age 72, adds:

> Many young people do not have respect for the old people because they know new things and they go to school. Old people did not always go to school but both the old and the young should be respected for what they know.

There is disagreement among the aged as to whether the past was better than the present and whether or not old people were treated better in the past. Don Pedro claims that old people think the aged were "more respected in the past" when *their own children* do not treat them with deference. "It is *their own fault*! Children must be taught to respect old people," is his simple explanation. His point is accented in one of the tales he is fond of telling his grandchildren:

> There was once a man who was very very rich. This man had an old father who was very poor and lived a life of suffering and hardship. One day the rich man noticed his old father in the yard, very cold and very sick. The rich man said to his own little son, "Go and get the blanket we use for the horses and give it to your grandfather. He is cold and the blanket will comfort him." The little son ran and took the blanket down from the wall and very carefully tore the blanket in half. He took half of the blanket to his grandfather and he replaced the other half of the blanket to the wall. When the rich man saw what his little son had done he shouted, "Why have you done this? Your grandfather is cold and I told you to take him the horse's blanket to keep him warm!" The little son answered his father: "Papa, I did as you told me but I wanted to save the other half of the blanket to give to you when you grow old and you are cold.

The personality patterns and individual skills of older Bojaqueños vary but most are able to find some area of activity or advisement that is performed best by an older person. This in turn usually meets their needs in important value areas. Older individuals who are able to perceive the areas of activity appropriate for the aged are rarely idle and do not lead reclusive or quiet lives. They also appear to suffer less from the mental strain imposed by feelings of dependency and diminishing self-esteem. At present, patterns of positive adjustment to aging are more common in Bojacá than those of dissatisfactory aging.

A MODEL FOR UNDERSTANDING THE AGING PROCESS

As Back (1976:409) has pointed out, "...it is always possible for society to arrange institutions such that either youth or age can be peaks or depressions in life." However, the occasional problems of adjustment to old age in Bojacá cannot be viewed as social pathologies or serious malfunctions in the social system. From a theoretical perspective, the aged are neither disengaging as described by Henry and Cumming (1961) nor are they assuming highly specialized or exalted roles reserved exclusively for their age group. Successful aging individuals are, instead, reducing their participation in some activities while increasing their contribution to other areas of village life. The knowledge and skills accumulated during adulthood are redirected in a manner appropriate to the individual's physical capabilities and in a fashion deemed appropriate by other members of the community.

Cognitive data on the aged in Bojacá also provided a means for interpreting the aging process that closely parallels Erik Erikson's model for identity crises among adolescents (1959). Erikson suggests that the transitions occurring during adolescence are multi-faceted and contain elements of biological change, psychological change, and change in the social expectations that others hold for the individual. In Erikson's model the successful resolution of the adolescent identity crises resulting from this triadic change leads to the next developmental stage of young adulthood.

In a general psycho-cultural perspective, growing old contains many of the elements of Erikson's model for adolescents. The aging adult experiences increasing degrees of biological change and psychological change as he or she passes from middle years into old age. The aging individual must also come to terms with changes in the manner in which he or she is perceived by others. Just like the adolescent, the older person is often expected to drop former roles and activities and assume new ones more appropriate to a new age category.

In comparing old age with adolescence, the changes of these two periods appear almost as mirror images. The adolescent experiences new biological growth and increasing physical ability coupled with newly developing role identities. The aging individual experiences decreasing physical ability and diminishing participation in society. Cognitive material from Bojacá revealed an understanding of both these patterns of change as being most particular to youth and old age. But the comparisons between the adolescent experience and old age, whether they be considered parallel or mirror image experiences, cannot be developed in depth. The similarities must be regarded as merely categorical ones: both periods in the life span tend to include an increase or peak of biological, psychological, and social change in the life of the individual.

With this limitation in mind, one additional question can be posed: If the changes of adolescence tended to produce an "identity crisis" in the adolescents Erikson studied, is it possible that aging individuals also experience some form of identity crisis as the result of the three types of change converging at this point in their lives?

The proliferation of gerontological literature concerned with the problems of aging in American culture and the polemics over what constitutes "successful" and "unsuccessful" aging in America would lead to the conclusion that older Americans often do suffer from identity problems. The same questions thought to be typical of the adolescent—Who am I? What shall I become? What are my relationships with the world around me?—are often recorded for informants presented in gerontological studies. However, unlike the adolescent, most old people have been familiar with some form of adult identity; whether it was a healthy or mature identity is irrelevant in this case. The adolescent is forming an adult identity for the first time and the transition between childhood and adulthood is much sharper and deserves Erikson's label "identity crisis." The transition between middle adult years and old age does not.

Because the aging adult has experienced some form of previous adult identity, the crisis that he or she might undergo with the process of aging could best be labeled "identity flux." The identity flux experienced among aging individuals is often recognizable in the current literature under the general heading of "unsuccessful aging." Unsuccessful aging is a concept used by gerontologists to describe individuals who are not successfully adapting or adjusting to old age. Those who appear to be aging unsuccessfully, or more precisely suffer from identity flux, are generally characterized as unhappy in their retirement, unhappy with the loss of former roles, depressed, anxious, or confused by their current status as an older person.

A greater opportunity for the resolution of any identity flux among aging Bojaqueños is made possible by shared expectations for age-appropriate behavior. Older and younger villagers disagree over some of the specific forms for respectful interaction between generations, but they agree that deference or respect is an essential quality of interaction with the aged. There is also occasional disagreement over when and how the aged should make contributions to community and family life, but it is agreed that the aged can perform valuable and necessary roles within these contexts. Bojaqueños of all age groups possess overlaping cognitive understanding for age-appropriate behavior that allows the older Bojaqueños to pursue continued activity in important value areas such as *cariño*, *respeto*, and *oficio*. The transition from one age grade to another is charted and understood by most old and young members of the community. Shared expectations for age-appropriate behavior constitute the principle deterent as well as the most available resolution for identity flux among the aged in Bojacá.

SUMMARY

Informal cognitive elicitation procedures are useful in providing insight into vague and abstract aspects of the aging experience. This study reveals that in a peasant community in the Colombian Andes there are areas of activity where older Bojaqueños can pursue age-grade expectations and find positive reinforcement from other members of the community. The cognitive data collected in Bojacá also demonstrates both the positive and negative aspects of aging in this community. Older Bojaqueños are neither discarded nor exaulted by other age grades, but they can cope with experiences of identity flux through the pursuit of the age-group expectations they share with younger Bojaqueños.

NOTES

1. This research was funded in part by the National Science Foundation and the Wenner-Gren Foundation for Anthropological Research.

5 The Coming of Age in Chinese Society: Traditional Patterns and Contemporary Hong Kong

CHARLOTTE IKELS
Harvard University

Inevitably when the plight of the elderly in an industrialized society is up for discussion, someone says, "yes, but in China..." The ethnographic veto is in full force. Charlotte Ikels, however, considerably weakens the punch of the "Chinese veto." On the basis of 20 months of fieldwork on aging in Hong Kong, Ikels is able to compare the current realities with those of the village and the non-industrial city in traditional China. These realities are considerably different than the idyllic accounts with which we are all familiar. Anthropologists have an enduring concern for the difference between ideal and real culture. One of the early lessons of anthropology is that informants will tell you one thing, but quite possibly they will do something a little different. Participant observation is a check of the ideal (what should be done) from the real (what is done). The ideal of filial piety and veneration of the old is, without doubt, pervasive in Chinese culture. As Ikels indicates however, it is not very clear to what extent it was ever achieved even in the traditional village, except by the wealthy.

If veneration is only an ideal that relatively few achieve, then how are the elderly treated and how do they gain security in old age? Charlotte Ikels examines the position of the elderly in three contexts which provide insights into the effects of urbanization and industrialization on social and cultural resources available for the aged in working out their security. In the traditional village the factors are present which reinforce a relatively strong position for the elderly. With urbanization most of the features present in the village that reinforced filial piety are gone. Pre-industrial Chinese cities did not have many old people since those who reached old age usually tried to return to their village. On the other hand, Hong Kong has more elderly and being old in Hong Kong is a far cry from the picture painted for the well-to-do in the rural countryside. Industrial Hong Kong is an environment fraught with insecurity for the aged and with factors that put a strain on intergenerational relations. Yet, these elderly are not abandoned. Because

of the greater insecurity in Hong Kong, Chinese aged must careful-
ly select and cultivate the child who will willingly respond when
parents need support.

By examining three contexts in one culture, Charlotte Ikels is
pursuing an anthropological goal of documenting and explaining
variation. Anthropologists have usually been concerned with vari-
ation of a crosscultural nature. It is only when we investigate soc-
ieties which are of a larger scale and greater complexity that we
have begun to ask questions of intra-cultural variation. China, in-
deed, is one of the world's great civilizations and the civilization
with the longest continuity. The next time the "Chinese veto" is
used, we will have the sophistication to ask, "What kind of Chin-
ese?" This is a lesson we will return to in Chapter 14 and 15. What
kind of American?

One of the most fundamental problems faced by every individual approaching the later stages of the life cycle is to guarantee
himself at least a minimal level of personal security when no longer able to provide for his own needs. While there is tremendous
individual variation in the rate of aging and in the extent of physical decline, each older person nevertheless suffers a loss of vigor
relative to his younger self. For most older people the essence of
the solution lies in accommodating to the shift from relative self-
reliance to reliance on others. Just who these others will be depends partly on cultural definitions and partly on personal resources. For example, older people with families can choose supporters from among their kin. If they have money, they can also
choose to buy care from professional care-givers. If they have
neither kin nor money, perhaps they can draw on friends and
neighbors or community organizations. In affluent countries, they
may have automatic support through pension systems or social
security programs.

The availability of care-givers is not sufficient to ensure their
use by older people. The values of the older person and of the society at large also play a major role in how the individual chooses
among the alternatives available to him. In looking at values, for
example, we can assume that the emphasis a society places on the
value of self-reliance will affect the willingness of a person to yield
his independence. Presumably the greater the emphasis on self-
reliance the greater the reluctance of the older person to assume a
dependent role, e.g. Clark (1972). In the United States, with its
traditional emphasis on self-sufficiency, extreme exponents of this
point of view can be found in the persons of elderly couples or
widows who, though frail and impoverished, refuse to give up their

homes and move in with their children or to accept public aid. Alternatively, the greater the emphasis placed on interdependence the easier it will be for the older person to yield to the authority of others.

There is, of course, another side to the coin, and that is that the values of a society also affect the willingness of potential care-givers to discharge their responsibilities. In a society with homogeneous values, care-givers and care-receivers should be ready to assume their reciprocal roles at about the same time. In a society with competing value systems, however, there may be serious differences of opinion as to when it is appropriate to activate these roles and even as to whether the parties involved have the respective obligations and rights associated with these roles. In the absence of strong cultural supports or meaningful sanctions, the elderly may find themselves in a precarious situation if the expected care-givers are unwilling to assume their responsibilities.

In the following analysis I will present the solutions which elderly Chinese have utilized or attempted to utilize in meeting the needs of their later years. I will look first at the traditional village context, then at the traditional urban context, and finally at the contemporary urban context of Hong Kong. The extent to which values and sanctions function to protect the elderly will serve as the focus of these sections.

VILLAGE SOLUTIONS

The emphasis the Chinese have traditionally placed on filial piety is both well known and frequently contrasted with the American emphasis on the cult of youth, e.g. Hsu (1953). What is less well known is the extent to which the norm was actualized in terms of obedience, veneration, or support. What limited evidence there is suggests that the image of the venerated elder surrounded by numerous progeny is essentially a depiction of the aspirations of the well-to-do. In traditional rural China, the demographic variables of fertility, morbidity, mortality, and migration operated to reduce the likelihood of any particular individual's attaining old age accompanied by a large number of surviving offspring. Economic factors, especially in South China, meant that many families could not support themselves on the fragments of land available to them. For over a century, South China has been an exporter of labor, sending adult sons to Southeast Asia, the United States, Europe, and—closest to home—Hong Kong. Parents of sons working overseas, although receiving financial support, were not in a position to exercise much control over their everyday lives. These demographic and economic qualifiers, however, are seldom taken into consideration by those contemplating the circumstances of the elderly in traditional Chinese society. The reader is advised to keep these qualifers in mind while considering the solutions Chinese have developed to deal with the problem of security in old age.

In the introduction I mentioned that the relative weights a society assigns to the values of independence and dependence can affect the provision of care for the aged, but in the case of the Chinese the concept of interdependence provides a more flexible tool with which to analyze social relationships. Interdependence is reflected in both intergenerational and peer relationships. In the early years of the parent-child relationship, the parents are clearly the providers of care, but many years later the parents will be the recipients of care from their children. In the case of peer relationships, on the other hand, the interdependence is less long-term and more discrete or situational in nature. If, for example, one party helps the other find a job or a place to live, the other will do likewise should the occasion for such assistance arise. The dynamic operating between the generations is different from that operating between peers. The one is based on the expectation of an ultimate pay-off on the initial investment of care whereas the other is based on a much more immediate expectation of reciprocity. One can determine very quickly whether a peer takes reciprocity seriously, and, if he doesn't, can take steps to replace him with someone more reliable. With children the situation is different. One could find out too late that they are not only unreliable but also irreplaceable. Therefore, it is extremely important to make it clear to children from the very beginning by means of ideology and strong sanctions that support of parents is not easily shirked.

> If a son should murder his parent, either father or mother, and be convicted of the crime, he would not only be beheaded, but his body would be mutilated by being cut into small pieces; his house would be razed to the ground, and the earth under it would be dug up for several feet deep; his neighbors living on the right and left would be severely punished; his principle teacher would suffer capital punishment; the district magistrate of the place would be deprived of his office and disgraced; the prefect, the governor of the province, and the viceroy would all be degraded three degrees in rank. All this is done and suffered to mark the enormity of the crime of parricide. (Doolittle 1966 I:140)

That these sentences were ever carried out is doubtful, but they illustrate how seriously such a crime was viewed and that a vigilant community had the responsibility to check unfilial conduct long before it reached the point of parricide. Ideally then, children, particularly male children, were the basis of security in old age.

But what of people lacking male descendants? Where could they turn for support? One of the most obvious alternatives was to rely on daughters and sons-in-law. Hopefully, parents could persuade one daughter to remain at home by bringing in a son-in-law, either an orphan or someone with many brothers, who, freed of the responsibility of providing for his own parents, could devote himself to his parents-in-law. In the absence of any descendants, one could adopt a child, preferably a fraternal nephew (Levy 1949:127) as this strategy minimized dispersal of the ancestral estate. Another alternative, especially for those who remained unmarried or were widowed without children, was to bind themselves to their natal or spouse's natal families as dependent aunts or uncles. During their productive years the fruits of their labors would be shared with the natal units, and in old age they would be sheltered by their nephews.

Other social relationships beyond the family could also be drawn on in times of need or old age. Two forms of fictive kinship, "sworn" sibling relationships and *kai* relationships, could be established to meet the needs of those lacking an active kin network. The model for sworn relationships is drawn from the novel *The Romance of the Three Kingdoms* in which the three heroes swear eternal brotherhood, but the model is not restricted to males. Sworn sisterhoods appear to have been common in the silk-weaving districts of Kwangtung province (adjacent to Hong Kong) during the first decades of this century. Women usually joined these sisterhoods at an early or middle age. Ideally they lasted until the partners died, but according to some observers (e.g. Sankar 1977), they were frequently unstable unless formally institutionalized by co-residence and economic interdependence. The common theme of *kai* relationships was that of need on the part of one and nurturance on the part of the other. The *kai* relationship of greatest significance to the elderly was that in which an older person *kai*ed a young adult, preferably one without parents of his own. The two would exchange gifts publicly with the senior providing services to the junior in the early years of the partnerships and the latter providing services to the senior in the later years. Supernatural sanctions and the force of public opinion encouraged the participants to fulfill their obligations.

Less personalized means of gaining support included relying on community organizations. In villages with strong lineage systems, a person could appeal to the lineage head for some support if only to live in the ancestral temple. A wealthy lineage might even have provided additional care through the proceeds of ancestral land held in common by the lineage (Chen 1936:27). Monasteries or nunneries, less common than ancestral temples, provided some accommodation for the destitute. Less regularized support could also be obtained from neighbors or through begging in public areas or around temples during festivals or the new year.

Conspicuously absent from the sources of support in old age was self-support. In the traditional rural village, few people were able to amass sufficient capital or property to live off its interest (e.g. Chen 1936:103). Those who were able to do so generally made their wealth available to their descendants, for those who were wealthy had no difficulty in acquiring descendants. A concubine could readily compensate for an infertile wife, and there were no shortages of adoptable children. Generally speaking, those who had wealth in old age also had descendants. Those who had no descendants were generally poor, and what little money they could put together went towards their funerals. Thus, social relationships were the main basis of support in old age, and villagers of all ages shared the ethic of interdependence.

That the values of a society, at least during relatively stable periods, must in some way function so as to promote the survival of that society is a basic assumption of anthropological theory. If this assumption is correct, then filial piety and interdependence must have had a functional basis in traditional village life. For many years researchers seeking information about the comparative status of the elderly in preindustrial societies were restricted to the findings of Simmons (1945) who, using the Human Relations Area Files, studied the role of the aged in 71 "tribes." Drawing primarily on the work of Simmons as well as on additional studies, Rosow (1965:21-22) concluded that the relative position of the aged is stronger when:

1. They own private property (or control it) on which younger people are dependent.

2. Their experience gives them a vital command or monopoly of strategic knowledge of the culture, especially in preliterate societies.

3. They are links to the past in tradition-oriented societies, especially when they are crucial links to the gods in cultures with ancestor worship.

4. Kinship and the extended family are central to the social organization of the society.

5. The population clusters in relatively small, stable communities (gemeinschaft societies).

6. The productivity of the economy is low and approaches the ragged edge of starvation.

7. There is high mutual dependence among the members of a group.

As we shall see below, all seven of these factors were present in traditional China and, under ordinary circumstances, operated to ensure a measure of security in old age.

Rosow's first variable is an economic one—the extent to which the old own or control private property on which the young are dependent. In village China the economic relationship between fathers and sons contributed greatly to the sense of obligation to parents. A son usually owed his occupation to his father or other close kinsman. In the case of a peasant, land or tenancy rights derived from the father; in the case of a craftsman, training usually derived from the father or other male relative (e.g., Lee 1953:274; Fei 1946: 141, 143; Chan 1953:208). Tools, skills, clientele, and trading partnerships were owed to senior kinsmen. Furthermore, so long as the father remained alive, he usually retained legal right to the land. Ideally family property was not divided up among the sons until after his death. If division did not occur earlier, it was normally with a stipulation regarding the care of the parents. The son assigned this particular responsibility could expect to receive a larger share of the estate than his brothers (Levy 1949:137). Thus, sentiment aside, Chinese sons had very practical reasons to fulfill their filial obligations.

The residential family and the economic family were not necessarily coextensive, and caring for parents did not always mean co-residence. In land-poor villages, a son frequently had to migrate to the city and send money back to his parents. In other cases where responsibility was rotated among a number of sons, the parents might live alone or with one son, in their shop for example, but take meals on a regular basis with the others (Hsu 1971:114; Cohen 1976:74-75). The significant index was the provision of care not the co-residence.

The second variable, monopoly or control of strategic knowledge, operated to ensure the elderly a needed place even when their physical strength had declined. Although traditional China was by no means a preliterate society, the relative scarcity of formally educated people meant that personal experience and the experiences of those in one's own community were the major sources of knowledge (e.g., Yang 1953:91-92).

Rosow's third variable, the extent to which the elderly are links with the past, is of particular significance since premodern China is well known for its focus on the past. From the time of Confucius onward, philosophers preached that peace and harmony would reign when the people returned to the ways of their ancestors. The

Chinese took special pride in noting their links with the past in the form of genealogies stretching back 20 or more generations. The achievements of the ancestors were spurs to achievement for the descendants (e.g., Hsu 1971). The elderly themselves were soon to join the ancestors and so to be in a position to exert influence on behalf of family members. Alternatively, should the behavior of the descendants be offensive, it was not unknown for them to return as vengeful ghosts (Ahern 1973:199-203). Strong supernatural sanctions reinforced the practical reasons behind filial piety.

Fourth, kinship and the extended family were central to the social organization of the Chinese village. Most Chinese villages were composed of the members of a few lineages, the founders of which had migrated to the area many years before. Some villages, especially those in the southern provinces such as Kwangtung, consisted of the male members of a single lineage plus their wives and unmarried daughters (e.g., Freedman 1970:1). In such circumstances, one's neighbors were also very likely to be one's kin as lineage and village membership were nearly coterminous. In this context, the misbehavior of any one person was an insult to the ancestors of everyone else and could jeopardize the relations of the entire community with the supernatural. Furthermore, the neglect of elderly lineage members, the last survivors of a nonproductive branch perhaps, reflected on the morality of the entire group. Therefore, there was a major incentive to develop collective solutions to provide for their needs.

Fifth, Chinese villages varied in size from several hundred to several thousand members. In most cases, it was possible to know something about everyone in the village or at least to be able to get such information at will. Anonymity was impossible, and serious delinquencies followed one for life. In addition, though some members left the village for employment in the cities, their families usually remained behind (e.g. Lang 1946:82). Village growth came about through reproduction and not in-migration. This stability of personnel meant that debts and favors were long remembered and that over the course of a lifetime an individual probably developed personal ties with nearly every family through at least one of its members. In times of need these personal ties could make the critical difference.

Rosow's sixth variable, the inverse correlation between local productivity and the position of the aged, seems at first glance paradoxical, but here the importance of the principle of interdependence is again clear. In a marginal economy the contribution of every person to the small gross product is highly valued. Elderly Chinese gathered firewood and medicinal herbs or tended chickens, and they could frighten birds away from the fields. So long as productivity exceeded consumption, there was a place for the old. Under conditions of prolonged hardship or serious disability, however, the elderly were particularly susceptible to infectious diseases and unlikely to pose a serious burden for long.

The seventh variable, the degree of mutual dependence, also operated to protect the aged. In the Chinese village, for example, the irrigating and the draining of the rice fields required extreme coordination and cooperation on the part of the villagers. Similarly, intensive cooperative labor was essential during the harvest particularly when the weather threatened (e.g., Pasternak 1972:20). In some parts of China, intervillage rivalries were so intense that pitched battles occurred necessitating the formation of village patrols (e.g. Freedman 1970:105-111). The need for cooperation put high priority on such character traits as reliability and loyalty. Clearly any person who was not good to his parents was also not good for the community, and it is this linkage which partly explains the community's interest in filial piety.

In summary, practical economic considerations, supernatural sanctions, structural factors, and the force of public opinion all combined to ensure that the village elderly were granted their due. But perhaps we have overlooked another very important motivator, namely, self-interest. Any person who failed to provide for his parents was not setting a good example for his own children and thus undermined his own security in old age.

TRADITIONAL URBAN SOLUTIONS

I have so far said little about the situation of the elderly in the cities of premodern China. The reasons for this omission are two: (1) there is a relative scarcity of material on this topic, and (2) there was a relative scarcity of the old in the cities. Clearly the first reason derives from the second. The premodern Chinese city was populated primarily by the young and middle-aged, most of whom were males unaccompanied by their families. According to Skinner (1977:535) in Canton in 1895, the sex ratio was 168 males per 100 females for the northeastern "gentry" districts of the city, and 224 males per 100 females for the southwestern "merchant" districts. Most men were in the city as sojourners sending their money back to the villages and returning there annually for the ancestral festivals or the new year, and most men expected to retire to their villages in old age. Even as late as 1936, Lang (1946:82) found that in Peking, a nonindustrial society:

> Wage earners and members of the lower middle class have intimate contacts with the soil. Many workers, apprentices, riksha coolies, servants, and others of this class belong to families living in the country: they send money to their rural homes, leave their wives and children with their old folks, and regard their sojourn in the city as temporary, even when they spend their entire lives there. Evidently a nonindustrial city does not induce many peasants' sons to establish their families in it, although there are exceptions.

Those who did spend their final years in the city did so because they had family in the city or had no one willing to provide for them in the countryside. This latter category faced a problematic future. (Skinner 1977:545).

Ideally the values operating in the urban context were the same as those operating in the rural: interdependence, filial piety, and respect for the past and those associated with it. However, given the fact that the social organization was so very different with regard to community size, stability of residence, and familiarity of neighbors, it was impossible to know the personal histories of everyone, let alone to have personal ties to them. The city was not, of course, so totally atomized as to lack personal relationships and notions of mutual assistance; it was rather that one had to make more conscious efforts to develop such relationships. In this context, an anonymous older person was assumed to be someone else's responsibility.

Newcomers to the city usually went first to live with relatives or fellow villagers who had gone before them, and some in old age were able to derive considerable support from such familiars. For others, however, a larger population base was necessary to provide some measure of social welfare, and this larger base was found in district and surname associations (e.g., Crissman 1967:15). In a provincial city, these district organizations usually consisted of the natives of a county or a cluster of neighboring counties. In a cosmopolitan city such as Peking or Shanghai, the inclusive "district" might have been an entire province. The surname associations recruited people with the same patronym regardless of place of origin and were in a sense clan associations. Even though no genealogical connections could be traced, the members were considered descendants of a common ancestor, and families with the same surname could not intermarry.

Both district and surname associations provided a means of keeping in touch with the home community by the channeling of remittances and the dissemination of news. They also sponsored credit associations and, of great interest to the elderly, burial societies. In the latter, participants were guaranteed a coffin, funeral, and transport back to the village or a local burial in exchange for small monthly payments. These organizations also introduced the newcomer to opportunities for building up his social networks, for in the city just as in the countryside, enduring personal relationships were the key to security in time of need.

Some old people gained a modicum of security through their work contacts. While craft and trade guilds were run by and for the business owners and were primarily concerned with business matters, they did on occasion perform meritorious acts such as providing a free burial or helping out a widow (e.g., Rhoads 1974:104 and Skinner 1977:533). But these formal organizations did not really offer much security for the ordinary aged worker. No union contracts provided for pensions or unemployment compensation. At best, the larger firms made lump-sum payments to retiring workers and considered their obligations at an end. Instead, the ordinary worker had to depend on personal relationships built up over a long period of time (e.g., Lamson 1934:138 and Fried 1953:152). For example, a shop employee who had worked for the same owner/manager for 25 or 30 years was not simply discharged as his usefulness declined. Normally his duties and remuneration were gradually reduced until perhaps he became little more than a "night watchman" sleeping on the floor in the front of the shop in exchange for his meals. Similarly, a woman who had faithfully served one master and his household for many years was not turned aside in her old age. For all practical purposes such long-term servants were members of the family and as such were kept on although their duties were greatly lessened.

Let me here stress the point that in the premodern period the elderly constituted a very small proportion of the urban population (and of the rural population also), and the period between the cessation of their "usefulness" to their employers and their deaths was probably quite short. Anyone so debilitated that he or she could perform no services about the house was an easy target for infectious diseases. Furthermore, since most of the elderly retired to their native villages, few employers had to worry about the buildup of a large group of aged employee-dependents.

Workers could also rely on each other in old age. An older worker might find shelter in another worker's family, particularly if they were from the same village. Temporary domestic servants sometimes maintained group quarters to which they could retire between jobs or in old age. These so-called *jaai tohng* (lit. vegetarian halls) could be religious or secular in nature (e.g., Yap 1962: 448-449). Another possibility was to establish fictive kin ties (*kai* relationships) with someone younger, but their endurance in the cities was more doubtful than in the countryside as the behavior of the partners was not so susceptible to public scrutiny.

Those in the weakest position in the city were elderly refugees and those with irregular employment histories. Refugees from famine in the countryside were not welcomed in the cities regardless of their age as at such times the streets were crowded with desperate beggars (e.g., Skinner 1977:346). A worker lacking adequate skills, a laborer whose strength was impaired by injury, or a servant who was insufficiently accommodating found employment infrequently. As soon as their services were no longer needed, they were discharged. Under these circumstances, they were never in a position to build up the affective dimensions of the employer-employee relationship, and thus found themselves stranded in old age.

In summary then, cities lacked substantial elderly populations. Most old people retired to their native villages. Those staying on were most secure when their families also lived in the city or when they had been able to establish long-term personal relationships with employers or coworkers. Those lacking these personal ties, an almost impossible situation in a village, were dependent upon the generosity of neighbors or the occasional welfare acts of formal organizations. For some the only certainty in old age was a burial.

SOLUTIONS IN URBAN HONG KONG

The British Crown Colony of Hong Kong contains over 4.5 million people and lies 90 miles southeast of Canton, the largest city in the adjoining Chinese province of Kwangtung. The Chinese imperial government ceded parts of Hong Kong to the British government in the middle of the nineteenth century following military action by British soldiers and merchants. The remaining predominantly rural and suburban parts of Hong Kong, known as the New Territories, were leased from China in 1898. This lease is due to expire in 1997.

The present population of Hong Kong is nearly 99 percent Chinese. According to the 1971 Census (Hong Kong Census and Statistics Department 1972:16), only 13.7 percent of those aged 40 or more were born in Hong Kong compared with over 95 percent of those under the age of 15. The vast majority of the older population was born and brought up in Kwangtung. These differences in place of birth are also reflected in differences in exposure to formal education. For example, according to the Census (p.64), 95 percent of the children aged 6—11 were attending schools in 1971, and 80 percent of the males and 69 percent of the females aged 12—16 were still in school. In contrast only 43 percent of those aged 60 or more had received any formal education, with old women six times more likely than old men to be illiterate.

The elderly are a large and increasing proportion of the population. Between 1961 and 1976 the total population of Hong Kong increased by 41 percent, but the elderly population (those aged 60 or more) increased by 163 percent to 398,180. Nearly 9 percent of all people in Hong Kong are 60 or more years old. Furthermore, life expectancy for males 60 years old in 1971 was 15.45 years; for women, 20.67 years (Working Party Report 1973:7). The infectious diseases characteristic of regions with impure water supplies, an abundance of insects, and an absence of antibiotics are no longer a major health problem in Hong Kong. Mortality figures are strikingly similar to those of other urban industrial societies, with cancer accounting for 24.1 percent of all deaths in 1975 (Hong Kong Census and Statistics Department 1976:1). According to preliminary By-Census data (personal communication), in 1975 the three leading causes of death among those aged 60 and over were circulatory system problems, cancer, and respiratory problems. The majority of these elderly deaths were preceded by a considerable period of invalidism, which necessitated relying on others, e.g. family members, community nurses, or institutions. While only 1.1 percent of elderly deaths fell into the suicide and self-inflicted injuries category, people aged 65 and over, who made up only 5.6 percent of the 1976 population, accounted for 21.7 percent of the deaths in this category.

Hong Kong is a far cry from the agrarian village. According to Podmore (1971:22), only 5 percent of the employed population are in the primary industries of agriculture and fishing. Manufacturing employs 40 percent; government and service occupations, 22 percent; and commerce, 16 percent. Densities of over 250,000 persons per square mile are not uncommon; Mong Kok district, for example, had a density of over 400,000 (Census 1972:28) in 1971. The extent to which industrialization and urbanization have been accompanied by Westernization, i.e., the adoption of the value system associated with the West, has been investigated by Agassi and Jarvie (1969) and Shively and Shively (1972). Both studies expressed doubts about the ability of the Chinese to remain unaffected ideologically, and the latter study concluded that a reorientation of values is definitely taking place and that it is associated with education more than with any other single factor. The potential for value conflict between the old and the young is therefore quite high.

The question which many Chinese parents now ask themselves is "Will my children provide for me when I am old?" The parental position of advantage enjoyed by those owning land has been radically altered in Hong Kong. Young people do not seek employment in agriculture but in commerce, industry, and the professions. While the children of shopkeepers may follow in the footsteps of their fathers, most young people obtain their jobs through friends or direct application (Mitchell 1972:172). Parental hostility can rarely interfere with employment opportunities. Furthermore, should children fail to live up to filial responsibilities, there is no wider kin network or solidary community able to play the role of enforcer on behalf of neglected parents. The employer is little concerned with his employees' home lives. While neighbors may become aware of bad relationships, there is no tradition authorizing direct involvement in the family life of nonrelatives.

Parental anxieties are most severe at two stages in the family life cycle: first, when children are in the process of marrying out, and, second, when advanced old age threatens parental well-being. When these two stages occur almost simultaneously, as when the youngest child does not marry until the parents are in their late 60's or 70's, a common pattern is continuous coresidence, particularly if there is only one surviving parent. When these two stages occur 10 or 20 years apart, however, there is tremendous concern about future relations. For example, among my informants it is increasingly the norm for children, including sons, to move out at marriage or a couple of years later at the birth of the first child. Often the move is just around the corner, and the two households continue to share meals on a regular basis. For the 45 percent of the population living in public housing estates, however, the moving out of the younger generation can have serious consequences.

Until the mid-1970's, public housing regulations required that newly married couples live elsewhere than in the parental unit. Housing regulations also restricted—and continue to restrict—accommodation to families having no fewer than four members at the time of entry into an estate. Newly married couples, therefore, were ineligible for housing anywhere in the estate. These rules were extremely unpopular and widely evaded. To bridge the gap between official policy and community sentiment, the rules were altered to allow one married child and his or her spouse to remain in the parental unit and ultimately to succeed to the tenancy. This new ruling has the effect of forcing adult children living in public housing estates to make major decisions about obligations to parents considerably sooner than those living in the private sector because if no child remains with the parents, the parents forfeit the tenancy completely. Yet protecting parental housing security means giving up the idea of a period of independent living by the newly married couple.

Although at present most parents can expect to spend at least part of their lives living independently of their children, this period is usually neither long nor characterized by isolation from the children. The period is likely to be short because the present cohort of elderly parents raised four or five children to adulthood, and these adult children generally do not leave home until marriage occurs, which is around the age of 22 for daughters and 28 for sons. Many parents in their 60's, particularly if theirs is a second marriage, still have unmarried children at home. Furthermore, unemployment, the absence of a pension, widowhood, or illness on the part of a parent or the need for household assistance on the part of a child are sufficient grounds for the reestablishment of coresidence. While elderly parents may be supported financially by their adult children, they, for their part, contribute a substantial proportion of the labor in these reunited households.

Stem families in Hong Kong are predominantly patrilineal though the parents of the wife, especially her widowed mother, comprise a frequent alternative form. The presence of the wife's parents is rarely a violation of the traditional Chinese rules and does not indicate a shift to bilaterality in an urban context. As in the past, reliance on daughters is a sanctioned alternative in the absence of sons. The economic circumstances of Hong Kong make the choice of sons rather than daughters as coresiders and supporters more practical. The labor force participation of women is much less than that of men, and even when performing the same work, they are often paid less. While daughters may be an important source of positive affect, in most cases they cannot be as supportive, in an economic sense, as sons.

That coresidence of parents and children is now optional and not obligatory means that the potential for conflict resulting from different attitudes and interests—the generation gap—can be controlled. Children who have poor relationships can now move out and minimize familial involvement, especially if they have siblings who are more closely involved. Indeed, the close ties of some children permit the looser ties of others. Another strategy for reducing potential conflict is parental relinquishment of control over decisions considered to be the most important by the child, i.e., the selection of job and spouse. Children also avoid disagreements by simply not consulting their parents on sensitive issues.

The later resumption of coresidence usually means the moving of the parent to the household of the child, i.e., to the household of someone accustomed to making most of the decisions. The thoughtful parent does not attempt to exert control in these circumstances. Support and respect continue to be given to elderly parents in Hong Kong, but such giving is clearly accompanied by parental relinquishment of real power over the younger generation.

The elderly traditionally sought relationships with individuals beyond the immediate family. Urbanization *per se* need not mean the absence of significant extrafamilial relationships. Indeed a number of studies (e.g., Mizruchi 1969, Gutkind 1969, and Hollnsteiner 1972) have indicated that many urban neighborhoods, particularly those inhabited by a stable low-income population, are characterized by intense local interaction. In such settings, the elderly without kin can frequently rely on assistance from neighbors while those with kin have a stable group of peers with whom to compare the experience of aging. Unfortunately the present circumstances in Hong Kong are destructive of such neighborhoods, for the government is carrying out an ambitious resettlement program by removing urban dwellers to the suburbs. This resettlement is carried out on a household basis with little attention paid to the fact that on-going social relationships are destroyed by not carrying out the scheme on a neighborhood basis. The elderly suffer most by this policy since they have few resources other than the immediate neighborhood to utilize in the development of extrafamilial ties. For those lacking families such a move can be devastating.

Relocation is especially severe for the present cohort of elderly since it is largely China-born and derived from a rural background. Preference in friends is for people from the same dialect region, and the preferred mode of friendship building is through careful observation of the candidate in a variety of situations over a long period of time. Public housing estates are not settled on a dialect basis, and they are so large, each having tens of thousands of residents, that it is difficult to distinguish between residents and casual visitors. Future cohorts should experience less difficulty for two reasons: (1) the relocation will abate, and those estates now newly settled will stabilize as tenants rarely abandon public housing, and (2) those now middle-aged are much more likely to have grown up in Hong Kong and to have acquired the personal skills necessary for the rapid conversion of acquaintances into friends.

Migration and relocation within Hong Kong many years after arrival have also affected familial relationships. Migration has meant the fragmentation of many families with some of the members still in China and others in Hong Kong. Old people separated from their descendants in China expect and receive little if any assistance from them. The aid flow even in old age is expected to go the other way— from those overseas to those in the village. Relocation within Hong Kong since it is frequently on a nonvoluntary basis has also been damaging to relations with kin. While most old people who have raised families in Hong Kong live either with or near at least one of their children, they are less likely to live near other kin such as siblings, cousins, or nephews and nieces. In part this is because of the absence of such kin, but even when they do reside in Hong Kong, interaction is quite limited. The patrilineage which in the village was the next corporate group to which an individual belonged and from which he could claim assistance is almost nonexistent in Hong Kong. This absence means that increasingly responsibility for family members rests exclusively with the household, i.e. the nuclear or stem family. Extended kin appear to be significant primarily for those people lacking spouses or descendants.

CONCLUSION

Hong Kong now has many of the features of an urban industrial society, but changes in material circumstances and ideology have not been accompanied by compensatory changes in the social sector. According to Burgess (1960:378) industrialization forced the countries of Western Europe, regardless of their differing cultural traditions, to develop special programs and services to meet the emerging needs of the elderly. All had to address problems of income, housing, health, and status deprivation. Hong Kong, however, has not yet addressed these problems seriously. Little (1974:8) categorized Hong Kong's services to the elderly as only a step ahead of those provided by Thailand, Iran, and Greece—all of which are considerably more traditional agrarian societies.

Yet the support networks upon which the older generation in Hong Kong must rely are being compelled to carry a much heavier burden than their rural predecessors. The following list points up some of the differences between traditional rural life and contemporary urban life which make adaptation to aging in Hong Kong a more challenging experience for both the elderly and their families:

1. *Personal Safety*. In the village, narrow lanes restricted traffic to a pace set by pedestrians. An individual with poor hearing, vision, or motor capabilities was in little danger. In Hong Kong congested city streets are dominated by undisciplined motorists. An individual with poor hearing, vision, or motor capabilities is in considerable danger every time he or she attempts to cross the street.

2. *Public Security*. In the village, neighbors and dogs quickly perceived the presence of strangers. In Hong Kong the mobility and density of the population make it difficult to distinguish neighbors and strangers.

3. *Public Opinion*. The homogeneity of the village meant a genuine value consensus. Deviators were noted and sanctioned. The heterogeneity of Hong Kong and the coexistence of competing value systems mean a weak and divided public opinion. Deviators go unnoted and unsanctioned.

4. *Public Health*. In the village, mortality was largely a function of infectious diseases to which the very young and the very old were especially vulnerable. Weakened unproductive old people were at worst a short-term burden to their families. In Hong Kong death is increasingly the consequence of chronic disease accompanied by a long period of invalidism. More and more old people are a long-term burden to their families.

5. *Knowledge of Surroundings*. In the countryside long residence meant familiarity with the various parts of the village. Physical changes in the appearance of the village were infrequent and gradual. A long-term resident could easily find his way around. In Hong Kong changes of residence make it necessary to become acquainted with new territory. Yet physical changes in neighborhoods are frequent and rapid, making it easy for a person to lose his way.

6. *Knowledge of Neighbors*. The small and stable population of the village meant the opportunity to interact with almost all of the other villagers or their families in the course of a lifetime. No one was a stranger, and almost everyone was bound in reciprocal obligations to everyone else. The large and shifting population of Hong Kong affords only limited opportunities for interaction with a few people over a long period of time.

7. *Support Networks*. The lineage villages of southeastern China were composed of villagers who were both relatives and neighbors. This double relationship meant a potentially wide support network in time of need. In Hong Kong the absence of kin due to mortality and migration patterns, or their noncontiguous residence if present, coupled with the instability of the urban neighborhoods means contraction of the support network to the immediate family, i.e., to descendants.

8. *Privacy*. Rural housing generally afforded separate sleeping areas for adult couples. Large areas of open space, e.g., rice fields, provided the opportunity to escape from noise, quarrels, or excessive interaction. In Hong Kong a severe housing shortage has resulted in overcrowding. Many couples live and sleep within sight and sound of others. The high population density makes it difficult to avoid noise or interaction with others.

While these eight contrasts are somewhat overstated for emphasis and are of greatest significance to those who suffer impairment,

I think they effectively illustrate the additional difficulties that old people in Hong Kong must face. Because of the traffic situation in Hong Kong an older person's life is in danger any time he attempts to cross the street. Hearing and vision deficits make him slower to perceive danger, and increased reaction time means that he cannot so readily avoid it once he does perceive it. At present old people make up about one-third of Hong Kong's annual traffic fatalities.

When old people go out for walks and begin to wander, their chances of getting lost are much greater than in the village. Buildings are torn down and replaced, shops fail and are succeeded by new shops with such rapidity that districts beyond one's every-day range become unfamiliar very quickly. Furthermore, in the village a wanderer is easily identified, and a covillager will either steer the old person back on the right track or notify the family of his whereabouts. In urban Hong Kong, however, a wanderer need only go around the corner to be in unknown social territory. Worries about injury or disappearance frequently lead families to restrict the older person's activities. Either he is accompanied on excursions or he doesn't go out.

Restricting an old person to home or its immediate vicinity does not alleviate all concern. Hong Kong abounds in burglars and robbers who use every ruse to gain entry into a building. Passing themselves off as coworkers or schoolmates of younger family members, they may be able to trick an unwary old person (or young one for that matter) into permitting them entry into the building. Though at least three of my informants were victims of robbery or attempted robbery, the elderly in Hong Kong do not constitute a preferred category of victim as they do in some urban areas in the United States. Most people fall victim to robbers lurking on staircases. Such robbers avail themselves of whomever comes up the stairs.

The lessened mobility of the elderly frequently means a diminished social life. The scarcity of siblings in this age group and their dispersion throughout Hong Kong even if present mean that there is no readily available extrafamilial source of emotional gratification. Yet given the attitudinal differences which exist between the generations, there is probably a high need for peers with whom to share one's difficulties. Unless the old person lives in one of the more stable neighborhoods, it can be difficult to operate in a social arena beyond the immediate family. This contracted sphere of social interaction can make the older person's constant presence in the home a source of friction as in overcrowded conditions it renders privacy impossible.

Fortunately most older people remain capable of making major contributions to the running of the household, e.g., doing marketing, laundry, or cooking, and otherwise freeing other household members to engage in money-making activities. The problems of reduced social networks and dependency are most acute in time of incapacitating illness. Given the shortage of services and facilities for those in need of skilled nursing or extensive personal care, the burden falls almost exclusively on the immediate family. If there are sufficient funds to pay for private care, the nature of the burden is primarily financial and may be comparatively light, but where there are no funds, the daughter-in-law or daughter may be forced to quit a job and to remain almost constantly on call. The absence of a wider support network makes it difficult for the primary care-giver to take off more than a few hours at a time. The old person lacking descendants is, of course, in an even more difficult situation.

Given the lack of pensions and the low levels of public assistance, even healthy old people must rely on their descendants, but the current atmosphere of insecurity means that parents now watch their children for signs of unreliability and try to determine which child is most likely to follow through on filial responsibilities. The elderly are so concerned about the nature of their relationships because they know that if for some reason the children should become alienated, there are few sanctions which they can bring to bear to awaken them to their filial responsibilities. While immediate neighbors may be aware of neglect or abuse, they are rarely in a position to apply sanctions. The offending child may live elsewhere, have gotten employment on his own, and appear a normally responsible person to his peers and neighbors who have no contact with his parents. As Bott (1971:390) has pointed out, this "individuated" quality of the urban family guarantees it privacy and freedom of action, but it also means that the most vulnerable members of the family have no extrafamilial supporters who will readily act on their behalf. While few descendants take advantage of their parents helplessness, enough do to result in newspaper stories of abandonment that give every old parent cause to ponder. Parents must now be calculating in their familial relationships whereas previously calculation was mainly the business of those without descendants.

This latter category remains in a precarious position. In the past there were culturally prescribed alternatives—various forms of long-term social relationships—upon which they could elect to rely, but attempts to follow these alternatives in Hong Kong today are less likely to meet with success. The public opinion which in the village witnessed and enforced the obligations of the partners in fictive kin relations is weak in Hong Kong. The removal of the partners from the neighborhood which witnessed the establishment of the ties greatly dilutes the incentive to carry on with the ties when they prove inconvenient. Since the older partner usually makes the initial investment of services in such partnerships, it is the older person who loses the most by the weakening of this traditional tie. Private charitable organizations are not able to finance expansion of their limited community services. Employers in new sectors of the economy feel few obligations to former employees. At best, these famililess older people must rely on each other or on their neighbors, an increasingly risky strategy given the emphasis on urban renewal and suburban resettlement.

Given the absence of any expanded opportunities for old people to be financially self-supporting and the shortage of medical services and facilities for long-term care, the elderly in Hong Kong have no choice but to follow the traditional strategies of reliance on personal ties. Yet at the very same time, the processes of urbanization and industrialization have increased the scope of the services this shrinking support network must provide. Surely the present situation in Hong Kong while, not so bad as local newspapers suggest, is also a far cry from the romantic ideal portrayed by Hsu (1953). Aging in contemporary Hong Kong is fraught with insecurity—a situation likely to persist for quite some time.

NOTES

1. An earlier version of this paper was presented in November 1978 at the annual meeting of the American Anthropological Association in Los Angeles and at the annual meeting of the Gerontological Society in Dallas.

6 Warriors No More: A Study of the American Indian Elderly

GERRY C. WILLIAMS
University of Oklahoma

Americans Indians are one of the reasons anthropology developed in the United States. Early American anthropologists spent long hours with older Indian men and women recording the events and cultures of yesteryear that were rapidly being swept aside by the expansion of the United States. Gerry Williams continues a theme developed by Charlotte Ikels. Just as change and industrialization have altered the ability of the Chinese aged to reach their ideal of secure old age through filial piety, change and incorporation into an industrial society has had profound implications for the American Indian aged. The net effect of America's expansion has been to radically alter Native American culture. People have been forced to migrate from native lands and have often been placed on reservations in the arid West. Subsistence of a traditional nature has been altered or made impractical. As a substitution for native culture, American Indians have been incompletely assimilated into American culture and remain as one of the most impoverished minorities in the United States.

Although the experience of tribes on reservations is different, the non-reservation Indians, as studied by Williams, parallel major historical patterns which have shaped the role of the elderly in White American society. Bonds of kinship are weakened by increased mobility and geographic dispersal. Still the contact and involvement of children and siblings with the older Indian does not diverge significantly from those patterns in industrial nations (see Chapter 14). Technology and progress which brings with it an emphasis on youth, has brought a distinctive pattern for the Indian. Many older adults are assuming positions of influence within their families. Since younger adults cannot find satisfactory employment, the old support their families through army pensions or social security. An emphasis on the values of productivity has devalued the old in white American society. Among the non-reservation Indians in Oklahoma, productivity has little relation to age as chronologically reckoned. It is ability and skills that count, not chronology.

> *Williams introduces a curious dilemma. At a time when* Indianness *and interest in cultural roots is in resurgence, the old find that they are very important repositories of past cultural lore and tradition. However, Williams' older informants are too young. Their Indian culture was disappearing while they were young. Demands for traditional lore and knowledge should give them an avenue for renewed importance and leadership. Unfortunately it is not a path they can take. Among other American Indian groups, this is an important source of self esteem for the aged.*

The past few years have witnessed an upsurge of anthropological interest in the study of the aged. This intensified desire on the part of anthropologists to acquire an understanding of the aging processes has resulted in numerous symposia at the annual American Anthropological Association meetings (San Francisco 1975; Washington, D.C., 1976; and in Houston 1977); as well as collected works of articles on the subject (e.g., Youmans 1967; Cowgill and Holmes 1972, et al.) As this article and others within this volume reflect, those field workers who have chosen to focus upon the study of the aged have done so within a wide range of cultural settings. For instance, researchers have dealt with the aged among the Bantu (Fuller 1972), the Japanese (Plath 1972), black Americans (Jackson 1971a), Irish (Streib 1972), Mexican Americans (Leonard 1967; Moore 1971a), American Indians (Levy 1967; Munsell 1972), and so on. As a result of these studies and others, a somewhat thoroughgoing crosscultural perspective is being established in which the details of the aged in diverse societal environments are becoming well documented.

Indeed, there are marked differences as we move from culture to culture in terms of this particular group's demographic, social, and economic characteristics. And quite possibly herein lies the anthropologist's major contribution to the study of the aged. That is, our focus upon non-Western, preindustrial (as well as the industrialized) cultures can give us a baseline and mode of comparison for arriving at theoretical statements as to the aged and related processes of social interaction. The cultural context, the adaptive strategies, and the wide range of social interactions that the anthropologist encounters and directs his research attention toward may reflect ultimately upon directional change, particularly if specific groups are viewed from an historical perspective.

Of course, the above observations are well known. For example, in terms of a study dealing with elderly minority groups, Kent (1971:26) states that at least at one level of analysis, the study of the aged must be dealt with in "relative terms"; that is, it is suggested that there is an "appropriate" way to age in every culture.

Anderson (1972) echoing this statement, but going one step further, outlines a crosscultural comparative focus. That is, in reference to the definitional aspects of aging, she points out that white Americans are considered to be old when they have reached a certain age, whereas in other societies the definition of "aged" is not necessarily chronological but is expressed in functional terms.

In this chapter we accept both Kent's and Anderson's central position that there is (1) an "appropriate" way to age in all cultures, or as another researcher has put it, "Each older person... [has a] ... social status and role structure, that is, assigned or assumed positions and tasks and accompanying responsibilities" (Twenie 1970); and (2) that white American society tends to define the aged in formal chronological terms. The latter (nonfunctional) stress manifests itself in general terms as a "warehousing" effect (Romano 1965) or, as Nader (1970) has put it, "the last segregation." In general, in American society youth and vitality are venerated (cf. Berger and Neuhaus 1970). Being defined as "old" brings negative appraisals in our society. Instead, youth and middle age are the most attractive years. In a society such as this, "...that prizes youth above seniority, that venerates knowledge more than wisdom, that accords status to work over leisure, and that, above all, abhors death, the very aged and spent find themselves at some major disadvantage...." (Simmons 1961-65:158). These attitudes effect our definitions and modes of adjustment toward the aged.

Clark and Anderson (1967) have argued that there are four historical factors which could be used to account for the role of the contemporary elderly in white American society. Briefly stated these factors are (1) a weakening of kinship ties brought about by an increasing internal migration of individuals and families; (2) rapid industrial and technological change which excludes the elderly from significant productive roles and emphasizes the fact that "progress" has blurred the need for the knowledge and skills of the elderly; (3) an increase in the number of aged and in the percentage of aged in the total population; and (4) the emphasis on productivity in American values makes it increasingly difficult for the elderly to feel needed—they are either physically unable to perform as well as they once did or are relegated to a relatively nonvalued status of old even though they are physically and mentally capable.

THE INDIAN ELDERLY

The focus of this paper is upon the Indian elderly. Specifically, data was collected from nonreservation Indians living in the state of Oklahoma. This minority group represents a small percentage of the

total population of the state and includes numerous tribal groupings. Unlike so many other Indian groups in the United States, the
Oklahoma Indian does not live within a reservation system. A complicated history of forced migrations, governmental removals, trea-
ty agreements, and promises resulted in the establishment of unita-
ry tribal lands (e.g., Cherokee, Choctaw, Creek, Chickasaw, and Se-
minole Nations) and ultimately individual Indian land allotments.

In what follows we attempt to use the four above-stated historical factors as outlined by Clark and Anderson (1967) in terms of
their relationship to Indian cultural values toward the aged. Primarily the paper is concerned with the changing patterns toward the
aged as well as the contemporary characteristics of this minority
group. A number of difficulties are immediately presented with a
study of this nature: (1) the difficulty of establishing patterns of
social ranking and interaction within the Indian community from a
historical/traditional perspective; (2) the interactions of this minority, through acculturation, to the industrial/modernized culture
within which they have functioned (particularly so with the somewhat less isolated nonreservation groups); and (3) the values and
particularly the definition of the aged and the aging process as defined from within. In general terms, we need to ask is old age a
"least" desirable period of life for the Indian elderly? Does old age
carry socially negative connotations? What are the sociocultural
characteristics of being old? And finally, what role does the aged
person play in this minority community?

KINSHIP

It is Clark and Anderson's contention that an overall weakening of
kinship ties brought about by increasing migrations of individuals
and families has affected the position and role of the aged individual in contemporary American society. How have migrations affected the Indian family?

There is little doubt that kinship ties within the Indian community have been ultimately affected by migrations of individuals
and families. From the early 1900's to the present, a trend from
ruralism to urbanism can be observed. Of the total Indian population, conservatively estimated at 113,000 within the state, 49 percent now reside in urban areas. This figure is 19 percent below the
figure for the general population of the state. The movement of the
Indian into urban areas can be dramatically illustrated with figures
on the *net migrations* of two areas: one rural, and the other urban.
In the urban area during a 10-year period from 1960 to 1970, we

find an overall increase in the Indian population of 517 per 1,000, whereas in the rural areas we find a loss of 83 people per 1,000 (Gann 1974). The Oklahoma Indian parallels the trend in white America toward increasing migrations of the individual and family.

Traditionally the grandchild-grandparent relationship was very strong; however, as one younger Indian summarized the situation today:

> [It] ...is being changed...My children live here...my father lives ...[in another town] ...and they don't see him that often simply for geographical reasons. A lot of families are spread out like that.

Demographic figures place the Indian family at an average size of 4.12 compared to 3.36 for the total population. The two figures seem to be rather close. The impression is that the Indian family in terms of size is also beginning to parallel the general population. This coupled with migrations seems to support the idea that kinship ties are changing within this group due to geographical mobility.

However, upon close inspection of informants' statements about family relationships we find quite a different picture, particularly among the rural populations. In the majority of cases the elderly have relatives near. Household composition may vary from a single generation to four generations living under the same roof. An elderly Indian might live alone, but a son next door, a daughter down the road, a sister in a nearby town. As one individual put it: "I live alone, but my son comes every day, my daughter every two weeks." In another example within an urban setting, an aged couple lived alone, but their daughters and nephews lived within the same city block. In general, although movements and family size support the idea of weakening kinship ties through migrations, upon close inspection of the Indian family, viewed outside of a specific household, we find close ties between generations.

In general, the old and relatively helpless Indian is not left alone, nor is there thought of abandonment which might have been the case at an earlier period in some of the hunting and gathering groups. Frequently the older relative is assisted by relatives and they may play a vital role in the day to day subsistence of their families. In many respects the old are more important today than they were in the past (cf. Goodwin 1942:517).

TECHNOLOGY AND PROGRESS

The industrial and technological changes which have occurred within American society in general have tended to create a situation in which the youthfulness of society is stressed rather than the experience and knowledge of the older generations. Progress in industry and technology has meant new opportunities for the young, often times at the expense of jobs for the older members of society. As was indicated earlier, youth and middle age are the most attractive years, with old age and retirement being viewed with negative connotations. In other words, social pressures brought about by a new value system resulting from our rapid industrial and technological progress has tended to blur the significance of the skills and knowledge of an older generation. We look to the youth of America for progress.

Obviously these changing attributes of the industrial and technological system of American society have had specific influences upon the Indian population in Oklahoma. The role of technological change and its effects upon the aged Indian can be best described using the base line of "allotments" for the late 1800's and early 1900's.

Historically, the communities within our sample practiced a mixed subsistence economy. Hunting and trapping were seasonal pursuits with agriculture being practiced as a supplementary activity. The planting of corn and the gathering of wild plants were the tasks of women. These activities were carried out on a family basis, usually in the form of a mother's and grandmother's joint garden patch. With allotments (of 160 acres) the males began to farm, although some hunting continued. Production remained basically for family consumption with one-half an acre or so being cleared for planting. Today gardens are planted, usually by the elderly, and their produce makes a contribution to the household. Hunting also still plays an economic role—it is not unusual to find meat drying behind a rural home.

Few of the rural Indians within our sample could subsist on their lands through agricultural pursuits alone. The Indian thus has been forced to participate in the American labor market. The result is that (1) 32 percent of all Oklahoma Indians have an income below the federal poverty level and (2) that 25 percent are unemployed although this figure varies—in one area the rate is as high as 74 percent. So-called progress has blurred the traditional economic pursuits of *all* age grades within the Indian community in Oklahoma.

In some instances, the elderly of today were able to obtain employment when they were young. These persons now, through retirement benefits, Social Security, or veterans' pensions are the sole source of steady income within many of the extended kin groups. This is an interesting twist to the *myth* that the young within eth-

nic groups economically support their old. In fact, the reverse is often the case. To illustrate this point, Goodwin (1942), writing on
the Western Apache, states:

> Many old men and women have monthly army pensions...and the
> first or second of every month sees them gathered...to receive and
> sign their checks, which, in many instances, serve largely to sup-
> port their families. Thus, old people are now often the wealthiest
> members of their families, *the reverse*...[emphasis added]...of
> former times.

Although Goodwin is speaking of reservation Apaches who served
in the capacity of scouts for the U.S. Army; the Army and civilian
retirement checks are significant forms of family income to Oklahoma Indians. The checks are from other Army duties (World War
I and World War II) and from private industry, but they are in many instances a primary source (and at times the only stable source)
for many Indian families.

In families where alcoholism is a problem, a phenomenon of the
middle-age group in the Indian community, the stability of the family is at times placed directly upon the elderly member of the
group, since younger family heads may disappear from the home
for periods of time. One individual illustrated the dependency role
of the young upon the old as follows: "My cousin works and had
all those kids and my grandmother takes care of them and does all
the cooking and cleaning. She takes care of everything while my
cousin is at work."

The care of the young similarly has historical depth as a *traditional role* assumed by the aged Indian. That is, the elderly played
a significant role in the teaching of the younger Indian. In this manner his knowledge was utilized in the education of the young. This
function was in many instances replaced by the Indian schools and
boarding homes which were forced upon many of the Indian families in the late 1800's and early 1900's. However, today with the
stress upon "Indianness" the old are being utilized once again for
their knowledge of past historical events and traditional cultural
values.

POPULATION INCREASE

Of the total Indian population of the state, 5.16 percent are males
over age 62, whereas 6.49 percent are females over age 62. Comparative figures for the general population of the state indicate that

13 percent are over age 62. The Oklahoma Indian aged population is slightly higher on a percentage basis, when compared with all Indian populations (including reservation groups) throughout the United States: 10.65 percent compared to 7.27 percent. Comparative figures for the United States in general as of 1974 places 10 percent of the more than 200 million people at age 65 or over (Kalish 1975: 14).

However, the utilization of these figures in terms of pressures upon the Indian community is highly suspect. There is simply no easy way to assess the impact of this group's growth (using these figures) since the Indian does not *type* or distinguish old age by these (numerical) categories. In other words, the fact that 10.65 percent of the Indian population in Oklahoma is over age 62 may tell us something about Indian longevity, but it tells us absolutely nothing about a growing group of dependents since the chronological dimension is not considered crucial, nor is the individual isolated as a less productive (or nonproductive) member of the society by this criteria. This point leads us to the final category with which this paper deals.

PRODUCTIVITY: TOWARD A DEFINITION OF OLD

We have made the observation that the elderly have in the past made economic contributions to the Indian family and that they continue to do so today.

Within generation segments, however, there appear to be conflicting ideas about the status and role of the aged. As the following quotations indicate, there is historical depth for the elderly's *functional* role within the social structure, a role which gave the aged a certain degree of respect and status.

> ...you got to look up to them, especially in some things, like medicine and songs because they are the only one who know those... My grandfather is clear on some things that are important like medicine and how to do meetings...[meetings refers here to the Native American Church ceremonies].

> Elderly has always meant those people who were the leaders of the tribe. The ones that ruled and decided what to do. They were the ones that did things. Yes, and they were the ones that gave advice. They were respected.

Both of the foregoing statements were made by younger Indians and their responses are somewhat of an idealization of the old.

Certainly conflicting attitudes are present in the Indian community. An elderly woman when questioned about her views of the aged within the current social setting made a typical response, also voiced by others, and observed by researchers in everyday and special social settings. That is, "...at the pow wows it's different now. The young people don't come by and talk much to the old people anymore...You no longer feel like you are somebody to be old."

The lack of respect for the aged can be attributed to a changing value system. Numerous individuals both young and old commented upon the loss of the "Indian culture" as a source of conflict between generations. Education and training in white schools, the adoption of Christianity, and in general the influence of white values can account in part for differing attitudes across generations.

Although some of the traditional power in areas such as group leadership has shifted, the elderly are still in many instances given respect and held in high esteem. The trend toward "Indianism" or a revitalization of the Indian cultural traditions may in part account for conflicting attitudes between generations. That is, we would expect an idealization of the aged for they are, chronologically at least, closer to an older form of social behavior which is now being stressed by the younger Indian. This stress upon the older Indians' knowledge of traditional behavior often times is an expectation which the aged Indian cannot fulfill. Individuals in their 60's and 70's today, except in a few instances, cannot begin to recall earlier forms of ceremonial behavior, past life-styles, or the movements and exploits of a hunting and gathering subsistence. In other words, demands are being made upon the aged which create stressful situations for the elderly—a renewed interest in them. But an inability on their part is turned into defensiveness on the part of the old toward the young. Although this explanation is here presented as only a hypothesis, if shown to be correct the idealized attitude as opposed to the actual would be further understood.

Younger, better educated individual Indians are becoming very active in leadership roles and in making policy decisions. In tribal elections young men are becoming members of tribal business councils and there are mixed reactions by the elderly to this trend. The elderly have been forced to give up a traditional role of leadership to the young. Political power, one measure of individual or group status, is thus shifting toward the younger generation.

Although conflict exists in many areas in which the elderly Indian participates, in general throughout the Indian community, the concept of an individual's productiveness is stressed. The Indian cultural value of individual performance does not stress age as a criterion for defining the old. There simply is no chronological definition. Rather, the individual's ability to function seems to be the essential criterion of evaluation: "Some are still considered young at 119 years of age"! The individual Indian is valued for his or her ability in most instances. They are given respect for their experience. Again, Goodwin's work (1942) dealing with reservation Apache reflects an attitude toward the elderly found within our sample. That is:

> Keeping track of ages and birthdays has been introduced by whites within reservation times; formerly, old age was not determined by the number of years an individual has lived. Age did not exempt men and women from work unless it made them physically incapable, and an old woman continued to cook, gather food, build dwellings, and tan hides as long as she could. An old man did likewise, but because hunting, raiding, and war necessitated great physical endurance, he was excluded from these activities at an earlier age than a woman was from her less violent tasks.

CONCLUSION

In American society there is a specific age criteria for defining who is old. The aged are set aside as a group, segregated and in some instances warehoused—in short, in many instances their productivity stops upon reaching a specific age.

In the Indian community in Oklahoma we did not find this segregation of the aged. The aged Indian is treated individually, not as a segregated group, and an individual's status is related to his or her ability to function. Furthermore, although a stress upon ability is central to defining old age among the Indians, the elderly individual is given respect even though their capabilities decline as time passes.

The four historical factors which have influenced the American position (and attitudes) toward the aged have only to a limited extent influenced the nonreservation Indian living in Oklahoma. The influence is not always in the same general direction. For example, although Indian families are migrating, "family networks" running between households indicate that the elderly are able to maintain and have significant kinship ties. They are seldom left alone or isolated from other kindred.

The Indian's participation in the labor market, it seems, has often had the effect of placing the aged in key economic roles, that is, of family provider. The increase in the percentage of aged within the Indian community, as indicated, has shown a steady trend upwards over the past two decades. The Indian living within two cultural traditions, with different values, has had to develop many strategies for survival and in some cases these strategies have created a reliance upon the old individual; in other cases it has meant that the older Indian's role within the community has changed. The old are far from being segregated or stored away.

The older Indian is in one respect placed in a highly valued position for his previous role of leadership and tribal knowledge. It is in the former area (group leadership) that the greatest amount of conflict is now taking place. The young are beginning to take over the traditional roles of leadership and power. However, the aged Indian still is able to make useful contributions to the community. As yet the negativism of age is not a strong aspect of the Indian value system.

NOTES

1. The field research upon which this paper is based was carried out from May to September, 1974, in Oklahoma. It was supported by a research grant from the National Science Foundation (Grant #GY-11477). We wish to express our thanks for that assistance.

7 Aging and Mutual Support Relations Among the Black Carib

VIRGINIA KERNS
*Virginia Polytechnic
Institute and State University*

In Chapter 5, Charlotte Ikels described how the Chinese ideal of
filial piety is not always realized in fact. Virginia Kerns further
develops this issue of real versus ideal cultural behavior in writing
about her research experience with the Black Carib. She found
that informants equated aging with debility and incapacity,
speaking in negative terms that have a very familiar ring to American ears. The same men and women subscribed to an ideal of filial responsibility which holds that sons and daughters should support and care for their aged parents. During the course of the year
that she spent living in a Black Carib community, Virginia Kerns
discovered that the reality of daily life conflicted with these
normative statements in a number of respects. Older men and women were actually a very diverse group, and few were pure dependents as she had initially been led to believe. As for younger men
and women, they were not equally mindful of their economic obligations to their parents. Virginia Kerns explains some of this
variation in terms of the differing degrees of success that older
women have in maintaining mutual support relations with their
adult children. Just as elderly Chinese carefully cultivate ties with
their adult offspring, so also do Black Carib women. Rather than
naively trust in a cultural ideal of filial responsibility, they actively
attempt to enforce that ideal. Lacking a national system of social
security, or the opportunity to be self-supporting, these women
obviously must depend on their children for support. Yet it would
be a mistaken notion to think of them as pure dependents, "char-
ity cases", who accept support from their sons and daughters
without reciprocating in any way. In fact, they often reciprocate
in kind. Older women attempt, with varying degrees of success, to
establish themselves as the centers of redistributive support systems for their adult children. Certainly they accept support, but
their adult children also turn to them for help when the need
arises. Grown sons and daughters represent social security for
their mother, and vice-versa.

Finally, Virginia Kerns raises another issue that we have en-
countered before, in the Introduction and in Part II, an issue
which we will see again in Part IV. This concerns the complemen-
tarity of qualitative data, obtained by intensive and sustained
observation, and quantitative data, gathered through extensive
surveys and questionnaires. Both of these have advantages and
drawbacks (as discussed in Chapter 1). Perhaps a major disadvan-
tage of survey research is that it tends to elicit cultural ideals, to
be biased toward the normative order. We have large quantities of
survey data on the elderly in industrialized societies, but it is dif-
ficult to judge how descriptive these are of the daily lives of older
adults. In the specific case of the Black Carib, Virginia Kerns
found very negative attitudes toward aging, similar to those that
abound in reports of survey research on the aged. By living with
and observing older women and men on a daily basis, however,
she was able to probe beyond those attitudes. Eventually, she saw
that the negative stereotypes and the ideal of filial responsibility,
from the perspective of older women, were highly utilitarian and
helpful in motivating and mobilizing support.

When I began my research with the Black Carib, I had what seems
in retrospect an unduly optimistic attitude about one of the tasks
at hand: learning about the social lives of older women and men.[1]
I assumed that it would be no more difficult to see the shared
pattern in their lives than in the lives of young men and women.
During the 15 months that I spent living with them, I gradually
abandoned this notion. I came to feel that, as a group, the old
were even more diverse than the young; they had had many years
to develop differently. A very few conformed to common Euro-
American conceptions of the aged: they were withdrawn, inactive—
in a word, "disengaged." But most older women and men, *to different degrees*, were not.

I found that attitudes toward aging, although easy to elicit,
provided little help in understanding this diversity. What was striking was that young and old alike expressed almost uniformly negative attitudes; with few exceptions, they found very little to re-
commend in growing old. Most described aging as an inevitable
and highly regrettable process, entailing the loss of physical and
sexual vigor, two much-admired qualities. As for attitudes toward
the aged themselves, young men and women tended not to generalize but to comment favorably or unfavorably about specific
individuals.

If my information on aging had been limited to the attitudes
and opinions that Black Caribs expressed, both in response to my

questions and in everyday conversation with each other, I would have (mistakenly) concluded that aging entailed uniform social consequences: disability and dependence. Living in a Black Carib community for an extended period of time gave me the opportunity to place these attitudes in context, to balance them against the diversity that I saw in the social lives of older men and women. What I saw did not correspond directly with what I heard about aging: attitudes did not describe the facts of daily life as I observed it.

Specifically, I found that what people said about aging, and the aged, was not always consistent with their behavior. Filial responsibility to parents is a cultural ideal espoused by all; and nearly all men and women express feelings of affection and obligation toward their parents. But descriptions of these ideals and attitudes cannot convey the variation and complexity that I saw in intergenerational relationships. Such descriptions say nothing about the efforts that aged women and men must make to enforce the ideal of filial responsibility, to ensure that their sons and daughters contribute to their support. Among the Black Carib, security at any stage in life is bound up with kinship. But what distinguishes older people, especially women, from their juniors is that their security is so closely related to lifelong, intergenerational relationships— more precisely, to their abilities and efforts to maintain relationships of mutual support with adult children.

BLACK CARIBS IN BELIZE

The Black Carib, or *Garifuna* as they call themselves, are descendants of enslaved Africans who escaped and interbred with Carib Indians in the West Indies during the seventeenth century. Since the late eighteenth century, they have lived along the Caribbean coast of Central America. Today some 80,000 Black Carib occupy about 50 towns and villages strung out unevenly along a narrow coastal strip extending from Belize (the former British Honduras) to Nicaragua.[2] Very few non-Caribs live in the four Black Carib villages in Belize, which number several hundred inhabitants each. The two towns, with populations of several thousand, have mixed populations, with Black Caribs forming the majority. Nationally, Black Caribs constitute less than 10 percent of the population of Belize.

The two Black Carib towns in Belize are administrative and commercial centers with a number of amenities—electricity, piped water, hospitals, markets—not found in the villages. Village residents make rather frequent trips to the towns, both to avail them-

selves of the goods and services offered there and for social purposes, to visit relatives. Some men and women also seek work in
the towns for want of local wage-earning opportunities.

No matter how long they may live and work elsewhere, for
most Black Caribs "home" is the community where they were
born and where, as a rule, their mothers and many other members
of their families live. A deep-seated localism prevails among Black
Caribs, which they express in pointedly negative comments about
other communities, and favorable ones about their own. So it is
that the residents of any particular village will claim that theirs
has the best location, enjoying full benefit of the trade winds and
escaping the heavy heat that oppresses other villages; they will
criticize other villages for being "bushy," overgrown with foliage;
and they will contend that people are more peaceful and industri-
ous, and life altogether more pleasant, in their own village as opposed to the others.

To an outsider like myself, these distinctions are very subtle
ones. Although I lived for more than a year in one Black Carib
village and made frequent and extended visits to others, I found
the similarities far more striking than any differences. In outward
appearance, they look much the same, with their modest frame
houses, and a few of the traditional thatch type, set along a sandy
stretch of beach, facing the sea. Aside from the houses, the only
structures of any consequence are a school, a Roman Catholic
church, a small community center, and perhaps a *dabuyeiba*, a
thatch building where certain death-related ceremonies take place.

One feature that all of the coastal villages share is their geographic isolation; only one is accessible by road, and that an un-
paved track that is frequently impassable during the wet season.
This isolation indirectly accounts for the most commonly cited
advantage of village life: the leisured rhythm of daily routine
which centers on domestic activities and concerns. Aside from the
rather frequent ceremonial events that take place in Black Carib
villages, there is little to interrupt this routine. The insularity of
these villages also accounts for what many see as their primary
drawback: the lack of local enterprise, which forces men and women to look for work outside their communities. Every household
needs some cash income, and young men and women, who must
leave the community if they are to find work, provide much of it
(cf. Gonzalez 1969). They seek employment as wage laborers in
a wide variety of skilled and unskilled fields, some in neighboring
settlements, other in different districts, still others abroad.

About three-quarters of the residents of Black Carib villages in
Belize are economic dependents, too young or too old to find

steady, gainful employment. While only a fraction, about one-tenth of the residents, are over 50 years of age, their presence in community affairs is disproportionate to their numbers.

THE AGED AND COMMUNITY LIFE

In Black Carib villages, as in most human populations, old women outnumber old men. Differential longevity aside, Black Caribs typically define women as old at an earlier chronological age than men. They suggest a number of markers—especially reproductive and productive incapacity, and to a lesser extent, physical appearance—in their definitions of old age; most of these pertain to women at an earlier chronological age.

Infertility and old age are so closely connected in Black Carib thought that they frequently use one as a metaphor for the other; and they consider that the onset of menopause and of impotence mark the advent of old age in women and men respectively. Although most women over the age of 50 freely admit to having passed menopause, men, whatever their age, are not so willing to concede the decline of their own reproductive powers. Of course, no real stigma attaches to menopause, while impotence is a matter for ridicule, or for good-natured teasing at best. As a rule, men claim to remain sexually active into their 60's. (So, for that matter, do many women.)

Permanent unemployment, the second marker of old age, is a far easier one to verify than the first. Black Carib women of any age have an extremely disadvantaged position in the labor market of Belize. Even in the favorable circumstance in which they find steady work, usually as domestics or seamstresses or shop clerks, they typically earn about one-third to one-half the wages of unskilled male workers. After the age of 45 or 50, women find themselves excluded from the labor market. Relatively few employment opportunities exist for women of any age, and employers candidly admit their preference for younger workers. They can enforce this preference only in the case of women because Belize suffers from a chronic shortage of male labor. Men can usually find employment so long as they are physically vigorous, as many are into their 60's and 70's. And even after they leave the labor force, men can earn money as self-employed fishermen.

Occasionally, Black Caribs also mention the changes in physical appearance that accompany advancing age, especially the slow greying of hair. More frequently, they observe that women generally look older than men of the same age, a fact which they attribute to the wearing effects of childbearing. To illustrate, a number of men and women independently mentioned a married couple who seemed to be approximately the same age, about 60 years old; but the man was "much older" than his wife, they said. In the course of taking a census in that community, I later learned that he was 70 and his wife 52. While this was an extreme case, I did find that I consistently underestimated men's ages, but not women's.

Here I am partially following the Black Caribs' own criteria and defining the onset of old age with permanent unemployment (either because of physical disability or age discrimination in the labor market) after the age of 50. By this definition, all of the 60-year-old women of my acquaintance were socially old, while many men of the same age were not. To judge from the dozen funerals I attended in various communities, Black Carib men, far more frequently than women, die before they are considered socially old in this sense.

Funerals and various other death-related cermonies are frequent events in Black Carib villages, in part because so many men and women return late in life to the communities where they were born; and they eventually die there. As they grow older, women increasingly involve themselves in these and the other religious activities that are the focus of community life (see Kerns 1977, in press.) The vast majority of Black Caribs are Roman Catholics, but they also maintain a flourishing system of indigenous rituals directed toward the placation of the ancestors. Many people attribute misfortune, especially sickness and death, to the *gubida*, the family dead, who punish neglect in this manner. Adults make simple and private offerings of food and rum in the home when individual ancestors request these, usually through dreams. Ancestors also occasionally demand more public and elaborate feasting. Older women are the usual organizers and most active participants in the numerous death-related rituals, as well as in the Roman Catholic ceremonies (a distinction that they do not make, viewing these as related elements in one system).

Not all old men and women participate in these ceremonies; some are skeptics, others simply display little interest in them. Those who do participate derive some prestige, but individually, commensurate with the nature of their participation and the extent of their knowledge about arcane ritual matters. This knowledge does not give them any particular authority or power outside the ceremonial sphere. While some people (whose numbers tend to be proportional to their age!) contend that old men and women deserve to be treated with courtesy, social reality does not invariably correspond with this abstract ideal. And even the notion of courtesy is a very limited one. It does not imply deference or any formal display of respect, only the polite use of kinship terms in address. Young people typically address their elders (not only old men and women but anyone of an ascendant generation) as "aunt" (*naufuri*) or "uncle" (*yao*). As the senior generation, old men and women are "aunt" and "uncle" to nearly everyone.

This simple courtesy aside, Black Caribs are very egalitarian and informal in their dealings with each other. Whether a man or woman of any age is generally treated with civility or not largely depends on his or her reputation, which derives from personal qualities other than age. A sharp wit, generosity, musical abilities, and linguistic skills rank among the most admired qualities; and they are not qualities specific to either gender or to any particular age. Old men and women have as much opportunity to develop and display these qualities as young men and women. In fact, according to many young people, their elders have a slight edge in the matter of music. Long years of practice, they say, explain the fact that old men and women are such proficient musicians, singers, and dancers.

Reputation also has a material basis. Although income levels fall within the same general range, villagers do differ in the degree of socioeconomic security which they enjoy. Some earn or receive support quite regularly, others more sporadically, and a handful are destitutes, without any reliable or reputable means of support. These last are alternately the objects of pity and contempt, frequently classified by other villagers as "beggars" who must depend on the beneficence of their neighbors for their daily food. To "beg" decreases one's social stature as much as to share elevates it.

Black Caribs have a very expansive ideology of sharing in which generosity is the central virtue, and the accusation of "stinginess" the ultimate slur. In daily life, however, exchange visibly centers on a rather narrow range of kin. Parents and children, and spouses as well, have an undisputed obligation to share with each other and support each other; and siblings are obliged to "help" each other as necessary, although in a more limited way. As for more distant kin, Black Caribs are apt to label their requests for money, food, or other goods as "begging." Of course, what petitioners see as a reasonable request ("We are cousins, after all," they may say somewhat righteously), those who are petitioned often describe as begging ("We are hardly kin, after all," they later explain privately, in a defensive manner).

Because everyone occasionally needs to look beyond immediate kin for help, everyone is occasionally accused of begging. And likewise, everyone is vulnerable to the charge of stinginess now and then; no one has the resources to respond to every request. But it is only the few chronic beggars, not all of them old, who suffer the general disdain of the community. These are a handful of men and women without either gainful employment or immediate kin. Some literally lack close relatives; others lack them figuratively, because they have alienated them.

For older women, who are excluded from the labor market, economic security hinges almost exclusively on relationships with kin. Those with adult children assume particular importance, especially for the many women without wage-earning spouses. Aging men and women who make too many demands upon people other than immediate kin arouse resentment and invite ridicule. Such cases are exceptional, and in my experience limited to one or two in each village. The following two are representative.

In one village, a 60-year-old, childless widow lived alone and led what can only be described as a hand-to-mouth existence, "depending for her daily food on the largess of her neighbors. Their only relation to her was through marriage; many years before she had married their kinsman and come to live in the village. People spoke of her with thinly veiled resentment. Why, they asked, did she choose to remain in their community when she could return to her own, and to kin from whom she could legitimately ask support? It was something of a rhetorical question since, in fact, her closest living relatives were several cousins. By local reckoning, as next-of-kin they had the strongest obligation to help her, but it was an obligation they would have given secondary consideration at best. Their primary obligations, after all, were to their parents, children, and spouses. In her late husband's village, the widow at least had her own house; in her natal community, both food and housing would have been problematic.

Another old woman, who lacked even her own house, provoked both ridicule and contempt because of her wholly indiscriminate and incessant demands for food and money. She happened to be related by blood to most other village residents, not a "stranger" who had married into the community; but she had no immediate kin living there. From an outsider's perspective, she acted senile. The Carib language lacks a precisely equivalent concept, and other villagers generally described her as "half crazy," a victim of sorcery rather than age. Children alternately teased her and fled at her approach: a stooped and abject figure, brandishing the proverbial cane at her small tormentors as they scattered in all directions. As for adults, when they spoke of her it was with more contempt than pity, for she made herself a burden to others, and unnecessarily, according to most. The woman's daughter, who lived in another village, had repeatedly tried to convince her mother to come live with her; but the old woman adamantly refused to do so, for reasons which she could not explain and which others claimed they could not discern. They would simply say with a shrug, "Crazy old lady. Why doesn't she go live with her daughter?" But despite these complaints, they fed her; and one woman gave her the use of a vacant house that she owned.

At the other end of the social spectrum from these two old women were the many women and men who were, to different degrees, supported by their adult children. Some possessed a measure of security that is not easily or quickly achieved under the unstable economic conditions which prevail in Belize (see Ashcraft 1972). Although much employment is seasonal or otherwise temporary, there is no national system of social security or unemployment insurance. For Black Caribs, kin are the only insurance.

MUTUAL SUPPORT RELATIONS

The parent-child relationship, as Black Caribs conceive of it, is *the* central social bond; and they emphasize its material aspects as much as its emotional importance. This is a distinction, in fact, drawn by an outsider but not by them. In daily conversation, and in song as well, they are apt to speak of both in the same breath and with the same words. (An *abaimahani* song, a type sung on the anniversary of a death, provides striking illustration of this. In it, the composer laments her mother's death with these words: "She left me/To face troubles/Without a hammock, without a sheet" [translation by Hadel 1972:195].)

What particularly distinguishes the parent-child relationship from others, aside from its emotional and material intensity, is its duration. Ideally, parent and child maintain a life-long relationship of mutual support, exchanging a variety of goods and services, and money as well. If one takes account of religious beliefs, then the exchanges between parent and child extend even beyond the span of life. Adults make ritual offerings to their deceased parents and other ancestors who, they explain, protect attentive descendants and punish the negligent. The fit between supernatural and social morality (again, an outsider's distinction) is very close here: filial responsibility pertains during life and also after the parent's death.

But just as filial responsibility is a cultural ideal, so is parental responsibility. While adults have an obligation to contribute to their parents' support, so their parents share a reciprocal obligation to help them during their times of need. What requires emphasis here is that like any cultural ideal, the ideal of mutual support is not invariably cultural fact. In part, the quality of support during old age is contingent upon the quality of the relationship over time. It also depends on the parents' continuing, active efforts to maintain an exchange relationship.

Social relationships involving intensive exchange—be they with adult children, spouses, or anyone else—develop over time. A man who did not support his children throughout their dependency, for example, would only be deceiving himself if he expected to receive substantial help from them during his, in old age. Situations of nonsupport do occur, largely because marital unions tend to be unstable, and frequently dissolve, during early adulthood. In such cases, children usually remain with their mothers. Few men have the means to support the children of previous unions, nor are they under any real compulsion to do so (see Kerns 1977:211ff.). So it happens that some older men indirectly receive support from the children of their current spouses (women with whom they formed stable unions in later life) rather than from their own sons and daughters.

Older women face an entirely different situation as they grow old. Unlike men, many of whom can earn some money by fishing, women have few skills which are marketable later in lilfe. A few earn money occasionally by petty trading, but this rarely amounts to much. As for depending on spouses for support, many older women are widowed or separated. With few exceptions, however, they do have adult children who, with increasing age, eventually become their exclusive source of support. The exchanges between women and their children are reciprocal, at least until extreme old age. What varies, from one woman to the next, is the level of exchange and the degree to which the women are able to reciprocate.

Essentially, a woman must strive to make herself a dependable source of help to her sons and daughters. She must show them that it is good policy to "bank on mother," who can provide services and help when they need it. In cases of marital separation, to choose a particularly common example, young men and women commonly turn to their mothers for material help, counsel, and child care services. Typically, a woman will offer in these circumstances to care for her daughter's dependent children, freeing the younger woman for wage work. The daughter's obligation is to send her mother money for the children's support, as well as for her own. Some older women also maintain their adult children during extended periods of unemployment due to sickness or,

more frequently, the seasonal nature of so much unskilled employment in Belize. To do so, a woman simply channels the support
which she receives from others to the son or daughter in need of
it. Although siblings directly exchange rather little as adults, they
may exchange a great deal indirectly, through the medium of their
mother.

Women are not equally adept in this role. To function effectively, they must receive support from a number of sources, so
that they are financially stable; and they must receive enough, so
that they are financially solvent. A woman without her own house,
or without multiple donors to her household, necessarily tends to
be a poor risk as insurance against hard times. She accepts support
but is hard pressed to reciprocate.

There are very few older women who do not own their own
houses (either solely, or jointly, with their spouses); and most do
have several adult children as potential contributors. But even in
these favorable circumstances, women cannot afford to sit idly by,
waiting for their children to visit, gifts in hand, or expecting remittances to arrive punctually, either through the mail or an intermediary. On the contrary, they must assert their needs to their children, who are often employed in other settlements and districts.
A negligent young son (and, to judge from the complaints I heard,
they are not exceptional) may receive visits on payday from his
mother—or, if she is indisposed, from his sister, acting as her
mother's emissary (cf. Gonzalez 1969:59). This can involve traveling
distances of two or three hundred miles round trip from neighboring settlements by freight truck, the only readily available means
of transportation. These are not easy journeys.

Women can also apply pressure by publicizing either the generosity or neglect of their adult children. A mother who feels herself neglected by any of her children will not conceal her displea-
sure from them or from others. Typically, she reminds her children not only of their obligations to her but also of the various
services that she provides for them. In an extreme case, she may
actually refuse to provide these any longer, although women more
frequently threaten this course of action than actually follow it.
The parent-child relationship is distinctive from others in being
based upon generalized reciprocity. That is, exchange appears to
be very "altruistic," and it is not always precisely balanced (see
Sahlins 1965). Relations with spouses and friends, in contrast, require balanced exchange and quickly disintegrate without it. Young
women usually leave their spouses in the event of nonsupport; and
according to community opinion, they do so justifiably. But what
women will not tolerate in a spouse they do tolerate in their off-

spring, not only because of maternal indulgence but for material reasons: only later in life can they afford it.

Women do try to maintain a degree of equivalency in their exchanges with adult children, and many are successful in this attempt. It is a strategy which clearly benefits their children as well as themselves. By providing well for themselves, these women also provide security for their sons and daughters. It is axiomatic, after all, that a mother is *the* dependable source of help, if she has the means, in any crisis—economic, marital, supernatural, or medical.

Crisis is certainly inevitable. There is scarcely an adult Black Carib who will not experience unemployment, marital separation, and sickness at some point; these are life experiences which few, if any, have the good fortune to escape. But crisis, despite its inevitability, lies vaguely in the future. In the immediate present, young men and women must provide support for many dependents—their children, spouses, and parents. This may explain the basic asymmetry which characterizes relationships between women and their adult children. It is not necessarily the exchanges themselves which are asymmetrical, but the effort expended in maintaining them. This maintenance role seems inevitably to devolve upon mothers, if only because the benefits offered are immediate, and the alternatives very limited. Few neglect to cultivate and sustain these relationships: visiting their children, offering care when they are sick, sending them food and gifts, fostering grandchildren, representing their descendants in ceremonial life. It is a labor of love, certainly, but one in which the distinction between altruism and pragmatism is particularly obscure.

CONCLUSIONS

The gerontological literature is full of generalizations, most of them negative, about the social consequences of aging. A fundamental problem with many of these generalizations is that they rest on insufficient evidence. They have developed out of research confined to Western, industrial societies; and they have developed primarily out of survey research, which can reveal the gross outline, but none of the nuances, of the everyday lives of elderly men and women. As a result, a great deal is known about attitudes toward aging and about the demographic characteristics of the aged, information which survey research is well-designed to provide. But our knowledge of the daily social behavior of old people (in noninstitutional settings, at any rate) might aptly be described as hearsay since so little of it derives from direct observation. Young people may well express their belief to researchers that the elderly have few activities and interests, but do they in fact? Or are these simply different than the activities and interests of the young? And if old people, in response to a questionnaire, choose to describe themselves as lonely, should we surmise that they are isolated and inactive? Or would frequent conversation, and sustained observation, suggest a different conclusion?

My own experience with the Black Carib has led me to believe that survey research must be balanced with ethnographic research, lest attitudes and ideals assume an analytical significance that is disproportionate with their cultural significance. There is no denying that the ideal of filial responsibility is an important one to the Black Carib, but certainly the efforts that aged parents must make to enforce this ideal are equally worthy of attention. These efforts argue against the popular conception of the elderly as passive dependents, and against the analogous academic notion that activity and interaction inevitably decrease with advancing age.[3] Observation suggests that the activity patterns of Black Carib men and women do *change* with age, but not that the level of social activity and interaction invariably decreases. Indeed, women tend to involve themselves more and more in ceremonial activities, and without abandoning their domestic concerns.

Perhaps it is generally true, as so frequently contended, that young people express negative attitudes toward aging and the elderly. Black Caribs themselves speak of aging in terms of incapacity rather than in any positive way; and a growing body of cross-national survey research shows the prevalence of negative attitudes among the young.[4] But survey research is capable only of revealing these attitudes; it cannot reveal whether aging men and women use their perceived disabilities to garner attention and aid from the young. Black Caribs certainly do so, and I suspect that it is a widespread strategy.

Peter Townsend's (1957:172) anecdote about an elderly British woman whom he interviewed on several occasions is a particularly telling example of how to accentuate the negative with positive consequences. He reports talking to the woman, who lived alone, while her daughters were visiting her. When he inquired whether she was ever lonely, she glanced at her daughters and said yes. During a subsequent interview when she was alone, she confided to Townsend that she was "never lonely really, but I like my children to call." Any Black Carib woman would understand the wisdom of this ploy, and probably every researcher should regard it as a cautionary tale.

NOTES

1. This paper is based on fieldwork which was carried out in Belize during 1974-75. I am grateful to the U.S. Office of Education for a Fulbright-Hays dissertation fellowship and to the Wenner-Gren Foundation for a grant-in-aid (#3058) which made my research possible.

2. Davidson (1976) describes the geographic distribution of these settlements. Gonzalez (1969) and Taylor (1951) provide detailed descriptions of two communities in their ethnographies.

3. For example, Lowenthal (1964:56) refers to the "well-established fact that social contacts decrease with advancing age" (cf. Havighurst et al. 1968:161)

4. See Arnhoff, Leon, Lorge (1964); Sharma (1971); Bengston et al. (1975).

8 Withdrawal and Disengagement as a Cultural Response to Aging in India

SYLVIA VATUK
University of Illinois
at Chicago Circle

Cultures, in all their variety, are the laboratory of anthropology. NonWestern, nonindustrialized cultures offer a challenge to theories developed in European and American culture which supposedly have universal validity. One such theory, "disengagement" theory, is one of the few formal hypotheses to crystallize in gerontology as an alternative to the longer standing "activity theory" which had loosely guided gerontological research since the late 1940's. Once formulated, disengagement theory managed to polarize gerontological thinking into two camps: disengagement versus activity.

Both theories are concerned about successful aging. Activity theorists stressed that successful aging is related to maintaining reasonable activity levels and substituting new roles for those lost with retirement. Conversely, the disengagement hypothesis maintained that withdrawal is a normal aspect of aging as an individual and society are preparing for the ultimate disengagement, death. Words flew. The ink flowed. Pitched battles were held over the appropriate measurement and interpretation of the data and, of course, the implications in policy and values. Now that the dust has settled, we can see that both were simple answers to complex questions and gerontology has been enriched by looking at other variables and factors affecting activity and its opposite, disengagement.

Sylvia Vatuk further enriches our understanding of aging by exploring the disengagement hypothesis in a cultural context, India, where withdrawal in old age is the cultural ideal. As outlined in the Hindu scriptures, during the last two periods of one's life (both referring to old age), one should withdraw from this worldly activity and interest. Since this normative order is congruent with the broad outline of disengagement theory, then disengagement as an ideal and normal process, should be reflected in the lives of Indians, if disengagement is universal and normal.

126

In the village of Rayapur, India, Sylvia Vatuk explores this question. As an anthropologist she looks at the ideal and how it guides the lives of her Indian informants in the context of the social organization of the village. Old age is seen as a period of rightful dependency with security contingent upon the support of an extended family (especially an adult son). As we have seen among the American Indians, Black Caribs, and in China, intergenerational relations are essential keys to a satisfactory old age. In Rayapur during this period of dependency there is not withdrawal and isolation. Only when older fathers turn over the family resources to their sons and older mothers give the keys to the family storehouse to their daughters-in-law, do we find something like withdrawal. This is a shift in the power between generations which is fraught with ambivalence for both young and old. Although the roles entailing responsibility and power are surrendered to the younger generation, this does not mean older Indians in Rayapur "dropout" and become the hermits of the forest. On the contrary, activity levels for the most part increase, but are in different areas than when younger. By giving up one's "burden" to the younger generation, older men and women are free to do other things. The ideal of withdrawal in India does not mean total cessation of social activity. It is a norm which encourages the old to transfer resources to the young and the young to care for and respect their parents who should be more concerned about spiritual affairs.

THE AGED IN NONINDUSTRIAL SOCIETIES

One of the more prominent issues being investigated by anthropologists interested in the study of aging is that of crosscultural variation in response to the pan-human experience of growing old. Among those who have investigated this topic in nonindustrial societies (as contrasted with the United States or modern Europe) research hypotheses have typically been framed in terms of the relationship between forms of social organization and the status of (or treatment accorded to) the aged (e.g., Simmons 1945; Goody 1976). Anthropologists who are concerned with the phenomenon of social change, and with understanding the social consequences of modernization for the transformation of formerly nonindustrial societies in the contemporary world, have also begun to explore the issue of old age and society within a dynamic, processual framework (e.g., Cowgill and Holmes 1972a). Although data on aging accumulated through research designed specifically to answer these kinds of questions are increasingly becoming available, it is nevertheless the case that, until very recently, most of the generalizations that have been made about aging in crosscultural perspective have been based upon sources in which material about the role of old people is merely incidental to more general discussions of social organization as a whole, or of such specific institutions as the family or political system.

But whatever the source, the most common view suggests that so-called "traditional" societies typically accord special respect and veneration to old people, that their social position is relatively high in comparison with that of the aged in our industrial societies, and that as urbanization and industrialization proceed throughout the world, adverse consequences for old people are to be expected. For example, in a recent collection of original essays by social scientists, most of them based on research in a number of industrial and non-industrial societies of varying levels of development, the editors of the volume present as a central hypothesis the proposition that the status of the aged is "high" in agricultural societies, but declines with "modernization." They explain this situation, in societies like that of India where the bulk of the population participates in an agrarian economy, through forms of family and extended kin group structure, and through the ability of the elderly to wield economic power, hold a monopoly of necessary knowledge and skills, and continue to perform useful social functions to an advanced age (Cowgill and Holmes 1972b:310).

While this hypothesis has much to commend it, and while it has provided the impetus for a number of useful crosscultural studies of the role of old people in social context, the more deeply one probes into the broader problem of aging in nonindustrial societies, the more evident it becomes that a model of this kind is insufficient for a full understanding of the social and cultural dimensions of the aging process in any one particular society, not to speak of "traditional" societies in general. The question of the overall social position of the elderly—or of any other social category of persons— is a multifaceted and extremely complex issues that cannot successfully be analyzed using a single hierarchical dimension of "high" to "low" status. It is necessary to deal with such an issue on a number of different levels, isolating the many distinct components of social status which are present, none of which are likely to be found to vary in precisely the same way along given dimensions. Furthermore, even if one is successful in introducing the necessary conceptual precision, one is seriously handicapped in testing an hypothesis of this kind in a setting of rapid social change because of the usual absence of any kind of longitudinal data. The kinds of documentary, statistical, or even literary data that may be used by social historians investigating similar questions as they relate to our own past are rarely available to anthropologists working in nonliterate (or even in many literate) primitive and peasant societies. One is inevitably reduced, therefore, to using synchronic comparisons to draw inferences about diachronic processes.

AGING IN INDIA

Until very recently there has been little research on the question of aging in India, although in the 1960's at least one attempt was made to bring together evidence from literary and sociological sources to shed light on the issue of the status of old people in that society (Rowe 1961). Probably the first published report of a field investigation designed specifically to study this issue is that of Harlan (1964). In this article, the author discusses the results of two sociological surveys of aging men and women in villages in Punjab, northern India, based on field materials collected there by students of Punjab University. The central purpose of this research was to test the hypotheses outlined above concerning the status of the aged in preindustrial societies, specifically with reference to degree of authority within the family, subjective feelings of well-being, formal village leadership, and informal influence. The findings are clearly not supportive of these widely accepted hypotheses. The aged in these villages generally tend to "occupy a precarious position" (1964:249)—they have little power inside the family or in the community as a whole, and express considerable insecurity and dissatisfaction about their physical and emotional conditions. Harlan stresses the importance of personal circumstances and traditional social structure in creating status problems for the aged in societies like that of India, even where ideals of family solidarity and reverence for age might lead one to expect a more sanguine reality.

Since Harlan's work a number of more extensive studies of aging in India have been carried out, for the most part by sociologists interested in a more broadly focused inquiry into the roles of old people in particular rural or urban communities (see, e.g., Marulasiddaiah 1969; Desai n.d.; Iyer 1971; Soodan 1975). In these studies, most of which were conducted by means of standardized interview schedules, such areas of concern are emphasized as residence patterns, economic status, occupation, social activities, health conditions, and general satisfaction with life among the elderly. While results of these studies are too many and too varied to be summarized here, it can be said that they all demonstrate the great complexity of the issue of the status of the aged in India, and point to the desirability of more intensive and theoretically refined investigations into specific, limited aspects of this broad issue. The present chapter attempts to do this with respect to the question of the relationship between certain traditional Hindu socioreligious values and the behavioral responses of old people to some of the socially and physiologically imposed stresses of the later years which have been highlighted in these earlier studies. Furthermore, it attempts to deal with this issue in the context of a theory about the nature of the aging process which was developed in the course of psychological research on aging in the United States, namely the theory of disengagement. It is thus at one level a descriptive study of aging in another culture, and on another a test of the validity of a gerontological theory through crosscultural comparison.

THE DEMOGRAPHIC BACKGROUND

In order to place the data from this particular study into the appropriate context, it is necessary to look at some basic demographic information on India's population, particularly that part of the population that can be considered "aged," and to outline some of the features of Indian social organization which help one to understand the status and social roles of the elderly. The Indian population, which according to the 1971 Census of India totaled almost 550 million persons, is a "young" population relative to the populations of the industrialized countries of the West. In other words, it is characterized by a predominance of people in the younger age cohorts, and a relatively small proportion of the total in the older category (see Figure 8.1).

Over 40 percent of the population is under the age of 15, while 6 percent is over 60. In total numbers, however, the problem of the old in India is of substantial magnitude, with approximately 32.7 million persons in this age category (India 1976). With an already lowered death rate, and prospects of continued success in the gradual reduction of the birth rate in coming years, projections are for a corresponding increase in the proportions of the aged to the total population.

A summary social profile of the characteristics of the aged population in India is meaningful only in conjunction with some understanding of social and cultural patterns related to marriage and its dissolution, parenthood, and family structure in addition to more obvious demographic factors. An examination of Census figures reveals that the never-married population is negligible in the older age categories, particularly for females. This fact reflects the virtual universality of marriage for young people in Indian society, which is accomplished in significant part by the customary arrange-

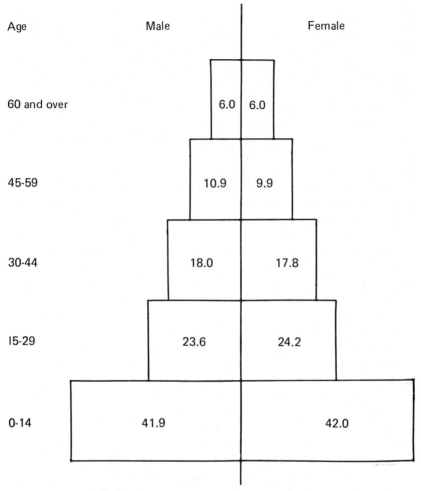

FIGURE 8.1 Population Pyramid of India.

Shown are percentages of total population in 15-year age
cohorts, as of Census of India, 1971

ment of marriages by the parents of young people in adolescence
or (in the case of boys) in the early 20's. Attitudes toward divorce,
and the former lack of legal provisions for the formal dissolution
of marriage for most Indians, help to explain the negligible numbers of aged persons reported in this status as well. Despite some
incidence of de facto marital separation, essentially all ever-married
persons are reported to the Census as currently married, unless
they are widowed.

There is in India, as in the industrial countries, a large disparity
in the proportions of widows among elderly females as compared

with the proportion of widowers in the older male population. In the first place, most Indian husbands are several years older than their wives at the time of first marriage as well as in subsequent unions. Furthermore, women widowed after the end of their child-bearing years almost never remarry, and many Indian caste groups forbid the remarriage even of young and childless widows. Thus the overwhelming majority of women over 60 years of age are widowed. Approximately 70 percent are so in the 60-64 age cohort, and this percentage rises to 85 for those over 70 years of age. On the other hand, men commonly remarry after the death of a spouse, even if they are elderly themselves; this fact, in combination with the usual age disparity between a man and his wife, helps to explain the striking statistics which show that even among men over 70 years of age, 60 percent are currently married. In the Western industrial societies, this kind of difference in marital status for aged men and women is partially accounted for by the greater survival rate of women, and by the consequent fact that women greatly outnumber men in the older age cohorts. However, this is not the case in India, where up to the age of 80 men continue to outnumber women (as they do at younger ages as well), and even over 80 years of age the sex ratio is not strikingly unbalanced in favor of females.

The practical consequences of these statistics for the situation of the elderly are many. Most obviously they mean that older men typically have a wife with whom to spend their declining years— in the usual case a woman younger than themselves, who is likely to be more robust and physically capable of providing care when necessary. The great majority of older women, on the other hand, lacking a spouse for support, must either live alone and provide for their own daily needs, or must rely on children or other relatives for companionship, support, and care in old age. For this reason, the problem of residence, support, and care of the aged is in India a female problem.

THE SOCIAL CONTEXT

The normal social expectation in India is that elderly persons will be cared for by their grown children, preferably their sons, and it is not surprising that in the absence of other forms of provision for old-age security, a high value is placed on having children, particularly males. Couples childless by design are almost nonexistent, but childlessness, or the failure of children to survive to adulthood, is by no means unusual. Reliable figures on the incidence of child-lessness in India are not available, but one study of a rural sample population shows that 22 percent of women have no living son, while 33 percent have only one (Collver 1963). When we combine this statistic with those presented on the incidence of widowhood, we must assume that substantial proportions of women in the older age cohorts are bereft of both husband and son, thus compounding the problem of residence and support for older women outlined above. The Indian social system does provide for alternatives, including adoption, polygyny, or divorce and remarriage—all of these to be availed of almost exclusively by men in their reproductive years who are without male issue. There is furthermore in India a broader conception of family solidarity than we are accustomed to in the United States, which recognizes the responsibility of nephews, grandsons, and others of the extended kinship network to take care of older persons in the absence of direct descendants. The ideal family system is one in which young men remain in the household of their parents after marriage, their wives joining this household and taking on the tasks of caring for their aged in-laws when this becomes necessary. Landed property is typically held in common by a father and his adult sons. On the former's death, it may be divided, equal shares going to each brother, unless they choose to continue to maintain a common household and to cooperate economically. In practice, however, there is considerable variation—by region, caste, economic level, and individual choice—as to the extent to which such patri-local extended families remain intact even throughout the lifetime of the senior couple. Although there is a substantial proportion of economically independent nuclear households in most Indian villages and towns studied by anthropologists or sociologists, it is nevertheless the case that this type of family is not the culturally sanctioned, ideal family form (see Dube 1955; Mandelbaum 1970; Kapadia 1966; Vatuk 1972). No positive cultural value is placed on a young couple's establishing themselves independently, and a strong cultural emphasis is on the duty of sons (and their wives) to provide for elderly parents, even if considerations of interpersonal conflict, economic well-being, or occupational convenience have dictated separate residences. Consequently, old parents are rarely expected to live on their own if they have living sons, and old persons without living children are expected to be taken in by whichever close junior relative may be available.

The strong emphasis placed in our society on self-sufficiency and independence for the old is entirely contrary to the Indian value system. Dependency for the old is not viewed in a negative light either by the old themselves or by those of the younger age groups, although obviously on an individual level there may sometimes be private resentment of the inconvenience and burden which must be incurred if this ideal is to be lived up to in practice. However, evidence from a number of studies which include data on the living arrangements of the aged in Indian rural and urban communities demonstrates that the ideal is in fact widely translated into practice, at least as far as the provision of shelter and sustenance is concerned. For example, in a study of three villages in north India, Raj and Prasad (1971), show only 7.6 percent of those over 50 living alone out of a sample of 327 persons in that age category. Almost half of these isolated individuals were childless, and it must also be taken into consideration that some of those in the younger age ranges may well join relatives when they reach a more advanced age and are unable to support or care for themselves. In a much larger study, a sample survey of approximately 2,000 persons over 60 years of age in the city of Delhi, Iyer (1971) reports only 5.8 percent living apart from any relative. The proportion of old persons living alone in the reports of other studies of the aged ranges from 3 to 14 percent (Desai n.d.; Soodan 1975; Marulasiddaiah 1969), the higher figure from a rural sample, in which it can safely be assumed that most of those living alone, in the sense of maintaining an independent household, are nevertheless in close proximity to relatives and life-long friends with whom they share many social activities as well as mutual help. The proportion of the elderly who are institutionalized in India is infinitesimal (none have been included in any of the samples reported on in the studies cited); the widely accepted principle that the proper place for the elderly is within a family setting is a primary explanatory factor in the almost total absence of such institutional facilities, even in the larger cities.

The important issues, then, are not limited to a consideration of where the old person lives and with whom he interacts on a day-to-day basis, but rather what the quality of that interaction is, what its satisfactions are felt to be, what points of strain and conflict are present for the older person within his family and immediate social environment. To answer these questions, it is most important to look at the value system, at cultural expectations about old age and the aging process, and to look at these not in isolation as direct determinants of behavior, but to seek their dynamic interplay with the social and economic system within which old people and their families live out their life cycles.

THE LIFE CYCLE IN INDIAN TRADITION

For the great majority of Indians, the relevant cultural values are to be found within the religious scriptures of Hinduism. In Hindu tradition a normative framework for the life cycle of both men and women is provided in the context of prescriptions in a number of texts for the ideal way of life, *varnāshrama dharma*, which may be translated "duties of social position and stage of life" (see deBary 1958; Basham 1954).

The first element in this compound concept, that of social position or rank (*varna*), refers to the four-fold functional division of traditional Hindu society into hereditary, hierarchically ordered categories of persons, whose special duties (*dharma*) toward society and the gods are outlined in some detail in the scriptures. The four relevant ranks and their respective functions are, in descending order of precedence, those of the Brahmans—priests and scholars; the Kshatriyas—rulers and warriors; the Vaishyas—agriculturalists, herders, traders, and the like; and the Shudras—servants to the other three. The three highest ranks are sometimes called collectively the "twice-born," in reference to the eligibility of their men for ritual initiation—in the form of a ceremonial rebirth—some time in late childhood or early adolescence. For the twice-born, the ideal life course is subsequently described in terms of four stages of life (*āshrama*), each of which has in turn its own appropriate set of duties or mode of living. These stages are outlined in the scriptures from the perspective of a male, but they assume his marriage, at the appropriate juncture, to a woman whose duties at each subsequent period will complement his own. In this way the traditional framework applies to both sexes, even though its prescriptions are more fully elaborated for men.

Briefly, there are four stages of life in the traditional normative scheme. The first is *Brahmacārya*; the emphasis in this period is on sacred learning, and a young man is expected to observe strict celibacy. The second, *Grhastha*, is the period of married life and parenthood, when a man and his wife assume the responsibilities of householders. During this stage, which is entered at the time of marriage, a man performs the special functions assigned to the social position (*varna*) into which he has been born, and takes an active role in the family and community of which he is a part. *Vānaprastha*, the third stage, is literally the stage of "dwelling as a forest hermit." In this period of life, which is said to begin when the householder "sees his skin wrinkled and his hair white, and the sons of his sons," (deBary 1958) then a man is exhorted to turn over the management of household affairs to his sons and retire, with or without his wife, to the forest. There he should spend some years in contemplation and devotion to the gods. He ideally begins to loosen the personal and social ties which have bound him to the world, a process which is completed in the final stage of life, *Sannyās*. This is a period of asceticism and renunciation of worldly ties, in which the twice-born Hindu male should end his days. He should live a solitary existence, having discarded all attachments to other human beings and to worldly goods and concerns, passing his days in meditation and the quest for spiritual perfection.

This framework or model for the ideal life cycle is one which, at least in its broad outlines, is familiar to Hindus of all social levels in contemporary India. While few lives as actually lived can be said to correspond in detail to the prescriptions of the Sanskrit texts, and whereas men do not plan their lives to follow precisely their directives, it is nevertheless clear that, in general, Hindus use the notion of the four stages of life normatively. Men and women tend, for example, to assess and evaluate their own lives and the lives of others in its terms, and they judge the appropriateness of various forms of activity and outlook at particular phases of the life cycle accordingly.

Of course, in speaking about the life cycle with religiously unsophisticated Indians one does not often hear it phrased in terms that are precisely those of the scriptures. There is a tendency to collapse the four stages of the sacred books into three: childhood, adulthood, and old age, ignoring the traditional distinction between the stage of withdrawal and that of renunciation. The terminology, too, tends to be translated into the modern language or dialect by those untrained in Sanskrit, so that, for example, in Hindi the word *burhappa* ("old age") replaces the Sanskrit terms for the latter stages of life. But nevertheless the traditional terms are familiar, and in slightly altered forms are also used on occasion to refer to the stage of adulthood (*girasth* in Hindi) and old age (*sannyās*). The latter is very widely used by older people to describe their own position with relation to the family of which they are a part, to characterize their own attitude toward this family, toward society, and toward life as such. It implies emotional and psychological detachment from the ordinary daily concerns of family life, noninvolvement, nonattachment, to worldly matters, particularly to those which involve conflict or material interests. Clearly their conceptions of the ideal old age are drawn very largely from the traditional prescriptions for the latter two stages of life, with their emphasis on the theme of gradual withdrawal and eventual renunciation of worldly ties and responsibilities. However, they do not emphasize the desirability of *physical* retreat which is so central to the scriptural statements—the nature of the retreat from life is seen as merely a social and psychological one, except in exceptional cases.

DISENGAGEMENT THEORY

When one examines the Hindu scriptural concept of the ideal life cycle, or its contemporary version as manifested in the words of religiously unsophisticated Hindu villagers, it becomes evident that they display significant parallels to some of the ideas put forward in the context of certain gerontological discussions of the nature of the aging process. I refer to so-called "disengagement theory," which postulates, in brief, that as a person ages a mutual withdrawal occurs between the aging individual and the society of which he is a part (Cumming and Henry 1961; Cumming 1964; Havighurst et al. 1964; Henry 1964; Maddox 1964). In its original formulation this theory was presented as describing an intrinsic developmental process, valid for all aging men and women, regardless of particular social or cultural milieu (Cumming and Henry 1961:17). The authors recognized, of course, that the precise timing or form of disengagement might vary from one society to another—depending upon the kind of social recognition accorded the older person or the degree of cultural valuation of age—but they nevertheless maintained that declining participation and emotional investment in the personnel and activities of young adult life is normal, inevitable, and indeed adaptive as one approaches the later years of life.

More recently the proponents of this theory themselves (see Cumming 1964; Henry 1964), as well as other researchers who attempted to test its validity, have seen the need to modify it, particularly to take into account personality variables. It has been suggested that to an important degree successful aging follows upon successful adjustment at other stages of the life cycle, and can best be viewed within the context of the total development of the personality. Some have sought to describe different "styles" of aging, that is, different ways of coping with the changes that inevitably confront the older person, any of which may prove successful depending upon a person's mode of adaptation over the entire life span (see Williams and Wirths 1963; Reichard et al. 1962; Maddox 1966; Neugarten, Havighurst, and Tobin 1968, for example). Although a number of gerontologists have pointed out the importance of considering cultural variables in the application of disengagement theory to the aging process outside of our own society, the most serious attempt to do this, using first-hand crosscultural data, is to be found in the work of Gutmann (1969, 1976). His latter study, dealing with old age among men of the Druze sect in Lebanon, is of special interest, particularly in that it presents pertinent psychological data in a cultural and social context.

The disengagement process, as postulated by Cumming and Henry and modified by subsequent investigators, has both psychological and social aspects, and since it describes an interactive phenomenon, requires consideration not only of the psyche and behavior of the elderly person, but also of the response by others in his community and social network to the aging man or woman's presence. The Hindu formulation of the proper stages of life, on the other hand, is more unidimensional; it prescribes a code for action *by* the individual, *for* his own spiritual well-being (as well as, by implication, for the welfare society as a whole). It is a *normative* concept which says nothing about psychological, developmental "reality." Nevertheless, the existence of such a conception among Indian Hindus, and its immediacy for those who are either approaching old age themselves or interacting with elderly relatives and associates, is of considerable relevance in the assessment of disengagement theory in crosscultural perspective.

AN ANTHROPOLOGICAL STUDY OF AGING IN INDIA

The heart of this chapter is an anthropological study of aging and the life cycle in India which was carried out in 1974—76 in a formerly agricultural village now part of the metropolis of New Delhi. As the population of this capital city mushroomed following India's Independence in the late 1940's, it absorbed, by expansion of its borders into the countryside, a large number of such villages, which today remain encapsulated and socially distinct though outwardly indistinguishable from the general urban sprawl. The village in which this research was done had been dominated by members of a caste known as Rayas. Most of the cultivable land had been owned by families of this caste, and other villagers of service and artisan castes performed their traditional occupations in return for an annual share of the harvest from the Raya landowners. Today the Rayas have received monetary compensation from the city of Delhi for the loss of their agricultural land to public housing construction, and most of them still live in their original homes in the village I have called Rayapur. They are for the most part economically well-off, and live in some respects an urban middle-class lifestyle. However, their very recent rural origins mean that the older Rayas are in many respects confronted with a situation of social change for which they are ill-prepared. It is this group of old people, and the families with whom they live, who constitute the primary focus of this research project.

THE RAYA AGED IN RAYAPUR

In studying aging and the life cycle in Rayapur, the definition of "old age" was treated from the beginning as one of the empirical questions to be investigated. Therefore, no a priori chronological age was established as a cutoff point for delimiting the study sample. Indeed, to do so would be to come up against the widespread ignorance of precise age, particularly among older females. It seemed most appropriate to single out for study those people who consider themselves old, and are so considered by others who know them and associate with them on a regular basis.

While the self-perception and the perception of others as old obviously varies from one individual to another, and tends to depend to an important degree on such external signs of aging as tooth loss and graying hair, general consensus in this Indian community seems to place primary stress on life-cycle criteria, at least in so far as the marking of the initial boundary of old age is concerned. Thus, the marriage of one's children—particularly of one's sons—and the birth of grandchildren, mark the beginning of old age in this society far more clearly than does the passing of a specified number of years. In chronological terms, this means that men and women in their mid-40's stand at the threshhold of old age, and begin to conform—and to be pressured by others to conform—to the role expectations for this stage of life.

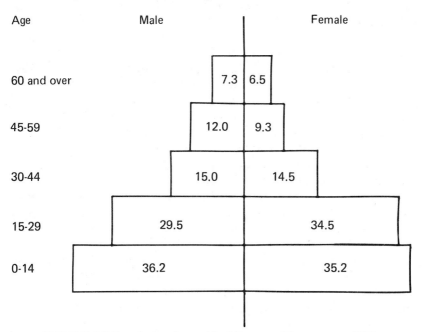

FIGURE 8.2 Population Pyramid of Rayapur (Owners: n = 543) by Percentages.

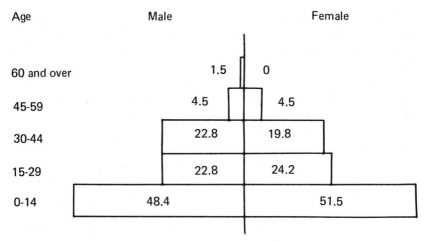

FIGURE 8.3 Population Pyramid of Rayapur (Tenants: n = 132)
by Percentages.

Despite the fact that my qualitative data in the pages to follow is based on interviews with and about old people as "old age" is defined intraculturally, I have for statistical and comparative purposes compiled from my household census of the community some figures on all persons reporting themselves to be 45 years of age and over, divided into 5-year age cohorts. The figures and tables thus give some information on the age distribution of Rayas in Rayapur, and of sex ratios, marital status, and residence patterns of those over 45 years of age. Note that in Figures 8.2 and 8.3 a distinction has been made between original Rayapur families (owners) and other Rayas (tenants) who are migrants to Delhi and live in rented accomodation in the village, often in the homes of relatives. Among the latter the elderly are very sparsely represented, reflecting the age-selective character of rural-urban migration. It may also be noted that among Raya women there is a negligible number of widows until one reaches the over-70 cohort (see Table 8.2). Chance may have played a role here, but a contributing factor is the practice of remarriage for women in this caste, after the death of a spouse, to a brother or other relative of the husband.

The old people of Rayapur live, with few exceptions, in so-called "joint" or extended family households of three and sometimes four generations (see Table 8.2). This is not to say that the majority of all Raya households are extended in structure, which they are not. The most frequent type of household for the elderly person includes an older married couple, one or more married sons and their wives and children, and one or more unmarried children of the older couple. Many such households also have additional

TABLE 8.1 Marital Status by Sex and Age Groups: Rayapur Rayas (Owners)

Age	Never married		Married		Widowed		Separated	
	M	F	M	F	M	F	M	F
45-49	0	0	92.3	100	7.7	0	0	0
50-54	0	0	100	100	0	0	0	0
55-59	0	0	100	80	0	20	0	0
60-64	25	0	75	86	0	14	0	0
65-69	17	0	83	100	0	0	0	0
70 and over	0	0	30	29	70	71	0	0

*Percentages (by sex) in each category.

TABLE 8.2 Marital Status and Residence Pattern: Rayapur Rayas (Owners)

			(Number of Persons)										
			Married						Widowed				
	Un-married		with marr. sons		with unmarr. children		with other		with marr. sons		with unmarr. children		with other relative
Age	M	F	M	F	M	F	M	F	M	F	M	F	M	F
45-49	0	0	1	4	10	6	1	1	1	0	0	0	1	0
50-54	0	0	5	3	5	4	0	1	0	0	0	0	0	0
55-59	0	0	4	3	6	2	1	0	0	1	0	0	0	0
60-64	1	0	3	5	0	1	0	0	0	1	0	0	0	0
65-69	1	0	5	3	0	0	0	0	0	1	0	0	0	0
70 and over	0	0	3	2	0	0	0	0	5	4	0	0	2	1

members, such as a widowed or separated daughter, an unmarried brother, or a daughter's child. In a few cases there is also the elderly parent of either husband or wife, making a four-generation family group. There are no examples of residentially independent old persons.

The older Raya men in Rayapur were almost all born there, and have lived there all of their lives, while the women were all born elsewhere, having come to Rayapur upon marriage, as is the custom in this region. With negligible exceptions, all of these older persons were engaged until fairly recently, for most of their adult lives, in agricultural pursuits. Women as well as men of this caste customarily work in the family fields, cut fodder for cattle, fetch water from the well for all household needs, as well as take care of all of the housekeeping, cooking, and childcare. Their village is located on a site poorly suited for agriculture in its soil and water supply, and it ranked very low in economic and prestige terms among the caste villages of Delhi and U.P. Now, on the contrary, its former land-owners are among the wealthiest and most influential members of the Raya caste. The urbanization of the village has brought about dramatic changes in occupational structure and life style, and the older persons on whom this study has focused find themselves in a position to enjoy almost total leisure and the good life in terms of physical comforts if not psychological satisfactions.

CONCEPTIONS OF THE IDEAL OLD AGE

The old people of Rayapur say that old age is ideally a time for rest and leisure, a time when work responsibilities should cease, and one should be able to sit back and let oneself be cared for by others. When speaking of a "good" old age, Rayapur men and women frequently use the concepts of "service" (*sevā*) and "comfort" (*arām*). These concepts are complementary to one another: the old person is said to enjoy comfort through being served by others, normally by his or her sons and their wives and children. This view involves a willing acceptance of dependency in old age—in psychological terms one could perhaps speak of a culturally legitimized regression to an earlier, childhood state of being nurtured by others. Attempts by the elderly of Rayapur to explain these concepts almost always failed to reach beyond the listing of such physical needs as food, shelter, and clothing, although there were other less direct indications that psychic, emotional needs were in fact no less pressing for these aged persons.

One of the difficulties in realizing an ideal old age of rest and nurture derives from the Indian family structure, in which aging parents are dependent on sons—and thus, in effect, upon daughters-in-law—to provide the routine physical care they require. Young women are of course socialized to the importance of their duty to care for the husbands' parents in old age, but the circumstances under which they live during the early years of marriage in the conjugal home, and the tensions that almost invariably develop between them and their mothers-in-law, in particular, often create animosities that persist into later years. In the conversations of the aging there is considerable cynicism expressed about the willingness of the young to provide, in the long run, the kind of service that they feel is their due. While most of the actual work involved in "serving" the old—namely providing the meals, washing the clothes, and so on, as well as nursing in time of illness—falls on the daughter-in-law, the son shares in the credit and blame for the quality of its performance. As several persons remarked in this regard: "If the son is good, everything will be fine. But there are very few sons like that nowadays. At most, one in a hundred will really care for his parents in their old age." Others pointed out that one's fate really lies in the hands of a stranger, the daughter-in-law one has brought into the family: "If she is that sort of woman, she will turn her husband's head against his parents and he will begin to neglect them." In fact, physical neglect of the old in this relatively affluent stratum is rare, but subjective feelings of neglect among the old, and actual neglect of their affective and social needs when they become physically feeble or incapacitated is not uncommon. It is doubtless observation of such situations that accounts for the often verbalized determination of the old "to die while my hands and feet are still working," in other words, before becoming a physical burden to others.

Related to this notion of old age as a time of release from burdensome work and responsibilities, is the idea that the old should voluntarily disassociate themselves from direct involvement in the management and direction of household affairs, and should let those who have assumed responsibility for the work also take on responsibility for decision-making. Such sentiments are voiced by young and old alike, but for each age group are founded in differing sets of motivations. The young are of course eager to be allowed to take over, particularly where, as in most Rayapur households, the son's earnings form a substantial part of the family income. The old, on the other hand, are in most cases not at all eager to give up a central role in the management of their household. Women are particularly loathe to turn over the keys to the household stores to a daughter-in-law whom they do not trust to conserve them wisely. But they nevertheless echo the traditional value of withdrawal, which provides ready justification for an attitude of resignation when the competition for dominance appears lost. When asked directly about their role in the household, elderly persons commonly began with a lengthy disclaimer to the effect that they left everything to others, that they had detached themselves from petty concerns, that they were devoted to religious worship, and were preparing to leave the world. Only lengthier discussion and close observation revealed the extent to which they were still "bound up in the life of a householder (*girasth*)," and the extent to which this involvement created worry and interpersonal conflict.

SOCIAL PARTICIPATION AND ACTIVITY
OF THE OLD IN RAYAPUR

In spite of the strong influence of the ethos of withdrawal from the world in old age, and the strong desire to rest and be cared for, it is in fact not easy to find persons for whom aging has caused a lapse into inactivity or declining social participation. The aged are in many respects more socially involved than the young in the extrafamilial network and in peer group interaction. For women the difference is quite marked, since in this society young married women are very much restricted to the home and only move outside of it on special occasions. Furthermore, release from the daily responsibilities of housework frees them for outside activities, including participation in religious worship and gatherings, for which previously they had little time, though possibly much inclination. It is possible to find more males than females who have actually relinquished family responsibilities and leadership to a greater or lesser extent. Doubtless this is at least partly an artifact of the absorption of the village of Rayapur into the city of Delhi and the consequent loss for these older men of the base of the only livelihood they knew. For most of them, there is no replacement for agriculture in terms of productive work in the context of the contemporary village situation. However, levels of activity remain high even for these men, if we consider their participation in day-long card games, frequent travel outside the village on family and caste business, and entertainment of visiting relatives and friends.

Older women in Rayapur normally continue to manage their own household as long as they are physically capable of doing so, and as long as the force of their personality is able to withstand the attempts of the daughter-in-law to usurp this right. Retirement for the older woman means in practice a re-division of labor when her sons marry—the younger woman or women take over the heavier, more onerous and tedious jobs of housekeeping, while the older woman takes over what they call the "outside" work: shopping, dealing with tradesmen and artisan specialists, managing ceremonial affairs, gift giving, and the family finances. Her control over the joint family purse is an important element in her day-to-day managerial authority. Care of milch animals is also in most families the province of older women. More than half of the households in which old people are present own at least one water buffalo for milk, and its feeding, watering, milking, and disposal of its wastes, takes several hours of a woman's day. Another major responsibility is the care of young children, particularly toddlers. Usually such a child will sleep with its grandmother at night and accompany her on errands and when she goes visiting. Grandmothers say that "the interest is dearer than the capital," to explain their close relationship with grandchildren.

Older men, on the other hand, appear at first glance to lead rather idle lives. Only a few of the younger men in the "aging" category are actively engaged in earning a living. For the most part, men of the grandparental generation among the Rayapur Rayas depend upon investments or rents or on the earnings of married sons for support. They remain in the village from morning to night, or visit other Raya villages on family business. Some are involved in court cases which occupy much of their time, while others are supervising the construction of homes in outlying suburbs of Delhi, which requires their continual presence at the site to oversee the process of building and material inventory. These older men commonly have a rather physically peripheral position in the joint household. When he comes into the house, the household mobilizes to take care of the senior man's needs. He is welcomed and catered to, his advice sought and decisions heard. But he is not expected to remain for long.

Many older men live for all practical purposes in an outbuilding, as is the custom in the rural area. This is usually located at some distance from the main house; here animals are tethered and men gather to talk, smoke, and play cards. They also sleep here at night, for men whose sons are married do not openly sleep in the house with their wives and ideally refrain from sexual relations altogether. This is another and crucial aspect of withdrawal in old age. When they become widowers they have even less place in the home, for their daughters-in-law must veil their faces before the father-in-law, and to spend time in the house would be to seriously inconvenience the daughter-in-law in the course of her household work.

Ideally the older men maintain that one should withdraw from active management of the household when the son is able to take over, but in most cases this does not actually seem to occur until the father is in his late 60's and the son a mature man with adolescent children. It is actually difficult to establish this without close observation within a family over a long period of time, for the strength of the ideal is such that interview reports are likely to misrepresent the actual situation. They are also likely to be contradictory: sons eager to affirm their idealized respect for the aged claim to follow the father's instructions on the most minute matters, while fathers disclaim any intentions of interfering with their sons' prerogatives of independence.

CONCLUSION

Without going into further detail about the activities and attitudes of the elderly in Rayapur, it is evident that we have a situation in which relatively high levels of social participation coexist within a framework of strong cultural values in support of social and psychic withdrawal by the aged from social ties and responsibilities and, concomitantly, from active managerial and authoritarian roles. The data raise a number of possible directions of inquiry. For example, we might ask to what extent there is evidence of conflict, either overt or otherwise, as a consequence of what appears to be a significant gap between ideal and actual behavior. Are there problems for the adaptation of the elderly—or for those with whom they interact and on whom they are dependent—arising out of difficulties in reconciling a normative prescription for "disengagement" with the evident desire of the elderly to continue, or even to increase in some areas, their levels of activity? Such problems seem to be actualized primarily in the arena of intergenerational relationships within the family and household, but there are a number of factors which tend to mute their overt expression. On the one hand, there is the force of equally strong cultural prescriptions of respect and obedience for one's elders. On the other hand, the inevitable physical decline that generally accompanies aging makes it impossible for many of the elderly to sustain the level of control and management that they might prefer. Withdrawal, expressed as a voluntary choice and buttressed by cultural prescription, then becomes a graceful way of giving in to the reality of a power relationship whose balance has already tipped against them. In this way, the theme of positive disengagement takes on a rhetorical function, enabling the parties to a potential conflict to avoid direct confrontation and a probable loss of face for the aged person.

To understand properly the role of the theme of withdrawal or "disengagement" in adaptation to the aging process in Indian society, it is necessary to make some conceptual refinements in the notion of "activity," as well as in that of "disengagement." With regard to the former it is clear that we must distinguish social activity per se from activity which involves the exercise of authority, dominance or management. While aging in Rayapur—or elsewhere in India—does not necessarily, or even typically, involve a decline in overall activity or social participation, it almost inevitably results in the older person relinquishing positions of control and authority, whether he does so willingly, or is forced to accede to the superior power of those younger than he. The process leading to such relinquishment is a truly mutually interactive one, between the old person and those in his immediate social environment, but in the more successful cases it takes place in the form of a voluntary retreat by the aged man or woman. Such a resolution is most successful not only because in an expedient sense it avoids the explicit conflict that a confrontation would involve, but because it enables the older person to make a positive affirmation of his adherence to central, culturally prescribed personal and spiritual goals.

A further distinction, with respect to the concept of "disengagement," is necessitated in the Indian context, because of the clear presence of two separate constellations or complexes of ideas—one involving the notion of rest, comfort, and dependency, while the other centers on the notion of withdrawal from the world's attachments and concerns. These two sets of ideas, which seem to be obviously related in a general sense, are revealed on closer examination to be quite different, and not necessarily implicated by one another. In the traditional schema emphasis is clearly upon the latter set of ideas. The purpose of the sacred texts, in their discussion of the life cycle, is to direct man how to live and how to prepare himself for the end of life. The ultimate goal for man in that context is spiritual, and the texts show no direct concern for man's worldly comfort or "life satisfaction" in the gerontologists' terms. While spiritual goals also have saliency for contemporary old people, the immediate concerns of bodily and emotional comfort seem to outweigh them for most people in the ordinary course of day-to-day life. While the notion that in old age one should be succored and cared for, that one should be in a position to "lay one's burden down" and have it taken up by others, has uniformly positive connotations for the elderly (although the realization of this ideal is not always possible in practice), the notion that one should free oneself from attachments to others and from concerns about family and community affairs creates sharply ambivalent feelings. Even those who accept this notion intellectually—and most old people are willing to agree that it is right and proper—have great difficulty following its implications in their interaction with other family members. In few instances are these ambivalences completely and successfully resolved. One reason for this is, of course, that the successful realization of a comfortable old age depends upon the performance of others, while successful renunciation depends on one's own will and mental effort.

In considering the issue of the cultural universality of the theory of disengagement in the aging process, it seems clear that this study lends support to those who have maintained that the way old people adapt to the stresses of the advancing years is affected in part by the way that their culture has led them to conceptualize this period of life, and by the kinds of cultural expectations they have formed in earlier years of what rewards and penalties old age should provide. Even in a society such as India, which in many ways provides a cultural framework peculiarly appropriate to a process such as is described by Cumming and Henry's theory, the realities of the social structure within which the aged live and have lived their lives, make conformity to the disengagement pattern impossible and even undesirable for the successful adaptation to aging of all but a few individuals who must be regarded as exceptional.

9 Ethnicity and Aging: Continuity Through Change for Elderly Corsicans

LINDA EVERS COOL
University of Santa Clara

Old people in traditional or nonindustrial cultures, by being embedded in a cohesive social structure of extended families, are accorded security in old age and have alternative roles and activities of value to themselves and the young. Do older adults fare as well and have opportunities in the city, especially industrial cities? The evidence from Hong Kong and from Oklahoma Indians indicates that old age in these contexts can be fraught with insecurity and poverty. Linda Cool explores this question among elderly Corsicans who have migrated from rural Corsica and settled in Paris. If urban dwellers, living in a large scale, socially heterogeneous environment are more atomistic and are less integrated with larger collectivities, then are not older urbanites more vulnerable to social isolation and disengagement?

Linda Cool continues and develops the theme of the last chapter: activity versus disengagement. As an anthropologist, she sees that this dichotomy has guided important research, but we have now progressed to the point where we can ask the question in a different way involving what we call the "methodology of the small". These techniques were perfected by anthropologists in tribal societies and are used to investigate smaller units in urban society. Linda Cool uses these techniques in her intensive interviews and participation with her older informants in both informal and formal contexts. She is concerned with an issue which has surfaced again and again in this volume. Survey research and the more intensive investigation of the cultural context can and should be combined. As Virginia Kerns argues, questionnaires elicit normative information which tells us very little about variation from the norms or even what these norms mean in the lives of our informants. Disengagement—activity is an issue, which if approached by survey techniques alone, manages to hide variation in social activity by focusing on the quantity of roles rather than quality.

Among her Parisian informants, Linda Cool finds variation and complexity. Ethnic identity is a very important component of the

Corsican experience in Paris. Ethnicity, however, is not one flat uniform variable, but is marked by degrees of participation identified as joiners, nonjoiners, and drop-outs as distinguished by participation in different kinds of activities that reinforce ethnic identity. Ethnicity is a resource to both elderly and younger Corsicans. One of the qualities discovered by Linda Cool is that there is a meaningful and valued exchange between young and old. The old have the cultural heritage the young want and, in turn, the old bolster their own value and self-esteem. Ethnicity, however, is a resource only to those who have it and in situations where ethnicity is a realistic strategy of a minority. It won't work for all older adults as we have seen among older nonreservation Oklahoma Indians who were too young to have acquired the vanishing culture that their young now want to rediscover.

Two major approaches have at least implicitly guided and given impetus to the majority of inquiries into the aging process. Activity theory, as initially elaborated by Cavan and associates (1949), was the first attempt to establish a working model for the elderly's relation to society. In essence, this viewpoint broadly posits a desire on the part of the aging individual to continue indefinitely his existing patterns of interaction and identification with society as a whole. But when, for reasons of physical, social and/or economic disruptions, the life-styles of middle age can no longer be maintained, the older person must adapt behaviorally to role loss by substituting other roles. In this manner, according to proponents of activity theory, the elderly can remain content, satisfied, and psychologically well-adjusted. Disengagement theory, on the other hand, is a consciously constructed rebuttal by Cumming and others (1961) to the then dominant activity approach. Their focus is rather on "normal" aging as a gradual and mutual withdrawal between the aging individual and the society. Although the disengagement process may be initiated by the individual or by the society, the result is the same—the slow but inevitable decrease in the number and complexity of the individual's roles over time.

These two approaches to the study of aging do not seem to be the diametrically opposed alternatives that their advocates claim. Both start from the assumption that old age is characterized by a generalized decrease in social roles and interaction. Their major difference lies in how they conceive the relationship between the individual and his society, that is, whether the elderly individual's eventual withdrawal from the social world is more a matter of his voluntary participation (as the disengagement theorists would argue) or of his forced retirement in spite of attempts to remain active (according to activity theorists). Yet neither approach explains why such a decrease occurs, or why some aging individuals seem to suffer less from its effects than others.

In spite of a call for its recognition (Maddox 1969:7-8), the issue of the heterogeneity of older people has been largely preempted by a desire to focus on homogeneity in the aging process. This is particularly the case since gerontologists have discovered what they believe to be a universal characteristic of aging in industrial nations, namely forced retirement of the elder members from the labor pool at a specific chronological age. The result has been the development of a stereotype of the old as a demoralized group deprived of its productive capacity and social identity. Social scientists, indeed all of society, have come to attribute this predicament to the sad, but inevitable, result of modernization and industrialization while overlooking the possiblilty of crosscultural (and intracultural) variation.

This study questions the case made for such an overextended uniformity in the aging process and suggests that older people are able to adapt to changing circumstances. By examining the situation of older members of the Corsican population in France, it seeks to determine if there are, in fact, other variables which may effect individual and group adaptation to the later stages of the life cycle. In particular, it develops an hypothesis concerning ethnic identity and ethnic group membership as potential mitigating factors which can act as buffers against the elderly's isolation and role loss in industrialized nations. Ethnicity becomes, in this perspective, an adaptive strategy that provides the older members of society with an exploitable social identity and a potential for ongoing interpersonal relationships even after retirement itself. It can also serve as the basis for power resources (defined here as valued knowledge of folk customs and ethnic history) which can be exploited for both social esteem and a sense of individual worth.

RESEARCH SETTING

To study ethnicity as a factor in the individual's capacity to adapt to growing old, three kinds of information are necessary: (1) where the people came from, (2) where they are now, and (3) how they got from there to here (Kalish 1971:82). To learn what it means to be old on the island of Corsica, the first research locale was the Niolo Valley, a mountainous region in the center of the island which historically has been dominated by a rural, pastoral economy. Because people from the Niolo tend to emigrate to Paris in search of jobs and the "good life" for themselves and their children, following well-established personal and regional chains of contacts, the French capital was the second research location and is the setting for this discussion.

This chain of migration, while it facilitated Corsican entry into the new situation of mainland life, was never able to establish truly Niolan or Corsican *quartiers* in Paris where one can go expecting to find a majority of residents from the island. This situation is a reflection of the difficulties for everyone (Corsicans included) of finding housing within easy access of one's place of work and within one's economic means as well as of the striking professional and economic diversity of the Niolans living there. During my seven months in the French capital, I was able to interview formally each member of a set of 74 Niolans aged between 55 and 92 years on two separate occasions (see Table 9.1 for an overview of the social characteristics of this sample set). These interviews gathered data on individual characteristics and on social interaction (particularly in kinship and ethnic-based networks and associations) as well as on self-assessed morale in old age (measured by the Life Satisfaction Index A of Neugarten, Havighurst, and Tobin [1961]). Fortunately, in the majority of cases my contacts with informants in Paris were not limited to the two more or less formal interview sessions. The Niolans extended invitations to me to return for dinner, for coffee, to attend family reunions, or to meet other friends. In addition, I regularly attended meetings and other formal and informal gatherings of the Niolans. Such activities add important depth to the research, for in this way I could observe both older and younger Niolans interacting under conditions more "normal" than the relatively formal interview sessions.

AGING AND EXCHANGE RELATIONS

One difficulty inherent in gerontological studies guided by the theoretical assumption of decreasing social roles and interaction on the part of the elderly is the tendency to focus on the *number* of roles performed by an older individual and on the *amount* of social interaction taking place. An evaluation of the *quality* rather than the mere *quantity* of roles played by an aging individual might counteract some of the explanatory deficiencies of existing gerontological theories. For example, in many societies power and influence are highly valued role qualities by which an individual exerts control over not only his own situation but also over the

TABLE 9.1 Social Characteristics of the Niolans in Paris

Total	74
Average age	68
Female	54%
Male	46%
Marital status	
Married	57%
Widowed	38%
Divorced/single	5%
Socioeconomic class (determined by job held before retirement)	
Upper	11%
Middle	34%
Lower	55%
Living arrangements	
Couples alone	34%
Individuals alone	17%
Couples with relatives	23%
Individuals alone	26%

larger group's activities. The paradigm of the exchange theory (Homans 1961, Blau 1964, Emerson 1962) views the problem of the aged as one of decreasing power resources as well as differential valuation placed on them by participants in social exchange, or interaction (Dowd 1975). Simmons (1960), for example, indicates that success in old age in rural-based, more traditional societies is grounded to a large degree in the elderly's continuing capacity to influence their juniors through the direct manipulation of such resources as knowledge, skills, and property rights. Maxwell and Silverman (1970) and Watson and Maxwell (1977) demonstrate cross-culturally that a relationship exists between esteem granted to elders and their control of information deemed useful by junior members of the society. In traditional Corsican society, for example, an older man was the absolute economic chief of his household through his ownership of key production materials (animals and land) and he retained respect as the community's major source of wisdom concerning animal husbandry and the affairs of men. Corsican women also exercised absolute command in their domain — the home. The arrival of a daughter-in-law particularly marked the end of a woman's perceived subservience to the needs of her husband and children and the beginning of her accession to the more valued role of power-broker of the hearth.

In Western industrial societies, the stereotypic belief is that most of the elderly have little to offer which may be viewed by younger people as useful or valuable: the aged's economic skills are often outmoded and their loss of income during retirement results in less monetary power. Thus the relative power of the aged in industrialized nations is commonly believed to diminish until "all that remains of their power resources is the humble capacity to comply" (Dowd 1975:587). Such compliance is often heralded as "proof" of the validity of the disengagement theory's assertions.

ETHNICITY AS IDENTITY

An individual's social identity is a function of his perceived or actual membership in categories or groups and of society's sanctioning this association. However, as the individual grows old, he may or may not be able to maintain the conventional identities of his earlier years. For example, a man forced to retire from work forfeits his role and identity as worker, loses the income perhaps necessary to maintain his earlier style of life, and may even drift away from previous work-oriented friendships. Likewise, as a married couple grows older, the likelihood increases that one partner will die, leaving the living partner without the role of spouse. Those older people who are unable to maintain a positive identity in the face of role loss are assumed to suffer debilitating effects, both social and psychological. Rose (1965), for instance, believes that older Americans are searching for group identity and support based on a rising consciousness of belonging to a minority group. To the extent that substitution of one social identity for another may be a mechanism by which the elderly can adapt to other role losses in society, Rose is correct. However, the new, substituted identity need not be that of being old per se. If one of the major quandries of old age is the acting out of an ambiguous "roleless role" (Burgess 1950; Rosow 1974) of being old, then a pattern of ethnic identity and interaction which continues from the younger years may help to mitigate some of the ambiguity and loss of identity associated with old age.

The ethnic group's historical uniqueness can furnish a context in which the aging individual may reinterpret his own life. In many ethnic groups throughout the world, youthful members are redefining their group's history, a fact which has important ramifications for the elderly members (Moore 1971b:90). In spite of the obvious successes of Niolan-born lawyers, doctors, and government officials,[2] the majority of older Niolans in Paris have been limited to jobs such as museum guards, *métro* workers, and *petits fonctionnaires* (low-grade civil servants). But the young Niolans' current reinterpretations of their people's collective history and problems now offer the elderly an opportunity to give a more positive meaning to their apparent lack of success and to remove the stigma of individual failure and personal inadequacy. The young now accuse the French government of failing to modernize the island, thereby forcing Corsicans to leave their homeland. "They [the elderly] are pioneers. They came here with nothing so that we could have a chance"—Niolan woman, 23, living in Paris.

Self-conscious attempts to explore the ethnic cultural heritage also provide opportunities for older Niolans to reinvent roles and power resources customarily allocated to their counterparts in more traditional societies: namely the roles of guardians and teachers of traditional knowledge and values—the bases of contemporary ethnic identity. Older Niolans in Paris customarily have performed the role of cultural broker (Wolf 1956:1075) linking new arrivals to the larger French culture, a function which reflects both their age and the fact that they have lived in the city longer and consequently know where to find jobs, housing, and other valuable urban resources. The rise of the young Niolans' interest in their ethnic background (and particularly in what makes them different from other French citizens) provides another meaning for the role of cultural broker—the elderly link younger people who never lived the old way of life on the island to their traditional (ethnic) culture. Thus, older Niolans offer the teaching of both instrumental (customs, knowledge of the economics of pastoral life, and so on) and expressive (language, family anecdotes, history) knowledge.

Rather than being ignored by Niolan networks and organizations in Paris, the old are encouraged to participate and are listened to with respect and interest. It appears that one of the keys to morale in old age may not only be the amount or type of social activity, but also (and perhaps more important) the individual's acceptance of the community in which he lives (and vice versa) as the focus of his social and personal identification. For example, the four members of the set with the lowest self-assessed morale are the ones who have not accepted their environment. They arrived in Paris late in life (after the age of 65) and were pressured into leaving the Niolo by their children "for the old people's good."

ETHNICITY AS PARTICIPATION

Ethnicity as identity can also provide the stimulus for group membership and involvement. Ethnic groups are a form of social organization: an ethnic group has a membership that identifies itself, and is identified by others, as constituting a collectivity distinguishable from other collectivities of the same order (Barth 1969:11). However, ethnic group membership may take at least three different forms among the Niolans in Paris depending upon the situational context, the individuals involved, and the needs of the actors: (1) informal interpersonal networks or groups based on a sentiment of brotherhood and friendship (or kinship),[3] (2) quasi-groups and informal interpersonal networks which continue to exist because of shared interest and a central meeting place,[4] and (3) formal associations with economic and/or political institutions defined by membership lists and collective goals.

This combination of formal associations and interpersonal networks is a balance between congregational and noncongregational ideologies and may well typify ethnic groups in other complex societies as well as France. The Niolans in Paris, for example, are dispersed throughout the city but overcome the problem of separation by making use of interpersonal networks based on friendship, kinship, and a sentiment of belonging with people from home (especially the village and region of origin). Such interpersonal ethnic networks are called upon for solution of a range of domestic and personal problems. In fact, Corsicans from all regions of the island emphasize the legitimacy and acceptability of "private" dyadic transactions for certain key activities: finding employment, obtaining special favors, or finding housing. The communication of common interest information and the presentation of a united front to the outside world are, on the other hand, the major functions of the formal associations.

Kinship and Friendship Networks. Numerous studies concerning urban family relationships (as evidenced by the frequency of contacts among family members who are not coresidents) and social class reveal close correlations between these factors. Individuals in the upper-middle class tend to report diminishing contacts with kin, and especially with collateral kin. One explanation for this phenomenon is the upward social mobility of the individuals (see, for example, Garigue 1958). Such findings appear to hold dire consequences for the social interaction of the aged, and particularly for older people who have no children of their own. However, this does not appear to be the case for the elderly Niolans in Paris. Rather, here the amount of reported social interaction with kinsmen does not vary significantly from socioeconomic class to class (see Table 9.2).

TABLE 9.2 Frequency of Contact and Socioeconomic Class

Frequency of Contact	Upper Class (N=8)	Middle Class (N=25)	Lower Class (N=41)	Total (N=74)
Daily	25%	28%	32%	30%
Weekly	37.5	52	32	39
Monthly	25	8	12	12
Once or twice a year	12.5	0	7	5
Rarely	0	8	15	11
Never	0	4	2	3

The fact of being a Niolan seems to ally immigrants in Paris even though their particular roles in the urban environment vary greatly, especially in terms of employment. As other research has shown (Laumann 1973:93), the average reported closeness of friends is *negatively* associated with occupational homogeneity--in other words, the more heterogeneous the friendship network is occupationally, the more likely it is that the respondent regards his friends as close. This may be because work-based friendships imply a more superficial relationship mediated by physical proximity and accessibility for much of the day. Friends with different occupations must seek each other out, which in turn reflects a higher valuation of the friendship. To the extent that a person chooses his friends on kinship or ethnic grounds, the more likely it is that his friends will be occupationally diverse.

The friendship of upper- and lower-class Niolans is not surprising from the point of view of the subordinate "friends." Since upper-class Niolans often act as patrons for new arrivals and for others who are not as fortunate as they, lower-class Niolans have a strong interest in making their wealthier counterparts retain a sense of solidarity and feel a full measure of their obligations. However, the interesting aspect is that the upper class individuals also claim the lower-class Niolans to be their *friends* and not just people they have sponsored in urban life. In many cases, such friendships represent continuing ties from childhood on Corsica. In addition, many of the outstanding Niolan successes in Paris are members of families that were well-to-do on the island--families that do not represent the traditional egalitarian picture painted by the Niolans of themselves. For members of these families, ties with poorer Niolans reinforce their claims of participation in the traditional way of life (now valued as the basis for contemporary claims to ethnic membership) which their families actually may not have known on the island—artisan skills, shepherding techniques, weaving, and so on. Ethnic respect is not automatically accorded to persons of high status in Paris, or on Corsica. The content and quality of their relationships with others, especially with their economic inferiors, also count among them and their peers. This respect is necessary if the upper-class individual is to compete successfully in ethnic institutions and to maintain his rural base for long-term power and security.

Strong family and parent-child bonds are important values in the Niolo and still create tight networks of solidarity among Niolans in Paris. In addition to their considerable resources for regular social contact with relatives and friends, all but a few elderly Niolans can find the assistance they need in special situations— someone to talk to about difficult problems and someone on whom they can rely in an emergency. Sixty-nine of the 74 sample members report that they have a confidante, either relative or friend. All but one of the elderly Niolans feel they have someone to call on in case of an emergency. Seventy individuals know of people on whom they could rely if they were sick, even for an extended period of time.

Informal or Quasi-groups. Upon arrival in Paris, Niolans seek to create and expand their networks of acquaintances in order to "get ahead" and to combat feelings of loneliness and homesickness. Unlike some urban migrants (for example, Price, 1975), Niolans usually arrive in Paris with strong networks of kin and friends. After becoming somewhat settled in the new environment, the Niolan migrant seeks to expand existing networks. The first possibility for such expansion by the Niolan male is the café, or bar. French bars differ from their American counterparts in many ways, but one of the most important differences is that regular attendance at a French bar does not carry a negative connotation of perpetual drunkenness. Regular participation in the urban "bar" culture is open to Niolan males of all ages (e.g., regular attendance at cafés is not related to age, chi square equals .13, n.s.). Although no women report that they regularly go to a bar, some state they do go occasionally with their husband or other male companion.

An alternative to the bar culture exists for Corsicans in Paris, an option which favors Niolan participation since it is managed by several young people from the Niolo. This is the Maison Corse, a place which serves the dual functions of tourist bureau for the island by day and meeting place for Corsicans after business hours. The first floor of the building is the tourist office. The basement, on the other hand, is a purely Corsican domain which is open every evening for meeting and drinking. There, young and old gather to talk, to sing traditional songs, and to meet friends. Once again, most women prefer the formal organization or their own networks of friends and kin, although younger women appear relatively frequently at the Maison Corse. The men represent all ages and walks of life. However, the young, men of retirement age, and individuals of the lower and middle classes are most prevalent. Some of the wealthier Niolans who serve as "patrons" and who want to extend their power bases use these gatherings at the Maison Corse to talk to their "constituents", renew ties, and to make further promises of aid in exchange for political support.

Formal Ethnic Organizations. Participation in voluntary associations is generally considered to be one of the effects of urbanization (Wirth [1938], 1964). This phenomenon appears to be associated with dense urban population and responds to the individual's need for more personal rapport and aid than that offered in daily urban life. For ethnic and other minority group members, participation in voluntary associations seems to assume even greater importance. For example, to compensate for discrimination met in other areas of life, blacks join more associations and are more active members than whites (Williams, Babchuck, and Johnson 1973: 637-676). One can view Niolan participation in voluntary associations in a similar manner. For the Niolans, the formal association is the Amicale Nioline (the French word *amicale* roughly translates into English as "association" or "grouping"). In Paris, this Niolan organization provides the medium for association, celebration, intra-aid, and regional and political activity. It is based partly on nostalgia for the homeland and concern for its welfare and partly on the perceived need for solidarity and interaction in the face of external discrimination.

REACTIONS OF OLDER NIOLANS TO THE PARISIAN MILIEU

The present study supports the belief that persons of similar status are more likely to form social interaction networks.[5] However, the argument developed here is that this similar status need not be that resulting from age or socioeconomic class alone, but may be based on a continuing identity. Some voluntary associations tend to exclude older people; examples include groups that are occupation-based, child-raising centered, and so on. This exclusion may not be intentional but rather may result from the different interests of younger and older people. However, the networks based on Niolan ethnicity encourage older people to participate in order to teach the traditional ways to the young. It seems that older people who maintain an interest during their working years outside the realm of the immediate work experience (politics, unions, hobbies, and so on) may adapt to enforced retirement more easily by turning to this outside interest. The finding that participation in voluntary associations relates to the psychological well-being of the elderly may be explained by suggesting that association membership functions to maintain or expand lifespace, to promote feelings of efficacy, and to reduce isolation through participation in wider networks.

We have seen that there are three types or levels of organizations open to Niolans based on ethnicity. However, these opportunities for solidarity fail to demonstrate the underlying diversity of individual participation. In fact, three types of participation are indicators of continuing identification with the ethnic group and the homeland. First is the ideal type of the joiners. Such individuals may participate in all three levels of ethnic activity, but the most important facet is their active membership in the formal club, the Amicale Nioline. The nonjoiners may participate in informal friendship networks and (or) in the unstructured quasi-groups at the bars or the Maison Corse. They do not, however, choose to participate actively in the Amicale. These two types are not mutually exclusive, in fact there is much overlapping (see Table 9.3). Finally, a third kind of participation, the dropouts, may be further subdivided into two types: those individuals who drop or ignore their ethnic identity and maintain no participation in ethnic activities, and those who drop their social relationships in general (examples of the so-called disengaged state).

TABLE 9.3 Niolan Ethnic Participation

1 Kinship/ Friendship Only	2 Informal Groups Only	3 Formal Groups Only	One and Two	One, Two and Three
29% (17)	2% (1)	4% (2)	29% (17)	36% (21)

The Joiners. As the name implies, the joiners actively seek out and participate in structured ethnic associations as well as in more informal kinship networks. Thirty-one percent of the set of aged Niolan informants in Paris actively participate in the Amicale Nioline by attending its regular meetings and its special events. Although they are of all ages and social classes, the joiners tend, in general, to be either young political militants (20 to 35 years old) who support regionalization and (or) autonomy for Corsica, or older, upper-level professionals (55 years and over). Members of the latter category particularly exemplify the Niolan success story in Paris: they live comfortably, receive recognition by others in their professions, and they enjoy the approval of Niolans in Paris and on the island (Table 9.4).

TABLE 9.4 Comparison of Joiners, Nonjoiners, and Dropouts

	Joiners (N=23)	Nonjoiners (N=35)	Dropouts (N=16)
Sex			
Male	57%	40%	44%
Female	43	60	56
Social Class			
Upper	26	0	13
Middle	44	20	50
Lower	30	80	38
Age			
55-64	52	46	44
65-74	35	26	19
75 plus	13	28	37

Although the joiners claim membership in the Amicale throughout their lives, their actual participation varies. Before age 30, there is strong, regular participation. This period corresponds to the individual's initial arrival in Paris and to his immediate need to find housing and employment. From the ages of 30 to 55 (corresponding roughly to the major portion of one's working life), active participation in the formal organization decreases. Ethnic membership and network participation do not end because kinship and friendship networks continue to flourish. However, individuals in this age bracket mention that both their interest in Amicale activities and the amount of time which they are able to devote to the organization lessen. Participation typically is limited to one or two special activities per year (usually the annual winter dance). After the age of 55, participation again picks up until it drops after age 75.

The age composition of one of the regularly scheduled meetings of the Amicale reveals the following pattern of participation: out of 36 in attendance, 28 percent were under 24; 11 percent were between the ages of 25 and 54; 19 percent were between the ages of 55 and 64; 31 percent were between the ages of 65 and 74; and 11 percent were over the age of 75. It is interesting to note that 39 percent (the first two age categories) of those in attendance were either students or were in their prime work years.

Participation in the Amicale's activities appears to be closely linked to the amount of time which an individual wishes (and is able) to devote to activities that extend beyond making one's living and raising a family. Younger people are particularly attracted to the meetings by a curiosity to learn about traditional Niolan folklore and about the island's distinctive values. In addition, they are more and more attracted by the increasing political orientation of the Amicale, particularly as it concerns the needs and rights of the island within the larger framework of the French bureaucratic system. Members over 55 generally play down this political component, preferring the attention and authority that comes with their knowledge of traditional ways of life on the island.

The Nonjoiners. The nonjoiners actively assert themselves to be Niolan and they help other migrants from their native region to the extent that they are able. However, they refuse to participate on more than a provisional basis in the Amicale's scheduled events because they do not like "club" life. The nonjoiners tend to be from the lower socioeconomic class; no members of the upper class belong solely to the category of nonjoiners (see Table 9.4). The nonjoiners may be divided into two somewhat overlapping groups. The first is composed of individuals who participate *only* in kinship and friendship networks. Ninety-four percent of this subgroup are women. This sub-category increases in size with age: 17 percent of the 55 to 64-year-olds, and 37 percent of those aged 75 years and over. The other subgroup of nonjoiners consists of individuals who participate in unstructured (quasi-) groups in addition to their involvement with Niolan kin and friends. Only one person claims that he participates in a quasi-group (a bar clique) but has no kin or other friends in Paris. He is alone in the city and lives in a tiny room, too small for company. Therefore he frequents a nearby Corsican-owned bar to talk with people and to pass the time.

Many of the nonjoiners have spouses who are not of Corsican ancestry. This helps to explain why participants in this level of ethnic activity do not belong to the structured clubs. The nonCorsican spouses find the kinship and friendship networks appealing, but they do not appreciate the sometimes excessively Niolan atmosphere of the Amicale.

The Dropouts. Although this category most obviously includes those individuals who simply choose not to participate in ethnic activities, the reasons cited by individuals are more complex. One major factor which causes a person to sever himself from his Niolan background is marriage to a person of a different ethnic heritage: 50 percent of the dropouts are married to nonCorsicans. A corollary to this aspect of denial of ethnicity is that individuals who marry nonCorsicans are most likely to be in the upper or middle class (62 percent of the dropouts belong to one of these socioeconomic classes). The group of middle-class individuals is composed particularly of people who have tried to succeed in the larger French society but have not quite "made it" according to French, Niolan, or their own standard of success. Social backgrounds continue to be important and difficult to disguise in France. An upwardly mobile Niolan might find his way blocked by his ethnic background or he might fear that this will happen. A response to such a situation is the creation of a new, unstigmatized identity by marrying a nonCorsican, changing one's surname, and practicing one's speech until the distinctive Corsican accent disappears (see Table 9.4).

A second major reason cited for not participating in ethnic activities is poor health. At first, this appears to offer support to the disengagement theory's claim that the old and society "need" to pull apart from each other due to the elderly's increasing incapacity to participate. All of the individuals in the present sample who state that they do not participate in ethnic networks because of poor health live in the household of one of their children and participate in family gatherings there. In effect, they are not as isolated socially as their statements originally lead one to believe. It seems that at least part of this reaction is due to the fact that these older people believe that they have no friends or contacts of their own outside of the immediate household. Four of the six individuals who claim to have no social interaction because of poor health arrived in Paris after the age of 65 and against their will (at the insistence of their children). These individuals have made little or no effort on their own to create friendships in the city. They have, in effect, given up interest in events and people. The two remaining dropouts state that they do not participate because they are not interested: ethnic identity does not constitute the only (or the most important) sense of belonging for them since they have numerous other roles to play (both are women in the 55- 64 year old group who are married to wealthy nonCorsicans).

LIFE SATISFACTION IN PARIS

The unsatisfactory health conditions of many of the dropouts as well as their feelings of being left out and of participating in (but not really belonging to) two worlds is reflected in their lower self-assessed satisfaction with life[6] (see Table 9.5). Other factors enter, for ethnicity is a variable like any other. In many studies of the aging process, individuals of the upper and middle classes are often predicted as having greater life satisfaction due to their level of income, education, and experiences in a variety of areas. This finding is somewhat substantiated here (Table 9.6).[7] However, upper- and middle-class individuals comprise 62 percent of the group of dropouts. Yet the mean life satisfaction score of the dropouts is lower than that of the lower-class informants.

TABLE 9.5 Life Satisfaction by Ethnic Participation

Ethnic Participation	Mean Life Satisfaction Score
Joiner	15.7
Nonjoiner	14.1
Dropout	12.8

TABLE 9.6 Life Satisfaction by Class

Class	Mean Life Satisfaction
Upper	16.1
Middle	15.6
Lower	13.2

Participation in ethnic groups and networks appears to be particularly important to the perceived life satisfaction of elderly individuals of the lower class, the individuals who are especially constrained by their environment (see Table 9.7). When ethnic participation of the upper- and middle-class informants is compared to their expressed life satisfaction, chi square statistics indicate no association other than that which might be expected to occur by chance.

TABLE 9.7 Aging Success in the Lower Class

Life Satisfaction	Regular Participation in Ethnic Groups or Networks	No Regular Ethnic Participation
Above median	17	1
Below median	10	13

Chi square equals 10.96, p < .001

The median life satisfaction score for Niolans in Paris is 14.44. This median is used as the baseline for defining those who are aging successfully in their own opinion and those who are not.

The mean life satisfaction scores also vary according to the age of the informant, with a decrease of reported morale accompanying increased age. However, chi square reveals little association when one relates age and scores above or below the life satisfaction median score: chi square equals 2.81, n.s. (see Table 9.8).

TABLE 9.8 Age and Life Satisfaction

Age	Mean Life Satisfaction
55-64	15.5
65-74	14.1
75 plus	12.9

CONCLUSION

Much anthropological and sociological literature concerning aging suggests that in a modern, industrial, urban society it is the implied threat or actual fact of social isolation which is the principal feature of the aged's decline (Townsend 1957; Clark and Anderson 1967; Shanas et al. 1968). Such alienation from the mainstream of one's society or culture, according to these authors, correlates with the constantly debilitating conditions of the elderly's physical and mental health. However, the present study has indicated that it would be wrong to believe that social isolation is invariably the outcome of growing old in the city. One simply cannot assume, as Rose's subculture approach to old age seems to take for granted, that once a person reaches old age he or she loses interest in everything but the fact of being old itself. To suggest that a group of people exists along a single dimension of common interest is unrealistic, just as it is inaccurate to assume that all older people are homogeneous in their interests, tastes, or needs.

Many older persons continue to maintain active roles in interpersonal associations. Old age, by nature, does not signal any weakening in the desire for contacts with family and acquaintances. Rather, like young people, the elderly seek a sense of continuity and community in relation to their world. However, in the city such interpersonal activities often take the form of complex and transitory relations with which the elderly may no longer be able to cope effectively. The disengagement and activity theories first appeared as a comment on the difficulty which many older people encounter while attempting to continue middle-age styles and levels of participation. What these theories overlook is that older citizens may (and often are able to) seek out alternative modes of action. The uniqueness of ethnicity in this regard is that it re-establishes social interaction at a level where the elderly can cope more successfully: namely, among kinsmen, through proximity, and within small-scale, informal organizations and networks.

A specific contribution of anthropology to the study of aging appears here. For in its search to understand the ranges of human behavior, anthropology usually focuses on the detailed study of small units and on how these units fit into the larger sociocultural framework. In pursuing such a perspective, anthropology exploits not only the advantages of the crosscultural perspective, but it also focuses attention on the diversity of adult behavior as it varies over time and space within a single culture. In the urban context, for example, the anthropologist analyzes not only the culture of the particular population set on which he or she is focusing, but also the nature of relations between that set and any other sets to which its individual members belong. Anthropology thus investigates the network (cellular) structure of a complex society by relating the constituent elements to the whole. It is this same network structure which seems to be best suited to the needs and capacities of older citizens. As Myerhoff and Simic have indicated, each cultural niche is a "distinct and unique resource subject to manipulation and individual interpretation and misinterpretation" (1978: 231).

This research suggests, then, that a stereotyped vision of society's older members is neither universal nor necessarily the case for that particular culture. The exchange of one social identity for another may well be characteristic of the mechanisms by which the old adapt in order to survive the loss of formerly sanctioned roles in society. Still, this new identity need not be that of old age per se. Substitution may be based on the progression to or the regression toward identities that hold out a measure of self-worth. These might include religious participation, organizational affiliation, or ethnic membership. The latter, in particular, provides a sense of personal continuity and communal belonging at a time in life when the older person begins to experience the diminution of his more conventional identities and roles founded on age, sex, and occupation.

Ethnic affiliation is not, however, a universal panacea for the problems of old age. At best, it offers the possibility for personal involvement and group membership for those individuals who seek it out. Participation is voluntary. To the extent that an older person keeps up (or resumes after an interruption during a busier time of life) his or her ethnic ties, there is a greater probability that a disengaged state may be avoided. Social relationships and organizational networks within the ethnic community of the city can serve, comparatively speaking, those same integrating functions of extended kin networks and traditional statuses often reserved for the elderly in rural, more traditional environments.

In Paris, the Niolan ethnic movement has assumed the care and respect of the elderly as one of its distinctive moral characteristics. To revere one's old relatives and to listen to their teachings are ways to indicate one's being Niolan. In effect, this respect for old people is a double-edge phenomenon as Lozier clearly has indicated: "Successful aging is based on the continuing existence of a social system in which behavior toward elders has social significance and social consequence for juniors" (1974:69). Both the old and the young benefit from such a situation: the old feel a renewed sense of self-esteem and social value, and the young find a more solicitous response from elders toward their grievances and opinions as well as reinforcement for *their* sense of belonging to the ethnic group.

While one might maintain that this reverence for the old is an anomalous case peculiar to Niolan ethnicity, I would argue the opposite position. Whenever an ethnic group depends for its special identity on a traditional heritage separate from that of the larger sociocultural context, its consciousness of belonging demands respect for the old as individuals who actually lived or were chronologically nearer that different life to which the membership collectively aspires. The old always represent proximity to that mythical time of ethnic purity before the contamination by the larger society and its values. However, the elderly's control of power resources is only valid and existent to the extent that the young value those resources. Moreover, the young members' reinterpretation of the group's ethnic history is as much a service to the elderly as to themselves. Their analysis of oppression and prejudice provides a framework to explain not only the group's collective frustrations in the larger society, but also the older members' personal lack of success in the pursuit of the better life. In this perspective, high morale in old age might not be so much the result of the individual's amount or type of social activity as it is his acceptance of the community in which he lives as a focus of his personal identity and social life. Ethnicity offers the old a continuing identity and source of control which may be compartmentalized during different stages of the life cycle but which remains available for use when needed or wanted. While ethnicity does not guarantee valued friendships for an older person, it does provide a backdrop for shared understandings and values, which are often the foundations of friendship. Such an identity and source of potential power (or control) is particularly important for those older people who have little else of positive value with which to identify in old age (i.e., those who are particularly constrained by their environment: the poor and the sick).

Future research must be undertaken to determine whether the "advantage" of ethnicity extends to other kinds of identities and interactional networks. Finding a place in society for the elderly that is meaningful to both the aged and to the larger social order is a problem which has yet to be solved. From our present limited perspective, we need to enlarge our view of the aged and their place in the social order. They can be more than the passive receptors of society's provisory benevolence which we have made of them.

NOTES

1. The research and studies forming the basis for this paper were funded by the Social Science Research Council Foreign Area Fellowship: Western European Program, July 1974—July 1975.

2. One notable success from the Niolo is André Rossi, who was formerly the Press Secretary of the Giscard government and recently has been appointed Minister of Foreign Trade.

3. This type of network seems to approach Mayer's definition of an "interactive quasi-group". This type of group is ego-centered in the sense that it depends on the existence of a specific individual as the focal point of the group. The actions of any member are relevant only so far as they are interactions between him and ego or ego's intermediary (Mayer 1966:97—98).

4. Mayer has called this type of quasi-group "classificatory". Common interests lie beneath this potential group to the extent that central interests and modes of behavior of the participants lead these individuals to interact and possibly to form definite groups at any time (Mayer 1966:97).

5. For example, Rosow (1967) and Blau (1971) stress that friendships and informal associations develop most easily among persons of like status. Rose (1965) believes that the most viable opportunity for creating associations in old age is among age peers. The argument continues that the social barriers between age groups are only a special case of the general social distance between people of unlike status.

6. The median Life Satisfaction score for the Niolans in Paris is 14.44. This median is used as the baseline for defining those individuals who are aging successfully in their own estimation and those who are not. Based on categories of joiners, nonjoiners, and dropouts versus those above or below the median score, chi square equals 11.82, $p < .01$. Thus, it appears that participation in ethnic networks and groups is associated with greater life satisfaction for these older Niolans.

7. Based on categories of upper, middle, and lower socioeconomic class versus those above and below the median score of life satisfaction, chi square equals 5.44, $p < .1$, an insignificant relationship judged by the standards orienting this research.

10 Old Age and Community Creation

JENNIE KEITH
Swarthmore College

A*t this point, we have focused on the relationships and interactions between older people and the rest of society (primarily younger people). As Jennie Keith points out, this is a product of the age-centrism of younger people. Researchers have only begun to explore the world of older adults from the point of view of older adults and the significance of relations of older people with older people. A definite boundary exists between young and old, reinforced by both through stereotypes. For example, recently I gave a talk to a group of college professors on anthropological research in retirement communities. One political scientist responded, "They sound just like people." Trying not to sound too incredulous, I replied "you've got it, they are people."*

Jennie Keith has it in this Chapter. We see the people quite clearly. By living in a retirement residence (Les Floralies), participating in the life of that community and charting the social and cultural order as it was being created, she sees the significance of peer relations. We shouldn't be surprised that her informants created a community or when friendship cliques form or when factional disputes tear the community into antagonistic camps. Nor should we be puzzled when we hear that the people at Les Floralies are interdependent, exchanging goods and services and identifying with each other. The fact that these older adults are taking charge of their lives and are concerned about their immediate present and the image of the future should not be startling. After all, we are looking at people who have had a lifetime of experience being human, negotiating a social and cultural world, and actively managing their affairs. Why should they abandon all of this, simply because they are people who happen to be old?

Les Floralies is not an isolated case as is apparent in comparisons with eight age homogeneous communities in the United States. Communities develop when certain features are present. Keith analyzes the effect of background and emergent factors upon community formation. The factors in each case are remarkably similar. Not only are they similar to each other, they are similar to the forces which create communities everywhere from squatter settlements to communities of nation states.

Jennie Keith demonstrates that old people can and do create communities and suggests that these communities may have special significance to their members who are often excluded in an age heterogeneous setting. Yet, these very communities are frequently branded by outsiders (usually younger) as the old folks home *or as a* geriatric ghetto. *It is our age-centrism again preventing us from seeing or even wanting to see. A very important lesson is to be learned here. Our limited theories and our images of older people have led us to underestimate the importance of many things including peer relations. In many respects the work of Jennie Keith, and of anthropologists like her, represent an anthropological corrective echoing the concerns of virtually every anthropologist in this volume. Jennie Keith calls for a creative combination of qualitative and quantitative research in order to know the cultural significance of what we are counting as well as knowing if what we are counting is worth counting. Furthermore, facts, figures, or descriptive accounts do not stand in isolation or magically fall together as the mosaic of a jigsaw puzzle. As insights and intriguing glimpses of a world we did not anticipate become more apparent, we must incorporate them into and construct a theory of age differentiation. A theory is necessary to integrate and guide research in aging in both simpler and in the modern complex societies.*

The word community has frequently been linked with various labels for older or retired people: retirement communities, adult communities, not to mention villages, towns, and worlds. The question which first led me into research with older people was whether community is ever an accurate description for collectivities of the aged, outside of an advertising campaign. Under what conditions and to what extent might separate residence become a setting for community among older people?

Anthropologists have traditionally been leaders in reporting closeup, inside views of little-known communities. Old people living together in industrial societies certainly fit into that "exotic" category, and anthropologists have provided much of the ethnographic information about them (Keith 1979). Crosscultural comparison based on extensive case studies is another research strategy central to anthropology. Because of the diversity of populations and settings in which we have observed old-age communities, it is now also possible to undertake comparative analysis of old age and community formation. In this chapter, I will present excerpts from my own ethnographic field study of old people in a new community, and, through a comparison with other age-homogenous settings, evaluate our current understanding of the conditions and consequences of old age as a basis for community.[1]

RESEARCH IN THE LES FLORALIES COMMUNITY

Like many anthropologists with a question about some little-known human group, I decided to move in on them: I lived for a year in Les Floralies, a new residence for retired construction workers just outside of Paris, France. Participant observation is the method anthropologists have found both most necessary and most productive in small settings about which very little preliminary information is available (Ross and Ross 1974). Following in this tradition, I lived in an apartment in the residence, ate meals in the dining room, and shared in all possible activities, both formal and informal: i.e., I learned to knit, played belote, worked in the kitchen, danced, watched television, walked to the corner cafe, attended Residents Committee meetings, visited, gossiped, and observed factional conflicts.[2]

Les Floralies as a Community. Because they live at Les Floralies, its 127 residents by definition share the territorial aspect of the community. The boundaries of this territory are also clearly marked for both outsiders and insiders: it is a building with a sign over the door and a fence around it. Local neighbors and merchants recognize residents as being from "the home." Residents in turn are protective of their shared space. They worry about outsiders who might intrude, and although they value freedom to come and go very highly, many would like to have the doors locked at least at night.

Community also has an affective dimension of we-feeling, and a behavioral and cognitive dimension of patterned social interaction, including shared expectations, norms and beliefs. Both social organization and we-feeling have developed to a high level in the residence.

Social Organization. The regular patterns of social living which define a social organization can be charted in many ways at Les Floralies. The residence is in a working-class suburb just across the eastern city limits of Paris. It is a 14-story glass and concrete building with studio and one-bedroom apartments. Two floors are reserved for people who cannot do their own housekeeping; the other apartments have kitchens and bathrooms. Everyone eats at least the noon meal in the dining room, which is the public arena for social contacts: both friendships and conflicts are made visible there. There are organized activities such as pottery classes, movies, a sewing club, and an elected Residents Committee as well as more informal card games, TV-watching in the lounges, and visiting. The most striking aspect of social life in the residence is its polarization into two factions, defined by pro- or anti-Communist attitudes. New arrivals are scrutinized for cues about their political identification (union membership, newspaper subscription, references to political figures), and then channeled into socialization by members of the appropriate faction. Those whose political orientation is never recognized remain social isolates.[3]

The flow of everyday contacts can be mapped into roles, groups, and factions; and attitudes about problems fundamental to continuation of these contacts— conflict, sexual relations, death, food-getting and sharing—can be described as widely shared norms and beliefs. Leaders, heroes, couples, workers are all roles which are clearly defined, and in terms derived from life inside the residence. There is even a well-known community drunk. Many friendship groups are recognized by other residents; and the faction borders which order so much of social life are not only evidence of social organization, but because of their redefinition in internal terms, also demonstrate the distinctiveness of this social order from its context. A ladder of social statuses is similarly both indicative of orderly, patterned interaction, and also, in its internal focus, further emphasizes the autonomy of social organization at Les Floralies.

The development of the Residents Committee as an institution is an important aspect of the emerging social organization, as well as a good example of the process. Originally defined very vaguely as a Social Committee concerned with recreation for residents, the Committee now is not only seen as a decision-making body for issues well beyond the area of recreation, but also as a mechanism for conflict resolution, and as an intermediary between staff and residents. A bitter election conflict was important in making the Committee more visible and more salient to many residents. Its triumph over petitioners for a separate leisure committee emphasized perceptions of its possible influence on the Director and consequently on the lives of other residents.

Specific incidents, such as a petition to hold Mass in the residence (hotly contested by the Communists) or requests for public funeral arrangements, were channeled through the Committee, and broadened its domain of action beyond recreation. Issues such as one man's right to bring a prostitute to his apartment, or another resident's invasion of the kitchen to shout complaints at the chef, were brought to the Committee, and set precedents for its role in conflict resolution. In both cases, the Committee asked the director to take action, which also strengthened the notion that it was appropriate for residents to reach the Director via someone on the Committee. In a mutually reinforcing spiral of events, the Committee is becoming more visible and more important to residents as its functions are expanded and defined.

Social organization at Les Floralies is also quite autonomous within the context of the surrounding society. Sources of social status, for example, are not a reflection of those current outside the residence. They also do not directly reject outside patterns, but rather emphasize the distinctiveness of this community by making many external sources of status simply irrelevant. There is no correlation between social status and age, health or contacts with people outside the residence. The old people with highest status at Les Floralies are those who participate the most in community affairs, either formal or informal.[4]

If staff members are looked at as representatives, or at least as members of the wider society inside the residence, it is also noteworthy that social organization among the old people not only goes beyond patterns imposed by the staff, but often exists in opposition to staff efforts. The possessive permanence of seating in the dining hall, central to informal socializing, persists in spite of staff proddings and invitations to residents to move around. Factional identities for activities organized by the staff (pottery class is non-Communist, flower-making for Christmas *is* Communist) clearly exceed their plans, and typically are completely unknown to staff members. Detailed beliefs spun out about food distribution (six slices of ham, one kilo of coffee per person, and so on) go far beyond staff intentions or knowledge, although they start from an activity, allocation of food, which is directed by a staff member. The entire web of informal relationships, friendship, mutual aid, couples, developed and exists outside of staff influence. The political factions which are key strands in this web of sociability are most definitely not approved by the staff; the director made several unsuccessful attempts at reconciliation or co-optation, each of which was duly interpreted by each faction as his susceptibility to manipulation by the other. Demands for a ritual recognition of death resulted from acute disagreement between the old people and a young administrator. The possibility of participation in funerals is now part of social life at Les Floralies because some of the old people recognized a need, and asked for a ritual response to it. Residents also express and enforce ideas, quite distinct from official rules, about how people should behave here. A drunken resident who frightened the women on his hall was ostracized in the dining hall although he had not broken any formal rule.

In other cases, an official rule may be manipulated by residents as a way of sanctioning disapproved behavior which the rule was in no way intended to cover: M. Fortin's whore, a threat to the community's image, but not a rule-breaker, became an illegal overnight guest, susceptible to banishment by the Director.

We-feeling. "We old people," "we working people," "we people who lived through the wars"—all these frequent uses of *we* provide the basis for the new one, "we residents." The sense of shared past and present experiences pulls these people together at the same time as it makes them feel distinct from others. Basic assumptions about the world, such as shortage of food, or division of the social spectrum according to symbols like Vichy and the Resistance, or Communists and non-Communists, are shared as automatically as the words to "Le Petit Vin Blanc." Physical aches, or the social pains of retirement or relationships with grown children, stimulate commiseration, often exchanged remedies, and at minimum a feeling of being understood and not suffering alone or as a deviant.

With a basis for we-feeling in their common historical, social and physical age, reinforced (or not fragmented) by their common social class, residents suddenly find themselves in a situation where, as they say, "we'll spend the rest of our lives." Their developing awareness of a shared fate is evidence for the we-feeling aspect of community at Les Floralies. The deep concern that the actions of any resident will affect the future of all the others is one expression of this feeling. The fight with the chef, the visiting whore, a handicapped woman who wanted to go on a trip with other residents, were all seen as possible threats to the entire community: staff members would be very angry with them all, the residence would be seen as disreputable, trips for everyone might be curtailed. Worries about the financial status of the residence are another indication of we-feeling, and also progressively bolstered it. In this case, an increasing number of residents saw themselves as more practical and experienced than the young Director, who they were afraid would spend so much on leisure "luxuries" that there would be too little left to pay for clothing. The fear that unwise budget decisions would have painful effects on everyone reflects a sense of common fate. The interpretation of what were seen as financial follies in terms of youth and inexperience emphasize age as a source of we-feelings. Even the fierce factional battles are a quickly dissolving contradiction to we-feeling. People fight about what is good for the community, because they feel tied to it, and to each other. The intensity of the battles is itself evidence for the force of those feelings.

FACTORS IN COMMUNITY FORMATION

Although the process of community formation is just beginning to be studied among older people, it has been quite thoroughly examined in other domains. Political scientists, for instance, have tried to understand what explains success or failure of attempts to build nations or to integrate them into larger communities (Merritt 1966; Coleman and Rosberg 1964; Deutsch et al. 1957). Observers of squatter settlements in many cities have asked when and how they become communities (M. Ross 1973). Utopian experiments offer another kind of evidence about factors which promote community creation (Kanter 1972). The conditions for community formation suggested by these kinds of research offer hypotheses about how the process might work among older people.

Conditions which promote we-feelings and social organization can be divided into those which are present or not among a collection of individuals at the beginning of the process– background factors; and those which may or may not develop over time– emergent factors. Social and cultural homogeneity of the individuals, the alternatives they perceive to living where they are, the difficulty and irreversibility of moving in, the size of the collectivity, the leadership skills available within it, and the material and social ties which may pull individuals away from the potential community are all background characteristics that can be identified early. Shared symbols, levels of participation in internal activities, proportions of social contacts shared with insiders, degree of interdependence among residents, their perceptions of threat from outside, participation in communal unpaid work, and the definition of status in internal terms are emergent factors which may develop with time.

COMMUNITY CREATION AT LES FLORALIES

Background Factors. The old people who moved into Les Floralies had many things in common besides their age. Age, of course, to begin with, has physical, social, and historical aspects. These people share the experiences of physical age, with its pains and techniques for coping with them; social age or stage in the social life cycle, with the emotional and financial adjustments of retirement and the problematic pleasures of relations with younger people, in particular, adult children; and historical age, with a common past branded by two world wars and a depression.

With the exception of 10 residents sponsored by the town in which the building is located, they are all either men retired from the construction trades or their wives and widows. Most of the women had also worked, either as domestics, or as sewing machine operators in garment factories. They are almost all French, and all spent their working lives in Paris. They are almost all poor; only 15 could afford to pay the $6-a-day for rent, activities, three meals a day, and medical care. The others turned over their assets to the public welfare program, which paid their costs at the residence and gave them back 10 percent of their original pensions as pocket money. The average monthly amount of this 10 percent is about $5.00.

Moving to Les Floralies was for most people a decision motivated by lack of alternatives. The letter telling them about the possibility of living at the residence for many represented an extraordinary, unhoped-for solution to problems of expropriation, loneliness, failing strength and poverty, combined with a strong desire to preserve independence.

The decision to move in, on the other hand, was a painful and difficult one, and was seen by almost everyone as irreversible. Privacy and an independent household are high values in France, and the vague notion of a collective life was frightening. As in the United States, the idea of special settings for older people in France also evokes images of the poor farm and the old folks home. Overcoming fears of entering the residence was a difficult process, made more difficult by the need for almost everyone to apply for social welfare in order to pay the fees. This required turning over assets, except for 10 percent of previous pensions as pocket money, and also involved an investigation of children's finances to see if they should pay a share of the costs. The bureaucratic struggle, the agony about imposition on children, and the perceived irreversibility of "going on welfare" added to the difficulty of the decision to come to Les Floralies. The decision was a costly one which required an important and irreversible investment, both psychic and financial.

Apartments at the residence are fully furnished, so that there is room for a minimum of additional objects. This restriction of possibilities for displays of ownership, as well as the extremely limited budgets of almost everyone in the residence, provided some of the restraint on material distinctions observed in many successful utopian communities. The dyadic ties which are considered a threat to community formation by many utopian planners are also mainly absent here. There are 14 married couples at Les Floralies, and one kin pair, an aunt and her niece. There are five couples who met in the residence, and who are recognized as couples only in the eyes of other residents, not in the legal terms relevant outside Les Floralies. These ties, which are rooted in participation in the residence, I think, bolster bonds of community rather than threaten them. In this sense, they are more similar to the distinctive sexual arrangements (celibacy or free love, fictional sibling ties) of many utopias than to the ties of married couples who arrive in the residence after many years together. One of the most dramatic evidences that utopias try to create something that has never existed in the real world is their attempt to break down the subgroup ties which in natural communities are the link between individuals and the community as a whole. Utopian experiments aim at tying the individual directly into the entire community, and they very often stumble on the obstacle of what are apparently very deeply-rooted habits of social participation via intimate ties to kin, sexual partners, and friends.

Since Les Floralies represents a case of unplanned community formation, it is probably more reasonable to expect it to follow the pattern of natural rather than utopian communities: the definition of subgroups should appear as part of the community creation process. However, the utopian examples do suggest that the importation of many exclusive subgroup ties from past life *outside* the new setting might be a hindrance to community formation, while the development of these ties *inside* the emerging community would not only increase its emotional salience for many individuals, but also add to the shared experiences and understandings which make the community a distinctive locus for social life. From this point of view, Les Floralies has a relatively low number of kinship, sexual, and friendship ties derived from the past, and a relatively high number defined in terms of present life in the residence.

Les Floralies was planned to house about 150 people; when I left, there were 127 residents. It certainly has the characteristic of small size, and its social relationships are face-to-face.

Several individuals with exceptional leadership skills provide the last of the background factors for community formation. The President of the Residents' Committee, the leader of the opposition faction, and several other militant faction members are talented, energetic leaders who both push and pull others into participation in residence activities, and also became themselves symbols of the emerging community.

Emergent Factors. A general judgment about participation in social life at Les Floralies is that it is both widespread and active:

many residents take part regularly in a variety of ways. At minimum, everyone shares a meal once a day. Both elections and parties attract almost universal participation. About 60 percent of the residents have very frequent informal social contacts; 32 percent are regularly involved in organized group activities; 27 percent work. Given this base-line of participation, it makes sense to look more closely at the specific kinds of activity which have promoted community formation in other settings. Do they also have an impact at Les Floralies?

Community-wide Events. Many community meetings, especially when they are daily, are characteristic of successful utopian experiments, i.e., of those which create stable communities. Frequent meetings which bring the individual into contact with the collectivity promote we-feeling. "Participation...makes a member more involved in the group, keeps him more informed of events, gives him a greater sense of belonging..." (Kanter 1972:99). Taking part in community-wide events, in particular political meetings, was also pointed out as one factor in the emergence of a remarkable community among squatters in Nairobi, Kenya (Ross 1973:77).

The time and place to start looking for the effect of this factor at Les Floralies is certainly noon in the dining room. Every resident is guaranteed participation in one group experience every day, since eating this meal in the dining room is obligatory. The significance of the dining room as a stage where friendship, conflict, leadership, and censure are made public removes any doubt that this meal represents spatial but not social togetherness. Even a person who sits and eats in silence is a spectator to the daily dramas of community life. People appear in the residence for the first time in the dining room; their progress toward social incorporation is marked by a permanent table place. Leavings as well as arrivals are learned about here, as the announcement of death is also made in the dining room. As people make their rounds of greeting, as those with problems stop by a leader's table, as conversation continues, the flow of information is both visible and audible. Banishment from social contacts is signaled by sitting at a table alone.

Meals are not the only community-wide events which take place in the dining room. Parties also go on there, and except for the one Mardi Gras dance which was defined as a Communist party function, there is usually extremely high and enthusiastic participation in these events. It was always far easier to count the few people who were missing, because they were ill or away from the residence, than to list those present. Memories of Christmas or New Year's celebrations, with details of who danced with whom, who was drunk, who sang, and so on, are one element in a developing repertory of shared experiences which is a basis for feelings of distinctiveness as a community. Appearing at one of these parties is often the occasion which marks, for a newcomer, first feelings of belonging, and for others, first real recognition of the new person.

The dining room was also the scene of elections for the Residents Committee, which offer another example of extremely high participation in a community activity. The elections added another landmark experience, peopled with villains and heroes, to the community repertory. Because they focused on the possibility of residents acting as decision-makers, the elections also raised the question of the "participation hypothesis" and its relevance to the residence. This hypothesis states that when members participate in making decisions which affect a group, they are more likely to value it and to feel solidarity among themselves (Verba 1961). Applied to the process of community formation, the hypothesis suggests that participation in decisions affecting the potential community should promote positive feelings toward it and toward other members.

Decision-making. A bitter, clandestine election campaign, a close to 100 percent turnout to vote, residents assembled in the dining hall to watch the votes counted and share in victory or defeat, and an unsuccessful attempt by the losing faction to create an alternative to the Committee, all focused the attention of many residents on the possibility of participation in making decisions. For most people at Les Floralies, those not in the militant core of a faction, this had been not so much an impossibility as something that had never occurred to them. The residence had a Director, so they assumed he made all the important decisions. Since they were welcomed by the Committee on arrival, everyone knew it existed, but certainly not as a powerful group of representatives.

Two specific issues demonstrate this awakening concern about decisions, a concern that could only develop after the elections and consequent conflicts posed the possibility of some resident influence. One complaint which was often expressed by people to whom I talked during the election period was that they never knew what went on in the Committee anyway. There were no reports made, and only rare (two per year) general meetings when residents could ask questions and bring grievances. This attack on the Committee was started by members of the "outgroup" Communist faction, but it became a very widespread subject of comment during and after the elections. The President and the Committee, incidentally, agreed with the need for reports and for general meetings, and had on their own made these requests to the Director for months. The force of factional divisions is neatly demonstrated as essential agreement is redefined into two positions. The Communists demand more information flow to restrain Committee dominance; the Committee members now say they need more information flow to protect themselves from accusations of being a power elite.

Expression of worry about budget mismanagement also increased after the elections. Again, this was an issue which members of the Communist faction used to attack the Committee by saying too much was spent on leisure and not enough for clothes. Committee members had frequently raised this same problem with the Director. Although there is wide concern about buying clothes, often discussed in terms of residents' age and experience versus the Director's youth and lack of practicality, the issue does not seem likely to blur faction alignments, since proposed solutions to the problem split along faction lines. The President and his supporters tend to think of the budget in zero-sum terms. Since there is only so much money, expenditures for leisure have to be cut back in order to have enough for necessities. The Communist position is that the residents have worked hard enough all their lives to be provided for now. Both clothes and recreation are supposed to be supplied, so if more money is needed, the retirement fund should increase the budget.

Resident participation in making decisions about life at Les Floralies is still at a relatively low level. However, awareness of the possibility of this participation, and conflict over which residents should be involved sharply increased, mutually stimulating each other, in the months following the elections. Since neither the conflicts nor the issues of general meetings and money for clothing show any signs of subsiding, it seems likely that concern about participation in decisions, and probably that participation itself, will continue to grow.

Work. The natural experiments in community formation provided by utopias show that communal, unpaid work can be a source of success. The experiments which resulted in stable communities were far more likely than the failures to have work systems which involved no wages, little specialization, and frequent communal projects. Working together for the good of the community appears to promote feelings of "connectedness, belonging, participation in a whole, mingling of the self in the group..." (Kanter 1972:93).

At Les Floralies, all residents do not work, so we cannot expect the effects to be so universal. However, the residents who do work share certain attitudes toward the community. For those who choose to work, this kind of participation seems to produce feelings of identification with the community as a whole, although not with all residents. People who work, for instance, are more likely to be highly loyal to the residence. The distinction between this feeling and attitudes toward other residents is enunciated in their response to the statement "We have a right to demand what we want in the residence." People who work tend to disagree ($r = .48$; $N = 64$).[5] Rather than answering only for themselves as workers, I think they are answering in terms of all residents, including the majority who do not work. They do not feel that the proper relationship between residents and the community is one of demanding, because they see themselves as on the receiving end of the demands from other residents. They express an identity with the community for which they work, consequently they disapprove the notion of "demands" which sets up a residence-residents opposition.

From a more general point of view, the presence of over 30 people with widely recognized work roles, of course, also strengthens the social organization aspect of community. There are many jobs whose definition is relevant only within the context of the residence—menu planner, food basket packer—and those which are carry-overs from outside activities—plumber, electrician—are performed only within the residence community, and within the residence system of nonfinancial reciprocity. Shared understandings about these roles are an important element in the distinctive social organization of the residence.

Interdependence. Cooperative brewing and selling of illegal beer is one reason for the high level of community achieved in a Nairobi squatter settlement. Awareness of interdependence was intensified by occasional police raids and the need to raise communal funds to bail out those who were arrested (Ross 1973:136-38). Interdependence, usually economic or military, is also a source of emerging community among nation states (Deutsch 1957). In general, awareness of interdependence promotes feelings of shared fate; and the mechanics of interdependence, the social contacts through which it is played out, promote the definition of social organization. Although exchanging hand-made underwear for a crocheted blouse, giving an arm en route to the dining room, or preparing meals during a neighbor's illness are not as dramatic examples of interdependence as co-operative moonshining, they have great significance for the people involved. Because of this significance, interdependence also has consequences for community at Les Floralies. Residents share three kinds of relationships which involve interdependence: help in sickness or with a handicap; reciprocity of goods and services; and social, emotional ties of friendship.

Help with Illness or Handicap. For a blind woman who is guided through her days by other residents, dependence on their help is heavy, and she is intensely aware of that fact. For many other people who are ill and then recover, the support they receive from friends and neighbors is also a deep source of reassurance. The actual care represented by housekeeping chores, errands, or meal preparation is greatly appreciated. However, the most important aspect of care is often the less tangible fact that someone is aware of the illness, will drop in to check up, and will act as a gadfly to insure staff attention. Residents did not feel secure without this knowledge. The fear of being ill or injured and lying alone and helpless, possibly even dying, without anyone knowing is a specter which recurred with frightening regularity in residents' conversations, often when they described their previous living conditions or those of some old person they knew outside the residence. The solace which the concern of friends and neighbors brought to this fear was a profound source of interdependence. It touched not only those who actually experienced illness and care, but also the others, who by observing these incidents could feel vicarious relief for their own possible future need.

Exchange of Goods and Services. Other non-emergency kinds of services and various material objects are also exchanged among residents. Products of knitting, crocheting, specialized sewing (e.g., of men's pants or women's underclothes), knowledge of herbal recipes, even ironing, are either exchanged against a specific item, or offered in friendship and reciprocated more generally by invitations to coffee or aperitif and with small gifts such as cigarettes or candy. For people whose incomes are miniscule, these exchanges often make possible having a new item of clothing, or an old one refurbished. The significance of this kind of reciprocity becomes clear with the realization that without it access to the item or the service would simply be impossible. The resident workers also perform many services, which are often seen as very difficult to obtain from the staff repairman. Repair of a leaky sink, a blown fuse, or a stubborn drawer makes life instantly more comfortable. It also provides a pleasant sense of arranging things between friends as compared with bureaucratic requests which emphasize the asker's dependent position vis-à-vis the staff, and to which responses come slowly if at all.

Participation in these transactions is not as widespread as in care for the ill or support for someone with a handicap. However, for those who do offer and receive things or services, the experience leads to feelings that life is more manageable and more pleasant because of relationships with other residents. Both kinds of interdependence are factors in community formation: the content of the exchanges leads to we-feelings; the social contacts through which they take place promote definition of social organization.

Social and Emotional Ties to Peers. The possibility of having social relationships with peers at all is for most residents greatly broadened because they are at Les Floralies. Interdependence in the most general sense, and perhaps the most important, is promoted by this availability of peers as friends and neighbors, sexual partners, and participants in the mutual process of defining appropriate norms for these and other social relationships in old age. Looking at interdependence in this way leads to the last of the participation factors suggested by other examples of community creation, the proportion of kinds of social contact shared by potential community members.

Range of Shared Contacts. Most residents do more kinds of things with each other than with anyone from outside. In some cases, of course, this is because residents have few active social ties outside Les Floralies. Many do, however, and although their emotional ties with specific individuals outside the residence, such as children, may be very strong, they almost never share the range of activities with these people that they do with other residents. Residents often share certain kinds of relationships with people both inside and outside Les Floralies. Help in an emergency, such as sickness, for instance, often comes both from children and from neighbors. The emotional significance of a visit from a child may be very great, but usually more actual assistance comes from neighbors who can attend to daily needs. Strong affective ties which develop inside the residence coexist with close relationships to children. Many of the contacts with people from outside the residence are shared with other community members. Shopping trips, a visit to the local cafe, or just going for a walk very frequently involve more than one resident; women in particular usually leave the residence with someone else. The arrival of guests in the residence is also often the occasion to invite friends and neighbors from Les Floralies for an aperatif or coffee.

Residents of Les Floralies share a high proportion of kinds of social contacts with each other. This proportionality is perhaps less than the perennial examples of community such as the Bushmen or the Pygmies, but far exceeds even the most closely knit urban neighborhood. They do not go outside of the residence to work; they leave rarely for entertainment, and then almost always with someone from Les Floralies. Political involvement pulls people inward, rather than sending them outside the residence. Battles are fought with inside rather than external enemies. Relationships between the sexes develop and are recognized inside the residence. There is no indication that people participate in community life to compensate for lack of outside ties, or that frequent contact with children or friends from outside is contradictory to intense involvement in life inside the residence. Emotional ties to children seem to be part of a distinct aspect of residents' social lives. They are different from, and therefore not in competition with emotional bonds with other residents. Many contacts with friends and relatives from outside Les Floralies actually take place at the residence, and are often shared with other community members.

It is because residents at Les Floralies share such a high proportion of their social contacts with each other that many of the other factors in community formation can operate here. Generally high levels of participation in community activities, concern with decision-making, interdependence, and the appearance of community symbols would be far less likely if residents engaged in only a restricted range of encounters, while most of their spectrum of social contacts lay outside Les Floralies. It is through sharing many kinds of contact that residents become aware of the commonalities which lead to we-feelings; and a distinct social organization becomes recognizable as this variety of social ties stabilizes into patterns, and evokes shared ideas about what the patterns should be and how they should be maintained.

Threat. Although the residents at Les Floralies do not face the bulldozers or nuclear coalitions which have stimulated feelings of community among squatters or nations under threat, they do feel threatened in certain ways which lead them to awareness of their shared fate. The residents, in terms of threat, are more similar to some utopians who wanted to create a better social world precisely because their position, for instance as a religious minority, was precarious in the wider society. Although these old people certainly did not come to the residence with the intention of creating a community as a haven, the community which is emerging there does gain some impetus from their feelings of being threatened by the world outside—or its representatives inside– and from the protection which the community offers against this threat.

Because they are old and poor, most residents are frightened by many aspects of living in the wider society. They are afraid of inflation, of being hurt or injured alone, of being attacked in the street. They also feel more diffuse kinds of threat from changing times. Developments in technology and the growing emphasis on education have shifted the value on their manual skills. They do not understand the youth of today and are afraid of what they will make of society. As old people and retired people they feel they have little status, and most of them feel helpless to do anything about it.

Many residents talk about the physical safety and security offered by Les Floralies. Although they feel uneasy about having so little cash, they also count on the financial security of living there, where they are promised food, clothing, and medical care as well as shelter regardless of economic ups and downs in French society. Because they are *all* old and retired, these sources of low status outside the residence become irrelevant, and can in a sense be escaped inside. Many residents are beginning to believe that they can have some control over their lives in the community, a possibility which is minimal, to say the least, in the world outside. Les Floralies offers protection from threats to physical and financial security, to status and sense of personal efficacy– all threats which continually faced these old people in the world outside.

The world outside is present in the residence in the persons and attitudes of the staff. There are two ways in which residents feel threatened by the staff; and we have already seen what they do to protect themselves. Financial decisions which seem to residents to emphasize luxury items such as a kiln over necessities such as clothing raise fears of the residence running out of money. Residents try to combat this threat by participation in decision-making to bring their own practical experience to bear on what they fear is the youthful impracticality of the Director. Residents also feel threatened by the attitudes of a staff member, such as the head nurse, who they complain often treats them with minimal respect, ordering them around or not bothering to close a door during a physical examination. She also poses another kind of threat because residents see her as disorganized and unreliable as a source of medical attention. Residents help each other in illness, not only offering care themselves, but often making sure that a nurse comes to visit and brings medication when it is needed. Protection against loss of dignity is more difficult. Residents do sometimes turn to faction leaders with complaints, and these complaints may then be transmitted to the Director. The most common solace which residents offered each other, according to my observation, was the catharsis of a gripe session, in itself a source and reinforcement of we-feelings.

Threat plays a role in the formation of community at Les Floralies as it does in other settings. The precarious position of the poor older person in French society is not as extreme as that of persecuted minorities or illegal squatters. The old people, as in many industrial societies, suffer more from neglect than from organized attack. However, the financial and physical insecurities of old age and poverty are extreme enough to make the residence seem the only alternative available to many people. This kind of "no place else to go" commitment promotes a sense of shared fate among residents as it does among squatters or utopians. Escape from the status consequences of age has resulted in an important aspect of distinctive social organization at Les Floralies, the irrelevance of age in its social status system. Reaction to perceptions of threat from staff actions and attitudes have stimulated participation in decision-making and interdependence, which in turn promote community formation.

Symbols. As people's lives intersect in an increasing number of dimensions, certain aspects of their lives together may be elevated to the status of symbols which repɪesent their common experiences and evoke emotional responses to them. The presence of these symbols, distinctive to members of the emerging community, then further promotes community formation by emphasizing their separateness and uniqueness both in terms of their shared experiences and of their feelings about these experiences. At Les Floralies, certain individuals and events are becoming symbols. The oldest woman in the residence is a symbol of the ideal community member, universally loved and respected. The worst possible community member is also a common point of reference, as is the President. Events like the elections also become shared landmarks used by residents to situate other events in time, or to explain the polarized state of social life.

COMMUNITIES OF OLD PEOPLE IN THE U.S.

"You mean they're *French?*" was the startled reaction of one researcher who heard me talking about the residents of Les Floralies. Since she had missed the beginning of the conversation, she assumed that these people who sounded so familiar to her must be old Americans, living in public housing like that she herself had studied. The similarities among communities of old people in widely different locations are remarkable. Of the seven U.S. residential setting for old people about which we have extensive ethnographic information, six are emphatically described as communities. "United against the outside world," "cohesive community," "vibrant community of old people," "communally cohesive," are typical portraits of environments ranging from mobile home parks in California and Arizona to public housing in San Francisco, private condominiums in California, and a Sephardic Home in New York. The seventh case, a tri-ethnic public housing complex in Miami, is not a true negative example, as it also has high levels of community within its ethnic subgroups, which are in turn linked through culture brokers.

The old people in all of these situations have created communities out of similar feelings and activities. Friendships, sexual ties, fictive kinship; distinctive norms about sex and death; internally focused conflicts; resistance to outside status ranking; reciprocity of goods and services; support for ill or handicapped; autonomous definition of roles and formal activities, all appear again and again.

COMMUNITY FORMATION IN THE U.S.

Tables 10.1 and 10.2 compare the process of community formation in these American cases to Les Floralies in terms of both background and emergent factors.[6]

Among the background factors, the clearest consistency is in the homogeneity and small size of these groups of old people. The ethnically heterogeneous public housing complex at Fresh Pond does not counter the significance of homogeneity to community formation, but does offer a view of this relationship in a more complex setting. Fresh Pond is described as comprising ethnic subcommunities, which are linked together, particularly for political opposition to HUD, by charismatic individuals who serve as culture brokers. Homogeneity plays a role within these subcommunities, as each ethnic group is more homogeneous than Fresh Pond as a whole in terms of other characteristics such as marital status, previous residence, religion, or education. Particularly strong subgroups have formed in certain buildings which are highly homogeneous, e.g. by sex, ethnicity, and marital status. The distinctiveness of Fresh Pond as a community is underscored by the fact that its ethnic heterogeneity is less of a threat to communal ties than it is in the society outside: "The relationships among the groups are more harmonious, and the boundary lines more fluid, than might be predicted by the ethnic politics of the surrounding area" (Kandel 1979). Research in public housing for the elderly in Milwaukee also supports the finding that under certain conditions, the commonalities of age-homogeneous residence may promote greater ethnic interaction and harmony than is usual in the wider society (Wellin and Boyer 1979).

Individuals with leadership skills are also mentioned by almost all the observers. Although the information is not complete for some other characteristics, most of what is available corroborates the Les Floralies experience. Especially persuasive evidence is available about the influence of threat, since Equus Estates and Casas del Oro, which vary in terms of that factor, were directly compared by the same anthropologist. Fry reports that Casas del Oro residents have "reacted by intensifying their social organization and social life" to financial threats resulting from the bankruptcy of the park's original developer (1979).

There are two exceptions to the consistent influence of these factors. First, the residents at Arden can resell their condominium apartments easily, which makes their decision to enter that setting more reversible than that required in the other cases. Since Arden is described as having a high level of community, this requires explanation. Irreversibility of the decision to enter an age-homogeneous setting may be less important to community formation among old people than theories about community creation in other contexts suggest. Or, perhaps there are other aspects to irreversibility than the financial; the residents of Arden are described as having cut many of their formal and informal ties with "outsiders." These might be difficult to revive for a person leaving Arden. Since the measures of community used in these various cases are not identical, and are not applied by the same observers, it is also of course possible that the level of community at Arden is not as high as in the other examples.

The second exceptional factor which operates differently at Idle Haven and the Sephardic Home than in the other communities is that of pre-existing social ties among residents. The proposition that socially exclusive ties among kin or friends are a threat to community is derived from utopian experiments. At Les Floralies very few people arrived in the residence with these kinds of ties. The relationships which developed at Les Floralies, however, seemed to be an important part of the community formation process, rather than any obstacle to it. The experiences of people at Idle Haven and in the Sephardic Home go farther. One-third of the Idle Haven residents who responded to the questionnaire had known someone in the park before they came. In addition, there were 12 extended family households, and 11 sets of relatives living in separate mobile homes. Kinship ties and lifelong friendship networks were also central to social life in the Sephardic Home.

These findings emphasize the fact that the original proposition about social exclusivity was derived from the study of utopias, which strive to immerse individuals in a direct rapport with the

TABLE 10.1 Background Factors in Community Formation

	Homogeneity	Perceived Alterna-tives	Invest-ment	Irre-versi-bility
Les Floralies (Ross 1977)	High occupation income nationality	Low	High	High
Idle Haven (Johnson 1971)	High class income ethnicity	Low	High	High
Merrill Court (Hochschild 1973)	High class religion ethnicity marital status sex place of origin income previous residence	?	?	?
Sephardic Home (Hendel-Sebestyen 1979)	High ethnicity religion place of origin previous residence	?	?	?
Arden (Byrne 1971, 1974)	High class ethnicity marital status political affiliation previous residence	Low	High	Low
Equus Estates (Fry 1979)	High class ethnicity marital status	?	Moderate	Moderate
Casas del Oro (Fry 1979)	High class ethnicity marital status	?	High	High
Fresh Pond (Kandel & Heider 1979)	Low income High within ethnic groups & some buildings	Low	?	?

TABLE 10.1 Background Factors in Community Formation (continued)

	Material Distinctions	Institutionality	Leadership	Pre-existing ties	Size
Les Floralies (Ross 1977)	Low	Moderate	High	Low	127
Idle Haven (Johnson 1971)	Low	Low	High	Moderate	360
Merrill Court (Hochschild 1973)	Low	Low	High	Low	43
Sephardic Home (Hendel-Sebestyen 1979)	?	Moderate	?	High	180
Arden (Byrne 1971, 1974)	?	Low	High	Low	5,011 sub-divisions of 150-250 move in together
Equus Estates (Fry 1979)	Low	Low	High	Low	50 mobile homes
Casas del Oro (Fry 1979)	Low	Low	High	Low	69 mobile homes
Fresh Pond (Kandel & Heider 1979)	Low	Low	High	Low	105

TABLE 10.2 Emergent Factors in Community Formation

	Participation in Community-wide Events	Contacts inside Community	Inter-dependence	Work	Decision-making	Status Definition Internal	Threat	Symbols
Les Floralies (Ross 1977)	High	High	High	Moderate	Moderate	High	Moderate	High
Idle Haven (Johnson 1971)	High	High	High	Present—extent not clear	Moderate	High	Moderate	?
Merrill Court (Hochschild 1973)	High	High	High	High	Moderate	High	Moderate	?
Sephardic Home (Hendel-Sebestyen 1979)	High	High	?	Present—extent not clear	High	?	?	?
Arden (Byrne 1971, 1974)	High	High	High	?	High	Present—extent not clear	Moderate	Present—extent not clear
Equus Estates (Fry 1979)	High	High	High	Low	Low	High	?	?
Casas del Oro (Fry 1979)	High	High	High	High	High	High	Moderate	?
Fresh Pond (Kandel & Heider 1979)	Moderate	High	High	?	High	?	?	?

community as a whole. In most natural communities, individuals are, on the contrary, linked into the community by just such mediating ties as kinship and friendship. In the light of these two other studies, the fact that there were very few pre-existing social relationships among residents at Les Floralies or in Merrill Court was probably not an important aspect of community formation.

The conditions under which pre-existing social relationships are likely to promote rather than threaten community are when everyone in the new setting shares them, e.g., the Sephardic Home, or when those who share them are a minority, e.g., at Idle Haven. If a majority share this kind of tie, it may become the dominant basis of social participation, and may make problematic the integration of other residents. When the people who share this kind of bond from the past are in the minority, it seems more likely that they will also be drawn into present social life in the new setting unless the tie has some particular salience in the new setting, e.g., married status in a situation where widowhood is an important basis for communal feelings and activities (cf. Jonas 1979). The universal continuity of social roles and relationships which is present in the Sephardic Home makes the question of contradictions between past and present social organization almost meaningless. An entire generation of a tightly-knit ethnic and religious community simply moves together—as they have changed neighborhoods before—into a new living arrangement, without interruption of their participation in kinship, friendship, or factional ties.

The degree of institutionality of an age-homogeneous setting is explicitly raised by the case of the Sephardic Home. The anthropologist who worked there argues that community exists, in spite of the institutional context, because of the ethnic, kinship, and religious ties among the residents. Looking at all the cases of community formation, including Les Floralies, the degree of institutionality appears as an important additional background factor.

Kleemeier has hypothesized that, in general, the degree to which special settings for older people are institutions with social control over their residents has a negative relationship to social activity (Kleemeier 1959:347-351). Spontaneous social activity is the least likely in the most institutional settings, so that if community formation is to take place among older people, the setting in which they are brought together should not be too institutional. Residents must feel some independence from the staff, which can happen in various ways. At the Sephardic Home, other roles and loyalties crosscut the staff-inmate distinction. At Les Floralies, potential domination by the staff is counteracted by residents' feelings that staff members are employees who can be fired; by perceptions of them as young, inexperienced and less competent than residents in certain domains; by identification with them as fellow workers or grandparents. At Idle Haven, residents bring informal influence to bear on the manager; the residents of Equus Estates ejected the manager from their dominant clique; and in other parks residents have organized formally in opposition to managerial policies, in one case extending their conflict to the California State Legislature. Certainly, mobile-home parks are not institutions, although they do have rules and regulations. In Arden, as in most condominiums, a residents board has control over the management firm which is paid to administer the community. Although there are HUD rules, public housing for the elderly is not usually managed by a resident staff in an institutional style.

Thorough reporting of a negative case signals a degree of maturity for a research enterprise. The study of old-age communities has reached this point with the recent description of two public housing environments, one in Cleveland and one in Leeds, England (Goist 1978). Although both are age-homogeneous, and although residents of both also have in common Eastern-European Jewish backgrounds, only the English residence has become a community. Comparison of the two both reinforces the importance of factors we have already identified, and also introduces new ones. The Cleveland building has no dining room or day center, both significant stimuli to social participation in other settings. Also, the director of the Cleveland residence is opposed to any attempt by the old people to organize activities or to share in decision-making: he threatens them with eviction. In addition, the anthropologist who spent three years with these old people is persuaded that their previous history of residential transience has prevented them from creating and maintaining friendship ties, which in turn has blocked their acceptance of an old-age role, which now obstructs peer bonds with their coresidents. The strongest link among the Cleveland old people appears to be sharing and not challenging idealized images of their children's success and concern for their parents. A fascinating reminder of the importance of qualitative information comes in the comparison with the English old people: services performed by the English and American children for their parents are virtually the same; but the perceptions of the old people are positive in one case, negative in the other.

OLD AGE AND COMMUNITY CREATION: SUMMARY

Old people do create communities; and they do it under the same conditions that promote community among many other groups, including utopians, suburbanites and urban squatters. Anthropological research in old people's communities reveals the same combination of universality and diversity that we have reported about in many other aspects of human life. The diversity in forms of community is great, and the variety of detail in rituals, speech, beliefs, and behaviors abundant. On the universal side is the consistent influence of similar factors in promoting community formation. As we have often done before on returning from a field visit to some exotic tribe, anthropologists working with old people report that, most fundamentally, they are people. They have the same need for community, and create it under the same conditions; the difference may be in its precious significance to them, who are so often excluded from community in modern societies.

CONCLUSION: ANTHROPOLOGY AND OLD AGE

We still know very little about social ties among older people. Perhaps through a kind of age-centrism, younger researchers have concentrated on the relationships of old people to younger members of society, in particular to their kin. Since the evidence we do have demonstrates so consistently that peer relationships can meet important needs for old people, we must learn more about their friendships, groups, and communities.

Anthropology has both technical and theoretical contributions to make in this endeavor. Extended, holistic study of age-homogeneous groups and communities is necessary for discovery of the conditions that promote development of peer solidarity and organization, and of the mechanisms through which these attitudes and behaviors emerge. The hypotheses we now have can be used to guide the selection of age-homogeneous situations that vary in terms of the factors hypothesized to promote formation of peer communities. Systematic comparison of settings varying along these dimensions will make possible evaluation of the contribution made by each, of their interrelations and of the timing of their relative effects. Further negative cases, in which age peers are available, but not "used," will also be important bases for comparison.

An essential extension of anthropological research on aging is to the majority of old people who do not live in separate residential settings (cf. Carp 1976). The kind of qualitative data we are beginning to acquire about those settings must also be obtained about the social lives of old people in more usual circumstances. The data we have so far are predominantly quantitative: how many and what kind of contacts old people have with what categories of individuals. Participant observation as well as ethnoscientific eliciting techniques and the mapping and interpretation of social networks should reveal the significance to old people of different types of ties to peers and others.

Anthropological study of old people could have important consequences for easing the pains—both physical and social— of aging in modern societies. The research discussed in this paper, for example, emphasizes the needs that old people, under certain conditions, can meet for each other. Identification of these conditions would make possible policies to promote them, and consequently more satisfying years in our lengthening lives. The surprise with which both writers and readers respond to communities of old people is also a reminder of how little younger people know about how aging looks to the old. Anthropologists are specialists at discovering such insider's views; and awareness of them is certainly crucial to policy-making that affects older poeple. We are also experienced at the documentation of diversity. Since, as Bernice Neugarten puts it, as we age we become "more so," older people are the *most* diverse group in our population. Any policy must take account of that diversity, and this is not possible without adequate information. Policy implications of the community studies reviewed here provide an example and a warning. The earliest report of the benefits of peer communities were received with shock: how could age segregation be beneficial? Now it is necessary to remind policymakers that age-homogeneous housing is not necessarily good for everybody, that we do not know how representative of other old people is the very small minority who live in these settings, that the most important housing requirement of older people is *choice*. (cf. Carp 1976).

Finally, an anthropology of aging will itself come of age when the conditions and consequences of age-border definition in industrial societies are interpreted in a general theory of age differentiation. Anthropologists have contributed important analyses of age organization in traditional societies of Africa and Latin America. Research on age grouping in industrial societies is, with the active participation of anthropologists, now reaching down the life course beyond adolescence to old age. Even preliminary comparison of age-graded relationships in these disparate settings suggests some tantalizing hypotheses, for instance, about age organization as a means of reduction or avoidance of conflict in other spheres such as kinship (cf. Spencer 1976; Messer 1968, Keith 1979), or about the causes and consequences of egalitarianism within age groups (Legesse 1979).

A major contemporary challenge to anthropology is the need for theories that can encompass data from a wider range of societal complexity. Age organization offers a focus for that challenge and a promising arena in which to meet it.

NOTES

1. Portions of this chapter have been previously published (Ross 1977) and are reprinted by permission.

2. This entire study is reported more fully in Ross 1977.

3. Socialization into the residence is analyzed in more detail in Ross 1975.

4. Social status is analyzed more fully in Ross 1975b and 1977. Also see these sources for detailed correlations between social status and other characteristics.

5. This is significant at the .05 level.

6. These tables are based on my own reading and scoring of the sources cited. Except where specifics are noted, the score is based on more general reports by the researcher, e.g., "An extraordinary amount of neighborly interaction occurs . . ." (Byrne 1974.139) or "They see their housing development as a sanctuary in a world increasingly troubled with hippies, political radicals, minority groups, and criminals--a haven where responsible adults who have worked for a living can safely uphold the middle class values of their own generation" (Byrne 1974:146).

11 Health Perception in the Elderly: Its Cultural and Social Aspects

EUNICE BOYER
Carthage College

Health undoubtedly is one of the major difficulties associated with aging. Modern medicine has effectively brought the acute diseases under control, leaving the chronic ailments and infirmities of old age as the most wide spread debilitators of the human body, primarily because more people are surviving to old age. Perception of health is not a simple matter. It is quite clear that perceptions of our physical well-being are culturally structured. As Eunice Boyer argues, health perception parallels a physician's evaluation, but it also is conditioned by involvement in roles and activities. In investigating this question, she extensively interviewed elderly informants in public housing projects for the elderly and conducted several months of fieldwork involving observation and open-ended interviewing.

Eunice Boyer continues a theme developed by Jennie Keith. We know amazingly little about the social ties of older people and the effects of the immediate environment upon older adults. In this chapter the author examines an environment, public housing for the elderly, which when viewed from the outside possesses a double negative stereotype of poverty and homogeneously old. Probing beyond this stereotype, Eunice Boyer sees an environment of opportunity; just as Keith found that old people create communities of peers, Boyer finds that these communities provide a setting which has positive effects on health perception. The isolating effects of physical impairment are minimized through the physical structure of the environment (i.e., there are elevators rather than stairs). Of even greater importance, is the availability of peers and avenues for participation. Both of these factors offer opportunities, which if taken, improve the perception of one's health.

A combination of quantitative analysis of survey data and more intensive qualitative data obtained through her observations, gives us insights into the effects of activity patterns upon health perception. Organizational membership, increases in activities after moving into the housing project, and contacts with close friends all positively effect the evaluation of one's health. The statistical techniques used also permit functional mobility to be controlled for or held constant. Even with the effects of this more objective mea-

sure of health minimized, the relationship between role and activities and health perception is clear. Although the objective measures of health and mobility are most important in shaping health perception (simply because they are hard to deny), roles and activities, too, have significant consequences for the interpretation of physical well-being. This is one of the benefits of age concentrated housing anthropologists have found as they explore the culture of these environments.

In the central and deteriorating sections of many American cities, publicly owned apartment buildings for the elderly poor arose like mushrooms during the 1960's. (Present government policy calls for rent-subsidized housing built and managed by private firms.) These housing projects represent a new venture in care of the elderly, an adaptation to the new circumstances which are found only in advanced industrialized nations. This study was made in six public housing projects in a middlewestern city.

The development of age-segregated housing for the elderly has been criticized as "ghettoization," as discriminatory and as isolating for the elderly. To do field work in buildings such as these is to reject this stereotype. The residents of the buildings are overwhelmingly satisfied with their residential arrangements and, if asked, reject integration with public housing for younger families. The residents are involved in overlapping networks which tie them together in relationships of mutual concern and help, of shared likes and dislikes.

Public housing for the elderly is not, of course, a utopia, nor is old age an ideal state for all of the elderly. Among problems which concern the residents, their own health and the health of friends are frequently mentioned. One's perception of his health is a major component of morale in old age. This paper explores the relationship between this self-perception of health and participation in meaningful social roles.

CHANGING ROLES FOR THE ELDERLY

In all cultures, the roles played by the individual change as he matures and then ages. We do not expect the same behavior from a child as from a young adult; similarly, we expect the mature or aging person to behave in different ways from the young adult. Anthropologists have not studied the transition from maturity to age in many societies, but there has been a general belief that old age brought a gradual shifting of work obligations to match the person's declining vigor, and that in most primitive societies the elderly were accorded high status, not just for their ability to continue working but for their knowledge of tradition and ritual. Simmons' study (1945) suggested that even in simpler societies not all the elderly are treated in the same way. Men receive different treatment than women, and in general old age itself does not bring respect and high status; these are reserved for those who have been respected in their middle years and who carry this respect with them into old age. Simmons also suggests that he has found no society in which the senile person, the person whom age has deprived of wit and capability, is more than tolerated.

Cowgill and Holmes (1972a) document the changes which modernization brings: with more old people in a society, there is less prestige associated with age per se, and the rapid changes associated with modernization make knowledge of tradition of less value. There is also the beginning of a shift from family provision for care and needed financial support toward provision of aid by government agencies.

Clark and Anderson (1967) find that within American culture, the very person who has absorbed the cultural values of work and ambition makes the poorest adjustment to old age and is most likely to be stigmatized as mentally ill because of a failure of adjustment to changed circumstances and to the loss of occupational and other roles which comes with old age and mandatory retirement.

Within societies such as the United States and western European countries, various forms of social insurance have lessened dependence on one's family for security in old age and have mitigated the extremes of poverty and incapacity by providing pensions and medical care for the elderly. In spite of this, most of the elderly suffer from a loss of status, of prestige, and of meaningful and rewarding roles. While this loss of status may apply to an entire generation, there are major differences within the post-65 generation which relate to their capacity to acquire new roles which will give new meaning to life in old age.

The changes in self-perception from young to old, from comfortably off to poor, from working to retired, and from well to ill may be comparable in that in every case the first stage is seen as more desirable than the second, and the individual loses a role or a concept of self which has been of value to him. Merton's theory of relative deprivation (1957:228—250) would seem to be applicable to the elderly. If a person associates for the most part with others who are old, not too well off, and who share the aches and pains of aging, his own state may not seem so bad. For this reason, age-segregated housing may contribute to morale.

HEALTH IN AGING

Traditionally old age has been expected to mean poverty and ill health, but today many older people pass the age of 65 in glowing health and continue for several years with barely diminished energy. Health among the elderly population is the outcome of a lifetime of experiences and health history; it is also influenced by one's present life situation, including availability of care. Operative factors include genetic endowment, hygienic and dietary practices of a lifetime, exposure to contagious diseases, medical and dental attention or its lack, work history and exposure to health hazards at work, and a number of other considerations.

The relationship between socioeconomic status and health in the elderly is by no means clear-cut. There has been a general agreement that in the United States the poor suffer more from ill health and that they have less adequate medical care and make less use of preventive medicine. The provision of financial supplements for health care is not seen as having changed this picture greatly.

It appears to be easier to change the means of paying for health care than to change the attitudes which result in the use or nonuse of available facilities. Mechanic (1972:146-151) finds that there are still major differences between socioeconomic classes in knowledge of disease, utilization of health services, and speed or delay in seeking treatment. He sees a crisis-type of symptom as triggering a demand for medical services in all socioeconomic classes. The poor are more likely to regard chronic aches and pains as inevitable parts of aging, while the more well-to-do view them as treatable.

Dovenmuehle (1970:29—39) reports from the Duke Longitudinal Study that poorer respondents in their sample of elderly were less healthy, with higher rates for impairment of vision, arteriosclerosis, cardiovascular disease, high blood pressure, and pulmonary disease. Only obesity and impairment of mobility due to arthritis showed no difference between socioeconomic groups.

If these studies are correct, we should expect that a sample from public housing would have received inadequate health care in the past and would be somewhat reluctant to utilize Medicaid or Medicare payments to pay for preventive medical care in old age.

How do health and illness differ among the elderly, as compared to the general population? While studies of health and aging have documented the fact that not all older people are poor and ill, we still cannot expect to find among the elderly the same amount of energy and relative freedom from impairment which might be regarded as "normal" for the general population. At the same time, the role and task demands which are made upon the elderly are also diminished, so that an older person may be able to fulfill his expected roles with diminished energy and health. Instead of an ill-well dichotomy, with wellness as normal and illness as deviant, we find a situation in which illness and wellness shade into each other along a health-illness continuum.

Subjective health or self-perception of health is certainly rooted in reality and reflects objective health conditions, but there is not a one-to-one congruence between measures of objective health and health perception. Rather, health perception seems to be influenced by a number of factors, including one's expectations of health in old age, one's adjustment to declining energy, cultural norms of activity or inactivity in old age, and whether one's situation is such that rewarding roles and activities can be continued into old age.

The literature on health and aging provides justification for regarding self-assessment of health as an important element in any analysis of health. First, whatever its relationship to clinical assessments of health, it represents the way the individual sees his own health at the time he is asked the question as to the state of his health. Second, there is good evidence that self-assessment of health is associated with objective measures of health. Maddox and Douglass (1973:87—92) report that the Duke Longitudinal Study found a "persistent, positive congruence" between physicians' assessment and self-assessment of health in the elderly. Where the two were inconsistent, the individual usually overrated his own health. Maddox and Douglass also found that there was stability of rating over time; responses to questions about one's own health were not given in ways which changed whimsically or rapidly over time. Finally, they found that the self-rating predicted future physicians' ratings better than the reverse; the physician's rating was more likely to change in the direction of the individual's self-rating than the reverse.

Palmore and Luihart (1972:68—79), Richardson (1973:207—215) and Tissue (1972:91—94) all find that self ratings of health are associated with the effects of illness on the individual's performance in society and are reasonably valid measurements of health status. In short, there is good reason for using health perception as a measure of subjective health.

We are proposing in this paper that the relationship between objective health and self-perception of health are both direct and indirect. (See Figure 11.1)

We are thus proposing a relationship in which objective health influences health perception directly (Model A) and also influences the roles and activities which the person is able to undertake (Model B). In turn, the resources which the person brings to aging (under resources we would list objective health, education, income, and previous participation in activities) will influence his ability to assume or retain satisfying roles in old age. We are here concerned not with resources as influencing roles, but with roles as influencing health perception.

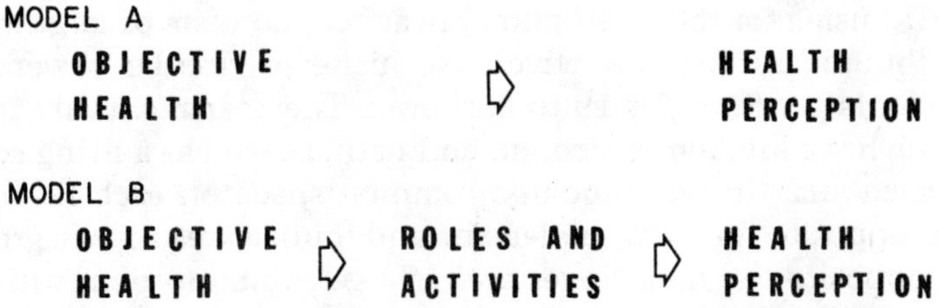

MODEL A

> **OBJECTIVE**   ⇨   **HEALTH**
> **HEALTH**   **PERCEPTION**

MODEL B

> **OBJECTIVE** ⇨ **ROLES AND** ⇨ **HEALTH**
> **HEALTH**   **ACTIVITIES**   **PERCEPTION**

FIGURE 11.1. Two models of the Relationship Between Objective Health and Self-perception of Health. Model A indicates a direct relation while Model B indicates an indirect relationship.

ADAPTIVE NICHE FOR THE AGING

Roles and activities for any population develop through the interaction of a particular population within a particular environment, forming a social structure which may share certain characteristics with other structures formed by similar populations within similar environments but which will always have unique characteristics. Within American society, some older people find a traditional niche within the extended family, living with a son or daughter and continuing to fill the traditional role of grandparent within a loving family. Others remain in independent housing, within their old community, which may be changing, demographically or socioeconomically. Still others find themselves, for the first time, within a niche whose other inhabitants are all elderly like themselves. Such a niche may vary from a "Sun City" retirement community for the well-to-do or for middle-income residents to public housing for the elderly.

This niche is peculiar to the United States and a few other countries, in which the secular decline of the death rate and in turn of the birth rate has produced a large proportion of elderly within the population. At the same time, mobility and the declining birth rate have made the traditional family arrangements for the elderly more difficult to maintain. Political pressure for such public housing projects relates to the number of the elderly; the system of pensions, Social Security, and welfare payments gives many poor people incomes which allow them to maintain an independent residence, especially if they are in partially subsidized housing.

THE ENVIRONMENT

Public housing for the elderly (in Milwaukee) consists of large apartment buildings, most of which are high-rise circular towers, 10 apartments per floor for 19 to 23 floors. The apartments are small, but each has a kitchen, bedroom, and bath, as well as a living room. In the circular towers the only common space on each floor is a bench opposite the elevators; chairs and lounge area on the ground floor opposite the mail boxes and a large common room with kitchenette available for planned group meetings give common space on the ground floor. This common room becomes a center for social interaction.

POPULATION—CHARACTERISTICS OF THE SAMPLE

Architecture alone does not explain the social structure which arises from social activity within a building, nor the roles found within this social structure. The nature of the population also determines the nature of the social structure. The sample on which this paper is based consists of 414 residents of six public housing projects within the city of Milwaukee. They were interviewed in a structured interview during May and June in 1973, and the author spent the next several months in field work which involved observation and open-ended interviews, especially within two buildings.

When we compare our sample with information concerning all occupants of public housing for the elderly in Milwaukee, we find that our sample is representative of residents of public housing. When we compare it with data from a study of all Milwaukee residents over 62 which was made by the Wisconsin Division on Aging and Family Services in 1971, it is clear that public housing attracts a population which is not typical of all elderly in the city of Milwaukee. Our population is predominantly female (83 percent), with a median age of 74 for the whole population. It is by definition made up of low-income residents of Milwaukee, with a median income under $2,000. The preponderance of those who are widowed (55 percent of the whole sample, 66 percent of women) suggests that the death of a spouse often precipitates a move into the semi-sheltered environment of public housing. Our sample is quite comparable to the larger Milwaukee population in education, with 66 percent having completed eight years of schooling or less.

INTERACTION WITHIN HOUSING

Several studies (Rosow 1967; Blau 1961; Rose 1962; Lopata 1973; Ross 1977) have stressed the adaptive value of age-concentrated housing, which gives greatly expanded opportunities for social interaction. The residents of any one housing project share certain problems and certain common traits such as age and social class, and in general the situation contributes to the rapid formation of social networks of friendship and sympathetic support. The residents are also cut off from former neighbors and associates by their move to the housing project. Each building becomes a microsociety within which the problems and advantages of congregate living are worked out by the population.

Within this particular niche, older women (as opposed to men) find that they have more, rather than fewer, opportunities for social participation. Not only is there a population which is made up of residents of similar background, but within these apartment buildings moderate physical impairment need not limit social participation. Within a neighborhood of single-family dwellings, even slight impairment may mean limitation of participation, as it may mean inability to take a bus, to climb stairs, or fear of walking a distance alone. Also, the density of the population increases chance social contacts. While some residents choose to remain in their apartments and to avoid as many contacts as possible, the easier way of life is to make friendly contacts with neighbors.

HYPOTHESES

1. The major hypothesis of this paper is that, with objective health held constant, the level of activity which a resident attains within the housing project and the roles he or she finds there will influence his or her health perception directly. The higher the level of activity, the higher the health perception.

2. Because the housing projects are essentially a woman's world, the health perception of women is expected to be higher than that of men.

3. The greater the number and frequency of contacts with friends, the higher the health perception of the residents is expected to be.

ANALYSIS OF DATA—
MULTIPLE CLASSIFICATION ANALYSIS

Analysis of data reported in this paper relies on Multiple Classification Analysis (Andrews, Morgan, and Sondquist 1967). This is a variation on multiple regression in which the grand mean of the dependent variable is computed and deviations from this mean are computed for every category of every independent variable. It is possible to input independent variables into the equation one by one, controlling for each added variable, so that the effect of each is entered into the equation in conjunction with the particular variable which is being tested and the net effects on the grand mean are determined.[2]

Multiple Classification Analysis can use any combination of nominal, ordinal, or interval scales in the independent variables. It provides the multiple correlation for the model as well as the proportion of variance explained for.the dependent variable. This becomes appropriate because we are considering nominal variables (e.g., sex) as well as ordinal. Each category of each independent variable is considered separately as it is associated with variation from the mean of the dependent variable. The multiple correlation coefficient, squared, gives the percent of variance in the dependent variables in the equation.

MEASURES OF HEALTH PERCEPTION

Mean Health Perception. The dependent variable used throughout this study, self-perception of health, is based on the response to the first question in the survey. This question was "We're interested in people's health and how their health problems are being taken care of. Would you say your health in general is excellent, good, fair, or poor?" To analyze the responses, an answer of "excellent" is scored as 4, "good" is 3, "fair" is 2, and "poor" is 1. The mean health perception for the entire sample is 2.31, and variations from this show the influence of categories of independent variables.

Index of Functional Mobility. The measure of objective health used throughout this study is based on the answers to five questions, which combine to give us an index comparable to the index developed by Katz et al. (1970) and to that used by Shanas et al. (1968). We asked our respondents five questions:

1.   Do you have trouble working around your apartment?
2.   Do you have trouble going up and down stairs?
3.   Do you have trouble getting around outside, weather permitting?
4.   Do you have trouble putting on shoes, bathing, and dressing?
5.   Do you have trouble using bathroom facilities?

The answers to these questions were rated as "no trouble," "some trouble," "need help," or "can't do," scored from 1 (can't do) to 4 (no trouble). The score on the Index of Functional Mobility thus ranged from a possible 5 (maximum incapacity) to 20 (no reported impairment in functional mobility). In comparison to the samples from the general population reported by Shanas et al., (1968), our population is relatively impaired, although no one has been institutionalized. (See Table 11.1)

TABLE 11.1 Comparison of National Sample with Milwaukee Public Housing Sample, Level of Reported Incapacity

Level of Incapacity*	National Sample* (percentages)	Milwaukee Public Housing Sample
No reported incapacity	63	35
Limited incapacity	22	31
Moderate incapacity	11	24
High incapacity	4	10

Divisions used are those used by Shanas et al. (1968:28).

Item Analysis of Index of Functional Mobility as Related to Roles. The effect of a high degree of impairment on health perception shows dramatically how the perception of health relates to functional mobility. (See Table 11.2) Those respondents who have

TABLE 11.2 Multiple Classification Analysis of Health Perception by Index of Functional Mobility

Degree of Loss of Functional Mobility*	Deviations from Grand Mean of 2.31	
	N	Gross
1. No limitation of functional mobility	145	+.52[†]
2.	77	+.27[†]
3.	86	-.32[†]
4.	64	-.46[†]
5. Very Low functional mobility	42	-.93[†]

[†]Significant at .05 level, t-test.
*Our first scoring was a four-part division which roughly paralleled that used by Shanas et al. (1968). Multiple classification analysis showed that the best scoring was as follows: (1) no impairment in functional mobility; (2); (3); (4); (5) Very low functional mobility.

no impairment, or report some trouble with only one task, have
health perception well above the mean. On the other hand, difficulty with as few as two activities begins to depress the individual's
perception of his own health.

We have arranged the items on the Index of Functional Mobility in the order of the degree to which they *raise* health perception
for the entire sample. The two items on which the largest number
of respondents report "some trouble" are going up and down stairs
and working around their apartments. To be able to perform these
tasks without difficulty gives the greatest increase in health perception. Next comes getting around outside. (See Table 11.3)

TABLE 11.3. Multiple Classification Analysis of Health Perception as Related
to Items Making Up Index of Functional Mobility.

Question:	Deviations from Grand Mean of 2.31	
Do you have trouble—	N	Gross Deviation
Going up and down stairs		
No trouble	176	+.41[†]
Some trouble	141	−.06
Need help	28	−.59[†]
Can't do	63	−.73[†]
Working around apartment		
No trouble	262	+.33[†]
Some trouble	91	−.46[†]
Need help	43	−.59[†]
Can't do	14	−1.17[†]
Getting around outside		
No trouble	303	+.24[†]
Some trouble	70	−.58[†]
Need help	20	−.72[†]
Can't do	17	−1.02[†]
Putting on shoes, bathing, dressing		
No trouble	341	+.14[†]
Some trouble	56	−.71[†]
Need help	4	−.07
Can't do	11	−.68[†]
Using bathroom facilities		
No trouble	366	+.07[†]
Some trouble	35	−.45[†]
Need help	8	−.69[†]
Can't do	4	−1.32[†]

[†]Significant at .05 level, t-test.

Putting on shoes, bathing and dressing, and using bathroom facilities are tasks with which most of the residents have no problems. These abilities seem to be taken for granted until they are lost; to perform them successfully does not raise health perception much. On the other hand, inability to perform these tasks has the most depressing effect on health perception. To be unable to use bathroom facilities is to lose the control over one's own bodily functions which has been intimately associated with status as an adult and self-sustaining personality; the negative effect on health perception is not surprising. To be unable to go up and down stairs is not of very great importance in the context of these housing projects, since elevators are available and are constantly used.

Sex and Health Perception. In general men are expected to have better health (or to claim better health) than women in old age (Shanas et al. 1968:53). In our sample, we find that men, rather than claiming better health, see their health as poor. This is true when a control for functional mobility is added, so that even though men have somewhat better functional mobility than women, they describe their health as poor more frequently. (See Table 11.4)

TABLE 11.4. Multiple Classifcation Analysis of Health Perception by Sex.

Sex	Deviation from Grand Mean of 2.31		
	N	Gross	Net*
Male	70	-.20	-.23
Female	314	+.04	+.05

*Net of Functional Mobility. Gross deviation refers to the deviation resulting from the addition of the first independent variable. All net scores reflect the influence of controlling for functional mobility.

When a control variable is added to the equation for Multiple Classification Analysis, if it is positively correlated with the first independent variable the variation from the mean will decrease. In Table 11.4 the variation of the male health perception score from the mean increases slightly when functional mobility is added as a control, primarily because men have less reported impairment than women. Since women make up the majority of the sample, their perception of their own health must be near the mean.

That the relatively few men who live in each project find themselves surrounded by women on each floor, in the lobby when they go for mail and find the "lobby group" of women in possession, at residents' meetings and card parties, is important. If it is true (LeMasters 1975) that the blue-collar world is still one of great sex segregation and male dominance, the adjustment to residence in a project with so few other males must mean a major role adjustment for men. Women, on the contrary, seem to find many new opportunities for leadership and for responsibility within the social structure of the housing projects. This is reflected in health perception.

Social Participation and Health Perception: Formal Organizations. Previous studies have usually found that participation in organizations is relatively low among the working class in the city. We find that in our sample only a minority of the men belong to any organization; for women the proportion of members is higher, and 51 percent, or 168, belong to at least one organization.

The type of organization preferred by those who have joined may give an indication of the interests of the residents. The Golden Age clubs meet within the buildings, holding weekly meetings, with a leader paid by the Board of Education. In spite of the convenience of such meetings, only 1 of 6 within the sample, or 69 out of 414, are members; Senior Citizens' groups, 18; fraternal organizations, 12; veterans' groups, 5. Only two respondents are members of employee unions or their retirees' auxiliaries. The effect of membership on health perception is shown in Table 11.5.

TABLE 11.5. Multiple Classification Analysis of Health Perception by Organizational Membership.

Number of	Deviation from Grand Mean of 2.31		
Organizations	N	Gross	Net*
Two or more	105	+.22[†]	+.20[†]
One	93	+.07[†]	+.10[†]
None	208	-.17[†]	-.15[†]

Eight who did not respond were removed from table.

*Net of Functional Mobility.

[†]Difference significant at .05 level, t-test.

Since it is possible that physical impairment may prevent organizational membership, Multiple Classification Analysis enables us to see if membership in organizations still increases health perception when functional mobility is added as a control. Table 11.5 shows that those who belong to no organization and those who belong to two or more differ significantly in their health perception. Those who belong to none have low health perception; the addition of functional mobility to the equation does not change the variation significantly. Those who belong to two or more also differ in the predicted direction, and again this is not due in any large part to good objective health. It would appear that it is not objectively poor health as shown by functional mobility which determines the effect of organizational membership on health perception.

Change in Level of Involvement in Activities. Specific organizations may be less important for the residents than their own assessment of their present level of activity as compared to their activities in earlier life. The adaptive niche of the housing projects offers encouragement for an increase in level of activity; those who take advantage of such opportunity should have higher health perception than those who do not do so. (See Table 11.6)

TABLE 11.6. Multiple Classification Analysis of Health Perception by Changes in Involvement in Activities after Moving to Housing Projects.

Relative involvement in Activities	Deviations from Grand Mean of 2.31		
	N	Gross	Net*
More involved	101	$+.29^{\dagger}$	$+.23^{\dagger}$
Same	130	$+.06$	$+.01$
Less involved	100	$-.21^{\dagger}$	$-.10^{\dagger}$
Never involved	70	$-.24^{\dagger}$	$-.26^{\dagger}$

Thirteen who did not respond removed from table.

†Significant at .05 level, t-test.

*Net of functional mobility.

Again, let us remember that if the variation *lessens* with the addition of functional mobility to the equation, the index of functional mobility is positively related to the first independent variable. Thus, those who are more involved with activities since moving to the housing projects have significantly higher health perception; because most of them have good functional mobility, the addition of this to the equation lessens the deviation somewhat, but it is still significant. There are two particularly interesting findings in Table 11.6. First, those who are less involved now than prior to housing project residence have low health perception, but they also have poor functional mobility so that health is apparently a limit on their active participation. Second, those who report that they have never been involved have low health perception but apparently do *not* have low functional mobility. So for those who respond to the situation in the housing projects, with a high density population of persons similar to themselves, and expand their interests and activities within the favorable adaptive niche of public housing, health perception apparently rises. Those who are not able to enter into new roles and activities have lower health perception in spite of good functional mobility. The use or nonuse of the opportunities for social involvement in this particular niche apparently affects health perception.

Interaction with Friends and Health Perception. The literature on friendship among the old is rather sparse; kin relations are assumed to be of more importance than friendship. Rosow (1967: 27–39) believes that working-class older people are more locally oriented than middle-class; they are much more dependent on neighbors for friendship, and age-concentrated housing is of great assistance to them in making friends. Lopata (1973:180) speaks of friendship as a great resource, which is more available to those with more education and social experience.

If Rosow is correct, age-concentrated housing such as we are studying should be characterized by much interaction among friends and by relatively few isolates. Most women in the housing projects claim at least one friend in the building. Often friends phone or stop by each other's apartments every morning, so that they provide a security check for each other. Some—usually those with more education but also the younger residents and married couples– orient their friendships outside the buildings and maintain cordial but rather distant relationships with their neighbors. Some, usually the leaders, feel an obligation to maintain friendly relationships with everyone in the building. Some are friendly with everyone on the floor, while others have one friend who is also a helper. There are small groups of congenial friends who play cards together regularly. Table 11.7 shows the relationship of contacts with friends to health perception.

TABLE 11.7. Multiple Classification Analysis of Health Perception by Contacts with Close Friends.

Number of Contacts with Friends	Deviations from Grand Mean of 2.31		
	N	Gross	Net*
No contacts	80	$-.28^\dagger$	$-.19$
Less than one a day	77	$-.14^\dagger$	$-.11^\dagger$
One or more a day	227	$+.12$	$+.08$

†Difference significant at .05 level, t-test.

*Net of functional mobility.

We find that the number of contacts with friends does influence health perception in the expected direction. Those with no contacts with friends have significantly lower health perception. This is not affected greatly by the addition of functional mobility to the equation. Given the density of the housing and the convenience of seeing others within the building, low functional mobility seems not to be a real barrier to contacts with friends.

Leadership Roles and Health Perception. We do not have survey data regarding leadership patterns in the housing projects, but we have ethnographic data based on a series of interviews with leaders in two buildings. This interviewing was done just after the Housing Authority, in response to federal guidelines, insisted that each building have an elected and formally organized Residents' Council, with officers, a budget for recreational expenditures, and elected delegates to a city-wide Residents' Council. We interviewed both formal and informal leaders in two buildings; in both of these, the leaders are women, although there are male leaders in other buildings.

The typical leader is a woman between 75 and 80 years of age, who has worked at some time in her life, and who is outgoing in personality. Some of the leaders maintain a series of activities outside the housing project; most of this group are in good health and perceive their health as good. A few, usually older and more disabled, limit their active social participation to the housing project but are very active there. All of the women we interviewed reported health somewhat better than seemed warranted by their functional mobility, and a corresponding high morale. These women have survived the death of children, the loss of a spouse, and the surrender of former homes and occupations but they continue to be optimistic and outgoing. All of them express a sense of responsibility to their elected posts. On the other hand, the recluses and isolates, those who seldom leave their apartments and who reject friendly overtures from neighbors, show health perception which is low as related to their reported functional mobility.

We interviewed at least one active leader who is confined to a wheel chair. At the time of our interview she was president of and pianist for the Golden Age Club. She is known throughout the building as a good cook who bakes and gives away her products, and as an active participant in building affairs. She is realistic about her health, especially about the limitation on her strength due to a heart pacemaker, but she is optimistic and uncomplaining.

Undoubtedly the characteristics which make for leadership reflect both the personality and past experience of the leader and the characteristics of the adaptive niche. The architecture of the buildings means that those with rather high impairment of mobility can still exercise active leadership. At the same time, those who are

youngest, in best health, and with the highest level of previous occupational and educational attainment are most likely to regard the
housing project as an apartment building rather than a community
and to look outside it for most of their associations. Continued residence, declining health, and the loss of friends and contacts in the
wider community may make the formerly outside-oriented more
dependent on other building residents.

Percent of Variance in Health Perception Explained. The importance of the relationship between functional mobility and health
perception is made clear by Table 11.8, since 26 percent of the variance in health perception relates to changes in functional mobility.
Beyond this, within the adaptive niche of public housing a total of
14 percent of variance is accounted for by roles and activities of the
residents.

TABLE 11.8. Multiple Correlation and Percent of
Variance in Health Perception

Variable	r	r^2
Functional mobility	.51	.26
Sex	.09	.008
Relative involvements	.22	.05
Number of organizations	.21	.04
Relationship to friends	.19	.04
Total roles & activities	.38	.14

Since there is feedback among various measures of roles and activities, the total influence of these variables is less than the sum of
the separate variables.

We should perhaps mention again the fact that there is a feedback between functional mobility and the person's ability to undertake roles and activities. Certainly, poor health limits participation;
limited participation lowers health perception. The addition of functional mobility as a control is an attempt to control for the effects
of objective measures of health.

SUMMARY

While the primary purpose of this paper has been to show the relationship between social roles and activities and health perception,
it has also been concerned with the life of the residents of the housing projects. Field work in these buildings shows that, far from being "warehouses" for older people who feel themselves to have been

discarded, the housing projects have become functioning communities, full of life and enjoyment. The residents, who might be described as underprivileged and rejected, establish networks of mutual support and aid. Leaders arise who are responsive to the needs of the residents.

It is possible that if the population of each project were less homogeneous, leadership roles might pass to the younger and better educated residents, and the members who had the demographic characteristics of our population might be pushed aside. The limits on income may give some residents a chance to develop leadership within the niche of public housing which they would not have in another community.

Also, the concentration of activities under one roof and the built-in aids (e.g., elevators) for the handicapped mean that impairment of functional mobility need not reduce participation. In another setting, limits on functional mobility might reduce health perception by limiting participation much more stringently.

Within the adaptive niche of public housing, it is clear that social participation is associated with better health perception; the characteristics of the environment and of the population have united to form a social structure within which roles and activities, as well as objective health, influence health perception.

NOTES

1. The research and studies forming the basis for this paper were conducted pursuant to a contract between the Department of Housing and Urban Development and the National League of Cities. The substance of such research is dedicated to the public. The author is solely responsible for the accuracy of the statements or interpretations contained herein.

The research was sponsored by the Urban Observatory, University of Wisconsin Extension Division, with the cooperation of the Department of Anthropology and the school of Nursing, University of Wisconsin-Milwaukee.

2. Multiple classification analysis is a variety of statistical analysis commonly referred to as analysis of variance. By using multiple regression, it is possible to examine the effects of the independent variable (the one that is affecting) upon the dependent variable (the one that is being affected and the one we want to explain). First, the mean for the dependent variable is calculated for all cases (the grand mean). Next, the independent variable is broken into distinct categories or levels. For sex this is male and female while for number of contacts this is none, less than one a day, and

more than one a day. The deviations from the overall mean of the dependent variable is calculated for the cases within each category of the independent variable. In other words, we examine the effect of the independent variable by examining the differences in the means of the dependent variables as expressed in terms of deviations, positive or negative, from the grand mean. Thus, in reading the tables, look at the grand mean and then look at the $+/-$ deviations to see the effect of the independent variable on the dependent variable.

12 Dependency and Reciprocity: Home Health Aid in an Elderly Population

KAREN JONAS
University of Wisconsin—Milwaukee

EDWARD WELLIN
University of Wisconsin—Milwaukee

Independence—dependence is an evaluative duality prompting people to affirm the positive, independence. One of the most common laments of older adults, especially Americans, is, "I don't want to be a burden, I want to be independent..." Dependency is one of the most pervasive problems of aging. It is a problem for older adults themselves, and for their families, friends and even society. The roots of this problem are planted in an elementary quality of social life. All social relations are interdependent with the interlinkages mediated by giving and taking or by the norm of reciprocity. Giving and taking are more or less balanced by sanctions, such as being called a free loader, directed against those who take too much. Dependence, or the inability to reciprocate and hold up one's end of a social relationship is a very real problem for both takers and givers.

We have seen this issue among the Chinese, the Black Caribs, and elderly Corsicans in Paris. Cultures work out solutions to this problem. Karen Jonas and Edward Wellin investigate the informal mutual aid networks in the same public housing projects for the elderly in Milwaukee as Eunice Boyer reported on in the previous chapter. Again anthropologists have come up with another surprise for the critics of age concentrated residences. In the informal mutual aid networks, Jonas and Wellin find interdependency with well articulated norms of reciprocity. Although materially impoverished, residents who need and receive care from friends and neighbors, actively reciprocate. Reciprocation is not always even, help episode for help episode. Where help giving becomes one way, the receiver has a number of alternative ways in which to hold up his/her end of the relationship.

As with other cultural phenomena, there are patterns. Jonas and Wellin systematically document these patterns in the quantitative analysis of their survey data. By careful use of the qualita-

*tive data obtained through months of observation, they are able
to resolve the apparent inconsistencies and probe deeper. Sex differences and degrees of prior acquaintance and intimacy are important features in structuring mutual aid networks. Females, in
giving aid are more likely to follow what the authors identify as
the mother hen pattern characterized by intimacy and long term
giving and taking of a diffuse nature (generalized reciprocity).
Males practice the customer pattern where intimacy is less intense
and reciprocation is immediate (balanced reciprocity). Where there
is no prior acquaintance, help may be given, but if demands persist, the norms are violated in that someone is trying to get something for nothing (negative reciprocity).*

*So what? The import of these findings is that for some older
adults, in a culture that emphasizes independence, the problem of
dependency is to a large extent resolved. As Jonas and Wellin
point out, everyone gains in this situation. Families gain in that
their older members remain independent and the quality of their
relationship improves. Public agencies (the state) gain since institutionalization is delayed or thwarted completely. The elderly also
gain in that by actively exchanging, their self-esteem is reinforced.
Thus, in an environment which is stereotyped as warehouses for
old people, we find networks of interdependent people maintaining their independence.*

"It's very important that I do not become a burden on somebody. That's the most important thing in my life today."
   Clark, quoting a San Francisco elderly informant (1972:272)

Being dependent, or a "burden", on others violates one of the pervasive values in American society, that of independence. To be dependent on others for the means of survival, without appropriate
reciprocation, has traditionally been regarded in our society as "a
confession of one's own incompetence or inadequacy and justification for . . . degradation in the eyes of the community" (Cowgill
1972a:243).

The norm of reciprocity (essentially, "one should help those
who have helped one") has been described as a universal, a principle that apparently occurs in the value systems and moral codes
of all societies (Gouldner 1960:171). Forms of reciprocity, often
studied under the rubric of exchange theory (Malinowski 1922;
Mauss 1954; Blau 1964; Sahlins 1965; Homans 1974; Dowd 1975;
Emerson 1976; Befu 1977) are seen as pervading the entire social
fabric and serving as networks that hold society together (Belshaw
1965:7). For contemporary Americans, with their strong cultural
emphasis on independence and general bias against dependency,
numerous empirical studies provide evidence that the norm of recip-

rocy exerts powerful effects throughout the society in structuring social relationships (e.g., Blau 1964; Homans 1961, 1974; Stack 1974).

Clark (1972:263-274) analyzes types of dependency and notes that in American society norms of reciprocity are held in cultural abeyance in only two types. One is developmental or transitional dependency, involving predictable periods of relative helplessness for affected individuals, when they require one-way care and resources from others, e.g., early childhood, critical phases of the child-bearing cycle, and senescence. The other is crisis-related dependency, generally unpredictable in occurrence and timing, such as sudden illness or injury, bereavement, and divorce. Both types of dependency tend to be institutionalized as permitting or requiring varying periods and intensities of essentially one-way support from others. However, the dependency is acceptable only if it is limited in time; should it persist beyond some culturally arbitrated period, the individual becomes a burden—the recipient of nonreciprocal support.

When we turn to questions of dependence and reciprocity among the elderly in our society, we find, to be sure, that many older persons enjoy good health, perform their usual activities with little restriction, and make few if any dependency demands on others. At the same time, the incidence of chronic illness and of long-term limitations in activity and mobility increase sharply with advancing age (Commission on Chronic Illness 1957; U.S. National Center for Health Statistics 1974, 1977). While only 1 percent of the noninstitutionalized population age 18-44 suffer chronic incapacities severe enough to require dependency on others for assistance in mobility and personal care, this figure rises to 12 percent among persons age 65-74 and to 26 percent in the population age 75 and older; furthermore, the lower the levels of education and income, the higher the frequency of chronic incapacity (Nagi 1976). Thus, it is the older, poorer, and less-educated segments of our noninstitutionalized population—those with the fewest resources to reciprocate help from others—who present the highest rates of disability and, if they are to avoid institutionalization, the greatest needs for long-term dependency.

Every society develops some set of patterns for the care and support of the elderly and incapacitated. Between them, Simmons (1945) and Cowgill and Holmes (1972) provide the basis for broadly delineating the evolution of societal arrangements for such care and support. Simmons surveys the place of the aged only in so-called "primitive" societies, i.e., in societies which share at least three attributes—little or no techno-economic modernization, the primacy of kinship in governing interpersonal relationships, and a low proportion of elderly in the population. Simmons finds that in such societies—irrespective of the form of the family, resources available to the elderly, or other cultural variations- aged men and women universally rely on younger kin for care and support (1945: 214).

Cowgill and Holmes also survey aging and its correlates cross-culturally but do so in a range of societies at different levels of modernization. They find that with advancing modernization—and with the interrelated factors of the reduced importance of kinship and increased proportion of elderly in the population—primary responsibility for the care and support required by elderly persons tends to shift from the family to the state. Although adult children in modern societies do retain some obligations for looking after aged parents, Cowgill and Holmes note that these obligations are often unclear and not wholly binding (1972b:307, 318-319).

In most societies, including our own, it can be argued that both the giver of support and the dependent can usually accommodate to dependency if at least one, or, preferably, two or more, of the following conditions are met: if (1) the dependency is of limited duration or intensity, (2) the dependent individual has something of value to exchange for help received, and (3) the participants share especially intimate socioemotional bonds, as among certain close kin.[2]

The object of the present inquiry is to examine patterns of dependence and reciprocity among an aggregate of elderly persons in a milieu in which, frequently, *none* of the foregoing conditions appear to be met. That is, we deal with a situation in which incapacitated individuals often require long-term support, possess few resources and apparently have little of value with which to reciprocate, and, for the most part, lack long-standing relationships or kinship ties with other elderly in the same setting. The opportunity to learn about various dimensions of the latter type of dependency situation was provided by a study of residents of public housing for the elderly in Milwaukee, Wisconsin. Among other things, the study investigated who provided and who received the care that sick or incapacitated persons received at home.

METHODS

The present research is part of a larger study of the general life situations and health needs of residents in 6 of the 13 public housing projects for the elderly in Milwaukee (Wellin, et al 1974). Two data-gathering approaches were used. One, the ethnographic, begun in late 1972 and still ongoing, involved informal and repeated interviews with a limited number of informants, occasional attendance at resident gatherings and activities, and observation in a range of situations. The second, or survey-research type, was based on standardized interviews and was carried out during spring 1973. The latter phase produced interviews with 414 respondents, constituting a carefully randomized sample of 37 percent of the residents of the six projects. Material in this paper draws on both sources of data.

THE HOUSING PROJECTS AND CHARACTERISTICS OF THEIR RESIDENTS

This study is limited to one of the niches occupied by the aged in contemporary American society— that of public housing for the elderly. Among the characteristics distinguishing that niche, three are especially prominent. For one, its primary support is *governmental*, through a combination of federal, state, and local arrangements. Secondly, the population consists of *dense and exclusive* concentrations of older persons. Thirdly, not all elderly but only those who meet stated criteria of *poverty* are eligible for residence.

Somewhat over 2,500 persons reside in Milwaukee's 13 public housing projects for the elderly. Dispersed throughout the central city, the buildings range in height from 8 to 24 stories and in capacity from 100 to over 250 apartments. Most apartments consist of living room, dining alcove, bedroom, kitchen and bathroom; some units, available only to married couples, have a second bedroom. Criteria for admission are based essentially on age and income. One must be poor and at least 62 years of age, although the minimum age is waived under certain conditions. While no specific requirements are laid down as to health status or functional mobility, those admitted must be able to function more or less independently.

One finds negative and stereotyped attitudes among many people in the community that elderly housing projects constitute "storage bins" for poor aged folk. Some residents say they shared these feelings when first admitted. Nonetheless, overwhelmingly, residents are pleased with the projects and their apartments, although somewhat less so with some of the neighborhoods in which projects are located. In fact, current occupancy rates approach 100 percent, and there are long waiting lists of applicants.

The median age of residents is 75 years, but the range of ages spans 35 years, or more than a full generation. The youngest residents are not yet 60, the oldest over 90. Women and widows predominate; 83 percent of residents are women, and of these two-thirds are widows. Most residents have had eight or fewer years of schooling; only a handful report education or training beyond high school. Although all residents meet poverty criteria, some are virtually destitute, while others appear to have reasonably adequate material resources. There is a large minority of black residents and, among whites, representation from many ethnic backgrounds. Length of residence in the projects varies from under one year to over eight years; the majority have been residents for about three to four years. Although nearly all residents had been able to function with minimal or no impediment when first admitted, about one-third (139 out of 414) had some degree of significant physical incapacity at the time of the interview, including 15 percent (61) who were severely hampered in physical function.

HELP AND CARE AT HOME

As part of the standardized interview, residents were asked whether, because of illness or indisposition, they had been helped or given care at home during the two weeks preceding the interview. If help had been received, residents were queried further as to who had helped, how often, and of what the help had consisted. In addition, respondents were asked whether they had given help to others during the same period; if they had done so, details were elicited as to whom they had helped, how frequently, and in what way(s).

Types of help received from all sources by ill or impaired elderly fall into four categories. In descending order of frequency, they are: *domestic chores*—preparing food for the ill person, cleaning or "neatening up" the latter's apartment (44 percent); *socioemotional support*- visits to talk with, read to, "cheer up," or "check up on" the incapacitated resident (24 percent); *personal care*- bedside nursing, administering medication, assisting with exercises, and the like (20 percent); *errands*—mainly to market or pharmacy (12 percent).

Sources of help, shown in Tables 12.1A and 12.1B, include two broad categories—*personal* networks of the ill person and *impersonal* (community agency and professional) sources. Personal network sources include neighbors/friends, and relatives, the latter comprising younger kin (mainly children and grandchildren) as well as same-generation kin (siblings); another personal-network source, only for residents married and living with spouse, is the wife or husband. Community and professional sources are primarily nurses and homemakers as well as, on occasion, social service workers and physicians.

TABLE 12.1. Sources and Frequency of home help over Two-Week Period as Reported by Recipients [A] and Givers [B] of Help

A.

Help RECEIVED from:	No. of Respondents Who Received Help from Each Source		Total Number of Help-episodes Received
Personal-network Sources		48	262
Neighbors/friends	16		85
Spouse	9		98
Siblings	8		44
Offspring & other younger kin	15		35
Community Agency/Professional Services		19	60
Nurse	5		32
Homemaker	9		23
Social service worker	3		3
Physician	2		2
Source not ascertained	2	2	4	4
Totals	69*		326

B.

Help GIVEN to:	No. of respondents Who Gave Help to Each Recipient		Total Number of Help-episodes Given
Recipient Within Housing Project		58	390
Neighbors/friends	44		254
Spouse	14		136
Recipient Elsewhere in Community		16	91
Siblings	7		48
Offspring & other younger kin	5		35
Friends	4		8
Recipient not ascertained	2	2	3	3
Totals	76**		484

*The 69 reported sources were named by 50 respondents.

**The 76 recipients were named by 64 respondents.

Note that Table 12.1A deals with the home help that both originates within and comes from outside the projects, as reported by *recipients* of help, while Table 12.1B shows the help that circulates within the projects as well as some aid that flows outward, as reported by *givers* of help, both over a two-week period. Table 12.1A reveals that personal-network sources are not only cited more often than agency or professional sources but provide over four times as many helping-episodes. Among relatives, younger kin are named more frequently than same-generation kin, i.e., siblings, but the latter provide help on more occasions. For married residents living with spouses, the latter is the primary and an extremely frequent source of aid.

Table 12.1B indicates that while most residents who help incapacitated others do so within the confines of the housing projects, nearly one-fifth of all helping episodes (91 of 484) are directed toward persons who live elsewhere in the community—siblings, offspring and their families, and friends.

The remainder of this chapter focuses on the most frequent and important type of aid revealed by our research— that which circulates among and between elderly residents of public housing. Only limited data are presented on assistance from agency and professional sources and from (and to) relatives and friends elsewhere in the community.

Comparison of Tables 12.1A and 12.1B reveals certain discrepancies. The major one is that neighbors/friends report *giving* help to neighbors/friends three times more frequently than the latter report *receiving* it from the former (254 episodes as against 85). A parallel but less marked discrepancy occurs among spouses— somewhat more help-episodes are reported to be given than received (136 as against 98). Close scrutiny of the data, plus follow-up interviews, reconcile the differentials. Among neighbors/friends, the discrepancy turns on differing definitions by givers and receivers of certain kinds of "help". Essentially, the chief area of disagreement is that of socioemotional support. It appears that a resident paying a call on an ill neighbor to cheer up, check up on, or simply "visit with" the latter often regards the visit as "helping" the neighbor. It is equally evident that the person visited is likely to define such visits as "normal" neighborly friendliness, not the rendering of sickroom assistance. Among spouses, the discrepancy revolves around differing role expectations as between wives and husbands. Wives tend to "minimize" reports of help-episodes given to and received from husbands; in general, wives seem to view much of the help they provide to be part of the expected wifely role and that received from her spouse to be part of ordinary husbandly aid.

Husbands, on the other hand, are likely to "maximize" reports of assistance, especially that given the wife when the aid requires the husband to assume duties ordinarily performed by his spouse.

Measures of Estimated Annual Frequency of Help. To expedite analysis in all the following tables, two measures of estimated annual frequency of help are used. Each measure—one of help *received*, as reported by recipients of help, the other of help *given*, as reported by help-givers—is based on the frequency of assistance episodes during the two weeks preceding the interview. Each reported frequency is extrapolated to a yearly basis by multiplying by 26 (26 x 2 = 52 weeks) but is otherwise unweighted.

The assumption underlying the extrapolation is that the home-help experience of the sample for a two-week period is a rough but reasonable approximation of 1/26 of such events for the preceding year for the population from which the sample is drawn. The specific two-week period fell within the span from late April to about mid-May, a period of fairly mild temperatures without weather extremes in Milwaukee. Although the assumption is not error-proof, we believe that the procedure provides a workable estimate of a year's patterns of home help for the population under study. In any event, inasmuch as the extrapolation factor is a constant 26, the procedure does not impair or bias the comparisons of the various subgroups.

Receivers of Home Help. It is important to note that, except between spouses, little direct exchange of help-for-help occurs; rarely does the principles operate of "you help me when I'm unable to help myself, and in return I'll do the same for you". For the most part, those residents who receive help and those who give it tend to be different individuals; it is unusual for the same person to be both receiver and giver of help. We next look at each aggregate separately—first the receivers and then the givers—analyzing each according to sex and age, marital status, and health status.

Examination and comparison of Table 12.2A and 12.2B show striking differences by sex but only inconsistent differences by age. Thus women report receiving assistance far more frequently than do men and receive it from every personal-network source as well as from community agencies. Men, on the other hand, receive little help from any source. Excluding help from one's spouse,[3] the mean for women is to receive help an estimated 15 times per year, for men only once.

Turning to age, we had expected advancing age to be associated with higher frequencies of home help. However, this is clearly

TABLE 12.2 Sources and Estimated Annual Frequencies of Help Received at Home for Females (A) and Males (B) by Age of Recipient

A.

Help RECEIVED from:	Age of FEMALE Recipients					
	Under 65	65-69	70-74	75-79	80 and older	Mean, all Females
	(28)	(55)	(87)	(95)	(64)	(329*)
Neighbors/friends	14	11	2	7	2	6
Siblings	14	0	3	4	1	3
Offspring	5	1	4	1	4	2
Community agencies	4	1	6	5	3	4
Total	37	13	15	17	10	15

*Fifteen females, age not ascertained, removed from table.

B.

Help RECEIVED from:	Age of MALE Recipients					
	Under 65	65-69	70-74	75-79	80 and older	Mean, all Males
	(9)	(9)	(15)	(19)	(14)	(66*)
Neighbors/friends	0	0	0	1	0	‡
Siblings	0	0	0	0	1	‡
Offspring	0	0	0	1	2	‡
Community agencies	0	0	0	0	0	0
Total	0	0	0	2	3	1

*Four males, age not ascertained, removed from table.

‡Frequency less than once per year.

not the case with women, and is only mildly so with men. Among women, the relationship between age and help-episodes is almost inverse—the youngest age-group receives help most frequently, the oldest least frequently, and the intervening age-groups are intermediate in frequency, varying inconsistently around the mean. Among men, the association between advancing age and frequency of help is fairly weak, in that the rare help-episodes are reported only by the oldest age-categories.

We have not dealt above with help between spouses, reserving it for our examination of the effects of marital status in Table 12.3A and 12.3B. Four marital statuses are represented in our population—currently married (and living with spouse), widowed, separated/divorced, and never married—with widowed females so predominating that one might aptly describe each housing project as essentially a "community of widows." Every other marital status is a relatively small segment, with the never-married among both sexes the smallest.

TABLE 12.3. Sources and Estimated Annual Frequencies of Help Received at Home for Females[A] and Males[B] by Marital Status of Recipient

A.	Marital Status of FEMALE Recipients				
Help RECEIVED from:	Married	Widowed	Separated/ Divorced	Never Married	Mean, all Females
	(35)	(228)	(48)	(27)	(338*)
Neighbors/friends	8	5	10	14	6
Siblings	21	1	0	2	3
Offspring	1	3	4	0	2
Community agencies	3	3	11	1	4
Spouse	32	··	—	—	—
Total	65	12	25	17	15*

*Six females, marital status not ascertained, removed from table.

B.	Marital Status of MALE Recipients				
Help RECEIVED from:	Married	Widowed	Separated/ Divorced	Never Married	Mean, all Males
	(29)	(19)	(13)	(8)	(69[†])
Neighbors/friends	0	1	0	0	‡
Siblings	0	0	0	0	0
Offspring	0	1	0	0	‡
Community agencies	0	0	0	0	0
Spouse	52	—	—	—	—
Total	52	2	0	0	1§

[†] One male, marital status not ascertained, removed from table.

[‡] "Total help received" excludes help from a spouse.

§ Frequency is less than once per year.

Table 12.3A shows the sources and estimated annual frequencies of home help received by females, according to the recipient's marital status; Table 12.3B presents corresponding data for males. Looking first at females, it is seen that *married women* are the most frequent recipients of help. Although they report help from every source, the assistance is rendered most often by the husband. The second most important source of help, an unexpectedly frequent one, is own-generation relatives, i.e., siblings, with relatively little help reported from offspring, i.e., adult children. *Separated/ divorced women* also report fairly frequent help received, but the pattern is different: they rely mainly on community agencies (nurses and homemakers) and almost as much on neighbors, supplemented by occasional help from offspring. For *never-married women*, neighbors are the single most important source of help. Finally, among the most numerous group, *widows*, help is reported from every source at relatively modest frequencies, more often from neighbors than from any others.

As to marital-status categories among men, *married males* report help received from only one source—their wives—from whom they receive assistance at a high rate. *Widowed men* report occasional help from siblings, neighbors, and offspring. However, men who are *separated/divorced* and *never-married* report no help received from any source whatever. It should be noted that whereas women in each marital status report assistance from community agencies, no men report help from this source.

How do patterns of home help vary according to the health of the receiver? Our measure of health is based on resondents' self-reports to the question: "Would you say your health in general is... excellent? Good? Fair? Or poor?" Our expectation, hardly a startling one, is that receivers of help are likely to be residents in poorer, i.e., in poor or fair, health. As Table 12.4 shows, this expectation is strongly borne out. That is, residents in "poor"health receive help more frequently, and from each source, than do residents in all other self-assessed health levels combined. In fact, except for infrequent assistance to persons in "good" health, *all* help flows *only* to those in "poor" and "fair" health.

TABLE 12.4. Sources and Estimated Annual Frequencies of Help Received at Home by Self-Assessed Health of Recipient

	Recipient's Self-assessed Health				
Help RECEIVED from:	Poor	Fair	Good	Excellent	Mean, Total
	(94)	(143)	(124)	(50)	(411*)
Neighbors/friends	10	7	3	0	5
Siblings	6	4	0	0	3
Offspring	5	1	2	0	2
Community agencies	12	2	0	0	3
Total	33	14	5	0	13

*Three cases, not ascertained as to self-assessed health status, removed from table.

To summarize findings to this point concerning the receivers of home help, recipients are more likely to be women than men and to be in poorer rather than better health. Women tend to receive assistance from all sources, from persons in their personal networks as well as from community agencies; the only men who receive significant amounts of home help are those who are married and living with spouse, and their wives are their only source of aid. Advancing age is not associated with the receipt of help among women and only mildly so with men.

Residents Who Give Help. Turning to the *givers* of help among residents of public housing for the elderly, Table 12.5A (women) and 12.5B (men) deal with estimated annual frequencies of help provided others, according to the age-bracket of the giver; help between spouses is excluded. Table 12.5A shows that just as women report receiving help from all sources, they also report *giving* aid to all categories of recipients—to neighbors and friends as well as to siblings and offspring. Their most frequent recipients are neigh-

TABLE 12.5. Estimated Annual Frequencies of Help Given to Others by Females(A) and Males(B) by Age of Giver

A.

Help GIVEN to:	Age of FEMALE Givers					
	Under 65	65-69	70-74	75-79	80 and older	Mean, all Females
	(28)	(55)	(87)	(95)	(64)	(329*)
Neighbors/friends	3	31	15	16	6	15
Siblings	13	1	5	4	0	4
Offspring	0	3	3	1	6	3
Total	16	35	23	21	12	22

*Fifteen females, age not ascertained, removed from table.

B.

Help GIVEN to:	Age of MALE Givers					
	Under 65	65-69	70-74	75-79	80 and older	Mean, all Males
	(9)	(9)	(15)	(19)	(14)	(66†)
Neighbors/friends	35	6	64	22	0	27
Siblings	0	0	0	0	0	0
Offspring	0	0	0	0	0	0
Total	35	6	64	22	0	27

†Four males, age not ascertained, removed from table.

bors and friends within the housing project; they provide help but much less frequently outside the project—to siblings, children and grandchildren.

Comparison of the tables shows that patterns of giving help differ sharply by sex. Men give help only to neighbors/friends but do so even more frequently than do women. As regards age, among women, if we exclude those under 65, the rate of helping others declines with advancing age; among men, however, there is no consistent association with age.

Data on the marital status of help-givers are presented separately by sex in Table 12.6. Among women, married females provide frequent assistance to their spouses and infrequent help to offspring, but almost none to neighbors. At the other extreme, never-married women give help fairly frequently but do so *only* to neigh-

TABLE 12.6. Estimated Annual Frequencies of Help Given to Others by Females (A) and Males (B) by Marital Status of Giver

A.

Help GIVEN to:	Marital Status of FEMALE Givers				
	Married	Widowed	Separated/ Divorced	Never Married	Mean, all Females
	(35)	(228)	(48)	(27)	(338*)
Neighbors/friends	1	16	12	31	15
Siblings	0	5	1	0	4
Offspring	5	2	8	0	3
Spouse	43	—	—	—	—
Total help GIVEN	49	23	21	31	22‡

*Six females, marital status not ascertained, removed from table.

B.

Help GIVEN to:	Marital Status of MALE Givers				
	Married	Widowed	Separated/ Divorced	Never Married	Mean, all Males
	(29)	(19)	(13)	(8)	(69†)
Neighbors/friends	0	13	54	101	26
Siblings	0	0	0	0	0
Offspring	0	0	0	0	0
Spouse	61	—	—	—	—
Total help GIVEN	61	13	54	101	26‡

†One male, marital status not ascertained, removed from table.

‡"Total help given" excludes help given to spouse.

bors. The separated/divorced are also fairly frequent providers of assistance, but divide their helping efforts about evenly between neighbors within the project and relatives elsewhere in the community. The majority group, widows, help neighbors fairly often and assist siblings and offspring also, but less frequently.

Patterns of giving help among men of different marital statuses can be described quite simply. Married males provide help *only* to their wives and do so at a high rate. Males in all other marital statuses, especially the never-married and divorced/separated, provide help *only* to neighbors/friends and do so also at a relatively high rate.

As indicated in Table 12.7, the primary donors of help, especially to neighbors, are residents in "good" and "excellent" health. However, to an extent, residents in "poor" and "fair" health also give some help to neighbors as well as to siblings and offspring.

TABLE 12.7. Estimated Annual Frequencies of Help Given to Others by Self-Assessed Health of Giver

Help GIVEN to:	Giver's Self-assessed Health				Mean, Total
	Poor	Fair	Good	Excellent	
	(94)	(143)	(124)	(50)	(411*)
Neighbors/friends	10	5	24	42	16
Siblings	4	6	0	0	3
Offspring	2	1	4	2	2
Total	16	12	28	44	21

*Three cases, not ascertained as to self-assessed health, removed from table.

Some kinds of help to others—running outside errands or providing assistance that involves physical exertion or stamina—require reasonably good health and functional mobility. Such aid is usually provided by the ill resident's relatives or by neighbors in good health. However, many small chores and forms of socioemotional support can be and are rendered an ill or incapacitated resident by a neighbor whose health is only somewhat less impaired. In short, one can help another person without leaving the premises, braving inclement weather, climbing stairs (projects have elevators) or, as noted, being in robust health. Thus, one woman with a heart ailment seldom leaves the building but collects mail and performs other services for several neighbors who are confined to their apartments. Another woman who walks with a cane rides the elevator regularly with a man more disabled than she (he requires two steel crutches) to make sure that he gets from and back to his apartment safely.

To summarize our findings concerning the givers of help, men exceed women in the number of help-episodes reported. However, married men help only their wives, and men living alone assist only other residents. Women help less often but distribute their help more broadly. While married women direct most of their assistance to their husbands, widows and the separated/divorced assist younger and own-generation relatives as well as neighbors. While residents in better health provide help to others much more frequently than do those in poorer health, the latter are also occasional sources of assistance to neighbors and relatives.

RECEIVING AND GIVING HELP: CONTEXTS AND RELATIONSHIPS OF HELPING PATTERNS

Having examined certain characteristics of receivers and givers of home-help during illness, let us turn to the contexts and relationships of helping patterns. The foregoing data, drawn largely from standardized interviews, show substantial differences betwen the sexes in the frequency, sources, and recipients of help. Data based on observation and other ethnographic procedures suggest that the quality and contexts of helping relationships also differ for men and women. Let us begin with women.

As noted by Anderson (1976), public housing projects for the elderly are essentially a female world, both numerically and in terms of their dominant social character. For any given resident, the probabilities are that five of every six neighbors are women. Furthermore, when groups of residents are observed chatting in the lobby, using laundry facilities, participating in the weekly card parties and bingo games, or interacting in many other situations, they are almost always or largely groups of *women.* Moreover, most of the women come from blue-collar backgrounds, in which their customary patterns of interaction were with other women.

Although there are several types of helping relationships among women, they have in common some degree of particularistic and diffuse interpersonal and emotional involvement. One pattern involves fairly active and healthy women shouldering responsibility to help one or more ill or incapacitated residents on a fairly regular basis. The specific help provided varies with given needs and circumstances but may include shopping or other errands, brief "check-up" calls, extended visits, or companionship. These are similar to relationships described by Johnson (1971) and Hochschild (1973) in other settings with dense concentrations of the elderly.

Characteristically, relationships to aid others are chosen and initiated by the helping individual and are usually with those residents with whom the helping person already has or subsequently develops some degree of emotional attachment. The helping person is often quite motherly and protective toward those she helps; one woman calls them, some of whom are older than herself, her "chicks". Because of the impaired health or mobility of those who receive help, the relationship is virtually never a directly reciprocal, or help-for-help, exchange. Nor is it solely a one-way relationship; in exchange for assistance, the helped person returns gratitude, positive affect, or such items as homemade baked goods or small gifts.

Although some women accept payment for services to an ill neighbor, this is not the norm and occurs only when there are extenuating circumstances, such as when it is known that the helper needs the additional pin money and the helped person can afford it. The norm, however, is to provide help without the expectation of monetary recompense. One 80-year-old widow makes it her business to pick up medicine or other items for several neighbors when she goes shopping. The day before her shopping trip, she visits them to find out what they might need. On one occasion, she made such a visit to a disabled neighbor who was being interviewed by the senior author. She stayed to chat and gossip for an hour; as she left, her neighbor somewhat surreptitiously pushed a list and a dollar bill into her hand. This incident serves to highlight the normative expectation in helping patterns among women. That is, emphasis is placed on the socioemotional transaction; even should payment occur, the monetary aspect is somehow made secondary.

Some women who regularly visit and help less healthy neighbors view these activities as a kind of "calling" or avocation, as their way of fulfilling a need to perform useful and needed services. One woman said that she helped others "because you never know when you might be in the same position". Another woman said that following her husband's death several years ago, she resolved to busy herself in regularly visiting and helping two or three ill residents.

As noted above, housing projects for the elderly are largely a female world; for most women residents, the project and their own apartments are, in Goffman's terms (1959) "center stage," to which important aspects of their lives are oriented, and where they conduct their significant "performances." By contrast, for many men, the project and apartment are "backstage," places mainly for storing one's props and for repairing to between performances. Thus, in general, the "neighboring" types of transactions that exist in the housing projects—visiting back and forth, exchanging goods or services, engaging in gossip, developing cohesive social networks —occur largely among women; men tend on the whole to be excluded, or exclude themselves, from them. To be sure, there are some men who are deeply involved in the interpersonal world of the housing project, and some women who participate minimally in it, but these tend to be exceptions.

While helping patterns among women depend on and reinforce personal and socioemotional relationships, corresponding patterns among men tend, by contrast, to emphasize impersonal and businesslike, including monetary, aspects. As noted in Tables 12.5B and 12.6B, men who live alone, especially the divorced/separated and never-married, are important sources of help to ill residents. For many of these men, helping activities tend to be assimilated to a "handy-man" role, in which more or less specific assistance is rendered to persons, largely women, who either temporarily or permanently cannot perform the tasks themselves. While such aid is often provided without payment being offered or expected, the help is given at least as often in the context of a relatively impersonal or "businesslike" transaction, in which a nominal fee is expected, offered, and accepted.

Among the men who own cars, there are several who have a more or less regular clientele, mainly women, for whom they provide a range of services, many of which require a need for transportation—driving residents to doctors' offices, on shopping trips, to church, and the like. A few men have fairly large numbers of clients or, as some men call them, "customers." The customers must arrange for the transportation in advance to ensure that the driver will be available. If the customer is physically impaired, the driver is expected to help her out of the building and into the car, deliver her to her destination, provide additional assistance if needed, wait until her business is finished, and then transport her home. Fees vary but usually range between 50 cents and a dollar.

The essential contrast between men and women helpers is perhaps best illuminated by the differing connotations of "chicks" and "customers." Each, of course, implies a kind of contract. The woman who tends her chicks is a "mother hen" who shares a socioemotional bond with them, provides a set of competencies and care to individuals who are vulnerable and need care, and receives evidences of socioemotional feedback in return for her help. On the other hand, the man who serves customers provides some range of services to persons who request them, usually on a relatively impersonal basis, in return for compensation which may range from a simple "thank you" to nominal payment.

Between spouses, the frequency of help is extremely high. Although there are married pairs among whom both partners are active and healthy, the fact that an ill or incapacitated resident lives with a spouse frequently permits the former to avoid or defer institutionalization well beyond the point that would be possible were he or she living alone. One typical case is that of a man whose wife is severely crippled with arthritis and who has taken over the entire domestic management of the household in addition to providing personal care for his wife. Another involves a woman whose husband is bedridden with cancer; without her care, according to neighbors, he would have been hospitalized long ago.

FRIENDS, NEIGHBORS, AND CORESIDENTS

Most residents recognize three categories of persons among other residents—friends, neighbors, and co-residents. The terms for the first two categories are often those employed by residents; for the third, there appears to be no agreed-on term. "Friends" are persons, usually few in number and of one's own sex, with whom one enjoys relatively high degrees of social reciprocity, interpersonal intimacy, and diffuse personal involvement. "Neighbors" refers to a larger number of persons, usually of both sexes, with whom various reciprocities occur in relationships marked by variable but limited reciprocity, intimacy and personal involvement.[4] "Coresidents," essentially all other residents of the project, are persons with whom there are degrees of social distance rather than intimacy, a general lack of personal involvement, and with whom reciprocity may involve little more than "passing the time of day." With respect to specific ego-alter relationships, the lines between friend and neighbor, and between neighbor and coresident, are often blurred and in states of flux. They are also occasionally subject to discrepant perceptions—as when A sees B as a neighbor, but B views A as a friend; or when C casts D as a coresident, but D perceives C in a neighbor role.

The foregoing categorizations have significant implications for helping patterns. Relations between friends sometimes involve frequent, regular, and indispensable assistance. In one case of close friends, for example, a woman with severe arthritis is helped into and out of bed twice daily, every day, by a woman who has been doing this for several years. Another case involves an 80-year-old woman who for about two years has been preparing dinner for and eating with a much younger woman who suffered a stroke; the younger friend reciprocates in several ways, including paying a greater share of the grocery bill.

Although help circulates within the projects between persons who relate to each other not as friends but as neighbors or even coresidents, such aid is governed by norms whose existence and strength become apparent when the norms are violated. Residents physically able to do so expect and are expected to help indisposed or incapacitated neighbors or coresidents on occasion, i.e., in a one-time crisis or on an irregular or infrequent basis. However, complaints are heard about neighbors or coresidents (i.e., persons with whom there is no prior intimacy or personal involvement) demanding too much help, or expecting it too frequently, or wanting one to provide what was initially a one-shot or infrequent service on a continuing basis.

To some extent, helping patterns within the projects can be sorted out in terms of Sahlins' distinctions between generalized, balanced, and negative reciprocities (1965:147-149):

> It is notable of the main run of generalized reciprocities that the material flow is sustained by prevailing social relations; whereas for the main run of balanced exchange, social relations hinge on the material flow... "Negative reciprocity" is the attempt to get something for nothing...[and]...is the most impersonal sort of exchange.

Thus generalized reciprocity often marks helping patterns involving two women who relate as friends, in which the help transactions are embedded in and serve as extensions of emotionally-toned interpersonal relationships. Balanced reciprocity frequently describes situations in which men are helpers—relatively impersonal and businesslike transactions in which some definite recompense is expected, offered, and accepted. Negative reciprocity, or something like it, seems to prevail in situations in which coresidents expect more than potential givers are prepared to offer.

Although this paper focuses on informal patterns and networks of aid among elderly residents of public housing, it should be noted that organized and institutionalized health and social services also occur. Services are provided by the Visiting Nurse Association, several schools of nursing, the health department, Project Involve (a local agency that serves the elderly), various social service agencies, and others. The Housing Authority staff also promotes various procedures for monitoring the health and safety of residents.

Friends outside the housing projects are occasionally helped by project residents. In addition, as we have noted, relatives living elsewhere in the community—both younger and same-generation kin—provide help to residents and, on occasion, are helped by them. Although many residents have adult children in the Milwaukee area and usually engage in many exchanges with them, most residents prefer to accept help from children only if the help can be rendered in the older person's apartment. One resident expressed the prevailing sentiment: "My children would do anything for me if I asked them, but I wouldn't want to live with any of them. If they had to take care of me, I would hate it as much as they would. It wouldn't work."

DISCUSSION AND IMPLICATIONS

In a setting sometimes stereotyped by outsiders as a dumping ground for poor elderly, we have found a viable community of peers involved in active exchanges between the relatively healthy and the ill. In this niche of public housing, problems of long-term dependency due to chronic incapacity are at least partially resolved by several kinds of reciprocities—*generalized* among women, often *balanced* when the helpers are men. In terms of cost-benefit considerations, we apparently have a situation in which for everyone concerned benefits appear to outweigh costs. Everyone seems to gain—relatives of elderly residents, agencies and programs supported by public funds, and the residents themselves.

The fact that peers assume some, often considerable, responsibility for the long-term support of disabled friends means that pressures on relatives are somewhat relieved, and the quality of the relationships between incapacitated parents and children and younger relatives may thereby be improved. Also, care by peers reduces, or at least defers, needs for institutionalization, which lightens otherwise costly demands on public funds. By no means least important, the givers/receivers of help are also the gainers. The givers have opportunities to play useful and needed roles, in return for rewards ranging from socioemotional gratification and heightened self-esteem to material compensation. At the same time, the receivers of aid are able to avoid or defer institutionalization (or living with relatives), retain a degree of independence by continuing to live in their own apartments, and maintain self-esteem by participating in varied reciprocities instead of being objects of one-way dependence.

As noted, this research has focused on but one of the niches in our society occupied by the elderly. There are other niches, each marked by somewhat different physical and social features, with populations of varying characteristics. There is a need to study and compare patterns of handling disability and dependence in the various niches. Rosow (1967) has made a beginning along these lines, studying apartment buildings with various concentrations of older people. Also, there are inner-city slum hotels and rooming houses, with a predominance of elderly single males (Stephens 1976), middle-class retirement communities peopled largely by retired married pairs (Jacobs 1974), working-class retirement communities (Hochschild 1973; Ross 1977), and others, including those niches in which the majority of elderly are found—individuals or pairs of spouses living in rented or owned quarters throughout the community as well as the numerous elderly, also dispersed, who live with younger relatives.

NOTES

1. The overall study from which present data are drawn was conducted pursuant to a contract between the U. S. Department of Housing and Urban Development and the National League of Cities, with the cooperation of the Milwaukee Urban Observatory. The authors are solely responsible for the accuracy of statements or interpretations in this paper.

2. However, as Clark points out, close kinship is not always or necessarily sufficient to legitimize an individual's "right" that his or her dependency claims be honored indefinitely (1972:270).

3. One source of help available only to currently married persons—the spouse—is not included in Tables 12.2A and 12.2B, but is presented in Tables 12.3A and 12.3B.

4. The present distinction between friend and neighbor is similar to that made by Keller (1968:25).

13 Age, Sex, and Death Anxiety in A Middle-Class American Community

CAROL M. SCHULZ
Johns Hopkins University

T hroughout this book we have been concerned with values and how they are manifest in social life. Values produce conflicts. when it is difficult or impossible for the positive to be attained. Carol Schulz, in this chapter, investigates another value dimension and another problem older adults must come to terms with—life and death. Although the negative, death, may come at any time, age is often taken as an indicator of our progression between life and death. In old age the probabilities and proximity of death become greater. People avoid the negative and affirm the positive. It is life that is emphasized while death is blocked out, denied, repressed, and not even talked about. Death is a nasty, five letter possibility.

Death anxiety, as a response to the possiblity, is investigated in a small, homogenous town in the Midwestern portion of the United States. Schulz effectively combines a dual research strategy of long term observation with a survey instrument. Her statistics would have been much less meaningful without the richness of her qualitative data based on observation. By placing her research in the context of a community, Schulz is able to look at death anxiety at all phases of human development and to isolate the cultural factors which explain the patterns in her data.

In her study Carol Schulz combines issues of communities and sex role differentiation appearing in the preceeding chapters. Communities are not only places in which to live, but they provide opportunities and structure avenues for problem resolution. However, communities may not offer resolutions to some problems. Carol Schulz discovers that the structuring of sex roles in her research community did not lead to a healthy resolution of the anxiety on the part of older men. Sex roles, by being complementary and minimizing conflict between men and women, also select for different styles of emotional expression as well as activities. Consequently older females are more accepting of the inevitable. Older men, who have repressed and denied death during

their working years, are faced with an unresolved anxiety that
surfaces following retirement.

What can be done about death anxiety, especially for older
males? Schulz suggests that continuity of roles or substitution of
roles be encouraged. Her informants tell her they want to feel
needed, to be useful, and to be desired by someone. These wants
are reminiscent of the values of affection, having duties and re-
sponsibilities, and having respect expressed by Kagan's informants
in Bojacá. Resolution of value conflicts is an individual and cultu-
ral affair. Individuals experience the conflict, culture provides the
guidelines and avenues for resolution.

"Aging" is actually a life-long developmental process, although
in the popular sense we think of aging as having to do with the elderly only. Regardless of which concept of aging is employed,
there is agreement that every person's life-long developmental process is a *continuum*, marked at some point by its inevitable end.
Death therefore has a rightful place in any study of human development, regardless of the age of the subjects. The "aged" are, of
course, statistically closer to death than younger persons. However,
on an individual basis, there is little prediction as to when a specific death will occur. For those who are young, death is unplanned,
and when it occurs, it is generally unexpected. For the older person death becomes less unexpected.

The awareness of one's finitude is undoubtedly a pan-human
characteristic. In American culture especially, we are much more
aware of the possibility of our deaths than we are openly willing
to admit. The older we become, the more conscious thought and
concern we invest in preparing for the "winding-down" stage of
our developmental process. A sense of closure is sought during this
last stage of life. Death therefore is an important point to consider
when studying the "aged." It is important *not* because the elderly
are preparing and waiting to die, but rather because they are preparing *to live* the completion of a natural cycle—their lifespan—in
a way which will give dignity and continued meaning to their lives.
Life and death are two undeniable parts of the same process which
we call human development. One cannot exist without the acceptance of the other. It might be argued that life cannot be sensed in
its ultimate fullness without the knowledge and acceptance of its
end.

Only recently have anthropologists begun to consider death as
a serious research topic. In the areas of understanding the cultural
meanings of death, the values and attitudes surrounding death and
the phenomenon of death anxiety, the anthropologist is in an appropriate position to delve into these issues. He or she is trained to

abstract the basic underlying values which lie at the core of a culture, as well as to outline the attitudes that are derived from that value system. When underlying value conflict is evident in a value system, cognitive mechanisms may be operating to reduce that conflict and let the value system maintain a dynamic equilibrium for the individual. The anthropologist can shed light on those cognitive and material aspects of the environment which shape certain characteristic cultural responses to aging and death. Our growing awareness of the etiology of one such response, death anxiety, may eventually bring into focus new alternative ways to view death and perhaps even change the status of "unclean" that death now holds in our contemporary American value system.

The following is one attempt at anthropological synthesis of aging, sex roles, and the response of death anxiety as seen on a community level. We shall begin with a basic orientation of the position that the death anxiety response holds in middle-class American culture.

DEATH ANXIETY IN AMERICAN CULTURE

Middle-class Americans live in a sociocultural environment in which death is commonly perceived as a "loss." For the individual's perception of personal death, this loss becomes a "loss of self," a very potent and central focus (Fulton 1964; Schulz 1977). Viewing personal death as a loss of self creates dissonance and anxiety for the individual who simultaneously advocates other values which emphasize the uniqueness and irreplaceability of the self. Not only is one's self unique, but, ideally, it is also productive and socially successful. Within this value system, the basic existential concepts of life and death are set into opposition. They become contradictory. The life values place a premium on youth, health, achievement, success, productivity and uniqueness of one's self. Death, on the other hand, is the negation of all that is positive in life. In order for the individual to embrace the contradiction, some form of compromise (mediation) has to occur between these two opposing sets of values. Some mediating concept or mechanism must intervene to reduce both the resulting value conflict and the psychological dissonance and anxiety. Death anxiety is the *response* of the individual to the life-death value conflict, and, as has been argued elsewhere (Schulz 1978), the means of compromise and mediation lie in reinforcing and bolstering one's sense of existence, one's concept of self. Affirming the sense of self is at some level basic to all cultures, regardless of value configuration. The *specific means*, however, of affirming the self can be found within the cultural framework of any given society. In American culture these means are extensions of the *success-achievement* core cultural life value.

The mediating, conflict-reducing mechanism of affirming the self appears to reduce the death anxiety response by suppressing conscious awareness of *one* of the conflicting concepts. The obvious concept to suppress is death itself. American culture has been quite successful in minimizing contact with and awareness of death-related phenomena. The reduction of death awareness and death anxiety is accomplished by the cognitive aspect of achievement motivation[2] and the behavioral aspect of success realization. These two aspects join to form a shield against conscious death awareness, thereby reducing the death anxiety response. This mechanism of attaching positive values of success and achievement to the self allows the individual to block out awareness of death by aspirations to productiveness and by the behavioral acting out of success attainment. In short, affirming the self through culturally acceptable and desirable means provides the individual with a phenomenological "immortality" of productiveness.

We shall extend this line of thought by examining the consequences of this achievement-oriented shielding against death anxiety for the elderly, especially the elderly male. Of major concern is the relationship of traditional sex-role differentiation in middle-class American culture on death perception and death-related affect in later life.

METHODOLOGY

A small semi-rural midwestern Protestant community was selected for a two-year period of intense participant observation. After one year of personal, face-to-face contact with a large segment of the 1,300 people in this community, a survey questionnaire was designed to gather quantifiable data on personal histories, and experciences with and attitudes about death. The instrument included two valid and reliable death anxiety measures (Collett and Lester 1969; Templer 1969) and a measure of achievement motivation (Mehrabian 1968).

The questionnaire, a self-report instrument, was administered to 264 adults (145 females; 119 males), randomly selected from 202 households in the community. This sample covers an age range from 18 years to 85 years. The refusal rate was less than 10 percent, a relatively small proportion considering the length of the instrument.

This combined research focus of traditional participant-observer fieldwork *and* questionnaire survey proved highly rewarding in theory construction as well as hypothesis testing. Selecting a community that was both conservative/traditional and socioeconomically homogeneous minimized the contaminating effects of interethnic and interracial class influences. The field work time allowed the construction of a fairly complex cultural framework. The community became both a quantitative data base as well as a qualitative frame for interpreting the quantitative results. It is desirable and productive to create this kind of a feedback mechanism between different methods of data acquisition. We shall now turn to some of the results of that survey which explore age, sex roles, and death anxiety.

AGE, IDEAL CULTURAL SEX ROLES AND DEATH ANXIETY

The relationship between achievement motivation (the self-affirmation variable) and death anxiety was examined across age for both sexes (Figure 13.1). The strongest inverse relationship was obtained during the peak productive years for males (age groups 20's—40's), indicating that the cognitive shield of "productive immortality" reaches highest efficacy in blocking out death awareness during the time of life when success aspirations are backed up by success-realization role playing (Schulz 1978). Such a relationship was not obtained for the females. It appears that females in our sample did not utilize this success-achievement mediator. This result was anticipated since middle-class American women who strongly adhere to the traditional sex-role of "homemaker" would not depend as strongly on success-achievement as a form of self-affirmation (Schulz 1978).

Sex-role definitions and expectations were clear-cut in this community. Males were the providers, competitors, "achievers," and breadwinners. Females were the homemakers, supporters, and maintainers of the domestic sphere, as well as those who lend support to the males in their role. Here traditional sex roles are complementary, with men and women having jurisdiction over separate spheres of activity and life. Sex roles are based on a division of labor and structured to minimize male-female competition.

This pattern of sex-role differentiation is learned early in life and is reinforced throughout adolescence and adulthood. This dif-

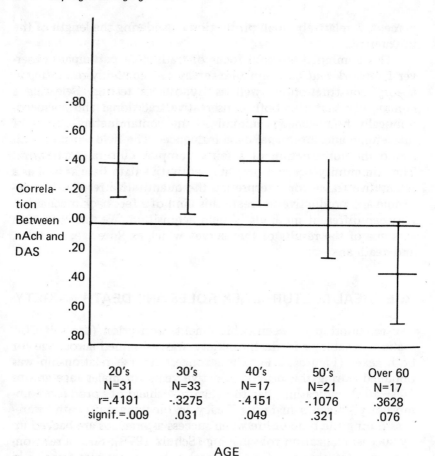

	20's	30's	40's	50's	Over 60
	N=31	N=33	N=17	N=21	N=17
	r=.4191	-.3275	-.4151	-.1076	.3628
	signif.=.009	.031	.049	.321	.076

AGE

[Confidence interval = .85]

FIGURE 13.1 Correlations Between Achievement Motivation
(nAch) and Death Anxiety (DAS) for Male Age Groups
(Schulz 1978, adapted by permission).

ferentiation is accompanied by the learning of appropriate sex-role
related affect. Emotional expression, especially negative affect
(such as fear), tends to be repressed in males, by whom it is interpreted as a "sign of weakness". On the other hand, although emotional expression is not wholeheartedly encouraged in the females
either, it is nonetheless allowed, and in some instances considered quite appropriate (such as an expression of fear) and in keeping
with the expected female role of psychological dependency.

This traditional pattern has rather interesting implications for
death anxiety and death-related affect in the elderly, especially the
elderly male. Although the "productive immortality" acts as a sup-

pressant of death anxiety during the peak productive years of the males' lives, the adherence to achievement motivation in later life is related to an increase (rather than a decrease) in death anxiety, as shown in the sharp drop of the curve in Figure 13.1.[3]

The change from a negative to a positive correlation between achievement motivation and death anxiety for males in later life may be explained by the lack of socially prescribed "productive roles" that characterizes senescence in our society, and this makes the striving for success and achievement somewhat futile and frustrating for the elderly male. Therefore, rather than acting to decrease his conscious death awareness and death anxiety, achievement orientation after retirement (and after having completed the "provider" role for his children) only increases his feelings of productive impotence, and in fact, increases both death awareness and death anxiety.

Both sex groups of this community sample responded to a 36-item death-concerns instrument (Collett and Lester 1969), which makes reference to a broad range of death fears. Approximately one- half of the items are worded in terms of acceptance and the other half in terms of avoidance or fear. This structural dichotomy was an outgrowth of the effort to control for response set, but it also serves as a convenient marker of the emotional directionality (acceptance/avoidance) of each of the concerns, regardless of its content. The 36 death concerns for the successive age groups for both sexes were factor-analyzed. The percentage of *avoidance* (consistent negative affect within the factor) factors, *acceptance* (consistent positive affect) factors, and the *mixed-reaction* (both positive and negative affect) factors were calculated, and are presented across age in Figures 13.2 and 13.3.

The percentage of mixed reaction factors (or, emotional "ambivalence") tends to decline with age for both sexes. The male group is especially interesting because the curve for mixed reaction factors across age roughly parallels that of the death anxiety mean scores across age (Figure 13.4). It has been noted elsewhere that emotional inconsistency ("ambivalence") appears to be directly related to self-reported death anxiety, especially for males (Schulz 1977).[4]

Another interesting sex difference becomes noticeable when we compare the percentage of avoidance and acceptance factors. Males in later life show a *marked increase in avoidance factors*, acceptance factors remaining stable throughout the lifespan. For the females, on the other hand, avoidance factors remain stable, while the *acceptance factors increase* in later life. This points to the fact that females become more positive toward death in general as they

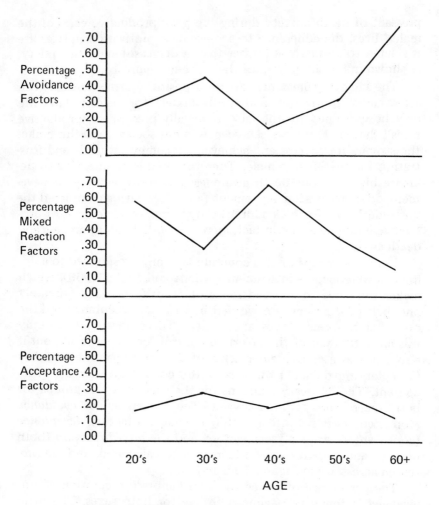

FIGURE 13.2 Percentage Avoidance, Acceptance and Mixed
Reaction Factors for Male Age Groups.

reach old age and death becomes imminent. These findings are cor-
roborated by strong feelings conveyed during informal interviews
throughout the field-work period. Males, on the other hand, become emotionally more negative toward approaching death. Perhaps an explanation can again be centered around sex-role expectation for emotional expression. Young men are expected to mask
and repress overt expression of fear, including death fear. To decrease the dissonance between what they may really feel and what
is culturally expected of them, men have to convince themselves,
consciously at least, that they are not afraid. Sufficient self-con-

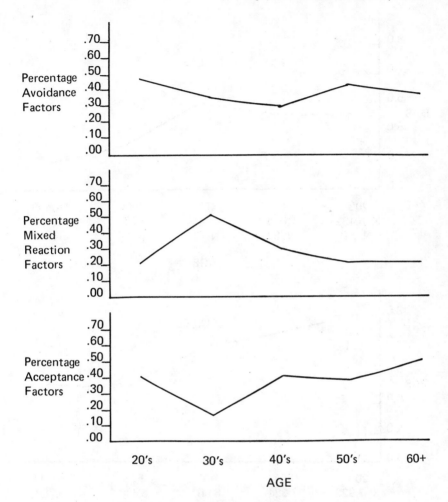

FIGURE 13.3 Percentage Avoidance, Acceptance and Mixed
Reaction Factors for Female Age Groups.

vincing of this sort could lead to a high degree of conscious masking of death fears and concerns. For a large portion of the male
lifespan, negative death-related affect is not dealt with openly or
directly. When the cultural expectation of the stoic, brave, provider male becomes attentuated, as it seems to with regard to the
elderly, the masking and repression is no longer a public necessity,
and death-related affect is allowed to surface.

Females are subject to different expectations for emotional expression. Their traditional sex role of dependency allows them

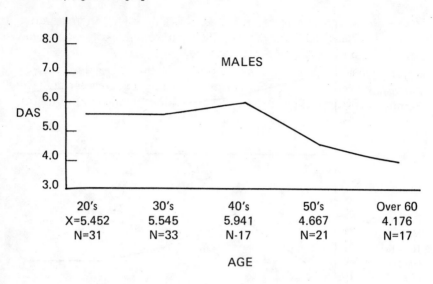

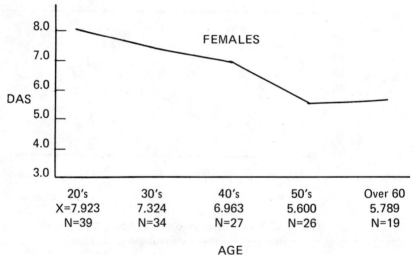

FIGURE 13.4 Death Anxiety (DAS) Mean Scores for Age Groups
(Schulz 1978, adapted by permission).

some overt expression of emotion (especially fear) throughout
their lives. Since they are allowed this expression, cognitive masking is not as necessary, hence not as strong as it is in males, and
many of these feelings, especially the strong negative affect *remains conscious,* and is in some sense "worked through" simply
because it is allowed to remain at a level of expression. It has also
been suggested that females are brought closer into contact with
potential death as a result of the birth experience (Sharon Rogers,
Alfred University, personal communication). By the time the fe-

males reach old age and death becomes imminent, their negative feelings toward death have been dealt with consciously, somewhat tempered, and perhaps even somewhat resolved.

Further explanation may be derived from the males' achievement orientation. The combination of a general decrease in achievement motivation (Figure 13.5) in later life, the decrease of cultur-

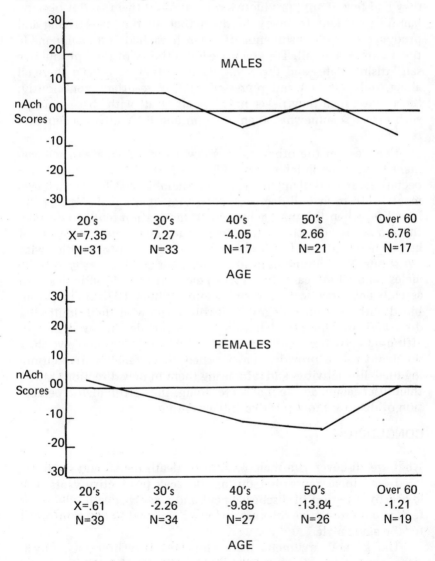

FIGURE 13.5 Achievement Motivation (nAch)
Mean Scores for Age Groups (Schulz 1978, adapted by permission).

ally prescribed productive roles and goals, as well as the awareness of the unfulfilled achievement goals set in youth, might all point to the futility of self-affirmation based on achievement in the face of approaching death. The negative emotional content, and perhaps an accompanying sense of bitterness, was evident in the old men of the community. They could not strive any more because they had few, if any, productive roles allotted them, and it became painfully evident to many of them that all the goal-striving and productive accomplishments of their lives had not really made them immortal at all. The cognitive immortality of the "productive self" disintegrates and the same old fears that have been there all along, only masked and repressed, simply resurface consciously. Since these men may never have openly dealt with these feelings, such affect is somewhat alien to them and difficult to accept and resolve.

Females, on the other hand, show a slight increase in achievement motivation in later years (Figure 13.5). Since the sex-role expectations are complementary, it is predictable that female achievement motivation will decrease when that of the males is high. In later life, when the male achievement motivation tends to decline, the female is cognitively free to pursue achievement interests of her own outside of the home without coming into conflict with her spouse's achievement needs. After their children are grown, females tend to increase their involvement in outside activities such as club and organization membership (Schulz 1975). This, combined with continued cognitive involvement with their adult children and growing grandchildren, keeps females involved in self-affirming activities at a time in life when the males perceive their dominant role ("provider") as finished. Since females are continuing their life activities and refocusing them in new directions rather than disengaging as the males are doing, the aged females' perception of death is more positive and accepting.

CONCLUSION

What we discover is a male pattern of death denial and death-related emotional repression during the peak productive years, followed by a period of disengagement and negative death-related affect, when productive roles are no longer assigned to and reinforced for the aging male.

The general argument from clinicians (psychologists, physicians, counselors, etc.) has been that repression of death awareness is "not healthy," just as any emotional repression is "not healthy." However, given the present American cultural life-death value configuration, repression of death awareness and death anxiety are *adaptive* in the broadest sense of the term, and even necessary for the reduction of individual cognitive dissonance, created by the life-death value antithesis created by the value system. The implicit message is that if we wished to alter the male pattern of repression and negative perception of death in later life, we would have to change more than just the individual's perception of death in old age. It would involve a revamping of traditional middle-class sex roles and the concomitant socialization approach to the expression of affect. Humankind, after all, is a product of cultural process, which tends to be conservative in the face of implemented change. We are not dealing with an isolated phenomenon, but rather with a complex interactive system of culture and the individual.

What, then, can be done to reintegrate elderly males into a *rewarding* continuation of their developmental process? An obvious approach is to ask these very men. The most common response revolved about the theme of wishing to feel needed and desired by someone. Performing a "useful" function was the way to become needed. When asked what they considered a "useful function," many equated this phrase with the work they performed prior to retirement. Of course, society no longer accepts their performance of these functions and we are caught in a circular web. They key to unlocking this defeating merry-go-round is to *create* a new, yet acceptable, set of options for "useful function." Traditional work-oriented functions are defined by the working-age sector of society. Mobilizing this portion of the society to create new options for the elderly will be a slow process. It may be more rewarding to create a social atmosphere in which the elderly make their own rules. Such subcultural settings already exist in age-homogeneous communities. Here the elderly are not set into competition with younger members of society. An older adult can define a social setting, new norms, and new alternative behaviors that are functional and that can be tailor-made for maximum personal well-being in the latter phases of human development. Such age segregation has its drawbacks in that it promotes isolation of the elderly from the rest of society, which brings into focus another value conflict in American society—segregation-integration and the melting-pot ideal (Ross 1977).

Another approach to integration through social "usefulness" is to place the elderly in the position of consultant, to be called upon for specific expertise when and as it is required by younger members of business and industry. A nationwide network of elderly business consultants is already in operation. The drawback to such an approach is that only a small segment of the elderly population qualifies for "expertship". What mechanism can exist for those who did not have professional careers?

The answer is not a simple one. The question may not even be appropriate. Reintegration is a complex issue involving an interplay of cognitive and perceptual restructuring (on the part of the elderly and those around them) and the creation of behavioral outlets for "usefulness." As the projection of citizens over the age of 65 increases in our society, this issue will become one of major focus to social planners in future years.

NOTES

1. The research upon which this paper is based is, in part, funded by the David Ross Research Grant, Purdue University.

2. A relationship between achievement motivation and fear of death has been suggested by Spilka and Pellegrini (1967). Lester (1970) has hypothesized a direct relationship between achievement motivation and fear of death, reasoning that persons who have the highest achievement motivation also have the most "to lose" by death, and therefore fear of death should vary directly with the "need to achieve." Lester did not substantiate his hypothesis; no significant relationship between the two variables was found. His sample, however, was an ad hoc group (primarily college students), and was not drawn from an already existing socially integrated community, where the inhabitants share a basic value orientation. In a community-based sample (Schulz 1978), a significant inverse relationship was obtained between these self-affirmation variables and self-reported death anxiety (using the DAS, Death Anxiety Scale, Templer 1969) for the males (Pearson Product Moment Correlation of -.21 between need for achievement and death anxiety, $p > .01$). No clear relationship was evident for the females. This study showed that for the males, self-reported death anxiety decreases with increased achievement motivation, as well as with increased education and income (the self-affirmation variables). Such an *inverse* relationship was expected in light of a mediating mechanism.

3. Both achievement motivation and death anxiety decrease with age for males; this direct relationship may, in part, be explained by the drop in score on both scales.

4. Emotional inconsistency ("ambivalence") seems to be related also to attitudinal inconsistency, which Lester (1967) found to be directly related to death anxiety.

14 Kin Relations of the Aged: Possible Consequences to Social Service Planning

MARIA SIEMASZKO
Catholic Charities of Chicago

W*hat can be done with our knowledge about older people? We have looked at age homogeneous communities, aid networks, ethnic resources, family networks, values, age norms and biological factors. We have examined these in Colombia, China, India, Belize, Paris, among the American Indians, and in the United States. What does all this have to do with aging here, right now, and in the not too distant future? Maria Siemaszko is somewhat distinctive among the contributors to this volume in that she is an anthropologist who is not employed by a university. Instead she works for a social service agency. She takes her anthropological perspective to the social services and brings the social services to anthropology.*

As an anthropologist interested in the design and delivery of social services, Siemaszko is first concerned with the resources older adults have available that may be reinforced and complimented by a social service program. Most obvious in a network of resources is the family. Puzzled by the stereotype that the family in industrialized society is in a state of dissolution, Siemaszko explores the recent research on family organization in urban America which posits that urban families are not the extended cohesive units their counterparts are in many horticultural and pastoral societies. Yet being smaller, more dispersed and nuclear does not mean that families are the isolated, insular and atomistic entities the post-World War II researchers forecast. Contemporary families are smaller, but they maintain a great deal of interaction and exchange, especially with older members.

Since family organization is a basic ingredient of a culture, Siemaszko asks if these family interaction patterns are distinctive subculturally? She investigates the kin network of a sample of Polish Americans and compares her results with those of known American and Polish samples. Differences do exist which are approximately halfway between the American and Polish sample. These differences partially condition the use of social services.

Also as Siemaszko points out, this cohort of Polish-American elderly is distinctive in that the effects of the diaspora of World War II are just becoming apparent.

As the year 2000 rolls around, there will be more older adults in America. Unquestionably the design of our social services will have to account for and accommodate the needs of this growing population. That population, however, is not uniform in resources or in culture, since people become even more heterogeneous as they age. We cannot force a heterogeneous group of people into the melting pot and expect one plan of action to resolve all problems. To plan these social services with the maximal economic efficiency and effectiveness, they must be culturally sensitive. They must acknowledge the resources people have and their receptivity to different kinds of assistance. Another side of the coin is in justifying programs. Stereotypes are used to paint dire circumstances under which some people are forced to live. While these images may have some objective basis and may assist in mobilizing support, they ignore much of the cultural variation. Stereotypes reinforce and maintain social boundaries by preventing us from seeing the humanity on the other side. We see the other, but we really do not comprehend the other. For the elderly this is especially tragic. Older adults, in accommodating to physical and psychological changes and to new arrangements in social roles, are shifting identities. As Siemaszko points out, this negative image can be incorporated into a self-image. It is also tragic that the young can only see a shell of a future. They miss the warmth, the vitality, and the social exchange that is in that future. To see through that stereotype is to see that older adults continue to be in charge of their lives and are preparing for tomorrow, and tomorrow, and tomorrow.

More than a decade of research has demonstrated that the American kinship system is indeed not disintegrating and that a majority of aged individuals receive support from kinsmen. Ironically, as we find the aged American individual in rather optimistic circumstances, public and government agencies see those 65 and over as deserted by kin and in need of supportive social services. Whereas many programs dealing with other aspects of our society are being cut back and phased out, proposals for replacing traditionally kin-based services to older adults are increasing in frequency and support.

On the surface, politics is a significant factor in the emergence of aging as a priority area. Although seniors make up only 10 percent of the total population, with the exception of the rich they are the segment of society with the most free time for voting, politicking and campaigning. But to leave politics as the single answer is simplistic, since because of their heterogeneity the elderly do not form a coherent voting block (Hudson and Binstock 1976). But the image of the elderly as alone, poor, and sick is a political force which cannot be ignored.

The research presented in this chapter intends to show that the aged in general have close kin units and call upon these units at times of crises, have routine vistiing and exchange of services, and basically live in the context of established American kin patterns. The kin relations of an American subculture, the Polish elderly, are measured and compared to the American kin system and suggestions are made for more efficient and culturally sensitive social service programs. We also speculate why Americans accept a seemingly untrue and pessimistic view of their own kin structure in reference to their elderly members.

THE EMERGING ELDERLY POPULATION

In 1900, persons over 65 comprised 4.1 percent of the population of the United States. By 1960–61, they comprised 9.2 percent of our population (United States Department of Health, Education, and Welfare, 1964:3). Currently (1970) the proportion of the aged is 9.9 percent. This means 20 million individuals, 8½ million men and 11½ million women, are 65+ years of age. Half of the older population is 73 years of age or older. In 1960, about 10,000 individuals reported themselves as 100 years of age or older. The older population as a whole is growing more rapidly than the total population. This is especially true for the 75+ age bracket. It is expected that the 65+ population will eventually reach between 15.2 and 18.5 percent of the total population assuming zero population growth and increases in longevity (Hauser 1976). Concerning the demographic data, Bratmen states:

> The age related and changing proportion of males to females, of white to other, of foreign born to native, etc., highlight the uniqueness of the older population and the necessity for planning based on knowledge and understanding.... Planning for and serving such a large but diverse and changing population demands careful attention to individual differences—planning for individuals rather than the average. (1970:17)

The facets of the study of the aged are many. They are not homogeneous nor proportionately found in our populations. Neugarten and Moore (1968) have noted that the aged are disproportionately found in rural counties, chiefly in the midwest, in older neighborhoods of large cities, and in the older suburbs. Only a very small proportion live in affluent retirement communities (about 2 percent). In these communities a subculture of the aged may be developing—one oriented to the use of leisure. But this is too small a number of aged individuals from which to generalize.

Additional dimensions to our knowledge of the aged are provided by Neugarten (1968:17 and 1975a) who predicted that today's aged will be different from future generations of aged. Future generations will probably be better educated, healthier, longer lived, and in higher occupational levels. They will be more accustomed to the politics of confrontation and will become a more demanding group. This may be a reaction to ageism. Covert forms of ageism (negative or hostile feelings towards an age group other than one's own) can be seen in attitudes Americans have about providing meaningful work or nonwork roles for older people; by the small percentage of the welfare dollar that is spent for services to the aged; and research on aging, which has been very slow to develop in both the biological and social sciences.

Thus we find the emergence of an enormous group of people for whom society has previously made no special provisions. Programs frequently are created which are based upon several assumptions about the elderly, which include such statements as most old people are in poor helath; they are physically isolated from their families; they want to continue to work; they live in poverty. Hence the elderly are often treated in policy formation as

a monolithic, homogenous group rather than as a heterogenous section of the population with diverse needs, with the result that programs for the elderly may offer too little flexibility and choice to those they are designed to serve (Friis, et al. 1968:2)

It is my contention that the most important factor in successful program planning for the elderly is the presence of significant others. This means that in dealing with elderly individuals and in planning programs for the elderly, one must count on these persons, make full use of them, and confer with them. The "significant others" compose or constitute one's social network.

SOCIAL NETWORK: THE ELDERLY AND THEIR KINSMEN

Social networks of older adults can be smaller or larger depending, of course, on the individual. For some extremely isolated persons, this network has shrunk to none or perhaps one individual. Ordinarily, however, the social network consists of the household of which he or she is a part, kin (children, grandchildren, siblings, etc.) to a greater or lesser extent, friends, acquaintances, and individuals with whom he or she have regular contact, such as shopkeepers, fellow roomers in a pension hotel, waitresses at the local restaurants, and other business or service personnel.

The portion of the social network of older people which we examine in this chapter is that of the kinship network. The specific relationships which are the focus of my research and analysis are the parent-child relationships of the aged, and the role of the children in maintaining their aged parents in financial, medical, and emotional aspects and needs. As Rosenmayr and Kockeis state this area of research has implications for the elderly:

> The connections are becoming apparent here between gerontological research and research in the family; indeed an overlapping of these two disciplines appears to us not as a regrettable, but as the fruitful and inevitable consequences of a suitable approach to the subject (1963:420).

Paradoxically, sociological and anthropological literature of the last 40 years has frequently lamented the death of the extended family in America and its replacement by an "unstable," "loose-knit," and "atomistic" nuclear family. Often the loss of an extended system is seen to adversely affect the life-style of the elderly in urban America. Sorokin, in 1930, for example, predicted the then future development of the nuclear family as follows:

> The family as a sacred union of husband and wife, or parents and children, will continue to decrease until any profound difference between socially sanctioned marriages and illicit sex relationships disappears. Children will be separated earlier and earlier from parents. The main socio-cultural functions of the family will further decrease, until the family becomes a mere incidental co-habitation of male and female, while the home will become a mere parking place mainly for sex relationships (Sorokin 1937:776).

Talcott Parsons furthers the implications of this view for the elderly (1942:102-103):

> The obverse of the emancipation, upon marriage and occupational independence of children from their families of orientation, is the depletion of that family until the older couple is finally left alone. This situation is in strong contrast to kinship systems in which membership in a kinship unit is continuous throughout the life cycle.

In a more recent article, however, Parsons states that even though the trend of the household has been that of isolation of the nuclear family, this does not really pose a problem for the aged because of "communications and the values of the American system" (1962:25). Even in the 1970's, scholars such as Robert A. Winch and Scott Green (1968) and Geoffrey Gibson (1972) view the American family as isolated and nuclear.

Contrary arguments to this pessimistic school of thought in terms of the industrial twentieth-century nuclear family include data obtained by recent historical research. These have demonstrated that relatively few functionally interdependent households existed in preindustrial England and in certain regions of France (Laslett, 1965). Often, individuals who managed to survive into their old age were left to live and die alone. Rudy Ray Seward investigated the colonial family in America. Using primary sources such as wills, cemeteries, and church records, Seward concludes that a vast majority of families were nuclear rather than extended (Seward 1973).

Ruth Benedict (1959) felt that the American family and marriage are remarkably well adjusted to American life. The freedom expressed in general American life is also reflected in our family life. Usually, it is very non-authoritarian in character: couples marry when they wish, with whom they wish, and have children for other reasons than family pressure. Benedict pointed out that so much talk about the American family as if it were in danger of falling apart—phrases like "saving the family" and "preserving the home"—is ridiculous. Families are everywhere, and through space and time they take on different forms. Ruth Benedict was one of the few observers of the family who did not take on a pessimistic view of the future of American family life.

Reaction to the pessimistic view of American family life has resulted in several empirical studies. The most important in this context are the following:

Eugene Litwak was one of the first to question the concept that Americans have an isolated nuclear family system (1965). In his studies he found that many Americans function in "modified extended families." The composition of these families consist of numerous nuclear families. They seem to be partially dependent on each other and often exchange services. The "modified extended families" are characterized as a kinship system differing from the isolated nuclear family and the classical extended family, falling somewhat in between.

Lillian E. Troll, in an article reviewing the major developments in the field of family sociology found that sociologists are discovering data that "make it clear that there is a modified extended kin structure in American society and that included therein are the older members of the family. The postparental couple—or the old conjugal unit is not isolated" (1971:254).

Sussman has concluded that the isolated nuclear family is a myth and that there exists in modern urban industrial societies "an extended kin system, highly integrated within a network of social relations and mutual assistance, that operates along historical kin lines and vertically over several generations" (1965:179). The extended kin family network is the basic social system in American urban society. Services to the old such as physical care, providing shelter, escorting shopping, performing household tasks, sharing of leisure time, and so on, are expected and practiced roles of children and other kin members.

Rosow (1970) has concluded that old peoples' relationship to their friends and neighbors is only secondary to that to their children. For financial assistance the old look only to their children. In cases of illness they look first to their children, but neighbors are second in importance. As the old see less of their children, they see more of their friends and neighbors. The old who are emotionally dependent on their children but do not see enough of them interestingly are precisely the ones who interact most frequently with their neighbors.

Finally, one of the phenomena of the last two decades or so is the emergence of the four-generational family. Townsend's analysis of this process suggests that our kinship structure is indeed changing more rapidly than supposed. He therefore speculates that any changes in family organization may have been affected more by changes in population structure than by changes in industrial and economic organization (1968a:257). Similarly, a study by Epstein and Murray documented the proximity of aged parents in the United States to at least one of their children (1967:163-179).

The most extensive study that examines kin relation of the aged is the three-industrial country study (Denmark, United States, and Great Britain) with a follow-up study of Poland, Yugoslavia, and Israel (Shanas, et al.:1968) and Shanas:1973). This study has examined many facets of the conditions of the aged. In considering the family and kinship relations of the elderly, it demonstrates that old people tend to live independently, but in close proximity to and in frequent contact with their children or substituent kin. Shanas found no evidence that adult sons and daughters have repudiated or rejected their elderly parents. This was determined from separate interviews of some 1,000 parents and their children. Shanas does show that adult children feel that meeting other needs is more important than meeting a parental need for financial help.

As we look over the empirical studies of the last decade it becomes evident that the kinship system of most American urban elderly has not atrophied. It has indeed become neolocal, mobile, and self-sufficient in structure. But when viewed in terms of how much communication and exchange actually transpires between nuclear families, the original Parsonian viewpoint becomes modified and the question of interaction becomes important. When these questions are asked, the response of most American family researchers is that we do indeed have many "significant others." These "significant others" more than likely want to be involved with their elderly kin and friends, want to assist in times of need, want to be involved in helping to plan for those more sickly and unfortunate, and need relief or assistance in caring for them. It is only reasonable that we include these kin and community resources in planning social service programs for the aged.

KIN NETWORKS AND POLISH ELDERLY

One of the basic goals in studying a subculture (Polish) is, of course, to determine whether American reactions to aging and help patterns for the aged are uniform within the country in order to ultimately be able to prepare sensitive and relative social service programs for our old. We look, therefore, for patterns. If the Polish subculture is different, then we must consider devising different programs. Avner and Weihl (1968) noted that such studies are beneficial in a culturally heterogeneous country (such as Israel, for instance) because "in such a society, the formal institutional structure is the same for all and can therefore be held constant. Variation in the collected data will have to be related to the fact of the inherent heterogeneity" (1968:17).

Kinship is an institution which has tremendous effects upon the formal structure of society. Peter Townsend (1957) in his analysis of the family life of old people in London illustrates the correlation between kin (the presence and lack of) to the use of institutions by the aged. Clearly, certain kinship structures make for lesser or greater reliance on other institutions. It is hypothesized that the kinship structures of various ethnic groups, in particular Polish-Americans, will not replicate those of the generalized American society. This, in turn, will affect the type of services and the use of those services by the Polish-American elderly.

Clark and Anderson (1967:283) support this formulation and attest to the variance in kinship expectations.

> On the whole, native-born subjects appear to grant greater independence to their children and even insist that their parental roles remain only peripheral in their childrens' lives. The nature of interaction between the generations seems to be somewhat formal

and dispassonate.... But other cultural systems program old age differently. Some of the immigrants in our sample come from areas of the world where kinship ties are the major sources of support and comfort in old age, where devotion and warm affective bonds persist, becoming even more intense with advancing years.

In view of the fact that 19 percent of all the populace of the United States is foreign-born (U.S. Department of Health, Education and Welfare, 1964) and with notably different ethnic patterns, this author undertook an exploratory study in order to compare the kinship ties of the Polish-American subculture with published data for the American population.

A neighborhood was selected which was reasonably representative of the ratio of elderly to the general populace and percentage of Polish-Americans to the general populace of Chicago. All of the respondents were 65 years of age or older. All of them claimed Polish as their ethnic affiliation and Polish-American as their nationality. About 25 percent of the interviews were in the Polish language and many more in a mixed Polish-English language. There is suspicion that this was done to test the authenticity of the interviewer. Participants came from every block of the sample area. Participants were chosen for their willingness to cooperate and if they did not exhibit obvious signs of mental disturbances. As part of the interview procedure, social services were offered where appropriate and very often accepted. These were in every case "soft" services such as information and referral services. The field work was completed in 1972–1973. Most of the data collected were compared to Shanas et al. (1968), United States data, and some of them were also compared to data retrieved from Poland (Piotrowski:1966 as referenced in Shanas 1968).

The Polish-American elderly proportionately do not live with their children or live as close to them as either the Polish or the American populations (Table 14.1A). Polish-Americans do not see their children as frequently within a 24-hour period (Table 14.1B). Of interest is that during the week the Polish-American elderly see their children as often as do the Polish and the American samples. Of interest also was that much of the visiting in the Polish-American sample was service-oriented. For example, the younger members often shopped or did heavy cleaning for their elderly parents while the elderly often repaid by watching children or baking specialties.

The Polish-American, like the Pole, proportionately do not see the siblings as often as the American (Table 14.1C). This can alternatively be explained by their kin being often scattered through-

**TABLE 14.1 The Proportion of Elderly Persons in Six Countries Who Have
Different Availability and Frequencies of interaction
with Children and Siblings[1]**

Those Whose Nearest Child Lives in the Same Household or Within 10
Minutes Distance

a.	Denmark	52%
	Britain	66
	United States	61
	Poland	70
	Polish-American	58
	Yugoslavia	73
	Israel	
	Western	55
	Oriental	84

Those Not Living With A Child Who Saw A Child Within the Last 24 Hours
and Within the Last Week

	Country	Saw Child Within Last 24 Hours	Saw Child Within Last Week
b.	Denmark	53	80
	Britain	47	77
	United States	52	78
	Poland	64	77
	Polish-American	56	79
	Yugoslavia	51	71
	Israel	48	76

Those Who Saw a Sibling Within the Last Week

	Country	Men	Women
c.	Denmark	32%	37%
	Britain	28	41
	United States	34	43
	Poland	33	38
	Polish-American	31	35
	Yugoslavia	48	40
	Israel	28	28

out the world or that this is not as an important kinship bond. The
sibling bond is an important one in Polish culture, but the diaspora
after World War II scattered many families throughout Europe, the
Americas, and Australia.

After determining the important members of a kinship system,
it is of value to analyze the frequency of interaction of these members. Of all widowed, separated and divorced respondents in the

TABLE 14.2

Percentage of Widowed, Separated and Divorced Persons with Different Numbers of Sons and Daughters, According to Distance from Nearest Child (Percentage Distribution)

	Number and Sex of Children					
	One Son Only	One Daughter Only	Two or More Sons	Two or More Daughters	Son(s) and Daughter(s)	All Widowed, Separated and Divorced Persons
*United States**						
Same household	26	46	35	46	46	43
Within 10 min.	20	9	26	30	30	26
11-30 min.	19	12	18	13	13	14
31-60 min.	14	4	9	4	4	5
More than an hour, less than a day	12	16	9	6	6	8
A day or more	9	13	4	1	1	4
Total	100	100	100	100	100	100
N=	74	115	78	573	573	840
Polish Population						
Same household	40	33	–	33	34	32
Within 10 min.	–	67	–	67	40	36
11-30 min.	60	–	50	--	13	21
31-60 min.	–	–	–	–	13	7
More than an hour, less than a day	–	–	50	–	–	4
A day or more	–	–	–	–	–	–
Total	100	100	100	100	100	100
N=	5	3	2	3	15	28

* United States figures obtained from Shanas, Ethel, Peter Townsend, Dorothy Wedderburn, Henning Friis, Paul Miljoj and Jan Strhouwer: *Old People in Three Industrial Societies,* New York: Atherton Press, 1968, p. 159.

American sample, 83 percent have at least one child within 30 minutes-travel. It is also interesting to note that a large percentage of only children (sons as well as daughters) stay close to the home of their parents in the Polish-American sample (Table 14.2).

Table 14.3

Percentage of Married Persons with Different Numbers of Sons and Daughters
According to Distance from Nearest Child (Percentage Distribution)

	One Son Only	One Daughter Only	Two or More Sons	Son(s) and Daughter(s)	All Widowed, Separated and Divorced Persons
United States *					
Same household	13	6	13	19	17
Within 10 min.	21	30	39	42	39
11-30 min.	45	20	15	17	17
31-60 min.	12	6	15	8	9
More than an hour, less than a day	22	23	15	11	13
A day or more	17	15	4	4	6
Total	100	100	100	100	100
N=	92	124	109	842	1,167
Polish Population					
Same household	–	–	–	30	19
Within 10 min.	–	–	50	30	25
11-30 min.	33	–	50	40	37
31-60 min.	–	–	–	–	–
More than an hour, less than a day	–	–	–	–	–
A day or more	67	100	–	–	19
Total	100	100	100	100	100
N=	3	1	2	10	16

*
United States figures obtained from Shanas, Ethel, Peter Townsend, Dorothy
Wedderburn, Henning Friis, Paul Miljoj and Jan Strhouwer: *Old People in
Three Industrial Societies,* New York: Atherton Press, 1968, p. 160.

Within the married population, 82 percent of the children of
Polish-Americans stay close to the home of their parents, whereas
73 percent of the American population have children staying within a half-hour of them (Table 14.3).

It is important to note that while proportionately more widowed than married persons lived with one of their children, fewer widowed than married lived within 10 minutes in the American
population. The opposite is true of the Polish-American population. According to Shanas, et al. and verified in the Polish-American figures, there seem to be consistent patterns to family structure (1968:153-155). Old people's marital status affects the com-

TABLE 14.4. Distance of Persons with Different Numbers of Sons and Daughters from Their Nearest Married or Widowed Child (Percentage Distribution)

Proximity of Nearest Child	One Son	One Daughter	Two or More Sons	More Than One Child—At Least One Daughter
*United States**				
Same household	8	21	10	16
Within 30 minutes	43	39	57	61
More than 30 minutes	49	40	33	23
Total	100	100	100	100
N=	141	221	185	1,395
Polish Population				
Same household	25	20	–	24
Within 30 minutes	50	60	67	59
More than 30 minutes	25	20	33	17
Total	100	100	100	100
N=	8	5	3	27

*United States figures obtained from Shanas, Ethel, Peter Townsend, Dorothy Wedderburn, Henning Friis, Paul Miljoj and Jan Strhouwer: *Old People in Three Industrial Societies,* New York: Atherton Press, 1968, p. 160.

position in the rest of the household. It can be said that a widowed person is less likely in both the Polish-American and American populations to live with a child than a single person is to live with a sibling (Table 14.4).

Interestingly enough, the Polish-American sample does not seem to have the parent-daughter, particularly the mother-daughter emphasis that the American population seems to have. Part of this is, no doubt, due to the higher proportion of only sons of the Polish-American family. On the other hand, it may also be partially due to the high status given to sons in Polish family structures.

Table 14.5 shows that the Polish sample proportionately seems to have the greatest kin contact, whereas the American sample has the least. Almost midway stands the Polish-American sample. These figures reflect a general feeling of "intimacy at a distance." The Polish sample seems rather high in terms of contact with one's children. This may be due to the fact that Polish families were resettled in village groups from the east to the west of Poland after World War II. Of special interest are the relatively low figures (compared to the American sample) of Poles and Polish-Americans who have no children and maintain no family contact. It seems that the Poles and the Polish-Americans can substitute intimate contact with other relatives when children are not available.

TABLE 14.5. Family Contacts of Men and Women Aged 65 and Over, Excluding Those Who Share a Home with Children*

Contacts	United States			Poland			Polish-Americans		
	Men	Women	All	Men	Women	All	Men	Women	All
Saw child during previous week	60	59	59	89	79	84	70	72	71
No contact with child but saw sibling or relative	7	9	8	3	3	3	10	7	8
Have no children, saw sibling or relative	12	17	14	5	11	8	10	10	10
Have no children, no family contact	21	14	18	2	6	4	10	7	8
Have neither children, sibling or relative	—	1	1	1	1	1	—	3	2

*United States, Poland figures obtained from Shanas, Ethel: "Family Kin Networks and Aging in Cross Cultural Perspective" in *Journal of Marriage and the Family,* Volume 35, Number 3, August, 1973, p. 510. Polish data gathered in 1966 by Jerzy Piotrowski.

——NOTE: These figures do not reflect those individuals who do not have children, but have regular contact with siblings in Europe or elsewhere; nor on those individuals who have seen their children greater than one week ago; nor those whose child lives wiht the elderly individual.

In measuring the intensity of older parent-child contact, the American sample seems to reflect the higher proportion of elderly who live with or saw their children in the 24-hour period. On the other hand, for general contact, the Polish-American sample reflect a proportionately higher rate of interaction from the period of two to three days (Table 14.6).

DISCUSSION OF FINDINGS COMPARED TO SHANAS ET AL. STUDY

After analysis, one could probably view the Polish-American sample as having more single people, more childlessness, more divorces, and less living siblings than the general American population. Obviously this does not make for a very close kin network and reciprocal behavior.

On the other hand, in terms of overall kin contact other than children with whom they live, the Polish-Americans have proportionately much more contact than the Americans. If one were to paint a picture of the Polish-American senior citizen, one would

TABLE 14.6. Percentage of Older Person Who Had Last Seen a Child
(Percentage Distribution)

Shortest Period Since Child Last Seen	United States*		Polish Population	
	Any Child Single or Married	Married Child	Any Child, Single or Married	Married Child
Today or yesterday	65.4%	58.9%	55.8%	51.2%
2-7 days	18.6	22.1	23.3	27.9
8-30 days	6.7	8.0	11.6	11.6
31 days-1 year	6.9	8.1	7.0	7.0
Not in last year	2.4	2.9	2.3	2.3
Total	100.0	100.0	100.0	100.0
N=	2,002	1,934	43	43

*United States figures obtained from Shanas, Ethel, Peter Townsend, Dorothy Wedderburn, Hennign Friis, Paul Miljoj and Jan Strhouwer: *Old People in Three Industrial Societies,* New York: Atherton Press, 1968, p. 162.

see a person who likes to live alone or with his or her spouse. They do not like to stay overnight at the homes of others, but then their children do not move far away as often as most Americans do. The children who live outside of their household come to see them more often than other Americans. Often their children live quite near them and regularly give them both service and financial support. They reciprocate with food and with watching grandchildren, and in cases of emergency. Kin relations are very close in the Polish-American subculture. Of course, one could raise the question as to how this behavior is related to socioeconomic background, and, therefore, question future patterns. Nevertheless, at present the data show a great deal of kin interaction.

After reviewing the data, the explanation for this diversity in kin relations can possibly be due to two factors. The first of these has already been discussed and this was the effect of World War II on the immigrant generation. The second might be explained as sampling error. We may have a cluster of persons whose normal behavior is non-kin oriented, who are transient, like traveling about, being alone, and individualistic. These individuals are often divorced or separated, do not have children, and have little sibling contact.

APPLICATION OF RESEARCH

A prime example of the type of application of kinship research and gerontology to social services for the aged is spoken of and constructed by Peter Townsend. He developed a general theory and applied it to 9,000 aged individuals. In this case the theory was:

An individual's behavior in non-familial as well as familial society is affected by the composition, the structure and the organization of the nuclear (or immediate) and the extended families to which he belongs. The specific form of this general hypothesis is that the likelihood of admission to an institution in old age, particularly a residential institution, is partly contingent on family composition, structure, and organization and not only on incapacity, homelessness, and lack of socioeconomic resources (1965, 164).

This proved quite applicable and correct. Sixty percent of all residents in old age institutions were childless. This general theory can, I believe, be applied to forecasting future institutional and bed needs by sampling the 50—60-age-range population characteristics.

In comparing the total kin network of the American and Polish-American samples, the data lead one to believe that the Polish-Americans are closer to their kin than the American sample. In comparing help given and received, the Polish-American sample receives more help from their kin and their kin are generally closer in terms of availability to them. An overly utopian picture of kin relations is not intended, but it does seem that even when children leave for different parts of the country or reside in the city's suburbs, at least one child stays behind and looks after the aged parents. Most of the needs of the aged individual, then, are met by those children who stay behind.

The unmet needs of the Polish-American senior citizens are numerous. But from the data and from observations based on participating in social service programs directed to Polish-Americans, one can conclude that it is rare that they have no one to care for them in sickness, no one to transport them to medical facilities, or no one to shop or cook or clean for them. Generally, such a need for social service is felt by the children of the aged who may have spent many months looking after the parents who in turn, under most circumstances, would be placed in nursing facilities. Quite often, the children feel that they need a break or additional help. Rarely do children see the care of aged parents as no longer primarily their responsibility. (Often when there are no children, there have been substitute relatives.) Rarely do the Polish aged express a need for these "hard" services in reference to themselves as individuals. Social services are seen as necessary when the family itself can no longer manage.

Felt needs of the senior citizens are often income-related. Most of the Polish-American sample was adamant in trying to maintain financial independence. There is also a great distaste of anything "smacking of welfare," especially for those who lived in the community during the depression. In general, the Poles are not a social-service-oriented group. They, unlike the Jewish population, do not have numerous programs as well as ethnic homes for the aged and nursing homes to meet the special needs of their own group. The Polish-Americans are usually most wary to take food stamps, to get a medical card from the state, or to receive financial assistance other than their pensions and what their children give them.

Another need that is often voiced, especially by the aged ladies, is for the company of other people. Seniors are in quite a predicament when they seek out human company other than that of their kin relations. Because they are often in financial need, they cannot afford to entertain at home nor to travel and pay for many outside activities such as senior citizens clubs.

Medical treatment is a great worry for these senior citizens. The old family doctors who spoke their language have died or retired. They are being replaced by specialists, or by doctors who charge too much in terms of the incomes of the aged. Most clinics where comprehensive and inexpensive care for the aged is available are in areas of the city which are difficult to reach and waiting for the services is usually long.

If we were to examine the distribution of social service delivery system for the aged in Chicago, it would be noted that most Slavic and Polish areas are relatively barren in terms of the presence of social service agencies. If it were possible to examine city-wide delivery and requests for service networks, it could be impressionistically predicted that Polish-Americans rarely request or use nearly the proportion of hard services (such as home help, hygenic services, transportation) as other areas and ethnic groups of the city use. It is argued that this is largely because their kinship networks are meeting these needs.

Unfortunately, services to the elderly often hinge on the availability of kin. This means that if a kinsman takes interest, provides assistance, and is vocal in planning or requesting services for an aged relation, these services on the part of the state are often not needed when these relatives are taxed to their limits. They are often made to feel shame for not providing enough or their unwillingness to continue such. Not only is this unfair to all individuals concerned, but it is also inefficient. For example, if a senior citizen lives with his working child, there is very little chance of receiving the financial benefits which they might otherwise be entitled.

In summary, it is argued that most social services are where they should be—that is, where the greatest needs are. One may, of course, speculate as to whether the greatest needs are in certain areas because people there have been accustomed to having their needs met by social service delivery systems. At any rate, since it is most certain that we are becoming a demographically aging society, there is very little doubt that planning and coordinating agencies will arise to chart and prepare for the needs of our future seniors. In planning for efficient and sympathetic programs, we must keep in mind kinship relations and how they function to meet some of the needs of the elderly.

CONCLUSIONS

The review of kinship in urban America has clearly shown that the American kinship system is indeed not deteriorating, that in fact there seems to be a lot of interaction between relatives, especially in regard to elderly kin. The data of our exploratory study substantiates our contention that there is a more intense relationship between Polish-Americans and their kin than in an "American" sample. Knowledge of this can assist in program planning, especially in areas where there is a high density of this ethnic group.

The question we then raise is to why there are the stereotypes of the aged that describe them as segregated, isolated, as people deserted by their kin, as helpless, poor, sick, and friendless. Why do we lump all persons aged 65+ into this category disregarding their ethnicity, socioeconomic standing, their education? Have they become the "in" group of the seventies? Is this stereotype encouraged and prosthelized because it makes securing funds for programs much easier? Most Americans can sympathize and relate to the elderly. They represent their grandparents and can easily be accepted as such by all segments of the population. This is in contrast to specialized programs for minority groups, unemployables, and abused or neglected children. The level of consciousness and guilt are raised high enough in order to move for programs for the elderly whereas programs for other groups may often raise objections, fears, or often in the case of children or the mentally disabled—utter abhorrence.

The unfortunate aspect of stereotyping the elderly is that seniors themselves will begin believing it and living with the assumptions that they are incapable, lonely, and needy. Although at present senior citizens may be able to gather and wield some political power, ultimately observations on older adults receiving social services lead us to conclude that the internalization of this stereotype will result in a poor self-image and a long-term dependence on services. In planning effective social services we should ascertain costs and benefits, not only for the social service agencies and the funds which support them, but for the individuals in need as well. Anthropological wisdom points to systematic cultural variation, as in the case of Polish-Americans, which defies being placed in a procrustean bed. There are strengths and weaknesses, cultural barriers in language and values, and there are resources. It is the recognition of these which will enable us to build maximally efficient social programs for older Polish-Americans and for older adults of other ethnic and minority groups. Efficiency should be culturally sensitive as well as economically sensitive to the tax dollar.

NOTES

1. Figures for Denmark, Britain, United States, Poland, Yugoslavia and Israel obtained from Shanas, Ethel: "Family Kin Networks and Aging in Cross Cultural Perspective" in *Journal of Marriage and the Family*, Vol. 35, No. 3, pp. 508 and 509.

15 Anthropology and Age: An Assessment

LOWELL D. HOLMES
Wichita State University

All of the contributors to this volume on gerontology are anthropologists. As Christine Fry has pointed out, this is somewhat unusual, for until very recently anthropologists seemed to show an almost studied neglect for the elders. They seemed interested in old people only as storehouses of knowledge about rapidly disappearing nonliterate societies. Franz Boas, the father of American anthropology, sent out eager students in ethnology with little more preparation than instructions to seek out the elders and ask them what things were like when they were young. In other words, the major emphasis was on reconstruction of traditional cultures and not the investigation of the contemporary roles, statuses, and social conditions of their elderly informants. A few studies in the area of tribal government called our attention to the existence of political organizations known as gerontocracies, but it was not until the publication of Leo Simmons' (a sociologist) book, *The Role of the Aged in Primitive Society*, that the specialized field of gerontology was recognized as a legitimate and appropriate area for anthropological investigation.

ANTHROPOLOGICAL PERSPECTIVES

Anthropology is a broad and complex discipline that studies the human animal in all phases of its life cycle and in all of its biological, social, psychological and cultural dimensions. While anthropologists in the past focused on nonliterate, preindustrial societies they no longer confine themselves to societies of any particular type nor to societies at any particular stage of cultural development. Anthropological studies do, however, continue to be crosscultural (worldwide) in their scope and holistic (taking the Gestalt or configurational view). It is a general approach to mankind but it also encourages a great deal of specialization in its practitioners.

Basically, there are two main divisions of anthropology- physical and sociocultural. Physical anthropologists, like Jeff Beaubier, concern themselves with human evolution, demographic factors, and biological mechanisms which regulate our bodies as we interact within a variety of sociocultural environments. Matters of genetic endowment, health, and longevity are to be found among their research interests, and occasionally their investigations shed light on puzzling questions like "Why can some Abkhasians (of the Caucasus) live to be 140 years old when most Americans never make 80?"

Social anthropologists (who study social interaction and social structure) and cultural anthropologists (who study cultural traditions) view the many societies of the world as so many experiments in human adjustment and survival in a variety of physical environments. It is right and proper that they include in their study each society's adjustment to the problem of growing old and the societal accomodations to its aged population. While social and cultural anthropologists have turned to so many new and different areas of specialization that anthropology has sometimes been defined as "what anthropologists do (and they do as they please)," there are also some traditional interests and approaches which are evident in this volume and in anthropology's approach to gerontology in general.

KINSHIP AND SOCIAL STRUCTURE

Anthropologists have had a long history of working in societies where the village structure, the social and political roles and the status system is based on kinship. Studies of social structure and its effect on the life style of old people are therefore natural areas of study for people like Maria Siemaszko, studying Polish and Polish-American family relationships, or for Jennie Keith, who turns her attention to the dynamics of community development and maintenance in eight retirement residences. While her societies are not based on kinship, they do unite their people in terms of common goals and common problems, and represent unique cultural systems not unlike many small self-contained societies for which anthropologists have evolved very effective investigative methodology.

STATUS AND ROLE

It was Ralph Linton who first brought the concepts of status and role to the attention of the world of social science, and it is not surprising that a major emphasis of anthropological gerontologists has been on analyses of roles and statuses of old people in relation to various variables such as geography, subsistence level, ideology, and modernization. Virginia Kerns follows this lead in her study of the unique status system which has been evolved by Black Caribs, and Gerry Williams describes the factors of poverty and "Indianness" which makes for an unexpected high status for elderly Indians on Oklahoma reservations. Eunice Boyer investigates a subject closely allied to status and role in her study of the relationship between role satisfaction and health, and Carol Schulz probes the topic even farther in her investigation of the correlation between role satisfaction and the acceptance or rejection of the idea of death in middle-class America.

Karen Jonas and Edward Wellin borrow somewhat from the interests of Sociology in their interaction analysis of aged living in a public housing complex in Milwaukee. Their focus is the documentation of patterns of mutual and unilateral aid. It is a study of who helps whom, why, and how often. Their goal is to isolate and analyze networks of individuals who relate to one another in special ways on special issues. The social network approach, now a well accepted anthropological research tool, also is evident in the work of Linda Evers Cool, who focuses on ethnic affiliations and how identifying with a given cultural tradition results in greater respect for that group's aged. Hers is a study of how shared cultural values and a consciousness of common roots can unite the young and the old under an ethnic banner.

COMPARISON AND CROSSCULTURAL ANALYSIS

Traditionally anthropology has studied the life ways of primitive or nonliterate people, but with the present state of world modernization few people of this description exist any more. It is therefore more accurate to describe anthropology today as comparative and crosscultural rather than as a discipline that limits itself to nonliterate tribal populations. Just as the British anthropologist Bronislaw Malinowski cast doubt on the universality of Freud's Oedipus complex by finding a society (the Trobriand Islands) which didn't seem to manifest it, anthropological gerontologists are finding that many generalizations and concepts developed by social gerontologists on the basis of life in one society (usually the United States) are valid only for that society and do not apply to mankind as a whole. As Clyde Kluckhohn phrased it, "Anthropology provides a mirror for man wherein he may see himself in all his infinite variety." This is anthropology's most important contribution to gerontology. Thus anthropological perspective derives from a careful analysis of Western and non-Western, industrial and preindustrial societies studied both synchronically and diachronically. Gerry Williams' study is a good example of a study incorporating synchronic analysis. Believing that "there is an appropriate way to age in every culture," he compares the role and status of reservation Indians in Oklahoma with their counterparts in American white populations. His focus is on a number of unique characteristics of reservation family systems, traditional and modern economic roles, and the emergence of a new interest in Indianness which influences the role and status of the aged in a new and unexpected way.

Kerns' study of Black Caribs also verifies the advantage of crosscultural studies in its presentation of data which challenges the long-revered "disengagement theory," the theory which holds that the aged must accept a decline in status and must relinquish leadership roles if societal equilibrium is to be maintained. Through this research we are provided with new insights into the range of heterogeneity which can exist in the operations of status and role determinations for aged members of societies. It is a fascinating story of one society's old people refusing to accept inferior status designations provided by its younger generations.

While Maria Siemaszko's study of Polish aged is a synchronic analysis—comparing a Polish-American sample with a European one and in turn with an American (i.e., Americans with no particular ethnic identification)—the research is also diachronically comparative in its historical concerns with the extent to which extended families existed in colonial America and the extent to which such families may or may not have functioned as highly supportive units in providing for the social, economic, and physical needs of the elderly. Her data show that the supportive role of the extended family (where it existed, and that was infrequent) is largely a myth, the probable creation of some modern sociological theorist.

Also crosscultural, but with the added dimension of moving across class and ethnic boundaries, is Jennie Keith's study of community structure and function in modern industrial society. Beginning with an analysis of Les Floralies—a residence for retired construction workers outside Paris—and then moving to a California mobile home park, a San Francisco apartment house residence, a home for Sephardic Jews in New York, and finally "an adult community" composed of condominium apartments in a northern California suburb, Keith finds that communities occupied predominantly by old people have a lot in common regardless of national, class or ethnic differences. All have (1) a common shared territory which is jealously protected against encroachment by outsiders, (2) a strong sense of in-group/out-group differences, (3) shared norms and common goals, and (4) clearly defined roles and statuses, i.e., a social structure.

CULTURAL RELATIVISM

Growing out of the anthropologist's emphasis on crosscultural analysis has come a philosophical attitude toward other cultures that greatly affects his methodology and his theoretical conceptualizations. This philosophical position is called *cultural relativism* and it represents an open-mindedness in accepting the diversity of culture around the world. Such relativism demands that no one culture be held up as offering the "right" or "natural" way of doing things. Moral or scientific judgements based on experience with but a single culture are suspected of being unfair and invalid. Having been trained in such a philosophical environment, anthropologists believe that problems and definitions associated with old age must be analyzed only in terms of the cultural context in which they occur. Behavior that indicates that aged are held in low esteem in one culture may mean something entirely different in another. The fact that the aged Eskimos were permitted to commit suicide when they no longer could keep up with the strenuous nomadic hunting life did not mean that they were held in low esteem. In fact, their families so respected them that they did everything in their power to postpone the day when the elder would make the fatal decision.

Cultural relativism is a theoretical position that also warns that cultural institutions cannot be easily transplanted from one culture to another. The Meals on Wheels program that has been so successful in the United States was received with little enthusiasm when taken to American Samoa. To begin with, volunteerism is not a Samoan characteristic as it is with Americans, and since there was no agency which could cook and deliver the food, elders were offered a free hot meal if they would come to the village school house where cooks in the children's hot lunch program would provide the additional meals to be consumed by the old folks. But high chiefs and their wives felt it beneath their dignity to eat with children or even to line up and be served as children.

In Linda Evers Cool's paper dealing with Corsicans in Paris, we find that the kind of disengagement so often noted in elderly middle-class Americans is just not present. Ethnic identification and ethnic group membership appear to be mitigating factors operating to reduce isolation and role loss for Corsican elders. Recent interest in seeking out and then finding pride in one's ethnic heritage have united the Corsican young (who want to learn) and Corsican old (who are seen as experts in traditional cultural matters).

Sylvia Vatuk's paper, however, provides us with a description of a tradition in India which might very well be called social and psychological disengagement. Deriving from age-old sacred Hindu texts, and associated with the privileges and responsibilities of the "twice-born" individual's retirement from household affairs and his rejection of attachments to other human beings and to worldly goods is viewed as positive and normal, contributing to his own well-being and the welfare of his society. It is not, as is the case in many Western societies, a withdrawal associated with loss of status and with the involuntary termination of a useful economic role on the basis of age. The lesson to be learned from this study is that disengagement must be understood and evaluated in terms of each and every cultural context in which it is found. Had the basic theoretical orientations of social gerontology been formulated by anthropologists, with their crosscultural perspectives and research experience, there would be no such thing as "the theory of disengagement." Disengagement should merely be understood as a phenomenon which may or may not be present in the society under investigation depending on its unique social, economic, and spiritual needs.

DEFINITIONS OF OLD AGE

Cultural anthropologists are also aware that even the answer to how old is "old" may vary greatly from one culture to another. In the United States there are few people who, if asked, would not say that old age begins at age 65, for that is the usual age of retirement from one's job and the age at which Social Security checks begin to arrive. The fact that some people look and behave much younger or older than their 65 years seems to have little impact on definitions of the advent of old age. But when one leaves the United States, one may find that definitions of old age can vary considerably. Most non-Western people think of folks as being young or at least middle-aged if they continue to carry out the responsibilities and activities required of them, and they think of people as being old when they can no longer perform their required duties. In other words, definitions of old age are functional (having to do with performance) rather than chronological (having to do with years). Samoans experience great difficulty in answering the question, "At what age do people become old in Samoa?" They have a term for old age (*matua*) but it is difficult for them to generalize in terms of years. Contrary to what might be found in some developing countries, these people usually know their exact age because they have been recorded by the government for better than 75 years, but they are not concerned with the mere passage of years. There are better ways to measure the life cycle.

LIFE-CYCLE ANALYSIS

It is the awareness that there are several ways to measure the life cycle that prompted Christine Fry to develop a multidimensional scaling analysis procedure. In her paper we are introduced to three indices for measuring the life cycle: *life time* (a chronological measurement of a series of changes in the life cycle), *social time* (age-graded statuses and roles occurring at different times during the course of the life cycle) and *historical time* (the events—social, political and economic—which affect the lives of members of a particular society). Two of these dimensions relate to a functional reckoning of aging and are in tune with the way nonliterate, preindustrial people view the unfolding of the life cycle. When applied in American society, this form of scaling permits a greater understanding of the cultural dimensions of age by supplementing the usual chronological measurement of age with the variables of family responsibility, and with commitment to careers, both of which may come at various times during one's life and play a role in establishing mileposts in the life cycle.

GERONTOLOGICAL MYTHS AND
THE SCIENCE OF ANTHROPOLOGY

It was said by some long-forgotten sage that since man is born without instincts and must learn his values, attitudes, and patterns of behavior from others, much of his life is destined to be oriented by myth or misconception. The problem becomes even more difficult when we try to understand human phenomena across cultural lines where communication is invariably garbled or totally absent. But even in our own society (one of the most segregated in the world in regard to age) we must admit that we know precious little about the social and psychological problems involved in old age. One of the more humbling experiences for a dozen or more social scientists at a recent workshop on gerontology at the University of Texas was the answering of questions on a Louis Harris survey instrument and trying to see how close they could come in guessing what the responses of 4,200 respondents had been to the questions "What is the worst thing about being over 65?" and "What is the best thing about being over 65?" Few if any of the workshop participants (some claiming to be gerontologists) scored very well on evaluating the relative importance of various negative and positive aspects of being old.

One of the more positive contributions of this volume is its role in showing us just how little we really know about our old folks. It is a myth-shattering and misconception-challenging book. Again and again, time-honored theories of social gerontology are shown to be culture-bound (and therefore not universally applicable) or completely false in the light of crosscultural data. One misconception that nearly all the authors comment on is that the elderly comprise a homogeneous group. This idea has undoubtedly developed from the fact that in our culture it is a common experience to be forced out of one's job at a particular chronological age (usually 65) and become the recipient of a small retirement income (Social Security), the amount of which forces nearly everyone but a fortunate few to "disengage" and curtail their social activities. The homogeneity we believe is characteristic of the aged may also result from our lack of contact and communication. There is a good chance that most social workers think all aged are poor, ill, lonely, or psychotic. Politicians, on the other hand, probably think that all elderly are aggressive and outspoken (like Grey Panthers), and people who run senior centers see only those who haven't enough imagination or adventure in their souls to have someplace else to go.

Maria Siemaszko's research goes a long way in dispelling notions of homogeneity among the aged. She notes that the elderly do not live more in one part of the country than another or more in one kind of a community than another. They are not all in retirement homes (only 4 percent are) and they vary greatly in the quality of their health, the quantity of their wealth and their degree of social and physical isolation. Ethnicity, her article tells us, adds another significant variable in the nature and quality of old-age life style. Even though most employers insist on retirement at age 65, it makes a great deal of difference whether you are a Polish-American or an American without a particular ethnic identity in the way your family relates to you during the retirement years. For example, Siemaszko points out that the degree to which the aged must rely on community agencies and institutions depends a great deal on the nature of the kinship system they participate in. While in the general American population there is a strong mother-daughter dyad, this is replaced among Polish-Americans with a strong emphasis on sons. Thus Polish-American elderly look more to males than to females for support, and males will, of course, meet needs that differ in kind from those met by female offspring. There is also greater kin contact among Polish-Americans, but the normal American pattern of the elderly having children live within a 10-minute walk is not the case with Polish-Americans, at least not in the Chicago area. This may very well be due to the fact that the elderly choose to remain in the old inner-city ethnic neighborhoods while younger generations have moved to the suburbs as a symbol of financial success and achievement. Siemaszko's findings are more than just interesting facts. The heterogeneity she spotlights makes us realize that there must be an ever-present awareness of cultural differences when planning or carrying out social services for the aged.

Virginia Kerns' study also speaks to the subject of societal heterogeneity in that it provides us with a case study of a people, the black Caribs of Belize, who have not been content to accept the stereotypes or the blanket status designations imposed upon them by younger generations. Here is a population that is neither homogeneous in their values or behavior, nor do they conform to the social scientist's expectations that the elderly are prone to disengage. Thus Kerns has shown us that a crosscultural perspective in the study of intergenerational interaction can provide data that "do not lend support either to the stereotype of passivity or to the related and equally widespread idea that activity and interaction inevitably decrease sharply with advancing age."

Charlotte Ikels' study also touches on intergenerational problems in a non-Western culture and introduces us to the difficulties associated with modernization and urbanization. And it sheds light on another important anthropological consideration—discrepancies between "the ideal" and "the real." Few places in the world present greater problems for families trying to maintain traditional relationships than urban Hong Kong. While filial piety and respect for the wisdom of age remain paramount within the Chinese value system, such ideas and their associated behavior are difficult to perpetuate where population density approaches 400,000 per square mile and where governmental restrictions and economic realities make intergenerational coresidence difficult if not impossible. The Hong Kong drama will be played out again and again in all parts of the world as traditional societies feel the disrupting influences of modernization. It is a human dilemma that the anthropologist as social gerontologist must come to know and understand if anthropology is to contribute to the betterment of the human condition internationally.

METHODOLOGY

Anthropologists have never had a complicated methodology, but they *have* used a more personal and intimate approach to their subjects than have most other social scientists. Compared to some social scientists who feel that "if you can't count it, it doesn't count," anthropologists have often collected their data by way of extended personal interviews and rap sessions. They also look upon questionnaires as bloodless affairs that demand that everything be responded to in terms of "strongly agree," "agree," "no opinion," and so on. Many of the people whose studies make up this volume lived with and participated in the society they were studying and thus were able to compare ideal responses of informants with real behavior and to observe genuine life situations and the operation of social structures on a day-to-day basis. Ever since Bronislaw Malinowski settled down to do field work in the Trobriand Islands in 1914 and attempted to "get inside the native's skin," anthropologists have been attempting to get the "people's view." Today this is known in anthropological jargon as the *emic* approach. While the name is new, it is a very old method which seeks to understand the subject's world as he or she perceives or experiences it. Dianne Kagan seeks such information in her ethno-linguistic search for linguistic categories or labels used by her subjects to function in their world and comprehend its complexities.

APPLIED ANTHROPOLOGY

The anthropologists who have contributed to this volume are not just ivory-tower academics who engage in gerontological studies as an elitist game to impress their students and colleagues. Nearly every one of the studies described here has its practical applications. Take the work of Jennie Keith, for example.

Debate has gone on for years in regard to the value of living in a residence exclusively for elders on the one hand or remaining in one's own home within a community composed of people of all ages. A recent survey of retired persons conducted by an annuity agency showed that there continues to be strong opposing opinions on this highly crucial issue. Quotes from this survey ran as follows: "Don't 'hole up' in a 'senior-citizen' enclave or retirement home until you must. Stay where you can get mad at the school kids cutting across your lawn." Attitudes toward retirement communities ranged from "God forbid!" (a man, age 73) to "I like being in a new community where we have all had to be friendly and outgoing if we are to have friends. We have so many activities run by retirees that we never feel left out" (a married woman, 65). A single woman (age 79) wrote, "Leisure villages are good for real estate operators, but it means segregating old age."

The studies of Jennie Keith and Eunice Boyer bear directly on this question. Both reveal real advantages for establishing segregated communities for the aged. Keith feels that it is a commonly held point of view that such residences for old people are depressing, unhealthy, and exist as a result of the aged being rejected by family and society. However, in her study of eight retirement communities in two countries, Keith finds that:

> All of these old people have turned to each other for many kinds of social needs. They are friends, lovers and factional adversaries; they protect each other in illness and emergency; they laugh, dance and mourn together. They evaluate each other in terms of the life they share, rather than according to the status ladders of the outside world where they are guaranteed a place on the bottom rung. That outside world is seen as dangerous in many ways: physically, financially, socially and psychologically; the community of age-mates is a refuge from all of these threats.

Boyer, in like manner, sees the senior citizen resident community in a positive light. She feels that rather than being a "ghetto" for a rejected minority these residential complexes usually incorporate construction features which allow residents to overcome mobility limitations thereby permitting more active participation. And the homogeneity of background gives greater opportunity for leadership and reduces isolation. Thus a more vigorous social life is permitted to develop and there is great opportunity for mutual aid and an exchange of services.

Karen Jonas and Edward Wellin's work provide information on the role of social networks in solving the ever-present problems of transportation, health care, and household maintenance. They believe that knowledge of how social and mutual aid networks develop, and the many forms they can take, can go a long way in determining what needs they will meet and what kinds of social service facilities are left to be provided by state and private agencies. Sometimes a combination of approaches may be called for. They state: "The health and welfare of elderly residents of such niches as public housing are probably best promoted through articulating the efforts and services of formal agencies and kinship sources with the informal networks of aid among neighbors."

Identifying and analyzing the role of networks is also an interest of Linda Evers Cool, who discusses their role in combating loneliness and encouraging social participation. Her research establishes the positive value of ethnic neighborhoods and minority associations such as the Amicole Nioline for Parisian Corsicans as a "medium for association, celebration, intra-aid, regional/political activity" and a source of new status for elders identifying with these groups.

What can be more practical and worthwhile in terms of modern Western values than attempts to promote a longer, healthier, and more vigorous life? But according to Beaubier, to do this we must understand the relationship between biological mechanisms regulating our bodies and how they are affected by social forces. And it is his interest as a physical anthropologist to show possible mechanisms whereby social phenomena actually do have physical bases that affect health and longevity of human groups.

Because we live in such a highly segregated society we are faced not only with interracial and interclass problems but also with problems of communication and adjustment between generations. Feeling that children in our society are robbed of the worthwhile experience of associating daily with elderly people, and thus not having a model for their own old age, Margaret Mead had been advocating a Grand Parent—Teacher Association for years.

Dianne Kagan's paper on peasant elderly in Bojaca, Colombia provides a case history of how one society outside our Western tradition has dealt with intergenerational differences. She states that the young and old in this society "disagree over some of the specific forms for respectful interaction between generations, but they agree that deference or respect is an essential quality of interaction with the aged." Reduction of intergenerational conflict is seen as possible through the sharing by different generations of cognitive expectations of age-appropriate activities. Hers is a methodology which could and should be brought to bear in our own society.

Few minorities are as little-known or as misunderstood as the American Indian. When one adds to the problem of depressed minority status the problems of being old, one encounters a vast problem area crying for the attention of the social gerontologist. Beginning with the realization that "there are marked differences as we move from culture to culture in terms of this particular group's demographic, social and economic characteristics," Gerry Williams shows how "the Indian living within two cultural traditions, with different values has had to develop many strategies for survival and in some cases these strategies have created a reliance upon the old individual; in other cases it has meant that the older Indian's role within the community has changed. The old are far from being segregated or stored away." As yet the negativism associated with old age found in most modern societies has not reached this aboriginal population. Perhaps that will require greater progress toward civilization.

FUTURE DIRECTIONS

This volume is not the final work that will come from anthropologists on the subject of social gerontology. It is only the beginning. The important thing is that we are now turning our analytical eyes more and more on our own society and assessing its problems and their solutions in terms of crosscultural perspective. And no longer do we look to the elderly merely as sources of traditional information. Some of our work will be pure research, designed to understand more about the human condition during the declining years, and some of our work will be practical and applied with an eye to solving problems of America's aged and the aged in other cultures. Whatever the purpose might be for our scientific activity, it will have the characteristics of being holistic, comparative, relativistic, and always striving to seek the people's points of view.

BIBLIOGRAPHY*

Adams, F.M. The Role of Old People in Santa Lemas Mazaltepec. *In* Aging and Modernization. D.O. Cowgill and L.D. Holmes, eds. New York: Appleton-Century-Crofts., 1972.

Agassi, J., and I.C. Jarvie. A Study in Westernization. *In* Hong Kong: A Society in Transition. I.C. Jarvie, ed., in consultation with Joseph Agassi, Pp. 129-163. London: Routledge & Kegan Paul, 1969.

Ahern, E. The Cult of the Dead in a Chinese Village. Stanford, Calif.: Stanford University Press, 1973.

Aldridge, G.K. Informal Social Relationships in a Retirement Community. *In* Marriage and Family Living 21:70-72, 1959.

Alger, J.F. Activity Patterns and Attitudes toward Housing of Families in Specially Designed Apartments for Aged Living in Ten New York City Projects. Ithaca, N.Y.: Cornell University Housing Research Center, 1959.

Anderson, B. The Process of Deculturation—Its Dynamics among United States Aged. *In* Anthropological Quarterly 45:4:209-216, 1972.

Anderson, R.A. Males in a Female World: Men in Public Housing for the Elderly. Doctoral dissertation, Department of Anthropology, University of Wisconsin-Milwaukee, 1976.

Andrews, F., J., Morgan and J. Sonquist. Multiple Classification Analysis: A Report on a Computer Program for Multiple Regression Using Categorical Predictors. Ann Arbor: University of Michigan, Institute for Sociology Research, 1967.

Arensberg, C. The Irish Contrymen. Blouchester: Peter Smith, 1937.

Arensberg, C., and S. Kimball. Family and Community in Ireland. Cambridge, Mass.: Harvard University Press, 1940.

Arley, N. Applications of Stochastic Models for the Analysis of the Mechanism of Carcinogenesis. *In* Stochastic Models in Medicine and Biology. John Gurland, ed. Pp. 3-44. Madison: University of Wisconsin Press, 1964.

Arnhoff, F., H. Leon and I. Lorge. Cross-Cultural Acceptance of Stereotypes towards Aging. Journal of Social Psychology 63:41-58. (1964)

Arth, M. An Interdisciplinary View of the Ages in Ibo Culture. Journal of Geriatric Psychology 2:33-39. (1968a) ——.

——. Ideals and Behavior: A Comment on Ibo Respect Patterns. The Gerontologist 8:242-244. (1968b)

Ashcraft, N. Colonialism and Underdevelopment: Processes of Political Economic Change in British Honduras. New York: Teacher's College Press, 1973.

*Additional references are listed following this Bibliography.

Atchley, R.C. Selected Social and Psychological Sex Differences in Later Life. *In* The Sociology of Age: Selected Readings. Robert C. Atchley and Mildred M. Seltzer, eds. Pp. 282-291. Belmont, Calif.: Wadsworth, 1976.

Avner, U., and H. Weihl. A Cross-Cultural Study in a Single Country. *In* Interdisciplinary Topics in Gerontology: Methodological Problems in Cross National Studies in Aging. Ethel Shanas and J. Madge, eds. New York: S. Kraeger, 1968.

Back, K.W. Personal Characteristics and Social Behavior: Theory and Method. *In* Handbook of Aging and the Social Sciences. Binstock and Shanas, eds. New York: Van Nostrand Reinhold, 1976.

Baltes, P.B., and L.R. Coulet. Status and Issues of a Life-Span Developmental Psychology. *In* Life-Span Developmental Psychology: Research and Theory. L.R. Coulet and P.B. Baltes, eds. New York: Academic Press, 1970.

Baltimore, D. RNA-Dependent DNA Polymerase in Virions of RNA Tumor Viruses. Nature 226:1209-1211. (1970)

Barth, F. Ethnic Groups and Boundaries. Boston: Little, Brown, 1969.

Bartlett, M.S. Stochastic Population Models in Ecology and Epidemiology. London: Methuen, 1960.

de Bary, W.T., ed. Sources of Indian Tradition, Vol. I. New York: Columbia University Press, 1958.

Basham, A.L. The Wonder that was India. New York: Macmillan, 1954.

Beaubier, J. High Life Expectancy on the Island of Paros, Greece. New York: Philosophical Library, 1976.

de Beauvoir, S. La Vieillesse. Paris: Gallimard, 1970.

Befu, H. Social Exchange. *In* Annual Review of Anthropology, 1977. Bernard J. Siegel, A.R. Beals, and S.A. Tyler, eds. Pp. 255-281. Palo Alto, Calif: Annual Reviews, 1977.

Belshaw, C.S. Traditional Exchange and Modern Markets. Englewood Cliffs, N.J.: Prentice-Hall, 1965.

Benedict, R. Continuities and Discontinuities in Cultural Conditioning. Psychiatry I, 161-67. (1938)

———. The Chrysanthemum and the Sword. Boston: Houghton Mifflin, 1946.

———. The Family: Genus Americanum. *In* The Family: Its Function and Destiny (revised edition). Ruth Nanda Anshen, ed. New York: Harper and Row, 1959.

Benet, S. Abkhasians: The Long-Living People of the Caucasus. New York: Holt, Rinehart and Winston, 1974.

Bengtson, V.L., J.J. Dowd, D.H. Smith, and A. Inkeles. Modernization, Modernity, and Perceptions of Aging: A Cross-Cultural Study. Journal of Gerontology 30:688-695. (1975)

Berger, P.L., and R.J. Neuhaus. Movement and Revolution. Garden City: Penguin Books, 1970.

Beyer, G.H., and F.H.J. Nierstrasz. Housing the Aged in Western Countries. Amsterdam: Elsevier, 1967.

Blau, P.M. Exchange and Power in Social Life. New York: John Wiley and Sons, 1964.

Blau, Z.M. Structural Constraints on Friendship in Old Age. American Sociological Review XXXVI: 429-439, 1961.

———. Old Age in a Changing Society. New York: New Viewpoints, 1973.

Bott, E. Family and Social Network: Summary and General Discussion. *In* Readings in Kinship and Social Structure. Nelson Graburn, ed. Pp. 389-391. New York: Harper & Row, 1971.

Bowers, A.W. Hidatsa Social and Ceremonial Organization. Smithsonian Institution, Bureau of American Ethnology Bulletin 194, Washington, D.C.: U.S. Government Printing Office, 1965.

Boyer, E.F. Factors Influencing Health Perception Among the Elderly in Public Housing. Unpublished Ph.D. dissertation. Milwaukee: University of Wisconsin, 1975.

Bratmen, H.B. The Older Population: Some Facts We Should Know (Publication #SRS-AOA-164-1971). Washington, D.C.: U.S. Department of Health, Education and Welfare, Administration on Aging, 1970.

Bultena, B.L. Age-grading in the Social Interaction of an Elderly Male Population. Journal of Gerontology 23:539-43. (1968)

———. Relationship of Occupational Status to Friendship Ties in Three Planned Retirement Communities. Journal of Gerontology 24:461-64. (1969)

———. Structural Effects on the Morale of the Aged: A Comparison of Age-Segregated and Age-Integrated Communities. *In* Late Life: Communities and Environmental Policy. Jaber F. Gubrium, ed. Pp. 18-31. Springfield, Ill: Charles C. Thomas, 1974.

Bultena, G.L., and V. Wood. The American Retirement Community: Bane or Blessing? Journal of Gerontology 24:209-17. (1969)

Burgess, E.W. Personal and Social Adjustment in Old Age. *In* The Aged in Society, Milton Derber, ed. Pp. 138-156. Champaign: University of Illinois Press, 1950.

———. Social Relations, Activities and Personal Adjustment. American Journal of Sociology 59:352-60. (1954)

———. Resume and Implications. *In* Aging in Western Societies. Ernest W. Burgess, ed. Chicago: University of Chicago Press, 1960.

———. Retirement Villages, Ann Arbor: Division of Gerontology. The University of Michigan, 1961.

Burton, M.L., and A.K. Romney. A Multidimensional Representation of Role Terms. American Ethnologist 3:397-407. (1975)

Butand, J.P., and B. Pons-Vignon. Les Retraitès Face aux Residences. C.N.R.O. Documents d'information et de Gestion 6. (1968)

Butler, J.A.V. Gene Control in the Living Cell. New York: Basic Books, 1968.

Butler, R.N. The Facade of Chronological Age. *In* Middle Age and Aging. B.L. Neugarten, ed. Chicago: University of Chicago Press, 1968.

Byrne, S.W. Arden: An Adult Community. Ph.D. dissertation. Berkeley: University of California, 1971.

——. Arden, An Adult Community. *In* Anthropologists in Cities. G. Foster and R. Kemper, eds. Boston: Little, Brown, 1974.

Cain, L.D., Jr. Life Course and Social Structure. *In* Handbooks of Modern Sociology. R.L. Faris, ed. Chicago: Rand McNally, 1964.

——. The Growing Importance of Legal Age in Determining the Status of the Elderly. The Gerontologist 14:167-174. (1974)

Calhoun, J.B. Population Density and Social Pathology. Scientific American 206:139-148. (1962)

——. Retirement Villages. Ann Arbor: Division of Gerontology, The University of Michigan, 1961.

Campbell, B.C. Human Evolution (2nd edition). Chicago: Aldine, 1978.

Carp, F.M. A Future for the Aged. Austin: University of Texas Press, 1966.

——. Housing and Living Environments of Older People. *In* Handbook of Aging and the Social Sciences. Robert Binstock and Ethel Shanas, eds. Pp. 244-271. New York: Van Nostrand, 1976.

Carse, J.P., and A.B. Dallery, (eds.). Death and Society. New York: Harcourt Brace Jonanovich, 1977.

Cavan, R., et al. Personal Adjustment in Old Age. Chicago: Science Research Associates, 1949.

Chan, W. Religious Trends in Modern China. New York: Columbia University Press, 1953.

Chandler, A.R. The Traditional Chinese Attitude Towards Old Age. Journal of Gerontology 5:239-44. (1950)

Changeux, J.P. The Control of Biochemical Reactions. Scientific American 212:36-45. (1965)

Chen, H. Landlord and Peasant in China. New York: International Publishers, 1936.

Chomsky, N. Syntactic Structures. The Hague: Mouton, 1957.

Clark, M.M. The Anthropology of Aging, A New Area for Studies of Culture and Personality. The Gerontologist 7:55-64. (1967)

——. Patterns of Aging Among the Elderly Poor of the Inner City. The Gerontologist 11:58-66. (1971)

——. Cultural Values and Dependency in Later Life. *In* Aging and Modernization. Donald Cowgill and Lowell Holmes, eds. Pp. 263-274. New York: Appleton-Century-Crofts, 1972.

——. Contributions of Cultural Anthropology to the Study of the Aged. *In* Cultural Illness and Health: Essays in Human Adaptation. L. Nader and T. Marelzki, eds. Washington, D.C.: American Anthropological Association. 1973.

Clark, M., and B.G. Anderson. Culture and Aging: An Anthropological Study of Older Americans. Springfield, Ill.: Charles Thomas, 1967.

Clark, M., and M. Mendelson. Mexican-American Aged in San Francisco: A Case Description. The Gerontologist 9:90-95. (1969)

Clausen, J.A. The Life Course of Individuals. *In* Aging and Society, Vol. 3: A Sociology of Age Stratification. M.W. Riley, M. Johnsen, A. Foner, eds. New York: Russell Sage Foundation, 1972.

Cluff, P.J., and W. Campbell. The Social Corridor: An Environmental and Behavioral Evaluation. Gerontologist 15:516-23. (1975)

C.N.R.O. Residence 'La Croix du Gué': La Vie Collective. Paris: C.N.R.O. Documents d'information et de Gestion, 1968(a).

——. Retired Persons and Homes for the Elderly. Paris: C.N.R.O. Documents d'information et de Gestion, 1968(b).

Cocolas, G.H. Biochemical Inhibitors of Aging. Component proposal *in* Pilot Research in Bio & Socioeconomic Gerontology, submitted to National Institute on Aging Bethesda, Md., November, 1978. Unpublished.

Cohen, M. House United, House Divided: The Chinese Family in Taiwan. New York: Columbia University Press, 1976.

Coleman, J., and C.J. Rosberg. Political Parties and National Integration in Tropical Africa. Berkeley: University of California Press, 1964.

Coles, R. The Old Ones of New Mexico. Albuquerque: University of New Mexico Press, 1973.

Collett, L.J. and D. Lester. The Fear of Death and the Fear of Dying. Journal of Psychology 72(2):179-81. (1969)

Collot, C. La Vie Collective: Solutions ou Palliatifs. Revue Francaise de Gerontologie 17. (1971)

——. Les Attitudes des Personnes Agées en Habitat Collectif. Revue de Gerontologie d'expression Francaise 3:32-6. (1972)

Collot, C., and H. Le Bris. Les Aspirations au Logement de Retraité. C.N.R.O. Documents d'information et de Gestion 30. (1975)

Collver, A. The Family Cycle in India and the United States. American Sociological Review 28:89-96. (1963)

Commission on Chronic Illness. Chronic Illness in the United States. Cambridge: Harvard University Press, 1957.

Conklin, H. Hanunoo Color Categories. Southwestern Journal of Anthropology 11:339-344. (1955)

Conner, K.A., and E.A. Powers. Structural Effects and Life Satisfaction Among the Aged. Journal Paper J-75586 of the Iowa Agricultural and Home Economics Experiment Station, Ames, Iowa, Project 1871. (n.d.)

Cottrell, L. The Technological and Societal Basis of Aging. *In* Handbook of Social Gerontology. C. Tibbitts, ed. Chicago: University of Chicago Press, 1960.

Cowgill, D.O. Aging in American Society. *In* Aging and Modernization. D.O. Cowgill and L. Holmes, eds. New York: Appleton-Century-Crofts, 1972(a).

———. A Theory of Aging in Cross-Cultural Perspective. *In* Aging and Modernization. D.O. Cowgill and L.D. Holmes, eds. Pp. 1-13. New York: Appleton-Century-Crofts, 1972(b).

———. The Role and Status of the Aged in Thailand. *In* Aging and Modernization. D.O. Cowgill and L.D. Holmes, eds. New York: Appleton-Century-Crofts, 1972(c).

———. Aging and Modernization: A Revision of the Theory. *In* Late Life: Communities and Environmental Policy. J. Gubrium, ed. Springfield: Charles C. Thomas, 1974(a).

———. The Aging of Populations and Societies. Annals, American Academy of Political and Social Sciences 415:1-18. (1974b)

Cowgill, D.O., and L.D. Holmes, eds. Aging and Modernization. New York: Appleton-Century-Crofts, 1972(a).

———. Summary and Conclusions: The Theory in Review. *In* Aging and Modernization. Pp. 305-323. New York: Appleton-Century-Crofts, 1972(b).

Crissman, L.W. The Segmentary Structure of Urban Overseas Chinese Communities. Man 2(2): 185-204. (1967)

Crow, J., and M. Kimura. Some Genetic Problems in Natural Populations. Proceedings of the Third Berkeley Symposium on Mathematic Statistics and Probability 4:1-22. (1956)

Cumming, E. New Thoughts on the Theory of Disengagement. *In* New Thoughts on Old Age. R. Kastenbaum, ed. New York: Springer-Verlag, 1964.

Cumming, E., and W.E. Henry. Growing Old: The Process of Disengagement. New York: Basic Books, 1961.

Cutler, Richard G. Evolution of Human Longevity and the Genetic Complexity Governing Aging Rate. Proc. Nat. Acad. Sci. U.S.A. 72, 11:4664-4668. (1975)

Datan. N., et. al. Climacterium in Three Culture Contexts. Tropical and Geographical Medicine. 22:77-86. (1970)

Davidson, E.H. Gene Activity in Early Development. New York: Academic Press, 1968.

Davidson, W.V. Black Carib (Garifuna) Habitats in Central America. *In* Frontier Adaptations in Lower Central America. M. Helms and F. Loveland, eds. Pp. 85-94. Philadelphia: Institute for the Study of Human Issues, 1976.

DeBusk, F.L. The Hutchinson-Gilford Progeria Syndrome. Journal of Pediatrics 80, 4(2):719. (1972)

Dempsey, D. The Way We Die. New York: McGraw-Hill, 1975.

Desai, K.G., and R.D. Naik. Problems of Retired People in Greater Bombay. Bombay: Tata Institute of Social Sciences (n.d.).

Deutsch, K., et. al. Political Community and the North Atlantic Area. Princeton, University Press, 1957.

Donfut, C., and C. Faucherand. Les Personnes Agées et la Vie Communautaire: Essai de Comparison. Revue Française de Gerontologie 15:35-8. (1969)

Doolittle, Rev. J. Social Life of the Chinese. 2 Vols. Taipei: Ch'eng-wen Publishing Co., 1966. Original edition published by Harper & Brothers Publishers, New York, 1865.

Dovenmuehle, R.S. Aging Versus Illness. *In* Normal Aging. E. Palmore, ed. Durham, N.C.: Duke University Press, 1970.

Dowd, J.J. Aging as Exchange: A Preface to Theory. Journal of Gerontology 30(5):584-594. (1975)

Dube, S.C. Indian Village. New York: Cornell University Press, 1955.

Dyson-Hudson, N. The Karimojong Age System. Ethnology 2:353-401. (1963)

Ehrlich, I.F. Life Styles Among Persons 70 Years and Older in Age-Segregated Housing. Gerontologist 12:27-31. (1972)

Eisenstadt, S.N. African Age Groups. Africa 24:100-113. (1954)

———. From Generation to Generation: Age Groups and Social Structure. New York: Free Press, 1956.

Elder, G.H., Jr. Age Differentiation and Life Course. Annual Review of Sociology, Vol. I. Palo Alto, Calif.: Annual Reviews, 1975.

Emerson, A.E. Human Cultural Evolution and Its Relation to Organic Evolution in Insect Societies. *In* Social Change in Developing Areas: A Reinterpretation of Evolutionary Theory. H. Barringer et. al., eds. Pp. 56-58. New York: Schenkman, 1965.

Emerson, R.N. Power-Dependence Relations. American Sociological Review 27:31-34. (1962)

———. Social Exchange Theory. *In* Annual Review of Sociology, 1976. A. Inkeles, J. Coleman, and N. Smelser, eds. Pp. 335-362. Palo Alto, Calif.: Annual Reviews, 1976.

Epstein, C.J., et. al. Werner's Syndrome: Review of Symptomatology, Natural History, Pathologic Features, Genetics, and Relationship to the Natural Aging Process. Medicine 45:177-221. (1966)

Epstein, L., and J.H. Murray. The Aged Population in the United States: The 1963 Social Security Survey of the Aged. Washington, D.C.: The United States Printing Office, 1967.

Erikson, Erik. Identity and the Life Cycle. New York: International University Press, 1959.

Evans-Prichard, E.E. The Nuer. Clarendon (U.K.): Oxford University Press, 1968.

Feder, S. Aging in the Kibbutz in Israel. *In* Aging and Modernization. D.O. Cowgill and L.D. Holmes, eds. New York: Appleton-Century-Crofts, 1972.

Fedio, P. Overview of Proceedings of Language and the Brain. Teaching Symposium presented by the Linguistics Society of America (LSA), 1972.

Fei, H. Peasant Life in China. New York: Oxford University Press, 1946.

Ferraud, D. Premier Bilan Medical à la Residence pour Anciens de la Buissonière. Revue Française de Gerontologie 15:103-10. (1969)

Fichet, M.F. Logement et Troisième Age. Gerontologie 4:10. (1971)

Finch, C.E. Cellular Activities During Aging in Mammals. New York: MSS Information Corporation, 1969.

———. Aging and the Regulation of Hormones. *In* Explorations in Aging. V.J. Cristofalo, J. Roberts, and R.C. Adelman, eds. Advances in Experimental Medicine and Biology. New York: Plenum, 1975.

Finch, C.E., and L. Hayflick, eds. Handbook of the Biology of Aging. New York: Van Nostrand Reinhold Co., 1976.

Fogel, L.J., A.J. Owens, and M.J. Walsh. Artificial Intelligence Through Simulated Evolution. New York: John Wiley & Sons, 1956.

Forner, A., and J. Kertzer. Transitions Over the Life Course: Lessons from Age-Set Societies. American Journal of Sociology 83:1081-1104. (1978)

Frake, C. The Ethnographic Study of Cognitive Systems. *In* Anthropology and Human Behavior. T. Gladwin and W.C. Sturtevant, eds. Washington, D.C.: Anthropological Society of Washington, 1962.

———. Notes on Queries in Ethnography. American Anthropologist. 66:132-145. (1964)

Feedman, A.M. and H.L. Kaplan, eds. Comprehensive Textbook of Psychiatry. Baltimore: The John Hopkins University Press, 1967.

Freedman, M. Lineage Organization in Southeastern China. London: The Athlone Press, 1970.

Fried, Morton H. Fabric of Chinese Society. New York: Praeger, 1953.

Friedman, E.P. Spatial Proximity and Social Interaction in a Home for the Aged. Journal of Gerontology 21:566-71. (1966)

———. Age, Length of Institutionalization and Social Status in a Home for the Aged. Journal of Gerontology 22:474-77. (1967)

Friis, H., P. Townsend and E. Shanas. Old People in Three Industrial Societies: An Introduction. *In* Old People in Three Industrial Societies. Shanas, et. al., eds. New York: Atherton Press, 1968.

Fry, C.L. Age Grading in a Complex Society: A Study of the Age Status Structure of the United States. Ph.D. dissertation. University of Arizona, 1973.

———. The Ages of Adulthood: A Question of Numbers. Journal of Gerontology 31:170-177. (1976)

———. Community as Commodity: The Age Graded Case. Human Organization 36:115-123. (1977)

———. Structural Conditions Affecting Community Formation among the Aged. *In* The Ethnography of Old Age. J. Keith, ed. Special Issue of Anthropological Quarterly, 52(1): 7-18 (1979)

Fuller, C.E. Aging Among Southern African Bantu. *In* Aging and Modernization. D.O. Cowgill and L.D. Holmes, eds. New York: Meredith, 1972.

Fulton, R.L. Death and the Self. Journal of Religion and Health 3(4):359-68. (1964)

Gann, R., Jr., ed. Oklahoma Indian Affairs Commission: Statistics for the Indian in Oklahoma, 1974.

Garigue, Philippe. Etudes sur le Canada française. Montreal: Presses Universitaires de Montréal, 1958.

Giacopassi, D. and R.F. Lovely. Factors Affecting Self-Assessments of Health among the Elderly. Unpublished paper, Midwest Sociological Association, Omaha, Nebraska, 1968.

Gibson, G. Kin Family Network: Overheralded Structure in Past Conceptualizations of Family Functioning. Journal of Marriage and Family 34:13-23. (1972)

Glass, D.C., ed. Environmental Influences, Proceedings of a Conference under the Auspices of the Russell Sage Foundation and the Rockefeller University. New York: Rockefeller University, 1968.

Goffman, E. The Presentation of Self in Everyday Life. Garden City, N.Y.: Doubleday, 1959.

Goist, D.F. Adaptive Strategies of the Elderly in England and Ohio. Paper presented at 31st annual meeting of the Gerontological Society. Dallas, Texas, 1978.

Goldstein, S.G. The Biology of Aging. N.E.J.M. (New England Journal of Medicine) 285, 1971.

Gonzalez, N.L. Black Carib Household Structure. Seattle: University of Washington Press, 1969.

Goodale, J.C. Tiwi Wives: A Study of the Women of Melville Island North Australia. Seattle: University of Washington Press, 1971.

Goodwin, G. The Social Organization of the Western Apache. Chicago: University of Chicago Press, 1942.

Goody, J. Normative, Recollected and Actual Marriage Payments among the LoWiili. Africa 39:54-61. (1969)

——. Aging in Nonindustrial Societies. *In* Handbook of Aging and the Social Sciences. R.H. Binstock and E. Shanas, eds. New York: Van Nostrand Reinhold, 1976.

Gordon, P. Adv. in Gerontol. Res. 3:199 (1971)

Gouldner, A.W. The Norm of Reciprocity: A Preliminary Statement. American Sociological Review 25:161-178. (1960)

Green, P.E., and Carmone, F.J. Multidimensional Scaling and Related Techniques in Marketing Analysis. Boston: Allyn and Bacon, 1970.

Gross, J. Aging of Connective Tissue, the Extracellular Components. *In* Structural Aspects of Aging. G.H. Bourne, ed. New York: Hafner Publishers, 1961.

Gubrium, J.F., ed. Late Life: Communities and Environmental Policy. Springfield, Ill.: Charles Thomas, 1974.

——. Living and Dying at Murray Manor. New York: St. Martin's Press, 1975.

Guemple, D.L. Human Resource Management: The Dilemma of the Aging Eskimo. Sociological Symposium 2:59-74. (1969)

Guillemard, Anne-Marie. La Retraite: Une Mort Sociale. The Hague: Mouton, 1972.

——. Comments. *In* Réunion des Chercheurs en Gerontologie Sociale. Paris: Caisse Nationale d'Assurance Vieillesse des Travailleurs Salariés, 1975. P. 43.

Guillemin, R. and R. Burgus. The Hormones of the Hypothalamus. Scientific American 227:24-33. (1972)

Gulliver, P.H. The Age Set Organization of the Jie Tribe. Journal of the Royal Anthropological Institute of Great Britain and Ireland 83:147-168. (1953)

——. The Turkana Age Organization. American Anthropologist 60:900-922. (1958)

——. Age Differentiation. International Encyclopedia of the Social Sciences. New York: Macmillan and Free Press, 1968.

Gutkind, P.C.W. African Urban Family Life and the Urban System. *In* Urbanism, Urbanization, and Change: Comparative Perspectives. P. Meadows and E.H. Mizruchi, eds. Pp. 215-222. Reading, Mass: Addison-Wesley, 1969.

Guttman, D.L. An Exploration of Ego Configurations in Middle and Late Life. *In* Personality in Middle and Late Life. B.L. Neugarten, ed. New York: Atherton Press, 1964.

——. Aging Among the Highland Maya: A Comparative Study. *In* Middle Age and Aging. B.L. Neugarten, ed. Chicago: University of Chicago Press, 1968.

——. The Country of Old Men: Cross-Cultural Studies in the Psychology of Later Life. *In* Occasional Papers in Gerontology. W. Donahue, ed. Ann Arbor: Institute of Gerontology, University of Michigan, 1969.

——. The Hunger of Old Men. Trans-Action 9:55-66. (1971)

——. Alternatives to Disengagement: The Old Men of the Highland Druze. *In* Culture and Personality: Contemporary Readings. Robert LeVine, ed. Chicago: Aldine, 1974.

——. Alternatives to Disengagement: The Old Men of the Highland Druze. *In* Time, Roles, and Self in Old Age. J.F. Gubrium, ed. New York: Human Sciences Press, 1976.

Guttman, L. The Structuring of Sociological Spaces. Transactions of the Fourth World Congress of Sociology 3:315-355. (1961)

Hadel, R.E. Carib Folk Songs and Carib Culture. Unpublished Ph.D. dissertation. Austin: University of Texas, 1972.

Hallowell, A. Review of Leo Simmons' The Role of the Aged in Primitive Society. Annals of the American Academy 244:229. (1946)

Hamer, J. Aging in a Gerontocratic Society: The Sedamo of Southwest Ethiopia. *In* Aging and Modernization. D.O. Cowgill and L.D. Holmes, eds. New York: Appleton-Century-Crofts, 1972.

Hamovitch, M.B. Social and Psychological Factors in Adjustment in a Retirement Village. *In* The Retirement Process. F. Carp, ed. Washington, D.C.: U.S. Department of Health, Education and Welfare, 1966.

Hampe, G.D., and A.L. Blevins, Jr. Primary Group Interaction of Residents in a Retirement Hotel. International Journal of Aging and Human Development 6:309-20. (1975)

Harlan, W.H. Social Status of the Aged in Three Indian Villages. Vita Humana 7:239-252. (1964)

Hart, C.W.M., and A.R. Pilling. The Tiwi of North Australia. New York: Holt, Rinehart and Winston, 1961.

Hauser, P. Aging and World-Wide Population Change. *In* Handbook of Aging and the Social Sciences. R.H. Binstock and E. Shanas, eds. New York: Van Norstrand Reinhold, 1976.

Havighurst, R. Successful Aging. Gerontologist 1:8-13. (1961)

Havighurst, R., et. al. Disengagement, Personality and Life Satisfaction in the Later Years. *In* Age with a Future. P.F. Hansen, ed. Philadelphia: F.A. Davis, 1964.

Havighurst, R., B. Neugarten, and S. Tobin. Disengagement and Patterns of Aging. *In* Middle Age and Aging. B. Neugarten, ed. Pp. 161-172. Chicago: University of Chicago Press, 1968.

Havighurst, R., et al. Adjustment to Retirement: A Cross-National Study. Assen: Van Gorcum, 1969.

Hayflick, Leonard. Current Theories of Biological Aging. Fed. Proc. 34, 1:9-13. (1975)

Hayflick, L. and P.S. Moorhead. In Vitro Population Doublings of Human Fibroblasts. Exp. Cell. Res. 25:585. (1961)

Henkin, R.K. The Neuroendocrine Control of Perception. *In* Perception and its Disorders, Proceedings of the Association for Research in Nervous Mental Disease. D. Hamburg, ed. Baltimore: Williams and Wilkins, 1970.

Hendel-Sebestyen. G. Role Diversity: Toward the Development of Community in a Total Institutional Setting. *In* The Ethnography of Old Age. J. Keith, ed. Special Issue of Anthropological Quarterly, 52:19-28, (1979).

Henry, W.E. The Theory of Intrinsic Disengagement. *In* Age with a Future. P.F. Hansen, ed. Philadelphia: F.A. Davis, 1964.

Hershey, D. Life Span and Factors that Determine It. Springfield, Ill.: Charles C. Thomas, 1974.

Hess, B. Friendship. *In* Aging and Society, Vol. 3: A Sociology of Age Stratification. Matilda White Riley, et al., eds. Pp. 357-393. New York: Russell Sage Foundation, 1972.

Hochschild, A.R. The Unexpected Community. Englewood Cliffs, N.J.: Prentice-Hall, 1973.

——. Disengagement Theory: A Critique and Proposal. American Sociological Review 40:553-569. (1975)

Hockett, C.F. Man's Place in Nature. New York: McGraw Hill, 1973.

Holliday, R. Growth and Death of Diploid and Transformed Human Fibroblasts. Fed. Proc. 34, 1:52. (1975)

Holmberg, A.R. Nomads of the Long Bow: The Siriono of Eastern Bolivia. New York: American Museum Science Books, 1969.

Holmes, L.D. The Role and Status of the Aged in a Changing Samoa. In Aging and Modernization. D.O. Cowgill and L.D. Holmes, eds. New York: Appleton-Century-Crofts, 1972.

——. Trends in Anthropological Gerontology: From Simmons to the Seventies. International Journal of Aging and Human Development 7:211-220. (1976)

Hollnsteiner, M.R. Becoming an Urbanite: The Neighbourhood as a Learning Environment. In The City as a Centre of Change in Asia. D.J. Dwyer, ed. Pp. 29-40. Hong Kong: Hong Kong University Press, 1972.

Homans, G.C. Social Behavior: Its Elementary Forms. New York: Harcourt, Brace & World, 1961.

——. Social Behavior: Its Elementary Forms. Revised Edition. New York: Harcourt Brace Jovanovich, 1974.

Hong Kong Census and Statistics Department. Hong Kong Population and Housing Census: 1971 Main Report. Hong Kong: Director of Medical and Health Services, 1972.

——. Annual Departmental Report 1975-1976. Hong Kong: Government Press, 1976.

Hoyt, G.C. The Life of the Retired in a Trailer Park. American Journal of Sociology 59:347. (1954)

Hsu, F.L.K. Americans and Chinese: Two Ways of Life. New York: Henry Schuman, 1953.

——. Under the Ancestors' Shadow. Stanford, Calif.: Stanford University Press, 1971. (Originally published in 1948 by Columbia University Press, New York.)

Hudson, R.B., and R. Binstock. Political Systems and Aging. In Handbook of Aging and the Social Sciences. R.H. Binstock and E. Shanas, eds. New York: Van Norstrand Reinhold, 1976.

Huntingford, G.W.B. The Nandi of Kenya. Clarendon (U.K.): Oxford University Press.

Republic of India, Office of the Registrar General. Census of India 1971. Series 1. Part II-C(ii) Social and Cultural Tables. New Delhi: Office of the Registrar General, 1976.

Ishida, R., and T. Takehashi. Increased DNA Chain Breakage by Combined Action of Bleomycin and Superoxide Radical. Biochemical Biophysical Research Communication. 66:11432. (1973)

Iyer, P.N. Project: Study of the Aged in Delhi—First Progress Report. Unpubl. mimeo. Delhi: Delhi School of Social Work, 1971.

Jackson, J.J. Negro Aged: Toward Needed Research in Social Gerontology. The Gerontologist II:2:52-57. (1971a)

——. Sex and Social Class Variations in Black Aged Parent-Adult Child Relationships. Aging and Human Development 2:96-107. (1971b)

Jacobs, J. Fun City: An Ethnographic Study of a Retirement Community. New York: Holt, Rinehart and Winston, 1974.

——. Older Persons and Retirement Communities: Case Studies in Social Gerontology. Springfield, Ill.: Charles C. Thomas, 1975.

Jacobs, R.H. One-Way Street: An Intimate View of Adjustment to a Home for the Aged. Gerontologist 9:268-75. (1969)

Jeffers, F., C. Eisdorfer and E. Busse. Measurement of Age Identification: A Methodologic Note. Journal of Gerontology 17:437-439. (1962)

Johnson, S.K. Idle Haven: Community Building among the Working Class Retired. Berkeley: University of California Press, 1971.

——. Growing Old Alone Together. New York Times Magazine. Nov. 11, 1973, p. 40.

Jonas, K. Factors in Development of Community in Age-Segregated Housing. *In* The Ethnography of Old Age. J. Keith, ed. Special Issue of Anthropological Quarterly, 52(1):29-38 (1979)

Jones, G.I. Ibo Age Organization, with Special Reference to the Cross River and Northeastern Ibo. Journal of the Royal Anthropological Institute of Great Britain and Ireland 92:191-211. (1962)

Kalish, R.A. A Gerontological Look at Ethnicity. The Gerontologist 11:78-87. (1971)

——. Late Adulthood: Perspectives on Human Development. Monterey, Calif.: Brooks/Cole, 1975.

Kalish, R.A., and S. Yuen. Americans of East Asian Ancestry: Aging and the Aged. The Gerontologist II:2:36-47. (1971)

Kandel. R.F., and M. Heider. Friendship and Factionalism in a Tri-ethnic Housing Complex in North Miami. *In* The Ethnography of Old Age. J. Keith, ed. Special Issue of Anthropological Quarterly, 52(1):49-60 (1979)

Kanter, R.M. Commitment and Community: Communes and Utopias in Sociological Perspective. Cambridge, Mass.: Harvard University Press, 1972.

Kapadia, K.M. Marriage and Family in India. Bombay: Oxford University Press, 1966.

Karlin S. and J. McGregor. On Some Stochastic Models in Genetics. *In* Stochastic Models in Medicine and Biology. Pp. 245-279. John Gurland, ed. Madison: University of Wisconsin Press, 1964.

Kart, C.S., and B.B. Manard, eds. Aging in America: Readings in Social Gerontology. Port Washington, N.Y.: Alfred, 1976.

Katz, S., T.D. Downs, H.R. Cash, and R.C. Grotz. Progress in the Development of the Index of ADL. Gerontologist 10:20-30. (1970)

Kazemier, B.H., and D. Vursje, eds. The Concept and the Role of the Model in Mathematics and Natural and Social Science. Proceedings of the Colloquium sponsored by the Division of Philosophy of Science of the International Union of History and Philosophy of Sciences. Utrecht: Utrecht University Press, 1960.

Keifer, C.W. Notes on Anthropology and the Minority Elderly. The Gerontologist II:94-98. (1971)

———. Lessons from the Issei. *In* Late Life: Communities and Environmental Policy. J. Gubrium, ed. Springfield, Ill.: Charles C. Thomas, 1974.

Keith, J., ed. The Ethnography of Old Age. Anthropological Quarterly 52(1) (1979)

Keller, S. The Urban Neighborhood. New York: Random House, 1968.

Kellogg, E.W., and I. Fridovich. Superoxide Dismutase in the Rat and Mouse as a Function of Age and Longevity. Journal of Gerontology 31:405-408. (1976)

Kent, D.P. The Elderly in Minority Groups: Variant Patterns of Aging. The Gerontologist II:2:48-51. (1971)

Kerns, V. Black Carib Women and Rites of Death. *In* Unspoken Worlds: Women's Religious Lives. Nancy Falk and Rita Cross, eds. New York: Harper and Row. In Press.

———. Daughters Bring In: Ceremonial and Social Organization of the Black Carib of Belize. Unpublished Ph.D. dissertation. Urbana: University of Illinois, 1977.

Kirk, L., and M. Burton. Meaning and Context: A Study of Contextual Shifts in Meaning of Maasai Personality Descriptions. American Ethnologist 4: 734-761. (1977)

Kleemeier, R. Moosehaven: Congregate Living in a Community of the Retired. American Journal of Sociology 59:347-51. (1959)

———. The Use and Meaning of Time in Special Settings: Retirement Communities, Homes for the Aged, Hospitals and Other Group Settings. *In* Aging and Leisure. Robert Kleemeier, ed. New York: Oxford University Press, 1961.

Kluckhohn, C. Values and Value-Orientations in the Theory of Action. *In* Toward a General Theory of Action. T. Parsons and E.A. Shils, eds. New York: Harper and Row, 1951.

Kohn, R.R. Principles of Mammalian Aging. Englewood Cliffs: Prentice Hall, 1971.

Krebs, H.A. and W.A. Johnson, The Role of Citric Acid in Intermediate Metabolism in Animal Tissues. Enzymologia 4:148-56. (1937)

Kutner, B., et al. Five Hundred Over Sixty. New York: Russell Sage Foundation, 1956.

Lamson, H.D. Social Pathology in China. Shanghai: The Commercial Press, 1934.

Lang, O. Chinese Family and Society. New Haven: Yale University Press, 1946.

Langford, M. Community Aspects of Housing the Aged. Ithaca, N.Y.: Cornell University Center for Housing and Environmental Studies, 1962.

Laslett, P. The World We Have Lost. London: Methuen, 1965.

Laumann, E.O. Bonds of Pluralism. New York: John Wiley and Sons, 1973.

Lawton, M.P. Ecology and Aging. *In* The Spatial Behavior of Older People. L.A. Pastalan and D.H. Carson, eds. Ann Arbor: University of Michigan Press, 1970.

———. The Relative Impact of Congregate and Traditional Housing on Elderly Tenants. Gerontologist 16:237-42. (1976)

Lawton, M.P., and B. Simon. The Ecology of Social Relationships in Housing for the Elderly. Gerontologist 8:108-15. (1968)

Lee, S. China's Traditional Family, Its Characteristics and Disintegration. American Sociological Review 18:272-280. (1953)

Legesse, A. Age Sets and Retirement Communities. *In* The Ethnography of Old Age. J. Keith, ed. Special Issue of Anthropological Quarterly 52(1): (1979)

LeMasters, E.L. Blue Collar Aristocrats. Madison: University of Wisconsin Press, 1975.

Lemon, B.W., et al. An Exploration of the Activity Theory of Aging: Activity Types and Life Satisfaction among In-Movers to a Retirement Community. Journal of Gerontology 27:511-23. (1972)

Leonard, O.E. The Older Rural Spanish-Speaking People of the Southwest. *In* Older Rural Americans: A Sociological Perspective. E.G. Youmans, ed. Lexington: University of Kentucky Press, 1967.

Lester, D. Inconsistency in the Fear of Death of Individuals. Psychology Reports 20:1084. (1967)

———. The Need to Achieve and the Fear of Death. Psychology Reports 27(2): 516. (1970)

LeVine, R. Intergenerational Tensions and Extended Family Structure in Africa. *In* Social Structure and the Family. E. Shanas and G. Streib, eds. Englewood Cliffs: Prentice-Hall, 1965.

LeVine, R.A. and W.H. Sangree. The Diffusion of Age Group Organization in East Africa. Africa 32:2. (1962)

Levine, S. Stress and Behavior. Scientific American 226:26-31. (1971)

Levy, J.E. The Older American Indian. *In* Older Rural Americans: A Sociological Perspective. E.G. Youmans, ed. Lexington: University of Kentucky Press, 1967.

Levy, M. The Family Revolution in Modern China. Cambridge, Mass.: Harvard University Press, 1949.

Lewis, C.M., and R. Holliday. Mistranslation and Aging in Neurospora. Nature 228:878. (1970)

Linschitz, H. The Information Content of a Bacterial Cell. *In* Essays on the Use of Information Theory in Biology. H. Quastler, ed. Pp. 251-262. Urbana: University of Illinois Press, 1953.

Linton, R. Age and Sex Categories. American Sociological Review 7:589-603. (1942)

Little, V.C. Social Services for the Elderly: With Special Attention to the Asia and West Pacific Region. A Preliminary Look. Paper presented at the annual meeting of the Gerontological Society, Portland, Oregon, 1974.

Litwak, E. Extended Kin Relations in an Industrial Democratic Society. *In* Social Structure and the Family Generational Relations. E. Shanas and G. Strieb, eds. Englewood Cliffs, N.J.: Prentice-Hall, 1965.

Looft, W.R. Socialization and Personality: Contemporary Psychological Approaches. *In* Life-Span Developmental Psychology: Personality and Socialization. P.B. Baltes and K.W. Schaie, eds. New York: Academic Press, 1973.

Lopata, H.Z. Widowhood in an American City. Cambridge, Mass.: Schenkman, 1973.

Lowdin, P.O. Quantum Genetics and the Aperiodic Solid. Some Aspects on the Biological Problems of Heredity, Mutations, Aging and Tumors in View of the Quantum Theory of the DNA Molecule. Quantum Chemistry Group, Preprint No. 85. Uppsala: Uppsala University Press, 1962.

Lowenthal, M.F. Social Isolation and Mental Health in Old Age. American Sociological Review 29(1):54-70. (1964)

Lowie, R. Plains Indians Age—Societies. New York: American Museum of Natural History Anthropological Papers, 1916.

Lozier, J., and R. Althouse. Social Enforcement of Behavior Toward Elders in an Appalachian Mountain Settlement. The Gerontologist 14:69-80. (1974)

Lwoff, A. Biological Order. Cambridge, Mass.: The MIT Press, 1962.

Maas, H.S., and J.A. Kuypers. From Thirty to Seventy: A Forty-Year Longitudinal Study of Adult Life Styles and Personality. San Francisco: Jossey-Bass, 1974.

Mack, A., ed. Death in American Experience. New York: Schocken Books, 1973.

Maddox, G.L. Disengagement Theory: A Critical Evaluation. The Gerontologist 4:80-82. (1964)

——. Persistence of Life-Style among the Elderly. Proceedings of the 7th International Congress of Gerontology 6:309-311. (1966)

——. Growing Old: Getting Beyond the Stereotypes. *In* Foundations of Practical Gerontology. Boyd and Oakes, eds. Pp. 5-16. Columbia: University of South Carolina Press, 1969.

Maddox, G., and E.B. Douglass. Self Assessment of Health: A Longitudinal Study of Elderly Subjects. Journal of Health and Social Behavior 14:92-97. (1973)

Malinowski, B. Argonauts of the Western Pacific. London: Routledge & Kegan Paul, 1922.

Mandelbaum, D.G. Society in India. 2 Vols. Berkeley: University of California Press, 1970.

Manil, P. La Tolerance dans la Cohabitation dans un Home de Vieillards. Revue de Gerontologie d'expression Française 17:31-44. (1970)

Marshall, V.W. Game Analysable Dilemmas in Retirement Village Living. International Journal of Aging and Human Development 4:285-91. (1973)

———. Socialization for Impending Death in a Retirement Village. American Journal of Sociology 80:1124-44. (1975)

Marulasiddaiah, H.M. Old People of Makunti. Dharwar: Karnatak University, 1969.

Mauss, M. The Gift: Forms and Functions of Exchange in Archaic Societies. Glencoe, Ill.: Free Press, 1954.

Maxwell, R.J. The Changing Status of Elderly in Polynesian Society. Aging and Human Development 1:127-46. (1970)

Maxwell, R.J., and P. Silverman. Information and Esteem. Aging and Human Development 1:361-392. (1970)

Mayer, A.C. The Significance of Quasi-Groups in the Study of Complex Societies. In The Social Anthropology of Complex Societies. M. Banton, ed. London: Tavistock Publishers, 1966.

Mayr, Ernst. Animal Species and Evolution. Cambridge, Mass.: Harvard University Press, 1965.

McAdam, D.W., and H.A. Whitaker. Language Production: Electroencephalographic Localization in the Normal Human Brain. Science 172:499-502. (1972)

McKain, W.C. The Aged in the U.S.S.R. In Aging and Modernization. D.O. Cowgill and L.D. Holmes, eds. New York: Appleton-Century-Crofts, 1972.

Mead, M. Culture and Commitment: A Study of the Generation Gap. New York: Doubleday, 1970.

Mechanic, D. Sociology and Public Health: Perspectives for Application. American Journal of Public Health 62:146-151. (1972)

Mehrabian, A. Male and Female Scales of the Tendency to Achieve. Educational and Psychological Measurement 28:165-73. (1968)

Merritt, R.L. Symbols of American Community, 1735-1765. New Haven, Conn.: Yale University Press, 1966.

Merton, R.K. Social Theory and Social Structure. Glencoe, Ill.: The Free Press, 1957.

Messenger, J.C. Inis Beag: Isle of Ireland. New York: Holt, Rinehart and Winston, 1969.

Messer, M. The Possibility of an Age-Concentrated Environment Becoming a Normative System. Gerontologist 7:247-51. (1967)

———. Age Grouping and the Family Status of the Elderly. Sociology and Social Research 52:271-79. (1968)

Miller, M.K., and S. Stokes. Health Status, Health Resources, and Consolidated Structural Parameters: Implications for Public Health Care Policy. Journal of Health and Human Behavior 19:263-279. (1978)

Mitchell, R.E. Levels of Emotional Strain in Southeast Asian Cities. 2 Vols. Taipei: The Orient Cultural Service, 1972.

Mizruchi, E.H. Romanticism, Rubanism, and Small Town in Mass Society. *In* Urbansim, Urbanization, and Change: Comparative Perspectives. P. Meadows and E.H. Mizruchi, eds. Pp. 243-251. Reading, Mass.: Addison-Wesley, 1969.

Moore, A. Life Cycles in Atchatlan: The Diverse Careers of Certain Guatemalans. New York: Teachers College, Columbia University, 1973.

Moore, J.W. Mexican Americans. The Gerontologist II:2:20-25. (1971a)

———. Situational Factors Affecting Minority Aging. The Gerontologist 11: 88-93. (1971b)

Morris, R.W. Cultural Attitudes toward the Menopause among a Non-Western Group of Women: A Study of Seventy-three Urban Chhatisgarhi Women. Unpub. M.A. thesis. Seattle: University of Washington, 1960.

Moss, G.E. Illness, Immunity, and Social Interaction. New York: Wiley-Interscience, 1973.

de Moussac, O. Les Residences pour Anciens du Batiment. Revue Française de Gerontologie 13:15-20. (1967)

Mumford, L. For Older People: Not Segregation, But Integration. Architectural Record 119:191-194. (1956)

Munsell, M.R. Functions of the Aged Among Salt River Pima. *In* Aging and Modernization. D.O. Cowgill and L.D. Holmes, eds. New York: Meredith Corporation, 1972.

Myerhoff, B., and A. Simic, eds. Life's Career—Aging. Cultural Variations in Growing Old. Beverly Hills: Sage Publications, 1978.

Nader, R. The Last Segregation. New York: Grossman Publishers, 1971.

Nagi, S.Z. An Epidemiology of Disability among Adults in the United States. Milbank Memorial Fund Quarterly 54(4):439-467. (1976)

Nahemow, N., and B. Adams. Old Age among the Baganda: Continuity and Change. *In* Late Life: Communities and Environmental Policy. J. Gubrium, ed. Springfield, Ill.: Charles C. Thomas, 1974.

Napior, D. Nonmetric Techniques for Summated Ratings. *In* Multidimensional Scaling: Theory and Applications in the Behavioral Sciences, Vol. I. R.N. Shepard, A.K. Romney and S.B. Nerlove, eds. New York: Seminar Press, 1972.

Needham, R. Age, Category and Descent. *In* Remarks and Inventions. R. Needham, ed. London: Tavistock, 1974.

Neugarten, B.L., ed. Middle Age and Aging: A Reader in Social Psychology. Chicago: University of Chicago Press, 1968.

———. Aging in the Year 2000, a Look at the Future. The Gerontologist 15(1): 1-40. (1975a)

Neugarten, B.L. Age Groups in American Society and the Rise of the Young-Old. *In* Political Consequences of Aging. F.R. Eisele, ed. Philadelphia: The Annals of the American Academy of Political and Social Science, 1974.

———. The Future and the Young-Old. *In* Aging in the Year 2000: A Look at the Future. B. Neugarten, ed. The Gerontologist 15:1:4-9. (1975b)

Neugarten, B.L., and N. Datan. Sociological Perspectives on the Life Cycle. *In* Life-Span Developmental Psychology: Personality and Socialization. P.B. Baltes and K.W. Schaie, eds. New York: Academic Press, 1973.

Neugarten, B.L., and G.O. Hagestad. Age and the Life Course. *In* Handbook of Aging and the Social Sciences. J.E. Birren, ed. New York: Van Nostrand Reinhold, 1976.

Neugarten, B., R. Havighurst, and S. Tobin. The Measurement of Life Satisfaction. Journal of Gerontology 16:134-143. (1961)

———. Personality and Patterns of Aging. *In* Middle Age and Aging. B. Neugarten, ed. Chicago: University of Chicago Press, 1968.

Neugarten, B.L., and J.W. Moore. The Changing Age Status System. *In* Middle Age and Aging. B.L. Neugarten, ed. Chicago: University of Chicago Press, 1968.

Neugarten, B.L., J. Moore and J. Lowie. Age Norms, Age Constraints, and Adult Socialization. American Journal of Sociology 70:710-717. (1965)

Norbeck, E. Age Grading in Japan. American Anthropologist 55:373-83. (1953).

Odum, H.T. Environment, Power, and Society. New York: Wiley-Interscience, 1971.

O'Malley, B.W., T.C. Spelsberg, W.T. Schrader, F. Chytil, and A.W. Steggles. Mechanisms of Interaction of a Hormone-Receptor Complex with the Genome of a Eukaryotic Target Cell. Nature 235:141-144. (1972)

Orgel, L.E. Aging of Clones of Mammalian Cells. Nature 243:441-444. (1973)

Pacaud, S., and M. Chapé. Les Rapports Sociaux dans la Vie Communautaire: Étude Sociometrique dans un Service Hospitalier. Revue Française de Gerontologie 11:359-98. (1965)

Palmore, E. The Honorable Elders: A Cross-Cultural Analysis of Aging in Japan. Durham, N.C.: Duke University Press, 1975.

Palmore, E., and C. Luihart. Health and Social Factors Related to Life Satisfaction. Journal of Health and Social Behavior 13:68-79. (1972)

Palmore, E., and K. Manton. Modernization and Status of the Aged. Journal of Gerontology 29:2, 205-210. (1974)

Parsons, P.A. The Genetic Analysis of Behavior. London: Methuen, 1967.

Parsons, T. Age and Sex in the Social Structure of the United States. American Sociological Review 7:604-616. (1942)

———. The Social Structure of the Family. *In* The Family: Its Function and Destiny. R.N. Anschen, ed. New York: Harper and Row, 1959.

———. The Aging in American Society. Law and Contemporary Problems 27: 22-35. (1962)

Pasternak, B. Kinship and Community in Two Chinese Villages. Stanford: Stanford University Press, 1972.

Paulme, D. Blood Pacts, Age Classes and Castes in Black Africa. *In* French Perspectives in African Studies, P. Alexaudie, ed. pp. 73-95. Oxford: Oxford University Press, 1973.

Peristiany, J.G. The Age Set System of the Pastoral Pokot. Africa 21:188-206. (1951)

Pihlblad, C.T., E. Beverfelt and H. Hellend. Status and Role of the Aged in Norwegian Society. *In* Aging and Modernization. D.O. Cowgill and L.D. Holmes, eds. New York: Appleton-Century-Crofts, 1972.

Plath, D.W. Japan: The After Years. *In* Aging and Modernization. D.O. Cowgill and L.D. Holmes, eds. New York: Meredith, 1972.

———. Ecstasy Year—Old Age in Japan. Pacific Affairs 46(3):421-430. (1973)

Podmore, D. The Population of Hong Kong. *In* The Industrial Colony. K. Hopkins, ed. Pp. 21-54. Hong Kong: Oxford University Press, 1971.

Prabhu, P.N. Hindu Social Organization. Bombay: Popular Prakashan, 1940.

Press, I., and M. McKool. Social Structure and Status of the Aged: Toward Some Valid Cross-Cultural Generalizations. Aging and Human Development 3:297-306. (1972)

Price, J.A. U.S. and Canadian Indian Urban Ethnic Institutions. Urban Anthropology 4(1):35-52. (1975)

Prins, A. East African Age Class Systems. Groningen: Wolters, 1953.

Proppe, H. Housing for the Retired and Aged in Southern California: An Architectural Commentary. Gerontologist 8:176-79. (1968)

Quastler, H. The Emergence of Biological Organization. New Haven: Yale University Press, 1964.

Radcliffe-Brown, A.R. Age Organization Terminology. Man 29:21. (1929)

Raj, B., and B.G. Prasad. Health Status of the Aged in India—A Study in Three Villages. Geriatrics 25:142-158. (1970)

———. A Study of Rural Aged Persons in Social Profile. Indian Journal of Social Work 32:155-162. (1971)

Reeves, A.G., and F. Plum. Hyperphagia, Rage, and Dementia Accompanying a Ventromedial Hypothalamic Neoplasm. Archives of Neurology 20:616-624. (1969)

Reichard, S., F. Livson and P. Petersen. Aging and Personality. New York: John Wiley and Sons, 1962.

Rheinstein, J. Duty of Children to Support Parents. *In* Aging in Western Societies. E.W. Burgess, ed. P. 442. Chicago: University of Chicago Press, 1960.

Rhoads, E.J.M. Merchant Associations in Canton. *In* The Chinese City Between Two Worlds. M.Elvin and G. W. Skinner, eds. Pp. 97-118. Stanford: Stanford University Press, 1974.

Richardson, A.H. Social and Medical Correlates of Survival among the Octogenarians: United Auto Worker Retirees and Spanish American War Veterans. Journal of Gerontology 28:207-215. (1973)

Richardson, J.M. Age and Need: A Study of Older People in North East Scotland. Edinburgh: Livingston, 1964.

Riley, M.W., M.E. Johnson, and A. Foner, eds. Aging and Society, Vol. 3. A Sociology of Age Stratification. New York: Russell Sage Foundation, 1972.

Robin, E.P. Discontinuities in Attitudes and Behaviors of Older Age Groups. The Gerontologist 11:177-184. (1971)

Robinson, H.W., and D.E. Knight. Cybernetics, Artificial Intelligence, and Ecology. New York: Spartan Books, 1972.

Romano-V, O.I. The Warehousing of People in Complex Society. Paper presented at the 64th Annual Meeting of the American Anthropological Association, Denver, Colorado, Nov. 18-21, 1965.

Romnay, A.K., and R.G. D'Andrade, eds. Transcultural Studies in Cognition. Special Publication of the American Anthropologist 66:Pt. 2. (1964)

Rose, A. The Subculture of the Aging. The Gerontologist 2:123-127. (1962)

——. Older People and Their Social World. Philadelphia: F.A. Davis Press, 1965(a).

——. The Subculture of the Aging. *In* Older People and Their Social World. A.N. Rose and W.K. Peterson, eds. Philadelphia: F.A. Davis, 1965(b).

Rosenberg, G.S. Poverty, Aging and Social Isolation. Washington, D.C.: Bureau of Social Science Research, 1967.

——. The Worker Grows Old. San Francisco: Jossey-Bass, 1970.

Rosenmayr, L. The Elderly in Austrian Society. *In* Aging and Modernization. D.O. Cowgill and L.D. Holmes, eds. New York: Appleton-Century-Crofts, 1972.

Rosenmayr, L., and E. Köckeis. Propositions for a Sociololgical Theory of Aging and the Family. International Social Science Journal 15:410-426. (1963)

Rosow, I. Retirement Housing and Social Integration. The Gerontologist 1: 85-91. (1961)

——. And Then We Were Old. Transaction 2(2):20-26. (1965)

——. Social Integration of the Aged. New York: Free Press, 1967.

——. Old People: Their Friends and Neighbors. American Behavioral Scientist 14:59-69. (1970)

———. Socialization to Old Age. Berkeley: University of California Press, 1974.

Ross, J-K. Learning to Be Retired: Socialization into a French Retirement Residence. Journal of Gerontology 29 (2):211-223. (1974a)

———. Life Goes On: Social Organization in a French Retirement Residence. *In* Late Life: Communities and Environmental Policy. J.F. Gubrium, ed. Springfield, Ill.: Charles C. Thomas, 1974(b).

———. Successful Aging in a French Retirement Residence. *In* Successful Aging. Proceedings of the Duke University Center for the Study of Gerontology Conference on Successful Aging. E. Pfeiffer, ed. Durham: Duke University Press, 1974(c).

———. Old People, New Lives: Community Creation in a Retirement Residence. Chicago: University of Chicago Press, 1977.

Ross, J-K., and M. H. Ross. Participant Observation in Political Research. Political Methodology 1:63-88. (1974)

Ross, M.H. The Political Integration of Urban Squatters. Evanston, Ill.: Northwestern University Press, 1973.

Rowe, W.L. The Middle and Later Years in Indian Society. *In* R.W. Kleemeier, Aging and Leisure. New York: Oxford University Press, 1961.

Rudolph, S.H., and L.I. Rudolph. Rajput Adulthood: Reflections on the Amar Singh Diary. Daedalus 105/2:145-168. 1976.

Sacher, G.A. Longevity, Aging, and Death: An Evolutionary Perspective. Kleemeier Award Lecture. Gerontologist, vol. 18, No. 2, (1978)

Sahlins, M.D. On the Sociology of Primitive Exchange. *In* The Relevance of Models for Social Anthropology. M. Banton, ed. Pp. 139-236. New York: Praeger, 1965.

———. Stone Age Economics.Chicago: Aldine, 1972.

Sangree, W.H. Age, Prayer and Politics in Tiriki Kenya. Oxford: Oxford University Press, 1966.

Sankar, A. Cantonese Domestic Servants in Hong Kong: The Role of the Vegetarian Hall in Preparing for Old Age. Paper presented at the annual meeting of the Association for Asian Studies, New Yrok, 1977.

Schally, A.V., and A. Arumura and A.J. Kastin. Hypothalamic Regulatory Hormones. Science 179:141-151. (1973)

Schooler, K.K. The Relationship between Social Interaction and Morale of the Elderly as a Function of Environmental Characteristics. Gerontologist 9:25-29. (1969)

Schull, W.J. Some Considerations in the Design of Genetic Studies. The Biology of Human Adaptability. P.T. Baker and J.S. Weiner, eds. Oxford: Clarendon, 1966.

Schulz, C.M. Free-Time Structuring As a Cognitive Defense against Death Anxiety. Working Paper 97, Institute for the Study of Social Change. W. Lafayette, Ind.: Purdue University, 1975.

———. Death Anxiety and the Structuring of a Death Concerns Cognitive Domain. Essence, Vol. 1:(3):371-88. (1977)

———. Death Anxiety Reduction througy the Success-Achievement Cultural Core Value: A Middle-Class American Community Case Study. Journal of Psychological Anthropology, Vol. 1, No. 3: 321-339. (1978)

Seguin, M. Opportunity for Peer Socialization in a Retirement Community. Gerontologist 13:208-14. (1973)

Selye, H. The Stress of Life. New York: McGraw-Hill, 1956.

Seward, R.R. The Colonial Family in America: Toward a Socio-Historical Restoration of its Structure. Journal of Marriage and the Family 35:58-70. (1973)

Shanas, E. The Health of Older People: A Social Survey. Cambridge, Mass.: Harvard University Press, 1962.

———. Problems in the Organization and Design of Cross-National Studies in Aging. *In* Interdisciplinary Topics in Gerontology. Vol. II. Methodological Problems in Cross National Studies in Aging. E. Shanas and Madge, eds. New York: S. Kraeger, 1968.

———. Family Kin Networks and Aging in Cross-Cultural Perspective. Journal of Marriage and the Family 35:505-511. (1973)

Shanas, E., et. al., eds. Old People in Three Industrial Societies. New York: Atherton, 1968.

Sharma, K.L. A Cross-Cultural Comparison of Stereotypes towards Older Persons. Indian Journal of Social Work 32(3):315-320. (1971)

Sheley, J.R. Mutuality and Retirement Community Success. International Journal of Aging and Human Development 5:71-80. (1974)

Shelton, A. Igbo Aging and Eldership: Notes of Gerontologists and Others. The Gerontologist 5:2-23. (1965)

———. Igbo Child-rearing, Eldership and Dependence: Further Notes for Gerontologists and Others. The Gerontologist 7:236-41. (1967)

———. The Ages and Eldership among the Igbo. *In* Aging and Modernization. D.O. Cowgill and L.D. Holmes, eds. New York: Appleton-Century-Crofts, 1972.

Shepard, R.N. The Analysis of Proximities: Multidimensional Scaling with an Unknown Distance Function. Psychometrika 27:219-246. (1962)

———. Introduction to Vol. I. *In* Multidimensional Scaling: Theory and Applications in the Behavioral Sciences. Vol. I. R.N. Shepard, A.K. Romney and S.B. Nerlove, eds. New York: Seminar Press, 1972(a).

———. A Taxonomy of Types of Data and Methods for Analysis. *In* Multidimensional Scaling: Theory and Applications in the Behavioral Sciences. Vol. I. R.N. Shepard, A.K. Romney, and S.B. Nerlove, eds. New York: Seminar Press, 1972(b).

Sherman, S. The Choice of Retirement Housing among the Well-Elderly. Aging and Human Development 2:228-38. (1971)

——. Mutual Assistance and Support in Retirement Housing. Journal of Gerontology 30:479-84. (1975a)

——. Patterns of Contacts for Residents of Age-Segregated and Age-Integrated Housing. Journal of Gerontology 30:103-07. (1975b)

Shively, A.M., and S. Shively. Value Changes during a Period of Modernization— The Case of Hong Kong. Hong Kong: The Chinese University of Hong Kong Social Research Centre, 1972.

Shneidman, E.S., ed. Death: Current Perspectives. Palo Alto, Calif.: Mayfield, 1976.

Simmons, L.W. The Role of the Aged in Primitive Society. New Haven: Yale University Press, 1945.

——. Attitudes toward Aging and the Aged: Primitive Societies. Journal of Gerontology 1:72-95. (1946)

——. Aging in Preindustrial Societies. In Handbook of Social Gerontology. C. Tibbits, ed. Chicago: University of Chicago Press, 1960.

——. Problems of Over-Aging. Duke University Council on Gerontology. Proceedings of Seminars, 1961-65. Durham, N.C.: Regional Center for the Study of Aging.

Simmons, R., and S. Klein. Gift of Life: The Social and Psychological Impact of Organ Transplantation. New York: John Wiley & Sons, 1977.

Singh, R.R. Welfare of the Aged. Indian Journal of Social Work 31:327-333. (1970)

Skinner, E. Intergenerational Conflict among the Mossi. Journal of Conflict Resolution 5:55-60. (1961)

Skinner, G.W. Introduction: Urban Social Structure in Ch'ing China. In The City in Late Imperial China. G.W. Skinner, ed. Pp. 521-554. Stanford, Calif: Stanford University Press, 1977.

Slater, P. Cross-Cultural Views of the Elderly. In New Thoughts on Old Age. R. Kastenbaum, ed. New York: Springer, 1964.

Smith, R. Cultural Differences in the Life Cycle and the Concept of Time. In Aging and Leisure. R. Kleemeier, ed. New York: Oxford University Press, 1961.

Sobel, H. Aging of Ground Substance in Connective Tissue. Science 167:205-208, 1967.

Sokolovsky, J., and C. Cohen. Networks Analysis and Therapeutic Intervention for the Urban Elderly. Paper presented at the 75th Annual Meeting of the American Anthropologists Association, Washington, D.C., 1976.

Sommer, R., and H. Ross. Social Interaction on a Geriatric Ward. International Journal of Social Psychology 4:128-33. (1958)

Soodan, K.S. Aging in India. Calcutta: Minerva Associates, 1975.

Sorokin, P.A. Social and Cultural Dynamics. New York: American Book Company, 1937.

Spencer, P. The Samburu. A Study in Gerontocracy in a Nomadic Tribe. London: Routledge & Kegan Paul, 1965.

———. Opposing Streams and the Gerontocratic Ladder: Two Models of Age Organization in East Africa. Man II:153-174. (1976)

Spilka, B., and R.J. Pellegrini. Death and Cultural Values. Paper presented at the American Psychological Association Convention, Sept., 1967, Washinton, D.C.

Spiegel, P.M. Theories of Aging. *In* Developmental Physiology and Aging. P.S. Timiras. New York: Macmillan, 1972.

Stack, C. All Our Kin: Strategies for Survival in a Black Community. New York: Harper & Row, 1974.

Stenning, D.J. Household Viability among the Pastoral Fulani. *In* The Developmental Cycle in Domestic Groups. J. Goody, ed. Cambridge: Cambridge University Press, 1971.

Stephens, J. Society of the Alone: Freedom, Privacy, Utilitarianism as Dominant Norms in the SRO. Journal of Gerontology 30:230-35. (1975)

———. Loners, Losers, and Lovers: Elderly Tenants in a Slum Hotel. Seattle: University of Washington Press, 1976.

Stewart, F. Fundamentals of Age-Group Systems. New York: Academic Press 1976.

Strehler, B.L. Implications of Aging Research for Society. Fed. Proc. 34, 1: 5-8. (1975)

Streib, G.F. Old Age in Ireland: Demographic and Sociological Aspects. *In* Aging and Modernization, D.O. Cowgill and L.D. Holmes, eds. New York: Meredith, 1972.

Sussman, M.B. The Isolated Nuclear Family: Fact or Fiction. Social Problems 6(4): 333-340.

———. Relationship of Adult Children with Their Parents. *In* Social Sturcture and the Family: Generational Relations. E. Shanas and G.F. Strieb, eds. Englewood Cliffs, N.J.: Prentice Hall, 1965.

Talman, Y. Aging in Israel, a Planned Society. *In* Middle Age and Aging. B. Neugarten, ed. Chicago: University of Chicago Press, 1968.

Taylor, D. The Black Carib of British Honduras. Viking Fund Publications in Anthropology, No. 17. New York: Wenner-Gren, 1951.

Teaff, J., M.P. Lawton and D. Carlson. Impact of Age Integration of Public Housing Projects upon Elderly Tenant Well-Being. Gerontologist 13, 3: 77-81. (1973)

Temin, H.M., and S. Mizutani. RNA-Dependent DNA Polymerase in Virons of Rouse Sarocoma Virus. Nature 226:1211-1213. (1970)

Templer, D.I. Death Anxiety Scale (DAS). Proceedings of the 77th Annual Convention of the American Psychological Association 4(2):737-38. (1969)

Tessler, R., and D. Mechanic. Psychological Distress and Perceived Health Status. Journal of Health and Human Behavior 19:254-262. (1978)

Teuber, H.L. Visual Field Defects after Penetrating Missile Wounds of the Brain. Cambridge, Mass.: Harvard University Press.

Thomas, E.M. GRASP—A Graphic Service Program. Proceedings of the 22nd National Conference, Association for Computing Machinery, 1967.

Tissue, T. Another Look at Self-Rated Health among the Elderly. Journal of Gerontology 27:91-94. (1972)

Townsend, P. The Family Life of Old People: An Inquiry in East London. London: Routledge and Kegan Paul, 1957.

——. The Effects of Family Structure on the Likelihood of Admission to an Institution in Old Age: The Application of a General Theory. *In* Social Structure and the Family: Generational Relations. E. Shanas and G.F. Strieb, eds. Englewood Cliffs, N.J.: Prentice Hall, 1965.

——. The Emergence of the Four-Generational Family in Industrial Society. *In* Middle Age and Aging. B. Neugarten, ed. Chicago: University of Chicago Press, 1968(a).

——. Problems in the Cross-National Study of Old People in the Family: Segregation Versus Integration. *In* Interdisciplinary Topics in Gerontology: Methodological Problems in Cross-National Studies in Aging. E. Shanas and Madge, eds. New York: S. Kraeger, 1968(b).

Troll, L.E. Family of Later Life: A Decade of Review. Journal of Marriage and the Family 33:263-290. (1971)

Twenie, E.E. Never Too Old: The Aged in Community Life. San Francisco: Jossey-Bass, 1970.

Tyler, S. Cognitive Anthropology. New York: Holt, Rinehart, and Winston, 1969.

U.S. Department of Health, Education and Welfare. Health, Education and Welfare Trends, 1963. Washington, D.C.: U.S. Government Printing Office, 1964.

U.S. National Center for Health Statistics. Limitation of Activity and Mobility Due to Chronic Conditions, United States, 1972. Department of Health, Education and Welfare Publication No. (HRA) 75-1523. Washington, D.C.: U.S. Government Printing Office, 1974.

——. Limitation of Activity Due to Chronic Conditions, United States,1974. Department of Health, Education and Welfare Publication No. (HRA) 77-1537. Washington, D.C.: U.S. Government Printing Office, 1977.

Uzzell, T., and D. Pilbeam. Phyletic Divergence Dates of Hominoid Primates: A Comparison of Fossil and Molecular Data. Evolution 25:615-635. (1971)

Van Gennep, A. The Rites of Passage. Chicago: University of Chicago Press, 1960. (Original published 1909.)

Van Hemmen, J.J., and W.V.A. Menling. Inactivation of Biologically Active DNA by X-ray Induced Superoxide Radicals and Their Dismulation Products—Singlet Molecular Oxygen and Hydrogen Peroxide. Biochemical, Biophysical Acta 402:133. (1975)

Vatuk, S.J. Kinship and Urbanization: White Collar Migrants in North India. Berkeley: University of California Press, 1972.

——. The Aging Woman in India: Self-Perceptions and Changing Roles. *In* Women in Contemporary India. A. de Souza, ed. Delhi: Manohar, 1975.

Verba, S. Small Groups and Political Behavior. Princeton, N.J.: Princeton University Press, 1961.

Verzar, F. The Aging of Collagen. Scientific American 213,3:104. (1969)

Von Mering, O. An Anthropomedical Profile of Aging—Retirement from Life into Active Ill Health. Journal of Geriatric Psychiatry 3:61-81. (1969)

Wake, S., and M. Sporakowski. An Intergenerational Comparison of Attitudes toward Supporting Aged Parents. Journal of Marriage and the Family 34: 42-48. (1972)

Walkley, R.P., et al. Retirement Housing in California. Berkeley, Calif.: Diablo Press, 1966.

Warner, L. A Black Civilization: A Social Study of an Australian Tribe. New York: Harper & Row, 1958.

Watson, J.D. Molecular Biology of the Gene. Second Edition. New York: W.A. Benjamin, 1975.

Watson, W.H., and R.J. Maxwell, eds. Human Aging and Dying: A Study in Sociocultural Gerontology. New York: St. Martin's Press, 1977.

Webster, H. Primitive Secret Societies. New York: Macmillan, 1908.

Weihl, H. Selected Aspects of Aging in Israel: 1969. *In* Aging and Modernization. D.O. Cowgill and L.D. Holmes, eds. New York: Appleton-Century-Crofts, 1972.

Weisburger, J.H., and G.M. Williams. Metabolism of Chemical Carcinogens. Cancer: Comprehensive Treatise. Etiology of Chemical and Physical Carcinogenensis. Vol. 2. New York: Plenum, 1975.

Wellin, E., R. Anderson, E. Boyer, J. Grommes, and K. Jonas. Health and the Elderly in Public Housing. Milwaukee Urban Observatory, 1974.

Wellin, E., and E. Boyer. Adjustments of Black and White Elderly to the Same Adaptive Niche. *In* The Ethnography of Old Age. J. Keith, ed. Anthropological Quarterly 52(1): (1979)

Weiner, N. Cybernetics. Paris: Hermann, 1958.

Williams, J.A., N. Babchuck, and D. Johnson. Voluntary Associations and Minority Status. American Sociological Review. 38:637-646. (1973).

Williams, R.H., and C.G. Wirths. Lives through the Years. New York: Atherton, 1963.

Wilson, M. Good Company: A Study of Nyakyusa Age Villages. London: Oxford University Press, 1951(a).

———. Nayakyusa Age Villages. Journal of the Royal Anthropological Institute 79:21-25. (1951b)

Winch, R.F., and S.A. Greer. Urbanism, Ethnicity, and Extended Familism. Journal of Marriage and the Family 30:40-45. (1968)

Winiecke, L. The Appeal of Age Segregated Housing to the Elderly Poor. International Journal of Aging and Human Development 4:293-306. (1973)

Wirth, L. On Cities and Social Life. Chicago: University of Chicago Press, 1964. Reprint of 1938 edition.

Wisconsin Division on Aging and Family Services. The Needs of Wisconsin's Older People: An Assessment of Wisconsin's Elderly. Vol. 1 and 2. Minneapolis: Mid-continent Surveys, 1971.

Wohlwill, J.F. The Age Variable in Psychological Research. Psychological Review 77:49-64. (1970)

Wolf, E. Aspects of Group Relations in a Complex Society: Mexico. American Anthropologist 58:1065-1078. (1956)

Wolf, S. and H. Goodell, eds. Harold G. Wolff's Stress and Disease. Springfield, Ill.: Charles C. Thomas, 1968.

Wolstenholme, G.E.W., and M. O'Conner, eds. Mutation as Cellular Process, A CIBA Foundation Symposium. London: Churchill, 1969.

Working Party on the Future Needs of the Elderly. Services for the Elderly. Hong Kong: Government Press, 1973.   (also referred to as the Working Party Report.)

Yap, P.M. Aging in Underdeveloped Asian Countries. *In* Sociological and Psychological Aspects of Aging. C. Tibbitts and W. Donahue, eds. Pp. 442-453. New York: Columbia University Press, 1962.

Yang, C. The Chinese Family in the Communist Revolution. *In* Chinese Communist Society: The Family and the Village. Cambridge, Mass.: MIT Press, 1953.

Youmans, E.G. Older Rural Americans: A Sociological Perspective. Lexington: Univeristy of Kentucky Press, 1967.

Zarit, S.H., ed. Readings in Aging and Death: Contemporary Perspectives. New York: Harper & Row, 1977.

ADDITIONS TO BIBLIOGRAPHY

Anderson, B. Stress and Psychopathology Among Aged Americans. Southwestern Journal of Anthropology 20:190-217, 1964.

Angrosino, M.V. Anthropology and the Aged: A Preliminary Community Study. The Gerontologist 16:174-180, 1976.

Cohen, C. and J. Sokolovsky. An Application of Network Analysis to Community-Based Treatment of the Urban Elderly. Forthcoming.

———. Health Seeking Behavior and Social Networks: The SRO Aged. Journal of the American Geriatric Society. Forthcoming.

Curley, R. Elders, Shades and Women: Ceremonial Change in Lango, Uganda. Berkeley: University of California Press, 1973.

Dougherty, M. An Anthropological Perspective on Aging and Women in the Middle Years. *In* The Anthropology of Health. E. Bauwens (ed.). St. Louis: C.V. Mosby, 1978.

Erickson, R. and K. Eckert. The Elderly Poor in Downtown San Diego Hotels. The Gerontologist 17:440-446, 1977.

Ganschow, T. The Aged in a Revolutionary Milieu: China. *In* Aging and The Elderly: Humanistic Perspectives in Gerontology. S. Spicker, K. Woodward and D. van Tassel (eds.). Atlantic Highland: Humanities Press, 1978.

Jacobs, J. An Ethnographic Study of A Retirement Setting. The Gerontologist 14:483-487, 1974.

Katz, S. Anthropological Perspectives on Aging. Annals 438:1-2, 1978.

Myerhoff, B. Aging and the Aged in Other Cultures: An Anthropological Perspective. *In* The Anthropology of Health, pp. 151-166. E. Bauwens (ed.). St. Louis: C.V. Mosby Co., 1978.

Roberts, W. All in the Family: The Older Person in Context. *In* The Anthropology of Health, pp. 177-191. E. Bauwers (ed.). St. Louis: C.V. Mosby, 1978.

Rogers, C.J. and Gallion, T.E. Characteristics of Elderly Pueblo Indians in New Mexico. The Gerontologist 18:482-487. 1978.

Sokolovsky, J. and C. Cohen. Measuring Social Interaction of the Urban Elderly: A Methodological Synthesis. Journal of Community Mental Health. Forthcoming.

——. The Cultural Meaning of Personal Networks for the Inner City Elderly. Urban Anthropology. Forthcoming.

Treas, J. Socialist Organization and Economic Development in China: Latent Consequences for the Aged. The Gerontologist 19:34-43, 1979.

Trela, J. and J. Sokolovsky. Culture, Ethnicity, and Policy for the Aged. *In* Ethnicity and Aging. D. Gelfand and D. Fandetti (eds.). New York: Springer, 1979.

Wilson, M. For Men and Elders: Change in the Relations of Generations of Men and Women Among the Nyakyusa-Nande People 1875-71, New York: Africana, 1977.

Wright, N. Golden Age Apartments: Ethnography of Older People. *In* The Cultural Experience, pp. 121-136. J. Spradley and D. McCurdy. New York: Social Science Research, 1972.

Author Index

Subject Index